적중100

영어 기출 문제집

중2

미래엔 | 최연희

Best Collection

구성과 특징

교과서의 주요 학습 내용을 중심으로 학습 영역별 특성에 맞춰 단계별로 다양한 학습 기회를 제
공하여 단원별 학습능력 평가는 물론 중간 및 기말고사 시험 등에 완벽하게 대비할 수 있도록
내용을 구성

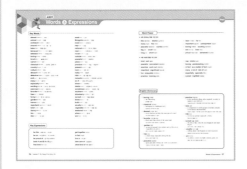

Words & Expressions

Step1 Key Words 단원별 핵심 단어 설명 및 풀이
Key Expression 단원별 핵심 숙어 및 관용어 설명
Word Power 반대 또는 비슷한 뜻 단어 배우기
English Dictionary 영어로 배우는 영어 단어

Step2 실력평가 단원별 수시평가 대비 주관식, 객관식 문제풀이

Step3 서술형 대비 학업성취도 및 수행능력평가 대비 서술형 문제풀이

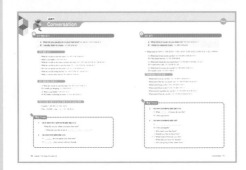

Conversation

Step1 핵심 의사소통 의사소통에 필요한 주요 표현 방법 요약
핵심 Check 기본적인 표현 방법 및 활용능력 확인

Step2 대화문 익히기 상황에 따른 대화문 활용 및 연습

Step3 기본평가 시험대비 기초 학습 능력 평가

Step4 실력평가 단원별 수시평가 대비 주관식, 객관식 문제풀이

Step5 서술형 대비 학업성취도 및 수행능력평가 대비 서술형 문제풀이

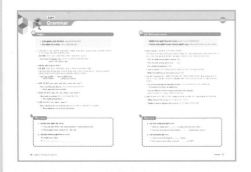

Grammar

Step1 주요 문법 단원별 주요 문법 사항과 예문을 알기 쉽게 설명

핵심 Check 기본 문법사항에 대한 이해 여부 확인

Step2 기본평가 시험대비 기초 학습 능력 평가

Step3 실력평가 단원별 수시평가 대비 주관식, 객관식 문제풀이

Step4 서술형 대비 학업성취도 및 수행능력평가 대비 서술형 문제풀이

Reading

Step1 구문 분석 단원별로 제시된 문장에 대한 구문별 분석과 내용 설명
확인문제 문장에 대한 기본적인 이해와 인지능력 확인

Step2 확인학습A 빈칸 채우기를 통한 문장 완성 능력 확인

Step3 확인학습B 제시된 우리말을 영어로 완성하여 작문 능력 키우기

Step4 실력평가 단원별 수시평가 대비 주관식, 객관식 문제풀이

Step5 서술형 대비 학업성취도 및 수행능력평가 대비 서술형 문제풀이
교과서 구석구석 교과서에 나오는 기타 문장까지 완벽 학습

Composition

|영역별 핵심문제|
단어 및 어휘, 대화문, 문법, 독해 등 각 영역별 기출문제의 출제 유형을 분석하여 실전에 대비하고 연습할 수 있도록 문제를 배열

|서술형 실전 및 창의사고력 문제|
학교 시험에서 점차 늘어나는 서술형 시험에 집중 대비하고 고득점을 취득하는데 만전을 기하기 위한 학습 코너

|단원별 예상문제|
기출문제를 분석한 후 새로운 시험 출제 경향을 더하여 새롭게 출제될 수 있는 문제를 포함하여 시험에 완벽하게 대비할 수 있도록 준비

|단원별 모의고사|
영역별, 단계별 학습을 모두 마친 후 실전 연습을 위한 모의고사

INSIGHT on the textbook

교과서 파헤치기

- 단어Test1~2 영어 단어 우리말 쓰기와 우리말을 영어 단어로 쓰기

- 대화문Test1~2 대화문 빈칸 완성 및 전체 대화문 쓰기

- 본문Test1~5 빈칸 완성, 우리말 쓰기, 문장 배열연습, 영어 작문하기 복습 등 단계별 반복 학습을 통해 교과서 지문에 대한 완벽한 습득

- 구석구석지문Test1~2 지문 빈칸 완성 및 전문 영어로 쓰기

이책의 차례 Contents

Lesson ③ **My Travel, My Way** 05~56

Lesson ④ **Giving a Hand** 57~108

Lesson ⑤ **Bravo! Brava!** 109~160

〈**Insight on the textbook**〉 교과서 파헤치기 01~58

〈책 속의 책〉 정답 및 해설 01~40

Lesson 3

My Travel, My Way

 의사소통 기능

- 경험 묻고 답하기
  A: Have you ever eaten pancakes?
  B: Yes, I have.

- 날씨 묻고 답하기
  A: How's the weather in London in March?
  B: It's rainy and cool.

 언어 형식

- to부정사의 형용사적 용법
  A B&B is a popular place **to stay** in England.

- 가주어 it
  It was just amazing **to see** the ring of huge stones.

Words & Expressions

Key Words

- **actually** [金ktʃuəli] 뷔 실제로, 정말로
- **admire** [ædmáiər] 통 존경하다, 감탄하며 바라보다
- **amazing** [əméiziŋ] 형 놀라운
- **anything** [éniθiŋ] 대 무엇, 아무것, 무엇이든
- **appear** [əpíər] 통 나타나다, 출연하다
- **around** [əráund] 전 ~ 둘레에, ~ 주위에, ~을 돌아
- **avatar** [金vətɑ:r] 명 화신, 아바타
- **become** [bikʌ́m] 통 ~(해)지다, ~이 되다
- **bungee jumping** 번지 점프
- **capture** [kǽptʃər] 통 잡다, 포착하다, 담아내다
- **chance** [tʃæns] 명 가능성, 기회
- **check** [tʃek] 통 살피다, 점검하다
- **cloudy** [kláudi] 형 흐린, 구름이 잔뜩 낀
- **college** [kálidʒ] 대학, 전문학교
- **create** [kriéit] 통 창조[창작/창출]하다
- **decide** [disáid] 통 결정하다, 결심하다
- **diary** [dáiəri] 명 수첩, 일기
- **different** [dífərənt] 명 다른
- **drawing** [dró:iŋ] 명 그림, 소묘, 데생
- **drive** [draiv] 통 (차량을) 몰다, 운전하다
- **during** [djúəriŋ] 전 ~ 동안[내내], (~하는) 중에
- **earth** [ə:rθ] 명 지구, 땅
- **else** [els] 뷔 또 다른, 다른
- **enough** [inʌ́f] 형 필요한 만큼의, 충분한
- **expect** [ikspékt] 통 예상[기대]하다
- **ever** [évər] 뷔 언제든, 한번이라도
- **famous** [féiməs] 형 유명한
- **field trip** 견학 여행, 현장 학습
- **finally** [fáinəli] 뷔 마침내
- **food** [fu:d] 명 식량, 음식
- **forecast** [fɔ́rkæst] 명 예측, 예보

- **foreign** [fɔ́:rən] 형 외국의
- **freezing** [frí:ziŋ] 형 꽁꽁 얼게[너무나] 추운
- **graduate** [grǽdʒuət] 통 졸업하다
- **guess** [ges] 통 추측하다, 짐작하다
- **huge** [hju:dʒ] 형 큰, 거대한
- **indoors** [indɔ́:rz] 뷔 실내에, 집안에
- **invite** [inváit] 통 초대하다, 초청하다
- **island** [áilənd] 명 섬
- **journal** [dʒɔ́:nl] 명 일기
- **market** [mɑ́:rkit] 명 시장
- **moment** [móumənt] 명 잠깐, 잠시, 순간
- **mostly** [móustli] 뷔 주로, 대개
- **mystery** [místəri] 명 수수께끼, 미스터리
- **object** [ábdʒikt] 명 물건, 물체
- **pack** [pæk] 통 (짐을) 싸다[꾸리다/챙기다]
- **perfect** [pə́:rfikt] 형 완전한
- **plate** [pleit] 명 접시, 그릇
- **portrait** [pɔ́:rtrit] 명 초상화
- **relax** [rilǽks] 통 휴식을 취하다
- **remain** [riméin] 통 남다, 남아 있다
- **scary** [skɛ́əri] 형 무서운, 겁나는
- **seafood** [si:fud] 명 해산물
- **simple** [símpl] 형 간단한, 단순한
- **touch** [tʌtʃ] 통 만지다, 건드리다
- **travel** [trǽvəl] 명 여행 통 여행하다
- **trip** [trip] 명 여행
- **turtle** [tə́:tl] 명 거북, 바다거북
- **university** [jù:nəvə́:rsəti] 명 대학교
- **vacation** [veikéiʃən] 명 방학, 휴가
- **weather** [wéðər] 명 날씨
- **windy** [wíndi] 형 바람이 많이 부는

Key Expressions

- **a few** 소수의, 약간의
- **a little** 좀, 약간; 약간의
- **a lot of** 많은
- **at last** 마침내
- **be full of** ~으로 가득 차다
- **get into** ~에 들어가다, ~에 타다

- **get to** ~에 도착하다
- **right now** 지금, 당장
- **set foot at[in]** ~에 발을 들여놓다
- **show up** 나타나다
- **stay[keep] indoors** 집안에 머물러 있다
- **such as** ~와 같은

Word Power

※ 날씨를 나타내는 단어

- □ **hot** (더운) → **cold** (추운)
- □ **warm** (따뜻한) → **cool** (서늘한)
- □ **fine** (맑은, 비가 안 오는)
- □ **mild** (온화한, 포근한)

※ 다음은 명사에 -y가 붙어 날씨를 나타내는 형용사가 되는 단어들이다. -y를 붙일 때 철자가 변하는 것이 있으므로 주의해야 한다.

- □ **sun** (해, 태양) → **sunny** (화창한)
- □ **rain** (비) → **rainy** (비가 오는)
- □ **snow** (눈) → **snowy** (눈이 오는)
- □ **cloud** (구름) → **cloudy** (구름이 낀, 흐린)
- □ **wind** (바람) → **windy** (바람이 부는)
- □ **fog** (안개) → **foggy** (안개가 낀)

English Dictionary

- □ **admire** 존경하다
  → to like and respect someone or something very much
  누군가 또는 무언가를 매우 좋아하고 존중하다

- □ **amazing** 놀라운
  → very surprising and making you feel pleasure, approval, or wonder
  매우 놀랍고 당신을 기쁨, 승인, 또는 놀라움을 느끼게 만드는

- □ **beach** 해변, 바닷가
  → an area of sand or stones beside the sea
  바다 옆에 모래나 돌이 있는 지역

- □ **chance** 가능성
  → the possibility that something will happen
  무슨 일이 일어날 가능성

- □ **create** 창조[창작/창출]하다
  → to cause something to happen or exist
  어떤 일이 발생하거나 존재하게 하다

- □ **decide** 결정하다, 결심하다
  → to choose to do something, usually after you have thought carefully about the other possibilities
  보통 당신이 다른 가능성에 대해 신중하게 고려한 후에, 무언가를 하기로 선택하다

- □ **drawing** 그림, 소묘, 데생
  → a picture made with a pencil or pen
  연필이나 펜으로 그린 그림

- □ **drive** (차량을) 몰다, 운전하다
  → to operate a car or other vehicle and control its movement and direction
  자동차나 다른 차량을 조작하여 그 움직임과 방향을 제어하다

- □ **food** 식량, 음식
  → what people and animals eat
  사람과 동물이 먹는 것

- □ **invite** 초대하다, 초청하다
  → to ask someone to come to something such as a party
  어떤 사람에게 파티와 같은 것에 와 달라고 청하다

- □ **island** 섬
  → a piece of land that is completely surrounded by water
  물에 완전히 둘러싸인 땅

- □ **market** 시장
  → a place where goods are bought and sold, usually outdoors
  보통 옥외에서 물건을 사고파는 장소

- □ **mystery** 수수께끼, 미스터리
  → something that is not understood or known about
  이해되거나 알려지지 않은 어떤 것

- □ **pack** (짐을) 싸다[꾸리다/챙기다]
  → to put clothes and other things into a bag, because you are leaving a place
  당신이 어떤 곳을 떠나기 때문에 옷이나 다른 것들을 가방에 넣다

- □ **relax** 휴식을 취하다
  → to spend time resting or doing something enjoyable especially after you have been doing work
  특히 일이 끝난 후 쉬거나 즐거운 일을 하면서 시간을 보내다

- □ **strange** 이상한, 낯선
  → unusual or unexpected, and making you feel slightly nervous or afraid
  이상하거나 예상치 못한, 그리고 당신을 약간 긴장시키거나 두려워하게 만드는

- □ **travel** 여행하다
  → to go from one place to another, often to a place that is far away
  한 장소에서 다른 곳, 종종 멀리 떨어진 곳으로 가다

01 다음 중 짝지어진 단어의 성격이 <u>다른</u> 하나는?

① wind – windy　　② health – healthy
③ snow – snowy　　④ fog – foggy
⑤ sun – sunny

02 다음 빈칸에 알맞은 말이 바르게 짝지어진 것은? ^{중요}

> • Ann has a lot _____ friends here.
> • I put on my seat belt as soon as I get _____ the car.

① into – at　　② of – into
③ on – in　　④ out – with
⑤ off – over

03 다음 영영풀이에 해당하는 단어로 알맞은 것은?

> a place where goods are bought and sold, usually outdoors

① mart　　② area
③ field　　④ market
⑤ factory

04 다음 짝지어진 단어의 관계가 같도록 빈칸에 알맞은 말을 쓰시오. ^{서답형}

> advise : advice = decide : _____

05 다음 우리말에 맞게 빈칸에 알맞은 것은?

> 나는 그의 사진을 몇 장 가지고 있다.
> ➡ I have _____ pictures of him.

① few　　② little
③ a few　　④ a little
⑤ a lot

06 다음 영영풀이에 해당하는 단어를 주어진 철자로 시작하여 쓰시오. ^{서답형}

> the possibility that something will happen

➡ c_____

07 다음 우리말에 맞게 빈칸에 알맞은 말을 쓰시오. ^{서답형}

> 내가 창문을 잠갔는지 가서 확인해 봐.
> ➡ Go and _____ that I've locked the windows.

08 다음 빈칸에 공통으로 알맞은 것은? ^{중요}

> • The parking lot is full _____ snow.
> • I can't think _____ her name at the moment.

① in　　② of
③ up　　④ about
⑤ at

01 다음 짝지어진 두 단어의 관계가 같도록 빈칸에 알맞은 말을 쓰시오.

(1) wind : windy = snow : _____

(2) hot : cold = warm : _____

(3) teach : teacher = create : _____

02 다음 우리말에 맞게 빈칸에 알맞은 말을 쓰시오.

(1) 마침내 여름방학이 왔다.
　➡ Summer vacation has come _____
　_____.

(2) Jane은 중국어를 좀 한다.
　➡ Jane speaks Chinese _____ _____.

(3) 더 이상 나는 집안에 머물지 않아도 될 것이다.
　➡ I won't have to _____ _____ any more.

03 다음 빈칸에 들어갈 알맞은 말을 〈보기〉에서 골라 쓰시오.

┌─ 보기 ─┐
pack　mostly　different　anything

(1) Would you like _____ else?

(2) The sauce is _____ cream.

(3) Did you _____ the camera?

(4) They are sold in many _____ colours.

04 다음 괄호 안의 단어를 문맥에 맞게 고쳐 쓰시오.

(1) It's not _____ raining now. (actual)

(2) That's _____, isn't it? (amaze)

(3) A _____ young woman is living next door. (mystery)

05 다음 빈칸에 알맞은 말을 〈보기〉에서 골라 쓰시오.

┌─ 보기 ─┐
get to　right now
is full of　catch a cold

(1) I'm coming down _____.

(2) We will _____ London at eight.

(3) The room _____ children.

(4) If you _____, you will cough a lot.

06 다음 영영풀이에 해당하는 단어를 주어진 철자로 시작하여 쓰시오.

(1) a_____ : to like and respect someone or something very much

(2) d_____ : a picture made with a pencil or pen

(3) f_____ : what people and animals eat

Conversation

교과서

1 경험 묻고 답하기

> **A** Have you ever eaten pancakes? 넌 팬케이크를 먹어 본 적이 있니?
> **B** Yes, I have. 응. 있어.

■ **경험 묻기**

'~해 본 적이 있나요?'라고 과거부터 현재까지의 상대방의 경험을 물을 때는 「Have you (ever)+과거분사 ~?」 형태인 현재완료 의문문으로 물을 수 있다.

■ **경험에 대한 물음에 대답하기**

경험이 있으면 Yes, I have. / Yes, I have+과거분사. 등으로 한다.
경험이 없으면 No, I haven't. / No, I have never+과거분사 / Not yet. 등으로 한다.

- A: Have you ever seen a bear? 너는 곰을 본 적이 있니?
  B: Yes, I have. / No, I haven't. 응. 본 적이 있어. / 아니. 본 적이 없어.

cf. '~에 가본 적 있니?'라고 묻는 표현은 Have you ever gone to ~?가 아니라 Have you ever been to ~?임에 주의한다.

- have been to: ~에 가본 적이 있다(경험) / ~에 갔다왔다(완료)
- have gone to: ~ 에 가버렸다(결과)

■ 경험을 나타낼 때는 다음과 같은 부사(구)를 함께 쓰는 경우가 많다. ever(지금까지), never(~한 적 없는), before(이전에), once(한 번), twice(두 번), 「숫자+times(~번, ~차례)」, many times(여러 번), often(자주)

- She has made fried rice many times. 그녀는 볶음밥을 여러 번 만든 적이 있다.

핵심 Check

1. 다음 우리말과 일치하도록 빈칸에 알맞은 말을 쓰시오.

(1) A: _____ you ever _____ *Les Miserables*? (너 '레미제라블' 읽어 봤니?)

　　B: Yes, I _____. (응, 있어.)

(2) A: _____ you _____ this food? (너는 이 음식을 먹어 봤니?)

　　B: No, I _____. (아니, 나는 못 먹어 봤어.)

② 날씨 묻고 답하기

> **A** How's the weather in London in March? 3월에 런던 날씨는 어떠니?
>
> **B** It's rainy and cool. 비가 오고 시원해.

■ 날씨 묻기
오늘 날씨가 어떤지 물을 때는 What's the weather like today?, 혹은 How's the weather today?라고 한다. 특정 지역의 날씨를 물을 때는 What's the weather like in+지역명? 혹은 How's the weather in+지역명?으로 나타낸다.

비슷한 표현

• What's today's forecast? 오늘 일기 예보가 어떻습니까?

■ 날씨 말하기
날씨에 대해 말할 때에는 비인칭 주어 it을 사용해 It's ~라고 한다. 날씨에 따라서 fine, sunny, warm, cool, hot, cold, cloudy, snowy, rainy 등의 표현을 사용한다.

• A: What's the weather like today? 오늘 날씨는 어떠니?
  B: It's rainy / sunny / hot / cold / cloudy / snowy.

cf. 현재진행형을 사용하여 '비가[눈이] 오는 중'이라고 말할 때는 「It's 동사원형+-ing.」라고 말한다. 또한 「It's+형용사.」 형태를 사용하여 말할 수도 있다.

• A: What's the weather like outside? 바깥 날씨 어떠니?
  B: It's raining. / It's rainy. 비가 내리고 있어.

cf. it은 날씨, 온도, 명암, 날짜 등을 말할 때 쓰는 주어로 인칭을 나타내는 주어가 아니기 때문에 비인칭 주어라고 한다.

핵심 Check

2. 다음 우리말과 일치하도록 빈칸에 알맞은 말을 쓰시오.

(1) A: _____ is the _____ in Cleveland? (클리브랜드의 날씨는 어때?)
   B: It's _____ and cold this time of year. (이맘때는 눈이 오고 추워.)

(2) A: _____ the weather _____ today? (오늘 날씨는 어떠니?)
   B: It's _____ and sunny. (덥고 화창해.)

(3) A: _____ the weather? (날씨가 어때?)
   B: It's _____ a lot. Let's stay at home. (비가 많이 와. 집에 있도록 하자.)

Listen & Speak 1 A-1

G: ❶Have you ever tried Indian food?

B: ❷Yes, I have, but I've only tried Indian curry.

G: ❸How was it?

B: ❹It was really hot, but I loved it.

G: 너 인도 음식을 먹어 본 적이 있니?
B: 응, 있어. 하지만 인도 카레만 먹어 봤어.
G: 어땠어?
B: 정말 매웠지만, 아주 좋았어.

❶ 경험을 나타내는 현재완료는 경험을 묻는 표현으로 사용된다.　❷ I have 다음에는 tried Indian food이 생략되었다.
❸ It은 Indian curry를 가리킨다.　❹ hot은 '뜨거운'이라는 뜻 외에 '매운'이라는 뜻이 있다.

Check(√) True or False

(1) The girl wants to eat Indian food.　　　　　T ☐ F ☐

(2) The boy has only tried Indian curry.　　　　T ☐ F ☐

Listen & Speak 1 A-2

G: ❶Bill, have you ever gone bungee jumping?

B: ❷No, I haven't. ❸How about you, Katie?

G: ❹When I visited New Zealand, I tried bungee jumping once.

B: ❺Wasn't it scary?

G: No, I liked it. I want to do it again.

G: Bill, 번지 점프하러 가 본 적 있니?
B: 아니, 없어. Katie, 넌 어때?
G: 뉴질랜드를 방문했을 때, 번지 점프를 한 번 해봤어.
B: 무섭지 않았어?
G: 아니, 좋았어. 또 하고 싶어.

❶ go bungee jumping: 번지 점프하러 가다　❷ I haven't = I haven't gone bungee jumping
❸ How about you?: 너는 어때?　❹ once: 한 번
❺ 부정의문문으로 Was it not scary?로 바꿔 쓸 수 있다.

Check(√) True or False

(3) Bill has ever gone bungee jumping.　　　　T ☐ F ☐

(4) Katie did bungee jumping once.　　　　　　T ☐ F ☐

Listen & Speak 2 A-1

B: ❶Mom, how's the weather today? Do I need an umbrella?

W: ❷It's quite cloudy outside. I'll check the weather forecast.

B: Thank you, Mom.

W: ❸Well, it's not going to rain today.

B: Good! Then, I don't need an umbrella today.

B: 엄마, 오늘 날씨 어때요? 우산이 필요한가요?
W: 바깥 날씨가 아주 흐려. 일기 예보를 확인해 볼게.
B: 고마워요, 엄마.
W: 음, 오늘은 비가 안 올 거야.
B: 좋아요! 그럼, 오늘은 우산이 필요 없어요.

❶ how's = how is　❷ It은 날씨를 나타내는 비인칭 주어로 우리말로 옮기지 않는다.
❸ be going to는 가까운 미래를 나타내는 어구이다.

Check(√) True or False

(5) It's quite cloudy outside now.　　　　　　T ☐ F ☐

(6) The boy needs an umbrella today.　　　　　T ☐ F ☐

Listen and Speak 2 A-2

W: Good morning, and ❶welcome to the weather forecast. ❷It's sunny outside, but we're expecting some rain in the afternoon. ❸Don't leave home without your umbrella. That's the weather forecast for today. Have a nice day.

❶ welcome to ~: ~에 오신 걸 환영하다 / weather forecast: 일기 예보
❷ It: 날씨를 나타내는 비인칭 주어 / expect: 예상하다
❸ Don't + 동사원형 ~: ~하지 마라

Communicate: A. Listen and Answer

Suho: ❶Anna, have you been to Australia before?
Anna: ❷Yes, I have. Actually, I lived in Sydney for a year.
Suho: Great! ❸How's the weather there in April? I'm going to visit Sydney on vacation next week.
Anna: ❹April is a great time to visit Sydney. In April, it's autumn in Australia.
Suho: Good. ❺I'm planning to spend some time on the beach and relax in the sun.
Anna: ❻Well, it often rains in April, but you may have some sunny days.
Suho: I'll take my hat and pack an umbrella, too.
Anna: ❼That's a good idea. Have a great time.

❶ Have you been to ~?: ~에 가 본 적이 있니?
❷ have = have been to Australia
❸ How's the weather there in April? = What's the weather like there in April?
❹ to visit Sydney는 time을 수식하는 형용사적 용법의 to부정사이다.
❺ be planning to: ~할 계획이다
❻ often은 빈도부사로 일반동사 앞에 위치한다.
❼ That은 지시대명사로 앞 문장의 내용을 받는다.

Communicate B. Make Your Own Dialogue

A: ❶Have you been to any special places in Korea?
B: Yes, I have. ❷I went to Ulleungdo last summer with my family.
A: How was the weather there?
B: ❸It was mostly sunny, but the weather changed often.

❶ have been to: ~에 다녀오다
❷ last summer: 지난 여름에
❸ It은 날씨를 나타내는 비인칭 주어이다. mostly: 주로, 대개

Progress Check 1

G: ❶Have you ever ridden a horse?
B: Yes, I have. How about you?
G: ❷No, I haven't. ❸How was it?
B: It was fun, but it was a little scary, too.

❶ ride − rode − ridden
❷ I haven't=I haven't ridden a horse
❸ it은 인칭대명사로 말을 탄 것을 가리킨다.

Progress Check 2

B: Mom, how's the weather today?
W: ❶It's quite cloudy outside. ❷I'll check the weather forecast.
B: Thanks, Mom.
W: ❸Well, it's going to rain in the afternoon.

❶ quite: 아주 / cloudy: 흐린, 구름이 많은
❷ the weather forecast: 일기 예보
❸ be going to: ~할 것이다

Progress Check 3

M: ❶Good evening, and welcome to the weather forecast. ❷It's raining right now, but we're expecting a sunny day tomorrow. ❸Don't leave home tomorrow without your hat.

❶ welcome to ~: ~에 오신 것을 환영합니다
❷ 현재진행형 문장이다. right now: 지금, 당장
❸ leave home: 집을 떠나다 / without: ~이 없이, ~을 사용하지 않고

● 다음 우리말과 일치하도록 빈칸에 알맞은 말을 쓰시오.

Listen & Speak 1 A. Listen and Check

1. **G:** _____ you ever _____ Indian food?

   B: Yes, I _____, but I've only _____ Indian curry.

   G: _____ was it?

   B: It was really hot, _____ I loved it.

2. **G:** Bill, have you _____ gone bungee _____?

   B: No, I _____. How _____ you, Katie?

   G: _____ I visited New Zealand, I _____ bungee jumping once.

   B: _____ it scary?

   G: No, I _____ it. I _____ to do it again.

Listen & Speak 2 A. Listen and Answer

1. **B:** Mom, how's the _____ today? Do I _____ an umbrella?

   W: It's quite cloudy _____. I'll _____ the weather forecast.

   B: Thank you, Mom.

   W: Well, it's not _____ to rain today.

   B: Good! Then, I _____ need an umbrella today.

2. **W:** _____ morning, and _____ to the weather _____. It's _____ outside, _____ we're expecting some _____ in the afternoon. Don't leave _____ without your umbrella. That's the weather _____ for today. _____ a nice day.

1. **G:** 너 인도 음식을 먹어 본 적이 있니?
   B: 응, 있어, 하지만 인도 카레만 먹어 봤어.
   G: 어땠어?
   B: 정말 매웠지만, 아주 좋았어.

2. **G:** Bill, 번지 점프하러 가 본 적 있니?
   B: 아니, 없어. Katie, 넌 어때?
   G: 뉴질랜드를 방문했을 때, 번지 점프를 한 번 해봤어.
   B: 무섭지 않았어?
   G: 아니, 좋았어. 또 하고 싶어.

1. **B:** 엄마, 오늘 날씨 어때요? 우산이 필요한가요?
   W: 바깥 날씨가 아주 흐려. 일기예보를 확인해 볼게.
   B: 고마워요, 엄마.
   W: 음, 오늘은 비가 안 올 거야.
   B: 좋아요! 그럼, 오늘은 우산이 필요없어요.

2. **W:** 좋은 아침입니다, 일기예보에 오신 것을 환영합니다. 밖은 화창하지만 오후에는 약간의 비가 예상됩니다. 우산 없이 집을 나서지 마세요. 오늘의 일기예보입니다. 좋은 하루 되세요.

Communicate A~B

A. **Suho** Anna, have you _____ to Australia _____?

Anna: Yes, I _____. Actually, I _____ in Sydney _____ a year.

Suho: Great! How's the _____ there in April? I'm _____ to visit Sydney on _____ next week.

Anna: April is a great _____ to _____ Sydney. In April, it's _____ in Australia.

Suho: Good. I'm _____ to spend some time on the beach and _____ in the sun.

Anna: Well, it _____ rains in April, but you _____ have some sunny days.

Suho: I'll _____ my hat and _____ an umbrella, too.

Anna: That's a good _____. Have a _____ time.

B. **A:** Have you _____ to any special _____ in Korea?

B: Yes, I _____. I went to Ulleungdo _____ summer with my family.

A: _____ was the _____ there?

B: It was _____ sunny, but the weather _____ often.

Progress Check

1. **G:** Have you ever _____ a horse?

   B: Yes, I _____. How _____ you?

   G: No, I _____. How _____ it?

   B: It was _____, but it was a _____ scary, too.

2. **B:** Mom, how's the _____ today?

   W: It's _____ cloudy outside. I'll _____ the weather forecast.

   B: _____, Mom.

   W: Well, it's _____ to rain in the afternoon.

3. **M:** _____ evening, and _____ to the weather forecast. It's _____ right now, _____ we're expecting a _____ day tomorrow. Don't _____ home tomorrow _____ your hat.

해석

A. 수호: Anna, 너 전에 호주에 가본 적 있어?
   Anna: 응, 있어. 사실, 나는 시드니에서 1년 동안 살았어.
   수호: 멋지다! 그곳의 4월 날씨는 어때? 난 다음 주 방학 때 시드니에 갈 거야.
   Anna: 4월은 시드니를 방문하기에 좋은 시기야. 4월에, 호주는 가을이야.
   수호: 좋아. 나는 해변에서 시간을 좀 보내고 햇빛을 쬐며 휴식을 취할 계획이야.
   Anna: 음, 4월에는 종종 비가 오지만, 맑은 날도 좀 있을 거야.
   수호: 나도 모자를 가져가고 우산도 챙길 거야.
   Anna: 좋은 생각이야. 좋은 시간 보내.

B. A: 넌 한국의 어느 특별한 장소들을 가본 적이 있니?
   B: 응, 있어. 나는 작년 여름에 가족과 울릉도에 갔어.
   A: 거기 날씨는 어땠어?
   B: 대체로 맑았지만, 날씨가 자주 바뀌었어.

1. G: 너 말을 타본 적 있니?
   B: 응, 있어. 너는 어때?
   G: 아니, 난 없어. 말 타는 거 어땠어?
   B: 재미있었지만, 조금 무섭기도 했어.

2. B: 엄마, 오늘 날씨 어때요?
   W: 바깥 날씨가 꽤 흐려. 일기예보를 확인해 볼게.
   B: 고마워요, 엄마.
   W: 음, 오후에 비가 올 거야.

3. M: 안녕하세요, 일기예보에 오신 것을 환영합니다. 지금은 비가 오지만 내일은 화창한 날씨가 예상됩니다. 내일 모자를 쓰지 않고 집을 나서지 마세요.

01 다음 두 문장의 의미가 같도록 빈칸에 알맞은 말을 쓰시오.

> How's the weather today?
> = _____ the weather _____ today?

02 다음 대화의 밑줄 친 우리말에 해당하는 것은?

> A: Jina, I'm going to Vietnam with my family this winter.
> B: Wow. That sounds like fun.
> A: <u>너 전에 그곳에 가 본 적 있니?</u>
> B: No, I haven't.

① Did you be there before?
② Had you been there before?
③ Have you been there before?
④ Have you gone there before?
⑤ When did you get there before?

03 다음 대화의 빈칸에 알맞지 <u>않은</u> 것은?

> A: What's the weather like outside?
> B: _____

① It's snowing.   ② It's very cold.
③ It's really cloudy.   ④ It will be very hot.
⑤ It's raining outside.

04 다음 대화의 빈칸에 알맞은 것은?

> A: Have you eaten this food?
> B: No, _____.

① I don't   ② I didn't
③ I haven't   ④ I hadn't
⑤ I loved it

01 다음 대화의 빈칸에 알맞은 것은?

> A: What's the weather like outside?
> B: _____

① It's fall.
② It's windy.
③ It's too cold to drink.
④ I like rainy days.
⑤ I dislike cold weather.

서답형
02 다음 대화의 빈칸에 알맞은 말을 쓰시오.

> A: _____ you _____ tried gimchi, Ann?
> B: Yes, I _____. It was very tasty.

03 다음 대화를 의미가 통하도록 알맞게 배열한 것은?

> (A) Well, it's going to rain in the afternoon.
> (B) Thanks, Mom.
> (C) Mom, how's the weather today?
> (D) It's quite cloudy outside. I'll check the weather forecast.

① (A) – (D) – (B) – (C)
② (B) – (C) – (D) – (A)
③ (C) – (D) – (B) – (A)
④ (D) – (B) – (C) – (A)
⑤ (D) – (C) – (B) – (A)

04 다음 대화의 빈칸에 가장 알맞은 것은?

> A: Have you seen the movie, *Avatar*, Sue?
> B: No, I haven't. _____
> A: Yes, it's my favorite movie.

① Do you?　　② Will you?
③ Had you?　　④ Have you?
⑤ What do you want to see?

 05 다음 대화의 빈칸에 알맞은 것은?

> A: How's the weather today?
> B: _____
> A: Really? I should wear my sunglasses then. Thanks.

① It's sunny and hot.
② I don't like sunny days.
③ It's cloudy and windy.
④ It looks like rain soon.
⑤ We have good weather in the fall.

[06~09] 다음 대화를 읽고, 물음에 답하시오.

> G: Bill, ___ⓐ___ you ever gone bungee jumping?
> B: No, I haven't. ___ⓑ___ about you, Katie?
> G: ⓒWhen I visited New Zealand, I tried bungee jumping once.
> B: Wasn't ⓓit scary?
> G: No, I liked it. I want to do it again.

06 위 대화의 빈칸 ⓐ에 알맞은 것은?

① do　　② did
③ were　　④ had
⑤ have

07 위 대화의 빈칸 ⓑ에 알맞은 것은? (2개)

① Why ② How
③ Who ④ Which
⑤ What

서답형

08 위 대화의 밑줄 친 ⓒ를 우리말로 옮기시오.

➡ _____

서답형

09 위 대화의 밑줄 친 ⓓ가 가리키는 것을 영어로 쓰시오.

➡ _____

[10~14] 다음 대화를 읽고, 물음에 답하시오.

Suho: Anna, have you ___ⓐ___ to Australia before?

Anna: Yes, I have. ⓑActual, I lived in Sydney for a year.

Suho: Great! ⓒHow's the weather there in April? I'm going to visit Sydney on vacation next week.

Anna: April is a great time to visit Sydney. In April, it's autumn in Australia.

Suho: Good. I'm planning to spend some time on the beach and ___ⓓ___ in the sun.

Anna: Well, it often rains in April, but you may have some sunny days.

Suho: I'll take my hat and pack an umbrella, too.

Anna: That's a good idea. Have a great time.

10 위 대화의 빈칸 ⓐ에 알맞은 것은?

① were ② go
③ be ④ been
⑤ gone

서답형

11 위 대화의 밑줄 친 ⓑ를 알맞은 어형으로 고치시오.

➡ _____

⭐중요

12 위 대화의 밑줄 친 ⓒ와 같은 뜻이 되도록 다음 문장의 빈칸에 알맞은 말을 쓰시오.

_____ the weather _____ there in April?

서답형

13 위 대화의 빈칸 ⓓ에 다음 영영풀이에 해당하는 단어를 쓰시오.

to spend time resting or doing something enjoyable especially after you have been doing work

➡ _____

14 위 대화를 읽고, 답할 수 없는 질문은?

① When did Ann go to Australia?
② Where did Ann live in Australia?
③ When will Suho visit Australia?
④ How is the weather in Sydney in April?
⑤ What will Suho take?

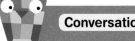

[01~02] 다음 대화의 빈칸에 알맞은 말을 쓰시오.

01

A: What's the weather _____ today?

B: _____ is warm and sunny.

02

A: _____ you ever slept in a tent?

B: No, I _____.

03 다음 대화를 의미가 통하도록 알맞게 배열하시오.

(A) It was really hot, but I loved it.

(B) Have you ever tried Indian food?

(C) Yes, I have, but I've only tried Indian curry.

(D) How was it?

➡ _____

[04~06] 다음 대화를 읽고, 물음에 답하시오.

B: Mom, how's the ___ⓐ___ today? Do I need an umbrella?

W: It's quite ⓑcloud outside. I'll check the weather ___ⓒ___.

B: Thank you, Mom.

W: Well, it's not going to rain today.

B: Good! Then, I don't need an umbrella today.

04 위 대화의 빈칸 ⓐ에 알맞은 말을 쓰시오.

➡ _____

05 위 대화의 밑줄 친 ⓑ를 알맞은 어형으로 고치시오.

➡ _____

06 위 대화의 빈칸 ⓒ에 다음 정의에 해당하는 단어를 쓰시오.

a statement of what is expected to happen in the future, especially in relation to a particular event or situation

➡ _____

[07~09] 다음 담화문을 읽고, 물음에 답하시오.

W: Good morning, and ___ⓐ___ to the weather forecast. It's ⓑsun outside, but we're expecting some rain in the afternoon. Don't leave home without your umbrella. That's the weather forecast for today. Have a nice day.

07 위 담화문의 빈칸 ⓐ에 알맞은 말을 쓰시오.

➡ _____

08 위 담화문의 밑줄 친 ⓑ를 알맞은 어형으로 고치시오.

➡ _____

09 What's the weather like in the afternoon? Answer in Korean.

➡ _____

Grammar

교과서

1 to부정사의 형용사적 용법

- A B&B is a popular place **to stay** in England. B&B는 영국에서 머무는 곳으로 인기가 있다.
- They need something **to drink**. 그들은 마실 것이 필요하다.
- I have a lot of homework **to do** tonight. 나는 오늘밤 해야 할 숙제가 많다.

■ to부정사의 형용사적 용법은 명사나 대명사 뒤에서 '~하는, ~할'의 뜻으로 쓰인다. 이 때 앞의 명사는 to부정사의 주어 또는 목적어 역할을 한다.

- I have no money **to give** you. [목적어] 나는 너에게 줄 돈이 없다.
  = I have no money that I can give you.

- He had no friends **to help** him. [주어] 그는 자기를 도와줄 친구가 하나도 없었다.
  = He had no friends who would help him.

■ to부정사의 수식을 받는 명사가 전치사의 목적어일 경우, to부정사 뒤에 전치사가 온다.

- Ann has elderly parents **to look** after. Ann은 돌보아야 할 나이 드신 부모가 있다.
- I want a small room **to live** in by myself. 나는 혼자 살 작은 방을 원한다.

■ -thing으로 끝나는 부정대명사는 「-thing+(형용사+)to부정사」의 어순을 따른다.

- I want something cold **to drink**. 나는 차가운 마실 것을 원한다.
- You feel that you have nothing **to wear**. 너는 입을 것이 아무것도 없다고 느낀다.

핵심 Check

1. 다음 괄호 안에서 알맞은 것을 고르시오.

(1) It's time (go / to go) to school.

(2) Jack has a lot of friends (helping / to help).

(3) Give me a pen (to write / to write with).

(4) Would you like something (to cold drink / cold to drink)?

2 가주어 it

> - **It** was just amazing **to see** the ring of huge stones.
>   거대한 돌들의 고리를 보는 것은 아주 놀라웠다.
>
> - **It** is easy **to bake** cookies. 쿠키를 굽는 것은 쉽다.
>
> - **It** will be nice **to become** a musician. 음악가가 되는 것은 멋질 거야.

■ 가주어 it

to부정사구가 문장 안에서 주어로 쓰일 경우, to부정사구를 문장의 뒤로 보내고 그 자리에 it을 쓴다. 이때의 it은 아무런 의미가 없는 주어로 '가주어'라고 하고, to부정사구를 '진주어'라고 한다.

- **To master** English in a month is impossible. 영어를 한 달 동안에 습득하는 것은 불가능하다.

  → <u>**It**</u> is impossible <u>**to master**</u> English in a month.
     가주어   진주어

cf. to부정사 이외에도 진주어로 명사절이 쓰일 때가 있다. 이때 명사절을 이끄는 접속사는 보통 that이 쓰인다.

- **It** is a bad habit **that** people read in bed. 침대에서 독서하는 것은 나쁜 버릇이다.

■ to부정사의 의미상의 주어

to부정사의 의미상의 주어가 문장의 주어와 일치하지 않는 경우, 일반적으로 「for+목적격」의 형태로 진주어 앞에 쓴다. kind, foolish, wise, honest, polite 등과 같이 사람의 성격을 나타내는 형용사가 보어로 쓰이면 의미상의 주어로 「of+목적격」의 형태를 쓴다.

- **It** is natural **for** your parents **to get** angry. 너희 부모님이 화를 내시는 것은 당연한 것이다.

- **It** is very kind **of** you **to help** me. 나를 도와주다니 넌 참 친절하다.

핵심 Check

2. 다음 괄호 안에서 알맞은 것을 고르시오.

(1) It is hard (understanding / to understand) his words.

(2) (It / That) is interesting to watch basketball games.

(3) It is good for your health (to exercise / exercise) every day.

(4) It is honest (for / of) you to say so.

(5) It is not easy (for / of) us to learn foreign languages.

01 다음 괄호 안에서 알맞은 것을 고르시오.

(1) There are many places (visit / to visit) in Jeju.

(2) Do you have anything (to do / doing) this evening?

(3) (It / That) is fun to travel to some countries in Asia.

(4) It is very kind (of / for) you to help me.

(5) It is hard (of / for) me to solve this problem.

> travel 여행하다
> solve 풀다

02 다음 밑줄 친 부분을 바르게 고쳐 쓰시오.

(1) It's difficult <u>exercise</u> every day.

　➡ _____

(2) It is impossible <u>finish</u> this work in an hour.

　➡ _____

(3) <u>That</u> is very important to learn a foreign language.

　➡ _____

(4) It was brave <u>for</u> him to save the child.

　➡ _____

(5) It was easy <u>of</u> me to answer all the questions.

　➡ _____

> exercise 운동하다
> impossible 불가능한
> save 구하다

03 다음 우리말과 일치하도록 빈칸에 알맞은 말을 쓰시오.

(1) 우리는 일정을 바꿀 시간이 없다.

　➡ We have no time _____ _____ the schedule.

(2) 그는 우리나라를 방문한 최초의 미국인이었다.

　➡ He was the first American _____ _____ our country.

(3) 나는 기차에서 읽을 책을 가져가고 싶다.

　➡ I want to bring a book _____ _____ on the train.

> schedule 일정
> country 나라

[01~02] 다음 문장의 빈칸에 알맞은 것을 고르시오.

01

> It is good for the health _____ early.

① get up　　　② got up
③ to get up　　④ to getting up
⑤ to be getting up

02 중요

> Do you have anything _____?

① read　　　② reads
③ reading　　④ to read
⑤ to be reading

03 다음 중 밑줄 친 부분의 쓰임이 나머지 넷과 다른 것은?

① He is always the first to come.
② He has nothing to write with.
③ He went to England to study English.
④ There are a lot of things for him to do.
⑤ He was looking for an apartment to live in.

04 서답형 다음 두 문장의 뜻이 같도록 빈칸에 알맞은 말을 쓰시오.

> I have a lot of letters _____ _____.
> = I have a lot of letters that I should write.

05 서답형 다음 두 문장의 뜻이 같도록 빈칸에 알맞은 말을 쓰시오

> To change the schedule is very difficult.

➡ _____ is very difficult _____ change the schedule.

06 다음 우리말과 같도록 할 때, 빈칸에 알맞은 말이 바르게 짝지어진 것은?

> 자전거를 탈 때는 헬멧을 쓰는 것이 안전하다.
> ➡ _____ is safe _____ a helmet when you ride a bike.

① It － to wear　　② This － wear
③ It － wears　　　④ It － wear
⑤ That － to wear

07 다음 중 밑줄 친 부분의 쓰임이 〈보기〉와 같은 것은?

> ┤ 보기 ├
> I have lots of books to read by next month.

① Jina has no chair to sit on.
② My hobby is to listen to music.
③ She is glad to get a letter from Tony.
④ He wants to play baseball after school.
⑤ I went to the market to buy some eggs.

서답형

08 다음 우리말과 일치하도록 주어진 단어를 바르게 배열하여 문장을 완성하시오.

너 뭐 좀 먹을래?
(anything / you / want / do / eat / to)

➡ _____

_____

중요

09 다음 중 어법상 어색한 문장은?

① It's almost time to go to bed.
② It's time to get aboard a plane.
③ It is time to eat dinner.
④ It's time for the children to going to bed.
⑤ It's time for my dad to buy a new car.

중요

10 다음 중 밑줄 친 it의 쓰임이 나머지 넷과 다른 하나는?

① It's important to be kind to others.
② Is it fun to play computer games?
③ It is not surprising for him to say so.
④ It's hard to believe, but it's a flower.
⑤ It's not easy to understand other cultures.

서답형

 11 다음 괄호 안에 주어진 말을 사용하여 우리말을 영작하시오.

그 기계를 고치는 것은 어렵다.
(it / difficult / fix / machine)

➡ _____

 12 다음 빈칸에 알맞은 말이 바르게 짝지어진 것은?

• It is very kind _____ you to say so.
• It is natural _____ a baby to cry.

① of – of   ② of – for
③ for – for   ④ for – of
⑤ for – with

13 다음 빈칸에 공통으로 알맞은 것은?

• It was honest _____ you to tell the truth.
• It is wise _____ her to make such a decision.

① of   ② for
③ with   ④ at
⑤ upon

서답형

14 다음 빈칸에 공통으로 알맞은 말을 쓰시오.

• You don't have _____ worry about it.
• I have no reason _____ be angry at you.

 15 다음 빈칸에 들어갈 동사의 형태로 적절한 것은?

It's necessary _____ on time.

① to be   ② is
③ be   ④ are
⑤ will be

16 다음 문장의 빈칸에 to를 쓸 수 없는 것은?

① It is natural for your mom _____ get angry.

② She hopes _____ visit her uncle.

③ He is kind enough _____ help us.

④ It is easy _____ speak English.

⑤ She made me _____ wash the dishes.

서답형

17 다음 문장에서 어법상 어색한 부분을 바르게 고쳐 쓰시오.

> I need a chair to sit.

_____ ➡ _____

중요

18 다음 중 밑줄 친 부분의 쓰임이 바르지 않은 것은?

① There is no bench to sit on.

② I have no money to give you.

③ Judy has a lot of friends to talk.

④ She doesn't have a house to live in.

⑤ Do you have a pen to write with?

19 다음 중 밑줄 친 부분의 쓰임이 나머지 넷과 다른 것은?

① It will soon be a new year.

② Is it easy to use this camera?

③ It is a lot of fun to ski in winter.

④ It isn't difficult to use the computer.

⑤ It is interesting to read English books.

20 다음 중 밑줄 친 to부정사의 쓰임이 다른 하나는?

① It is important to try your best.

② My dream is to be a singer.

③ I want a house to live in.

④ I decided to study Spanish.

⑤ It is very kind of you to help me.

서답형

21 다음 주어진 어구를 이용하여 〈보기〉와 같이 문장을 쓰시오.

┌─── 보기 ───┐
(boring / watch news on TV)
➡ It is boring to watch news on TV.

(pleasant / listen to music)
➡ _____

22 다음 빈칸에 들어갈 말이 바르게 짝지어진 것은?

• It's time for our children _____ to bed.
• You don't have _____ an umbrella with you.

① go – take   ② to go – taken
③ going – taking   ④ going – to take
⑤ to go – to take

서답형

23 다음 문장에서 어법상 어색한 부분을 찾아 바르게 고쳐 쓰시오.

> It is necessary for you going there as soon as possible.

_____ ➡ _____

Grammar **25**

01 다음 두 문장의 뜻이 같도록 빈칸에 알맞은 말을 쓰시오.

> To cook French food is difficult.
> ➡ _____ is difficult _____ cook French food.

02 다음 빈칸에 공통으로 알맞은 말을 쓰시오.

> • Mike had no time _____ do his homework.
> • I'm going to buy some paper _____ write on.

03 다음 주어진 단어를 바르게 배열하여 문장을 완성하시오.

(1) (bake / is / cookies / to / it / easy)
   ➡ _____

(2) (a magazine / on / he / read / the train / bought / to)
   ➡ _____

04 다음 밑줄 친 단어를 알맞은 형태로 고쳐 쓰시오.

> It is strange for her receive fan letters.

➡ _____

05 다음 괄호 안에 주어진 말을 사용하여 우리말을 영작하시오. (가주어 – 진주어 구문을 사용할 것.)

(1) 주말마다 그를 방문하는 것은 쉽지 않았다.
   (visit, easy, every)
   ➡ _____

(2) 다른 나라에서 사는 것은 재미있는 경험이다.
   (it, exciting, live, another)
   ➡ _____

06 다음 괄호 안에 주어진 어구를 이용하여 우리말을 영어로 옮기시오.

(1) 그녀는 가수가 되려는 강한 욕망을 갖고 있다.
   (strong desire, be, singer)
   ➡ _____

(2) 나는 이 문제를 해결하기 위해 모든 노력을 할 것이다. (every effort, solve)
   ➡ _____

(3) 우리는 이야기할 것이 있었다.
   (something, talk about)
   ➡ _____

(4) 나는 쓸 종이를 한 장 원한다.
   (want, write)
   ➡ _____

(5) 제게 뜨거운 마실 것을 좀 주십시오.
   (please, something, drink)
   ➡ _____

07 다음 빈칸에 알맞은 말을 〈보기〉에서 골라 쓰시오. (중복해서 사용할 수 없음.)

보기
| to | on | with | it |

(1) _____ is hard to follow good advice.
(2) Do you have anything to write _____?
(3) I need a knife to cut the rope _____.
(4) I have a lot of things _____ do today.

08 다음 문장에서 어법상 어색한 것을 찾아 바르게 고쳐 쓰시오.

(1) He doesn't have time play with his friends.

_____ ➡ _____

(2) It is important of you to study hard.

_____ ➡ _____

[09~10] 다음 우리말을 참고하여 문장을 완성하시오.

09
이 도시에는 방문해야 할 장소가 많이 있다.
➡ There are many places _____ _____ in this city.

10
너는 공부를 열심히 하는 것이 중요하다.
➡ It is important _____ _____ to study hard.

11 다음 두 문장의 뜻이 같도록 빈칸에 알맞은 말을 쓰시오.

To learn to ride a bike was not difficult.
➡ _____ was not difficult _____ to ride a bike.

12 다음 빈칸에 공통으로 알맞은 말을 쓰시오.

- It's time for my brother _____ come home.
- You don't have _____ water the flowers.

13 다음 문장에서 어법상 어색한 것을 찾아 바르게 고쳐 쓰시오.

(1) It was stupid for you to believe the rumor.

_____ ➡ _____

(2) It isn't necessary of you to come here today.

_____ ➡ _____

14 다음 주어진 단어를 이용하여 우리말을 영어로 옮기시오.

그곳은 24시간 동안 많은 물건들을 파는 장소이다.
(it's / a place / to sell / things)

➡ _____

Reading

My Special Travel Journal

Hi, I am Lucy Hunter, and I live in London. Last week, my family went on a vacation for three days. During our trip, I made simple drawings in my journal. That was a great way to capture all the special moments.

August 5

At last, we set foot at Stonehenge, one of the most mysterious places on Earth. After a two-hour drive from our home in London, we finally got to Stonehenge. It was just amazing to see the ring of huge stones. How did those huge stones get there thousands of years ago? What were they for? I guess Stonehenge will remain a mystery for a long time.

Lucy's Drawing Tips

Don't try to make perfect drawing. A few colors will be enough.

August 6

In the morning, we walked around the Cotswolds. It started to rain in the afternoon, so we decided to stay indoors at our B&B. A B&B is a popular place to stay in England. It feels more like a home than a hotel.

go on a vacation 휴가를 가다
during ~ 중에
simple 간단한, 단순한
journal 일기
capture 담아내다, 포착하다
special 특별한
moment 순간
set 놓다, 두다
mysterious 신비스러운
amazing 놀라운
ring 반지, 고리
huge 거대한, 큰
thousands of 수천의
guess 추측하다, 생각하다
remain 남아 있다
mystery 미스터리, 신비
tip 충고
perfect 완전한
enough 충분한
decide 결정하다
feel like ~처럼 느껴지다

 확인문제

● 다음 문장이 본문의 내용과 일치하면 T, 일치하지 <u>않으면</u> F를 쓰시오.

1 Lucy's family went on a vacation last week. ☐

2 Lucy wrote interesting poems in her journal. ☐

3 Lucy's family went to Stonehenge. ☐

4 Stonehenge was an old temple. ☐

5 Lucy's family stayed indoors at their B&B on August 6. ☐

The owner invited us for afternoon tea today. The dining table was full of cookies, cake, bread, and cheese. While I was busy eating, Mom was admiring the beautiful cups and plates. I ate too much, so I couldn't eat anything for dinner.

Lucy's Drawing Tips

It is O.K to draw everyday objects like cups and plates in your journal.

August 7

Our last stop was Oxford. We first visited Christ Church College. It has become a world famous place to visit since it appeared in the *Harry Potter* movies. In the movies, Harry and everyone else eat dinner at the Hall of Christ Church. We also saw portraits of famous people who graduated from the college. When we were outside the building. I walked to the famous olive tree and touched it. "Because I touched this tree," I said, "I will get into Oxford University!" Then, my brother said to me with a smile, "I can't wait to see your portrait on the wall."

Lucy's Drawing Tips

Create your own avatar. Your drawing journal will become much more interesting.

owner 주인
invite 초대하다
be full of ~으로 가득 차다
while ~하는 동안
be busy -ing ~하느라 바쁘다
admire 감탄하며 바라보다
plate 접시
everyday 매일의, 일상적인,
object 사물
become ~이 되다
appear 나타나다, 출연하다
else 또 다른, 다른
portrait 초상화
graduate 졸업하다
college 대학
touch 만지다, 대다
smile 미소, 웃음

확인문제

● 다음 문장이 본문의 내용과 일치하면 T, 일치하지 않으면 F를 쓰시오.

1 Lucy's mom wanted to buy the beautiful cups and plates. ☐

2 Lucy's family visited Christ Church College. ☐

3 Christ Church College appeared in the *Harry Potter* movies. ☐

4 Lucy didn't touch the famous olive tree. ☐

● 우리말을 참고하여 빈칸에 알맞은 말을 쓰시오.

1 Hi, I am Lucy Hunter, and I _____ in London.

2 Last _____, my family went on a _____ for three days.

3 During our _____, I made simple drawings in my _____.

4 That was a great _____ to capture all the _____ moments.

5 At last, we _____ foot at Stonehenge, one of the most _____ places on _____.

6 After a two-hour _____ from our home in London, we _____ got to Stonehenge.

7 It was just _____ to see the _____ of huge stones.

8 How did those huge _____ get there _____ of years ago?

9 What were they _____?

10 I _____ Stonehenge will remain a _____ for a long time.

11 Don't try to make a _____ drawing.

12 A few _____ will be enough.

13 _____ the morning, we walked _____ the Cotswolds.

14 It _____ to rain in the afternoon, _____ we decided to stay indoors at our B&B.

15 A B&B is a _____ place to _____ in England.

1	안녕, 나는 Lucy Hunter이고 런던에 살아요.
2	지난주에 우리 가족은 3일 동안 휴가를 갔습니다.
3	여행 중에 나는 일기에 간단한 그림을 그렸어요.
4	그것은 모든 특별한 순간을 포착하는 훌륭한 방법이었어요.
5	마침내, 우리는 지구에서 가장 불가사의한 장소 중 하나인 스톤헨지에 발을 디뎠다.
6	런던에 있는 집에서 차로 두 시간을 달려서 우리는 마침내 스톤헨지에 도착했다.
7	원형으로 둘러싸 있는 거대한 돌들을 보는 것은 정말 놀라웠다.
8	어떻게 그 거대한 돌들이 수천 년 전에 그곳에 도착했을까?
9	그것들은 무엇을 위한 것이었을까?
10	스톤헨지는 오랫동안 미스터리로 남을 것 같다.
11	완벽한 그림을 그리려고 하지 마세요.
12	몇 가지 색깔이면 충분할 것입니다.
13	아침에 우리는 코츠월드 언덕을 돌아다녔다.
14	오후에 비가 오기 시작해서, 우리는 B&B의 실내에서 머물기로 결정했다.
15	B&B는 영국에서 체류하는 곳으로 인기가 있다.

16 It feels more _____ a home than a hotel.

17 The owner _____ us for afternoon tea today.

18 The dining table was _____ of cookies, cake, bread, _____ cheese.

19 While I was _____ eating, Mom was _____ the beautiful cups and plates.

20 I ate too _____, so I couldn't eat _____ for dinner.

21 It is O.K. to _____ everyday objects _____ cups and plates in your journal.

22 Our last _____ was Oxford.

23 We first _____ Christ Church College.

24 It has _____ a world famous place to visit _____ it appeared in the *Harry Potter* movies.

25 In the _____, Harry and everyone _____ eat _____ at the Hall of Christ Church.

26 We _____ saw portraits of famous people _____ graduated from the college.

27 _____ we were _____ the building, I _____ to the famous olive tree and touched it.

28 "Because I _____ this tree," I said, "I will _____ into Oxford University!"

29 Then, my brother _____ to me with a _____, "I can't wait to see your _____ on the wall."

30 _____ your own avatar.

31 Your drawing _____ will become _____ more interesting.

16 그것은 호텔이라기보다는 집처럼 느껴진다.

17 주인은 오늘 오후의 다과회에 우리를 초대했다.

18 식탁에는 쿠키, 케이크, 빵, 그리고 치즈가 가득했다.

19 내가 먹느라고 바쁠 때, 엄마는 아름다운 컵과 접시를 감탄하며 바라보고 계셨다.

20 나는 너무 많이 먹어서 저녁으로 아무것도 먹을 수 없었다.

21 당신의 일기에 컵과 접시 같은 일상적인 물건들을 그려도 괜찮습니다.

22 우리가 마지막으로 머문 곳은 옥스퍼드였다.

23 우리는 먼저 Christ Church College를 방문했다.

24 이곳은 해리포터 영화에 등장한 이후 방문해야 할 세계적으로 유명한 장소가 되었다.

25 영화에서 Harry와 다른 모든 사람들이 Christ Church의 회관에서 저녁을 먹는다.

26 우리는 또한 그 대학을 졸업한 유명한 사람들의 초상화를 보았다.

27 우리가 건물 밖으로 나왔을 때, 나는 유명한 올리브 나무로 걸어가서 그것을 만졌다.

28 "이 나무를 만졌기 때문에, 난 옥스퍼드 대학교에 들어갈 거야!"라고 말했다.

29 그러자 오빠가 웃으면서 "벽에 걸린 네 초상화가 빨리 보고 싶어."라고 내게 말했다.

30 여러분 자신의 아바타를 만드세요.

31 그림일기가 훨씬 더 재미있을 거예요.

● 우리말을 참고하여 본문을 영작하시오.

1 안녕, 나는 Lucy Hunter이고 런던에 살아요.

➡ _____

2 지난주에 우리 가족은 3일 동안 휴가를 갔습니다.

➡ _____

3 여행 중에 나는 일기에 간단한 그림을 그렸어요.

➡ _____

4 그것은 모든 특별한 순간을 포착하는 훌륭한 방법이었어요.

➡ _____

5 마침내, 우리는 지구에서 가장 불가사의한 장소 중 하나인 스톤헨지에 발을 디뎠다.

➡ _____

6 런던에 있는 집에서 차로 두 시간을 달려서 우리는 마침내 스톤헨지에 도착했다.

➡ _____

7 원형으로 둘러서 있는 거대한 돌들을 보는 것은 정말 놀라웠다.

➡ _____

8 어떻게 그 거대한 돌들이 수천 년 전에 그곳에 도착했을까?

➡ _____

9 그것들은 무엇을 위한 것이었을까?

➡ _____

10 완벽한 그림을 그리려고 하지 마세요.

➡ _____

11 몇 가지 색깔이면 충분할 것입니다.

➡ _____

12 스톤헨지는 오랫동안 미스터리로 남을 것 같다.

➡ _____

13 아침에 우리는 코츠월드 언덕을 돌아다녔다.

➡ _____

14 오후에 비가 오기 시작해서, 우리는 B&B의 실내에서 머물기로 결정했다.

➡ _____

15 B&B는 영국에서 체류하는 곳으로 인기가 있다.

➡ _____

16 그것은 호텔이라기보다는 집처럼 느껴진다.

➡ _____

17 주인은 오늘 오후의 다과회에 우리를 초대했다.

➡ _____

18 식탁에는 쿠키, 케이크, 빵, 그리고 치즈가 가득했다.

➡ _____

19 내가 먹느라 바쁠 때, 엄마는 아름다운 컵과 접시를 감탄하며 바라보고 계셨다.

➡ _____

20 나는 너무 많이 먹어서 저녁으로 아무것도 먹을 수 없었다.

➡ _____

21 당신의 일기에 컵과 접시 같은 일상적인 물건들을 그려도 괜찮습니다.

➡ _____

22 우리가 마지막으로 머문 곳은 옥스퍼드였다.

➡ _____

23 우리는 먼저 Christ Church College를 방문했다.

➡ _____

24 이곳은 해리포터 영화에 등장한 이후 방문해야 할 세계적으로 유명한 장소가 되었다.

➡ _____

25 영화에서 Harry와 다른 모든 사람들이 Christ Church의 회관에서 저녁을 먹는다.

➡ _____

26 우리는 또한 그 대학을 졸업한 유명한 사람들의 초상화를 보았다.

➡ _____

27 우리가 건물 밖으로 나왔을 때, 나는 유명한 올리브 나무로 걸어가서 그것을 만졌다.

➡ _____

28 "이 나무를 만졌기 때문에, 난 옥스퍼드 대학교에 들어갈 거야!"라고 말했다.

➡ _____

29 그러자 오빠가 웃으면서 "벽에 걸린 네 초상화가 빨리 보고 싶어."라고 말했다.

➡ _____

30 여러분 자신의 아바타를 만드세요.

➡ _____

31 그림일기가 훨씬 더 재미있을 거예요.

➡ _____

[01~04] 다음 글을 읽고, 물음에 답하시오.

Hi, I am Lucy Hunter, and I live in London. Last week, my family went _____ⓐ a vacation _____ⓑ three days. _____ⓒ our trip, I made simple drawings in my journal. ⓓThat was a great way to capture all the special moments.

01 위 글의 빈칸 ⓐ에 알맞은 것은?

① on　　　　　② to
③ at　　　　　④ by
⑤ for

02 위 글의 빈칸 ⓑ와 ⓒ에 알맞은 말이 바르게 짝지어진 것은?

① on – During　　② in – During
③ on – While　　④ for – During
⑤ for – While

서답형
03 위 글의 밑줄 친 ⓓThat이 가리키는 것을 우리말로 쓰시오.

➡ _____

서답형
04 일기에 간단한 그림을 그리는 것의 장점을 우리말로 간단히 쓰시오.

➡ _____

[05~09] 다음 글을 읽고, 물음에 답하시오.

At last, we set foot at Stonehenge, one of the most mysterious places on Earth. (①) After a two-hour drive from our home in London, we finally got _____ⓐ Stonehenge. (②) It was just amazing to see the ring of huge stones. (③) What were they for? (④) I guess Stonehenge will remain a _____ⓑ for a long time. (⑤)
Lucy's Drawing Tips
Don't try to make a perfect drawing. _____ⓒ colors will be enough.

05 위 글의 ①~⑤ 중 주어진 문장이 들어갈 알맞은 곳은?

How did those huge stones get there thousands of years ago?

①　　　②　　　③　　　④　　　⑤

06 위 글의 빈칸 ⓐ에 알맞은 것은?

① at　　　　　② to
③ on　　　　　④ for
⑤ over

서답형
07 위 글의 빈칸 ⓑ에 다음 정의에 해당하는 단어를 주어진 철자로 시작하여 쓰시오.

something that is not understood or known about

➡ m_____

08 위 글의 빈칸 ⓒ에 알맞은 것은?

① Few   ② A few

③ Much   ④ Many

⑤ A little

09 위 글의 내용으로 보아 대답할 수 없는 질문은?

① Where did they go?

② Is Stonehenge a mysterious place?

③ How long did it take them to get to Stonehenge from their home?

④ What were the ring of huge stones for?

⑤ What is Lucy's drawing tip?

[10~15] 다음 글을 읽고, 물음에 답하시오.

(①) In the morning, we walked around the Cotswolds. (②) ⓐIt started to rain in the afternoon, so we decided to stay indoors at our B&B. A B&B is a popular place to stay in England. (③) The owner invited us for afternoon tea today. (④) The dining table was full ____ⓑ____ cookies, cake, bread, and cheese. (⑤) ____ⓒ____ I was busy eating, Mom was admiring the beautiful cups and plates. ⓓI ate too much, so I couldn't eat anything for dinner.   I = Lucy

10 위 글의 ①~⑤ 중 주어진 문장이 들어갈 알맞은 곳은?

It feels more like a home than a hotel.

①   ②   ③   ④   ⑤

11 위 글의 밑줄 친 ⓐ와 같은 용법으로 쓰이지 않은 것은?

① It's ten past twelve.

② It was raining this morning.

③ It is very dark in the room.

④ It's two miles to the beach from here.

⑤ It is in Mike's house.

12 위 글의 빈칸 ⓑ에 알맞은 것은?

① in   ② of

③ off   ④ with

⑤ from

13 위 글의 빈칸 ⓒ에 알맞은 것은?

① If   ② During

③ Since   ④ While

⑤ Though

서답형

14 위 글의 밑줄 친 ⓓ와 같은 뜻이 되도록 다음 문장의 빈칸에 알맞은 말을 쓰시오.

I couldn't eat anything _____ I ate too much.

15 위 글의 내용으로 보아 대답할 수 없는 질문은?

① Where did they walk?

② When did it begin to rain?

③ Where did they stay?

④ Why did the owner invite them for afternoon tea?

⑤ What was Lucy's mother admiring?

[16~20] 다음 글을 읽고, 물음에 답하시오.

(①) Our last stop was Oxford. (②) We first visited Christ Church College. (③) ⓐ It has become a world famous place to visit _____ ⓑ _____ it appeared in the *Harry Potter* movies. (④) ⓒWe also saw portraits of famous people who graduated the college. (⑤)

16 위 글의 ①~⑤ 중 주어진 문장이 들어갈 알맞은 곳은?

> In the movies, Harry and everyone else eat dinner at the Hall of Christ Church.

①   ②   ③   ④   ⑤

서답형

17 위 글의 밑줄 친 ⓐ가 가리키는 것을 영어로 쓰시오.

➡ _____

중요

18 위 글의 빈칸 ⓑ에 알맞은 것은?

① when   ② as
③ if   ④ while
⑤ since

서답형

19 위 글의 밑줄 친 ⓒ를 어법상 어색한 것을 고쳐 다시 쓰시오.

➡ _____
_____

20 위 글의 내용에서 언급되지 않은 것은?

① 우리가 마지막으로 들른 곳은 옥스퍼드였다.
② 우리는 Christ Church College를 방문했다.
③ Christ Church College는 영국에서 가장 인기 있는 관광지 중의 하나이다.
④ Christ Church College에서 Harry Potter 영화를 촬영했다.
⑤ Christ Church College에서 이 학교를 졸업한 유명 인사들의 초상화를 볼 수 있다.

[21~24] 다음 글을 읽고, 물음에 답하시오.

_____ ⓐ _____ we were outside the building, I walked to the _____ ⓑ _____ olive tree and touched it. "Because I touched this tree," I said, "I will get into Oxford University!" Then, my brother said to me with a smile, "I can't wait to see your portrait on the wall."

Lucy's Drawing Tips
Create your own avatar. Your drawing journal will become ⓒmuch more interesting.

I = Lucy

21 위 글의 빈칸 ⓐ에 알맞은 것은?

① When   ② Though
③ If   ④ Because
⑤ Since

서답형

22 위 글의 빈칸 ⓑ에 다음 정의에 해당하는 말을 쓰시오.

> very well known

➡ _____

23 위 글의 밑줄 친 ⓒ와 바꿔 쓸 수 <u>없는</u> 것은? (2개)

① many   ② even

③ very   ④ far

⑤ a lot

24 위 글의 내용과 일치하지 <u>않는</u> 것은?

① Lucy went out of the building.

② Lucy touched the olive tree.

③ Lucy wants to enter Oxford University.

④ Lucy's brother can see her portrait on the wall.

⑤ Lucy advises us to create our own avatar.

[25~30] 다음 글을 읽고, 물음에 답하시오.

Last winter, I went to Laos with my family. (①) We visited ⓐa lot of beautiful temples and went to the night ___ⓑ___ in Vientiane. (②) We also enjoyed their ⓒtradition food. (③) ⓓIt was a lot of fun to try new things in a foreign country. (④) I hope I will have a chance to visit Laos again. (⑤)   I = Minsu

25 위 글의 ①~⑤ 중 주어진 문장이 들어갈 알맞은 곳은?

Then, we moved to Vang Vieng and went river tubing.

①   ②   ③   ④   ⑤

26 위 글의 밑줄 친 ⓐ와 바꿔 쓸 수 있는 것은?

① few   ② many

③ much   ④ a few

⑤ little

27 위 글의 빈칸 ⓑ에 다음 정의에 해당하는 단어를 쓰시오.

a place where goods are bought and sold, usually outdoors

➡ _____

28 위 글의 밑줄 친 ⓒ를 알맞은 어형으로 고치시오.

➡ _____

29 위 글의 밑줄 친 ⓓ가 가리키는 것을 우리말로 쓰시오.

➡ _____

30 위 글의 내용으로 보아 대답할 수 <u>없는</u> 질문은?

① Who did Minsu go to Laos with?

② Why did Minsu visit temples?

③ What did Minsu do at Vang Vieng?

④ What food did Minsu enjoy?

⑤ What does Minsu hope to do?

[01~05] 다음 글을 읽고, 물음에 답하시오.

August 5

At last, we set ___ⓐ___ at Stonehenge, one of the most mysterious places on Earth. ___ⓑ___ a two-hour drive from our home in London, we finally got to Stonehenge. It was just ⓒ(amazed, amazing) to see the ring of huge stones. How did those huge stones get ⓓ<u>there</u> thousands of years ago? What were they for? I guess Stonehenge will remain a mystery for a long time.

Lucy's Drawing Tips

Don't try to make a perfect drawing. A few colors will be enough.

01 위 글의 빈칸 ⓐ에 다음 정의에 해당하는 단어를 쓰시오.

> the part of your body that is at the ends of your legs, and that you stand on

➡ _____

02 위 글의 빈칸 ⓑ에 알맞은 전치사를 쓰시오.

➡ _____

03 위 글의 괄호 ⓒ에서 알맞은 것을 고르시오.

➡ _____

04 위 글의 밑줄 친 ⓓ가 가리키는 것을 영어로 쓰시오.

➡ _____

05 What is Lucy's drawing tip? Answer in Korean.

➡ _____

[06~08] 다음 글을 읽고, 물음에 답하시오.

Hi, I am Lucy Hunter, and I live in London. Last week, my family went ___ⓐ___ a vacation for three days. ⓑ(For, During) our trip, I made simple drawings in my journal. ⓒ<u>That was a great way to capture the all special moments.</u>

06 위 글의 빈칸 ⓐ에 알맞은 전치사를 쓰시오.

➡ _____

07 위 글의 괄호 ⓑ에서 알맞은 것을 고르시오.

➡ _____

08 위 글의 밑줄 친 ⓒ에서 어법상 <u>어색한</u> 것을 고쳐 다시 쓰시오.

➡ _____

[09~15] 다음 글을 읽고, 물음에 답하시오.

August 6

In the morning, we walked around the Cotswolds. It started to rain in the afternoon, so we decided ⓐ(staying, to stay) indoors at our B&B. A B&B is a popular place to stay in England. It feels more ____ⓑ____ a home than a hotel. The ⓒown invited us for afternoon tea today. ⓓThe dining table was full of cookies, cake, bread, and cheese. While I was busy eating, Mom was admiring the beautiful cups and plates. I ate too much, ⓔso I couldn't eat nothing for dinner.

Lucy's Drawing Tips
ⓕIt is O.K. to draw everyday objects like cups and plates in your journal.

09 위 글의 괄호 ⓐ에서 알맞은 것을 고르시오.

➡ _____

10 위 글의 빈칸 ⓑ에 알맞은 말을 쓰시오.

➡ _____

11 위 글의 밑줄 친 ⓒ를 알맞은 어형으로 고치시오.

➡ _____

12 위 글의 밑줄 친 ⓓ와 같은 뜻이 되도록 다음 문장의 빈칸에 알맞은 말을 쓰시오.

The dining table was filled _____ cookies, cake, bread, and cheese.

13 위 글의 밑줄 친 ⓔ에서 어법상 어색한 것을 고치시오.

_____ ➡ _____

14 위 글의 밑줄 친 ⓕ를 우리말로 옮기시오.

➡ _____
_____

15 What was Lucy's mom doing when she was busy eating? Answer in English.

➡ _____

[16~18] 다음 글을 읽고, 물음에 답하시오.

We went on a field trip ____ⓐ____ Namhae last month. ⓑIt was just amazing to see so many beautiful islands. We also visited Namhae German Village. We'll never ⓒ(forget, remember) that trip.

16 위 글의 빈칸 ⓐ에 알맞은 말을 쓰시오.

➡ _____

17 위 글의 밑줄 친 ⓑ가 가리키는 내용을 우리말로 쓰시오.

➡ _____

18 위 글의 괄호 ⓒ에서 알맞은 것을 고르시오.

➡ _____

구석구석

Link - Share

We went on a field trip to Namhae last month. It was just amazing to see so
~로 현장 학습을 갔다 　　　　　　　　지난달　가주어　　　　　　　　진주어

many beautiful islands. We also visited Namhae German Village. We'll never
　　　　　　　　　　　　　　　　　　　　　　　　　빈도부사는 일반동사 앞에 위치한다.

forget that trip.

구문해설 · amazing: 놀라운 · island: 섬 · village: 마을 · trip: 여행

해석

우리는 지난달에 남해로 현장
학습을 갔다. 그토록 아름다
운 많은 섬들을 보는 것은 아
주 놀라웠다. 우리는 남해 독
일 마을도 방문했다. 우리는
그 여행을 절대 잊지 못할 것
이다.

Write

Last winter, I went to Laos with my family. We visited a lot of beautiful
　　　　　　　　　　　　　　~와 함께　　　　　　　　　　　많은(=lots of. many)

temples and went to the night market in Vientiane. Then, we moved to Vang
　　　　　　　　　　　　야시장

Vieng and went river tubing. We also enjoyed their traditional food. It was a
　　　　　　　　　　　　　　　　　　　　　　　　　　　　　　가주어　　= much

lot of fun to try new things in a foreign country. I hope I will have a chance to
　　　　　　진주어　　　　　　　　　　　　　　　　　　　　　　　to부정사의 형용사적 용법(~할)

visit Laos again.

구문해설 · temple: 사원, 절 · traditional: 전통적인, 전통의 · foreign: 외국의 · country: 나라
· chance: 기회

지난 겨울, 나는 가족과 함
께 라오스에 갔다. 우리는 아
름다운 절들을 많이 방문했
고 Vientiane의 야시장에 갔
다. 그리고 나서, 우리는 Vang
Vieng으로 옮겨서 강에 튜브
를 타러 갔다. 우리는 또한 그
들의 전통 음식을 즐겼다. 외
국에서 새로운 것을 시도하는
것은 매우 재미있었다. 나는
라오스를 다시 방문할 기회가
있기를 바란다.

Culture Project

September 15, 1835

We finally arrived on this island. There are many animals to study here.
　　　　　　　　　　　　　　　　　There are + 복수 명사 ~: ~가 있다　　to부정사의 형용사적 용법(~할)

Today, I saw some strange turtles. It was amazing to watch them.
　　　　　　　　　　　　　　　　　　가주어　　　　　　　진주어　　= some strange turtles

구문해설 · finally: 마침내 · arrive: 도착하다 · strange: 이상한 · amazing: 놀라운

1835년 9월 15일
우리는 마침내 이 섬에 도착
했다. 여기는 조사할 동물들이
많다. 오늘, 나는 몇몇 이상한
거북들을 보았다. 그들을 보는
것은 놀라웠다.

01 다음 중 짝지어진 단어의 관계가 나머지 넷과 <u>다른</u> 것은?

① final – finally
② slow – slowly
③ kind – kindly
④ friend – friendly
⑤ actual – actually

02 다음 빈칸에 들어갈 말로 적절하지 <u>않은</u> 것은?

• Did you _____ hear anything like that?
• Is there _____ room for me?
• What _____ did he say?
• Do you really _____ me to believe you?

① else
② ever
③ appear
④ expect
⑤ enough

03 다음 짝지어진 두 단어의 관계가 같도록 빈칸에 알맞은 말을 쓰시오.

cold : hot = same : _____

04 다음 빈칸에 들어갈 말이 바르게 짝지어진 것은?

• This is the line to get _____ the theater.
• Watch _____! There's a car coming!

① in – on
② to – off
③ into – out
④ to – after
⑤ into – for

05 다음 영영풀이에 해당하는 단어는?

a piece of land that is completely surrounded by water

① ground
② ocean
③ garden
④ earth
⑤ island

06 다음 문장의 밑줄 친 부분과 바꿔 쓸 수 있는 것은?

<u>At last</u>, the guests began to arrive.

① Usually
② Finally
③ Actually
④ Extremely
⑤ Especially

07 다음 우리말에 맞게 빈칸에 알맞은 말을 쓰시오.

그의 나이를 추측해 볼 수 있겠니?
➡ Can you _____ his age?

08 다음 중 의도하는 바가 나머지 넷과 <u>다른</u> 하나는?

① Have you seen the movie before?
② Have you had my spaghetti before?
③ Has our teacher gone home?
④ Have you ever been to China?
⑤ How many times have you been to the park?

[09~10] 다음 대화의 빈칸에 알맞은 것을 고르시오.

09

A: _____
B: It's raining.

① Do you like summer?
② Is it sunny today?
③ What's the weather like outside?
④ Do you like the windy weather?
⑤ Can you see the blue sky?

10

A: Have you ever tried Italian food?
B: _____ It was very tasty.

① Yes, I do.
② Yes, I have.
③ No, I don't.
④ No, I haven't.
⑤ Yes, I did.

11 다음 대화의 순서를 바르게 배열하시오.

(A) No, I haven't. How was it?
(B) Have you ever ridden a horse?
(C) Yes, I have. How about you?
(D) It was fun, but it was a little scary, too.

➡ _____

12 다음 빈칸에 들어갈 말로 적절하지 <u>않은</u> 것은?

A: How's the weather over there in London?
B: It's rainy. How about Seoul?
A: _____

① It's raining, too.
② It's sunny and warm.
③ It's windy and cloudy.
④ It's a beautiful city.
⑤ It's snowy and cold.

[13~16] 다음 대화를 읽고, 물음에 답하시오.

B: Mom, ⓐhow's the weather today? Do I need an umbrella? (①)
W: It's quite cloudy outside. (②)
B: Thank you, Mom. (③)
W: Well, ⓑit's not going to rain today. (④)
B: Good! Then, I don't need an umbrella today. (⑤)

13 위 대화의 ①~⑤ 중 다음 주어진 문장이 들어갈 알맞은 곳은?

I'll check the weather forecast.

①   ②   ③   ④   ⑤

14 위 대화의 밑줄 친 ⓐ와 바꿔 쓸 수 있는 것은?

① what's the weather today?
② what is it today?
③ how is it today?
④ what's the weather like today?
⑤ how's the weather like today?

15 위 대화의 밑줄 친 ⓑ와 같은 뜻이 되도록 다음 문장의 빈칸에 알맞은 말을 쓰시오.

it _____ rain today

16 Does the boy need an umbrella? Answer in English.

➡ _____

[17~18] 다음 문장의 빈칸에 알맞은 것을 고르시오.

17
> It is very dangerous _____ climb the mountain.

① to
② in
③ of
④ for
⑤ with

18
> Do you have anything _____ tomorrow?

① do
② did
③ doing
④ to do
⑤ to doing

19 다음 빈칸에 공통으로 알맞은 것은?

> • It was stupid _____ you to believe him.
> • It is clever _____ him to solve the problem.

① at
② of
③ for
④ from
⑤ with

20 다음 대화의 빈칸에 알맞은 말을 쓰시오.

> A: I think _____ _____ difficult to find the things I want to buy.
> B: You know, they have information desks.

21 다음 중 어법상 어색한 것은?

① Jane kept her promise to enter a university.
② Kathy wants someone to travel with.
③ Mike wants interesting something to read.
④ Linda doesn't have a pen to write with.
⑤ She was the first woman to land on the moon.

22 다음 중 밑줄 친 부분의 쓰임이 〈보기〉와 다른 것은?

> ┤ 보기 ├
> Jake has a lot of homework to do today.

① I need somebody to talk to.
② Frank must be crazy to quit his job.
③ I don't have time to chat with you.
④ She couldn't find any chairs to sit on.
⑤ Do you know the way to get to City Hall?

23 다음 중 밑줄 친 부분의 쓰임이 나머지 넷과 다른 것은?

① It is necessary for you to study hard.
② It is too cold to go swimming in the lake.
③ It's good to try to solve the problem.
④ It is difficult for us to achieve the goal.
⑤ It is dangerous to walk alone at midnight.

24 다음 문장에서 어법상 어색한 부분을 바르게 고쳐 쓰시오.

> Kirk needs a ball pen to write.

_____ ➡ _____

25 다음 우리말을 영어로 바르게 옮긴 것은?

> 냉장고에는 먹을 음식이 많이 있다.

① There are a lot of food to eat in the refrigerator.
② There are a lot of food eating in the refrigerator.
③ There is a lot of food eating in the refrigerator.
④ There is a lot of foods to eat in the refrigerator.
⑤ There is a lot of food to eat in the refrigerator.

26 다음 단어를 바르게 배열하여 문장을 완성하시오.

> anything / myself / to make / slimmer / look

➡ I will do _____.

27 다음 두 문장이 같은 뜻이 되도록 빈칸에 알맞은 말을 쓰시오.

> To finish this work is very important.
> = _____ is very important _____ finish this work.

[28~31] 다음 글을 읽고, 물음에 답하시오.

> Last winter, I went to Laos with my family. (①) We visited ⓐa lot of beautiful temples and went to the night market in Vientiane. (②) Then, we moved to Vang Vieng and went river tubing. (③) We also enjoyed their traditional food. (④) I hope I will have a chance ⓑvisit Laos again. (⑤)   I=Minsu

28 위 글의 ①~⑤ 중 다음 주어진 문장이 들어갈 알맞은 곳은?

> It was a lot of fun to try new things in a foreign country.

①   ②   ③   ④   ⑤

29 위 글의 밑줄 친 ⓐ 대신 쓸 수 있는 것은? (2개)

① many   ② few
③ much   ④ a little
⑤ lots of

30 위 글의 밑줄 친 ⓑ를 알맞은 형태로 고치시오.

➡ _____

31 위 글의 내용으로 보아 알 수 없는 것은?

① Minsu went to Laos last winter.
② Minsu's family visited beautiful temples.
③ Minsu did shopping at the night market in Vientiane.
④ Minsu's family went to Vang Vieng.
⑤ Minsu wishes to visit Laos again.

[32~37] 다음 글을 읽고, 물음에 답하시오.

August 7

Our last stop was Oxford. We first visited Christ Church College. It ___ⓐ___ a world famous place to visit since it appeared in the *Harry Potter* movies. In the movies, Harry and everyone else ⓑ<u>eat</u> dinner at the Hall of Christ Church. We also saw portraits of famous people ___ⓒ___ graduated from the college. When we were outside the building, I walked to the famous olive tree and touched it. "ⓓ<u>Because</u> I touched this tree," I said, "I will get into Oxford University!" Then, my brother said to me with a smile, "I can't wait to see your portrait on the wall."

Lucy's Drawing Tips
Create your own avatar. Your drawing journal will become ⓔ<u>much</u> *more interesting.*

32 위 글의 빈칸 ⓐ에 알맞은 것은?

① becomes   ② became
③ is becoming   ④ has become
⑤ had become

33 위 글의 밑줄 친 ⓑ 대신 쓸 수 있는 말을 쓰시오.

➡ _____

34 위 글의 빈칸 ⓒ에 알맞은 것은? (2개)

① whom   ② who
③ that   ④ what
⑤ which

35 위 글의 밑줄 친 ⓓ 대신 쓸 수 있는 것은?

① As   ② If
③ When   ④ Though
⑤ While

36 위 글의 밑줄 친 ⓔ 대신 쓸 수 <u>없는</u> 것은? (2개)

① far   ② very
③ even   ④ many
⑤ a lot

37 위 글의 내용으로 보아 대답할 수 <u>없는</u> 질문은?

① What was their last stop?
② Why is Christ Church College famous?
③ Who graduated from Christ Church College?
④ What did Lucy do when she was outside the building?
⑤ What did Lucy's brother say to her?

[38~39] 다음 글을 읽고, 물음에 답하시오.

September 15, 1835

We ⓐ<u>final</u> arrived on this island. There are many animals to study here. Today, I saw some strange turtles. ⓑ<u>It</u> was amazing to watch them.

38 위 글의 밑줄 친 ⓐ를 알맞은 형으로 고치시오.

➡ _____

39 위 글의 밑줄 친 ⓑ가 가리키는 것을 우리말로 쓰시오.

➡ _____

01 출제율 90%

다음 중 짝지어진 단어의 관계가 나머지 넷과 다른 것은?

① warm : cool
② different : same
③ remember : forget
④ huge : large
⑤ indoors : outdoors

02 출제율 95%

다음 두 문장이 같은 뜻이 되도록 빈칸에 알맞은 것은?

A bus appeared around the corner.
= A bus showed _____ around the corner.

① in
② up
③ out
④ off
⑤ onto

03 출제율 90%

다음 짝지어진 두 단어의 관계가 같도록 빈칸에 알맞은 말을 쓰시오.

create : _____ = decide : decision

04 출제율 85%

다음 우리말에 맞게 빈칸에 알맞은 말을 쓰시오.

다른 누군가에게 도와 달라고 부탁해 봐.
➡ Ask somebody _____ to help you.

05 출제율 95%

다음 중 영영풀이가 잘못된 것은?

① earth: the planet on which we live
② invite: to ask someone to come to something such as a party
③ relax: to feel more calm and less worried or tense
④ travel: to go from one place to another, often to a place that is far away
⑤ carry: to put clothes and other things into a bag, because you are leaving a place

06 출제율 100%

다음 빈칸에 알맞은 것을 모두 고르시오.

A: _____
B: It's snowing.
A: Really? I should wear my snow boots. Thanks.

① How's the weather today?
② What weather do you like today?
③ What's the snowy weather today?
④ What's the weather like today?
⑤ What does the cloud look like?

07 출제율 95%

다음 대화의 빈칸에 알맞은 것은?

A: _____
B: No, I haven't, but I've heard of it many times.

① How often have you been to Namsan?
② Did you go to Namsan?
③ When did you go to Namsan?
④ Have you ever been to Namsan?
⑤ How many times did you visit Namsan?

[09~10] 다음 대화를 읽고, 물음에 답하시오.

> Suho: Anna, have you ⓐ<u>be</u> to Australia before?
>
> Anna: Yes, I have. Actually, I lived in Sydney for a year.
>
> Suho: Great! How's the weather there in April? I'm going to visit Sydney on vacation next week.
>
> Anna: April is a great time to visit Sydney. In April, it's autumn in Australia.
>
> Suho: Good. ⓑ<u>I'm planning to spend some time on the beach and relax in the sun.</u>
>
> Anna: Well, it often rains in April, but you may have some sunny days.
>
> Suho: I'll take my hat and pack an umbrella, too.
>
> Anna: That's a good idea. Have a great time.

08 위 대화의 밑줄 친 ⓐ를 알맞은 어형으로 고치시오.

➡ _____

09 위 대화의 밑줄 친 ⓑ를 우리말로 옮기시오.

➡ _____
_____

10 위 대화의 내용과 일치하지 <u>않는</u> 것은?

① Anna는 호주를 방문한 적이 있다.
② Anna는 시드니에서 1년간 산 직이 있다.
③ 수호는 다음 주에 시드니를 방문할 예정이다.
④ 4월에 호주의 날씨는 가을이다.
⑤ 4월의 시드니 날씨는 대체로 화창하다.

11 다음 문장에서 어법상 어색한 부분을 바르게 고쳐 쓰시오.

> Mary needs some paper to write.

_____ ➡ _____

12 다음 빈칸에 알맞은 말이 바르게 짝지어진 것은?

> • It was wise _____ you to agree to the proposal.
> • It is impossible _____ us to win the game.

① of – of
② of – for
③ for – for
④ for – of
⑤ for – with

13 다음 빈칸에 들어갈 동사의 형태로 적절한 것은?

> It's necessary for you _____ the piano every day.

① practice
② practiced
③ practicing
④ to practice
⑤ to practicing

14 다음 두 문장이 같은 뜻이 되도록 빈칸에 알맞은 말을 쓰시오.

> To solve this puzzle is very difficult.
> ➡ _____ is very difficult _____ solve this puzzle.

15 다음 중 〈보기〉의 밑줄 친 It과 쓰임이 같은 것은?

> ─── 보기 ───
> <u>It</u> is very important to check the weather forecast every day.

① <u>It</u> is freezing here.
② <u>It</u> is not my lost puppy.
③ <u>It</u> was built by them.
④ <u>It</u> rained a lot yesterday morning.
⑤ <u>It</u> is fun to play soccer with my friends.

16 다음 중 어법상 어색한 문장은?

① I need a chair to sit.
② Columbus was the first man to discover the American Continent.
③ We have no house to live in.
④ He has a wish to become a pilot.
⑤ She forgot to bring something to write with.

17 다음 우리말을 영어로 바르게 옮긴 것은?

> 로마에는 방문할 장소가 많이 있다.

① There is many places visit in Rome.
② There are visiting many places in Rome.
③ There are many places visiting in Rome.
④ There are to visit many places in Rome.
⑤ There are many places to visit in Rome.

18 다음 중 밑줄 친 부분의 쓰임이 나머지 넷과 <u>다른</u> 하나는?

① He drove very quickly <u>to get</u> there on time.
② Katherine is coming to Seoul <u>to visit</u> us.
③ I'm going to the park <u>to walk</u> my dogs.
④ There's nothing <u>to be</u> afraid of any more.
⑤ I went to the post office <u>to send</u> the parcel.

[19~20] 다음 글을 읽고, 물음에 답하시오.

> Hi, I am Lucy Hunter, and I live in London. Last week, my family went on a vacation ___ⓐ___ three days. During our trip, I made simple drawings in my journal. That was a great way ⓑ<u>to capture</u> all the special moments.

19 위 글의 빈칸 ⓐ에 알맞은 것은?

① in   ② for
③ to   ④ at
⑤ during

20 위 글의 밑줄 친 ⓑ와 같은 용법으로 쓰인 것은?

① We wished <u>to reach</u> the North Pole.
② He made a promise <u>to come</u> again.
③ He was excited <u>to see</u> the scenery.
④ The boy grew up <u>to be</u> a poet.
⑤ We decided <u>to go</u> fishing in the river.

[21~26] 다음 글을 읽고, 물음에 답하시오.

August 5

ⓐAt last, we set foot at Stonehenge, one of the most mysterious places on Earth. After a two-hour drive from our home in London, we finally ⓑgot to Stonehenge. It was just amazing to see the ring of huge stones. ⓒHow did those huge stones get there thousand of years ago? What were they for? I guess Stonehenge will ___ⓓ___ a mystery for a long time.

Lucy's Drawing Tips
Don't try ⓔ(making, to make) a perfect drawing. A few colors will be enough.

출제율 95%

21 위 글의 밑줄 친 ⓐ 대신 쓸 수 있는 것은?

① In fact   ② In contrast
③ As a fact   ④ As a result
⑤ In the long run

출제율 100%

22 위 글의 밑줄 친 ⓑ 대신 쓸 수 있는 것은?

① arrived   ② reached
③ received   ④ appeared
⑤ happened

출제율 85%

23 위 글의 밑줄 친 ⓒ에서 어법상 어색한 것을 고치시오.

_____ ➡ _____

출제율 90%

24 위 글의 빈칸 ⓓ에 알맞은 것은?

① seem   ② look
③ remain   ④ appear
⑤ belong

출제율 95%

25 위 글의 괄호 ⓔ에서 알맞은 것을 고르시오

➡ _____

출제율 85%

26 위 글의 내용으로 보아 알 수 없는 것은? (2개)

① 스톤헨지는 세계에서 가장 신비한 곳들 중의 하나다.
② 런던의 집에서 스톤헨지까지 가는 데는 자동차로 두 시간 걸렸다.
③ 스톤헨지에서 거대한 돌들의 고리를 보았다.
④ Lucy는 그 거대한 돌들의 용도를 알았다.
⑤ 머지않아 스톤헨지의 미스터리가 풀릴 것이다.

[27~29] 다음 글을 읽고, 물음에 답하시오.

We went on a field trip to Namhae last month. ⓐIt was just amazing to see so many beautiful islands. We also visited Namhae German Village. We'll never forget that trip.

출제율 95%

27 위 글의 밑줄 친 ⓐ를 우리말로 옮기시오.

➡ _____

출제율 90%

28 When did they go to Namhae? Answer in English.

➡ _____

[01~03] 다음 대화를 읽고, 물음에 답하시오.

W: ⓐHave you gone to any special places in Korea?

M: Yes, I have. I went to Ulleungdo last summer with my family.

W: ⓑHow was the weather there?

M: It was mostly sunny, ⓒ the weather changed often.

01 위 대화의 밑줄 친 ⓐ에서 어법상 어색한 것을 고치시오.

_____ ➡ _____

02 위 대화의 밑줄 친 ⓑ와 같은 뜻이 되도록 다음 문장의 빈칸에 알맞은 말을 쓰시오.

_____ was the weather _____ there?

03 위 대화의 빈칸 ⓒ에 알맞은 접속사를 쓰시오.

➡ _____

04 다음 대화의 순서를 바르게 배열하시오.

(A) Mom, how's the weather today?
(B) Thanks, Mom.
(C) It's quite cloudy outside. I'll check the weather forecast.
(D) Well, it's going to rain in the afternoon.

➡ _____

05 다음 우리말의 의미에 맞도록 주어진 어구를 이용하여 영작하시오.

(1) 매일 일기를 쓰는 것은 쉽지 않다.
 (it, easy, keep, every)
 ➡ _____

(2) 나는 내 남동생이 찍는 사진들을 좋아한다.
 (photographs, which, takes)
 ➡ _____
 _____

06 다음 〈조건〉에 맞게 괄호 안의 단어를 이용하여 우리말을 영어로 옮기시오.

┌─ 조건 ─────────────────┐
1. 주어진 단어를 모두 이용할 것.
2. 필요시 관사를 붙이거나 단어를 추가 할 것.
3. It으로 시작할 것.
4. 대·소문자 및 구두점에 유의할 것.
└────────────────────────┘

(1) 내가 자동차를 주차하기는 어렵다.
 (difficult, me, park, car)
 ➡ _____

(2) 헬멧을 쓰고 자전거를 타는 것이 안전하다.
 (safe, ride, bike, with, helmet)
 ➡ _____

(3) 다른 나라에서 사는 것은 흥미진진한 경험이다.
 (exciting, experience, live, another, country)
 ➡ _____
 _____

07 다음 하루 일과표를 보고 빈칸에 알맞은 내용을 완성하시오.

8:00 a.m.	school
12:10 p.m.	lunch
5:00 p.m.	playground
6:30 p.m.	homework

(1) It's 8 a.m. It's time _____.

(2) It's 12:10 p.m. It's time _____.

(3) It's 5 p.m. It's time _____.

(4) It's 6:30 p.m. It's time _____.

[08~12] 다음 글을 읽고, 물음에 답하시오.

August 6

In the morning, we walked around the Cotswolds. ⓐIt started to rain in the afternoon, so we decided to stay indoors at our B&B. A B&B is a popular place to stay in England. ⓑIt feels more like a home than a hotel. The owner invited us for afternoon tea today. The dining table was full ⓒ_____ cookies, cake, bread, and cheese. While I was busy eating, Mom was admiring the beautiful cups and plates. I ate too much, so I couldn't eat ⓓ(something, anything) for dinner.

08 위 글의 밑줄 친 ⓐ와 같은 뜻이 되도록 빈칸에 알맞은 말을 쓰시오.

> We decided to stay indoors at our B&B _____ it started to rain in the afternoon.

09 위 글의 밑줄 친 ⓑ가 가리키는 것을 영어로 쓰시오.

➡ _____

10 위 글의 빈칸 ⓒ에 알맞은 전치사를 쓰시오.

➡ _____

11 위 글의 괄호 ⓓ에서 알맞은 것을 고르시오.

➡ _____

12 What did they do in the morning? Answer in English.

➡ _____

[13~15] 다음 글을 읽고, 물음에 답하시오.

Last winter, I went to Laos with my family. We visited ⓐa lot of beautiful temples and went to the night market in Vientiane. Then, we moved to Vang Vieng and went river tubing. We also enjoyed their traditional food. It was a lot of fun to try new things in a foreign country. ⓑI hope I will have a chance to visit Laos again.

13 위 글의 밑줄 친 ⓐ를 한 단어로 바꿔 쓰시오.

➡ _____

14 위 글의 밑줄 친 ⓑ를 우리말로 옮기시오.

➡ _____

15 Who did the writer go to Laos with? Answer in English.

➡ _____

01 다음 주어진 상황에 맞게 〈to부정사〉와 괄호 안의 단어를 이용하여 〈보기〉처럼 문장을 완성하시오.

> 보기
>
> I'm hungry. I need some food to eat. (eat)

(1) I'm very thirsty. _____ (drink)

(2) There's no chair here. _____ (sit)

(3) Tony feels lonely. _____ (talk)

02 다음 어구들을 연결하여 〈보기〉와 같이 한 문장으로 쓰시오.

• impossible	• him	• to visit	• his hometown
• kind	• foreigners	• to watch	• Korean
• difficult	• us	• to agree	• the work on time
• stupid	• her	• to finish	• the poor
• possible	• you	• to help	• to the proposal
• necessary	• me	• to learn	• the game

> 보기
>
> It is impossible for him to visit his hometown.

(1) _____

(2) _____

(3) _____

(4) _____

(5) _____

03 다음 Jessica의 이번 주 일정표를 보고, 내용에 맞도록 문장을 완성하시오.

Mon.	Tue.	Wed.	Thu.	Fri.
movie / watch	a piano lesson / take	a baseball game / watch	a piano lesson / take	four comic books / read

(1) Jessica has _____ _____ _____ _____ this Monday.

(2) Jessica has _____ _____ _____ _____ on TV this Wednesday.

(3) Jessica has _____ _____ _____ _____ on Tuesday and Thurday.

(4) Jessica has _____ _____ _____ _____ on Friday.

단원별 모의고사

01 다음 영영풀이에 해당하는 단어로 알맞은 것은?

> to cause something to happen or exist

① make ② repair ③ fix
④ create ⑤ prepare

02 다음 중 우리말 뜻이 <u>잘못된</u> 것은?

① at last: 마침내
② a little: 좀, 약간; 약간의
③ right now: 잠시
④ a lot of: 많은
⑤ set foot at: ~에 발을 디디다

03 다음 빈칸에 공통으로 알맞은 것은?

> • The bathtub was full _____ hot water.
> • Tom is fond _____ Kathy.

① at ② to ③ for
④ of ⑤ with

04 다음 짝지어진 두 단어의 관계가 같도록 빈칸에 알맞은 말을 쓰시오.

> arrive : arrival = decide : _____

05 다음 빈칸에 공통으로 들어갈 말을 쓰시오.

> • Mary didn't show _____ for the meeting yesterday.
> • I'm planning to clean _____ the park with my dad.

[06~08] 다음 대화의 빈칸에 알맞은 것을 고르시오.

06

> A: Have you ever caught a big fish?
> B: _____ I wish to catch it someday.

① Yes, I have.
② No, I haven't.
③ I caught a big fish.
④ Yes, my uncle caught a big fish.
⑤ I caught it and put it back.

07

> A: _____
> B: No, I haven't.

① Do you have a sister?
② Does he live with his grandparents?
③ Have you ever seen a bear?
④ Which country have you travelled?
⑤ Are you happy with the new class?

08

> A: What's the weather like there?
> B: _____

① I like hot summer.
② I got a bad cold.
③ I enjoy skiing here.
④ I should wear a coat.
⑤ It's cold and sometimes it snows a lot.

[09~10] 다음 대화를 읽고, 물음에 답하시오.

G: Bill, have you ever gone bungee jumping?
B: No, I haven't. ___ⓐ___ about you, Katie?
G: When I visited New Zealand, I tried bungee jumping once.
B: Wasn't it scary?
G: No, I liked it. I want to do it again.

09 위 대화의 빈칸 ⓐ에 알맞은 것은? (2개)

① How   ② Who
③ What   ④ Why
⑤ Which

10 위 대화의 내용으로 보아 알 수 없는 것은?

① Bill은 번지 점프를 해 본 적이 없다.
② Katie는 뉴질랜드를 방문한 적이 있다.
③ Katie는 번지 점프를 해 본 적이 있다.
④ Bill은 두려워서 번지 점프를 시도해 보지 않았다.
⑤ Katie는 다시 번지 점프를 하기를 원한다.

[11~13] 다음 문장의 빈칸에 알맞은 것을 고르시오.

11

My brother has many things _____ tonight.

① do   ② does
③ doing   ④ to do
⑤ to be doing

12

Kate is looking for a friend to travel _____.

① at   ② in   ③ with
④ on   ⑤ for

13

Alice and Ken are going to enter Berkeley. They need a dormitory _____.

① live   ② to live
③ to live in   ④ to live with
⑤ to living

14 다음 빈칸에 주어진 단어의 알맞은 형태를 쓰시오.

Is it possible _____ the project by tomorrow? (finish)

15 다음 밑줄 친 부분의 쓰임이 〈보기〉와 같은 것은?

┌─ 보기 ─────────────────┐
I have nothing special to eat in my bag.
└──────────────────────────┘

① She packed her bag to go home.
② I was happy to find my cell phone.
③ The man needs someone to look after his cat.
④ To eat breakfast is good for your brain.
⑤ We went to the school store to buy some snacks.

[16~17] 다음 중 어법상 알맞지 <u>않은</u> 문장을 고르시오.

16
① The man needs a piece of paper to write on.
② Amy has no house to live in.
③ There's nothing to worry about.
④ Give me a pen to write with.
⑤ You seem to have important something to tell me.

17
① It's hard to climb the tree.
② It's great fun skate on ice.
③ It's fun to watch a baseball game.
④ It's important for us to study English.
⑤ It's interesting to take a trip to strange lands.

18 다음 괄호 안의 단어 형태가 바르게 짝지어진 것은?

> • I have something (tell) you.
> • Do you have anything (read)?

① tell – read
② tell – to read
③ to tell – read
④ telling – read
⑤ to tell – to read

19 다음 밑줄 친 ⓐ, ⓑ를 어법상 올바른 형태로 쓰시오.

> I think shopping on the Internet is good.
> It's easy ⓐ<u>find</u> the things I want to buy.
> It's also easy ⓑ<u>find</u> good prices.

ⓐ _____ ⓑ _____

[20~23] 다음 글을 읽고, 물음에 답하시오.

> Our ①<u>last</u> stop was Oxford. We ②<u>first</u> visited Christ Church College. It has become a world famous place to visit ___ⓐ___ it appeared in the *Harry Potter* movies. In the movies, Harry and everyone ③<u>other</u> eat dinner ④<u>at</u> the Hall of Christ Church. We ⑤<u>also</u> saw portraits of famous people ___ⓑ___ graduated from the college.

20 위 글의 밑줄 친 ①~⑤ 중 어법상 어색한 것은?

① ② ③ ④ ⑤

21 위 글의 빈칸 ⓐ에 알맞은 것은?

① for ② when
③ during ④ since
⑤ while

22 위 글의 빈칸 ⓑ에 알맞은 것은?

① who ② that
③ what ④ whom
⑤ which

23 위 글의 내용으로 보아 알 수 <u>없는</u> 것은?

① 우리가 마지막으로 들른 곳은 옥스퍼드였다.
② 우리는 Christ Church College를 방문했다.
③ Christ Church College는 Harry Potter 영화에 나왔다.
④ Harry Potter는 Christ Church College의 학생이다.
⑤ 우리는 Christ Church College를 졸업한 유명한 사람들의 초상화를 보았다.

[24~27] 다음 글을 읽고, 물음에 답하시오.

_____ ⓐ _____ we were outside the building, I walked to the famous olive tree and touched it. " _____ ⓑ _____ I touched this tree," I said, "I will get into Oxford University!" Then, my brother said to me with a smile, "I can't wait to see your _____ ⓒ _____ on the wall."

Lucy's Drawing Tips
Create your own avatar. Your drawing journal will become _____ ⓓ _____ *more interesting.*

24 위 글의 빈칸 ⓐ와 ⓑ에 알맞은 말이 바르게 짝지어진 것은?

① If – Because
② As – Though
③ When – Because
④ Since – Because
⑤ When – While

25 위 글의 빈칸 ⓒ에 다음 정의에 해당하는 단어를 쓰시오.

a painting, drawing, or photograph of a particular person

➡ _____

26 위 글의 빈칸 ⓓ에 알맞지 <u>않은</u> 것은?

① very
② far
③ even
④ much
⑤ a lot

27 Why is the olive tree famous? Answer in Korean.

➡ _____

[28~30] 다음 글을 읽고, 물음에 답하시오.

Last winter, I went to Laos with my family. (①) We visited <u>a lot of</u> beautiful temples and went to the night market in Vientiane. (②) We also enjoyed their traditional food. (③) It was a lot of fun to try new things in a foreign country. (④) I hope I will have a chance to visit Laos again. (⑤)

I=Minsu

28 위 글의 ①~⑤ 중 다음 주어진 문장이 들어갈 알맞은 곳은?

Then, we moved to Vang Vieng and went river tubing.

①   ②   ③   ④   ⑤

29 위 글의 밑줄 친 부분을 한 단어로 쓰시오.

➡ _____

30 위 글의 내용으로 보아 대답할 수 <u>없는</u> 질문은?

① Where did Minsu go last winter?
② Where did Minsu go in Vientiane?
③ Was it a lot of fun to try new things in a foreign country?
④ What was their traditional food?
⑤ Does Minsu wish to visit Laos again?

Lesson 4

Giving a Hand

 의사소통 기능

- 도움 요청하기
  Can you do me a favor?

- 감사하기
  Thank you for sharing your umbrella with me.

 언어 형식

- 목적격 관계대명사
  He was the person **who[whom]** Kenneth respected the most in the world.

- so ~ that ... 구문
  He was **so** happy **that** he jumped for joy.

Words & Expressions

Key Words

- **activity** [æktívəti] 몡 활동
- **actually** [ǽktʃuəli] 뷔 실제로, 정말로
- **always** [ɔ́ːlweiz] 뷔 항상, 언제나
- **bath** [bæθ] 몡 목욕, 욕조
- **believe** [bilíːv] 동 믿다, 생각하다
- **board** [bɔːrd] 몡 판자, 널
- **build** [bild] 동 (건물을) 짓다, 건설[건축]하다
- **childhood** [tʃáildhùd] 몡 어린 시절
- **clean** [kliːn] 혱 깨끗한 동 닦다, 청소하다
- **close** [klouz] 혱 가까운, 친한
- **comfortable** [kʌ́mfərtəbl] 혱 편한, 편안한
- **condition** [kəndíʃən] 몡 상태
- **create** [kriéit] 동 창조[창작]하다, 만들어 내다
- **daughter** [dɔ́ːtər] 몡 딸, 여식
- **disease** [dizíːz] 몡 질병, 병
- **driver** [dráivər] 몡 운전자, 운전기사
- **error** [érər] 몡 실수, 오류
- **favor** [féivər] 몡 호의, 친절
- **fix** [fiks] 동 고정시키다, 수리하다
- **generation** [dʒènəréiʃən] 몡 세대, 대
- **gift** [gift] 몡 선물, 재능
- **happiness** [hǽpinis] 몡 행복, 만족, 기쁨
- **heavy** [hévi] 혱 무거운 (↔ light)
- **heel** [hiːl] 몡 발뒤꿈치, 뒤꿈치
- **homeless** [hóumlis] 혱 노숙자의
- **invention** [invénʃən] 몡 발명, 발명품
- **inventor** [invéntər] 몡 발명가, 창안자
- **joy** [dʒɔi] 몡 기쁨, 환희
- **just** [dʒʌst] 뷔 그저, 단지, 방금
- **local** [lóukəl] 혱 (특정) 지역의, 현지의
- **lucky** [lʌ́ki] 혱 운이 좋은, 행운의
- **material** [mətíəriəl] 몡 (물건의) 재료
- **nothing** [nʌ́θiŋ] 때 아무것도[단 하나도] (~ 아니다)
- **perfect** [pə́ːrfikt] 혱 완전한, 완벽한
- **person** [pə́ːrsn] 몡 사람, 개인
- **plant** [plænt] 몡 식물, 초목
- **pleasure** [pléʒər] 몡 기쁨, 즐거움
- **pressure** [préʃər] 몡 압력, 압박
- **project** [prádʒekt] 몡 프로젝트, 과제
- **proud** [praud] 혱 자랑스러워하는, 자랑스러운
- **purpose** [pə́ːrpəs] 몡 목적
- **respect** [rispékt] 동 존경하다 몡 존경
- **safety** [séifti] 몡 안전, 안전성
- **sensor** [sénsər] 몡 센서, 감지기
- **share** [ʃɛər] 동 함께 쓰다, 공유하다
- **shock** [ʃɑk] 몡 충격 동 쇼크[충격]를 주다
- **shopping** [ʃápiŋ] 몡 쇼핑
- **signal** [sígnəl] 몡 신호
- **still** [stil] 뷔 아직(도), 여전히
- **succeed** [səksíːd] 동 성공하다 (↔ fail)
- **support** [səpɔ́ːrt] 동 지지하다, 지원하다
- **trial** [tráiəl] 몡 시험, 실험
- **truly** [trúːli] 뷔 정말로, 진심으로
- **trusty** [trʌ́sti] 혱 신뢰할 수 있는
- **understand** [ʌndərstǽnd] 동 이해하다, 알아듣다
- **until** [əntíl] 접 ~할 때까지 전 ~까지
- **volunteer** [vὰləntíər] 몡 자원 봉사자
- **wander** [wándər] 동 거닐다, 돌아다니다, 헤매다
- **worry** [wə́ːri] 동 걱정하다, 걱정[불안]하게 만들다
- **worse** [wəːrs] 혱 더 나쁜, 더 심한 뷔 더 심하게

Key Expressions

- **at first** 처음에는
- **be thankful for** ~에 대해 감사히 여기다
- **cheer up** 힘을 불러일으키다, ~을 격려하다
- **come over to** ~에 오다
- **come up with** (해답 등을) 찾아내다[내놓다]
- **feel like -ing** ~하고 싶다
- **for[with] joy** 기뻐서

- **give up** 포기하다
- **grow up** 성장하다, 자라다
- **keep an eye on** ~을 계속 지켜보다
- **look for** ~을 찾다
- **take care of** ~을 돌보다, 뒷바라지하다
- **thank A for B** A에게 B에 대해 감사하다
- **wander off** 여기저기 쏘다니다

Word Power

※ 별개의 단어를 쓰는 남성명사와 여성명사

- □ **son**(아들) – **daughter**(딸)
- □ **king**(왕) – **queen**(여왕)
- □ **husband**(남편) – **wife**(아내)
- □ **nephew**(조카) – **niece**(조카딸)
- □ **boy**(소년) – **girl**(소녀)

- □ **uncle**(삼촌) – **aunt**(숙모)
- □ **bull**(황소) – **cow**(암소)
- □ **dad**(아빠) – **mom**(엄마)
- □ **rooster**(수탉) – **hen**(암탉)

English Dictionary

- □ **always** 항상, 언제나
  - → at all times 항상
- □ **believe** 믿다
  - → to accept or regard something as true
    원가를 사실로 받아들이거나 간주하다
- □ **build** (건물을) 짓다, 건설[건축]하다
  - → to make something by joining things together
    사물들을 함께 결합해서 어떤 것을 만들다
- □ **childhood** 어린 시절
  - → the period of a person's life when they are a child
    어떤 사람이 아이이던 시절
- □ **comfortable** 편한, 편안한
  - → making you feel physically relaxed when you use something
    당신이 무언가를 사용할 때 신체적으로 편안함을 느끼게 만드는
- □ **create** 창조하다, 만들어 내다
  - → cause something to happen or exist
    어떤 것이 발생하거나 존재하게 하다
- □ **driver** 운전자, 운전기사
  - → the person who is driving a vehicle
    차를 운전하는 사람
- □ **gift** 선물
  - → something that you give someone as a present
    당신이 누군가에게 선물로 주는 것
- □ **heavy** 무거운
  - → weighing a lot
    무게가 많이 나가는
- □ **heel** 발뒤꿈치, 뒤꿈치
  - → the back part of your foot, just below your ankle
    발목 바로 아래에 있는 발의 뒷부분
- □ **inventor** 발명가
  - → a person who has invented something, or whose job is to invent things
    무언가를 발명했거나, 무언가를 발명하는 것이 직업인 사람
- □ **joy** 기쁨, 환희
  - → a feeling of great happiness 대단한 행복감
- □ **perfect** 완전한, 완벽한
  - → as good as something could possibly be
    어떤 것이 가능할 수 있을 만큼 좋은
- □ **plant** 식물, 초목
  - → a living thing that grows in the earth and has a stem, leaves, and roots, especially one that is smaller than a tree or bush
    땅에서 자라고 줄기, 잎, 뿌리를 가진 생물, 특히 나무나 덤불보다 작은 생물
- □ **pressure** 압력, 압박
  - → force that you produce when you press hard on something
    어떤 것을 세게 누를 때 당신이 만들어 내는 힘
- □ **project** 프로젝트, 과제
  - → a task or problem in school that requires careful work over a long period of time
    학교에서 장기간에 걸쳐 주의 깊은 연구가 필요한 임무 또는 문제
- □ **safety** 안전
  - → the state of being safe from harm or danger
    해로움 또는 위험으로부터 안전한 상태
- □ **support** 지지하다, 후원하다
  - → to agree with someone, and perhaps help them because you want them to succeed
    다른 사람의 의견에 동의하고, 어쩌면 그들이 성공하기를 원하기 때문에 그들을 돕다
- □ **worry** 걱정하다
  - → to keep thinking about problems that you have or about unpleasant things that might happen
    당신이 가지고 있는 문제나 일어날지도 모르는 불쾌한 것들에 대해 계속 생각하다

01 다음 중 나머지 넷을 대표할 수 있는 단어는?

① corn   ② plant
③ carrot   ④ rose
⑤ flower

02 다음 빈칸에 알맞은 말이 바르게 짝지어진 것은?

> • _____ first she didn't seem to notice me.
> • We should be thankful _____ our parents.

① To – with   ② For – at
③ At – to   ④ At – for
⑤ For – with

03 다음 영영풀이에 해당하는 단어로 알맞은 것은?

> to walk around a place in a casual way, often without intending to go in any particular direction

① jump   ② move
③ wander   ④ travel
⑤ wonder

04 다음 짝지어진 두 단어의 관계가 같도록 빈칸에 알맞은 말을 쓰시오.

> low : high = light : _____

05 다음 우리말에 맞게 빈칸에 알맞은 것은?

> 그들은 일자리를 찾고 있다.
> ➡ They are looking _____ work.

① at   ② for
③ down   ④ to
⑤ with

06 다음 영영풀이에 해당하는 단어를 쓰시오.

> to cause something to happen or exist

➡ _____

07 다음 우리말에 맞게 빈칸에 알맞은 말을 쓰시오.

> 비가 그칠 때까지 기다리자.
> ➡ Let's wait _____ the rain stops.

08 다음 빈칸에 공통으로 알맞은 것은?

> • She grew _____ in Boston.
> • She doesn't give _____ easily.

① in   ② of
③ up   ④ about
⑤ at

01 다음 짝지어진 두 단어의 관계가 같도록 빈칸에 알맞은 말을 쓰시오.

(1) boy : girl = son : _____
(2) safe : safety = active : _____

02 다음 우리말에 맞게 빈칸에 알맞은 말을 쓰시오.

(1) 기뻐서 내 가슴이 터질 지경이야.
➡ My heart will burst _____ _____.
(2) 여름에 영국에 오지 그러니?
➡ Why don't you _____ _____ _____ England in the summer?
(3) 나는 Mary에게 편지를 써서 그 선물에 대해 감사의 뜻을 전해야 한다.
➡ I must write and _____ Mary _____ the present.

03 다음 빈칸에 들어갈 알맞은 말을 〈보기〉에서 골라 쓰시오.

┌── 보기 ──┐
build   someone   share
still   understand
└────────────┘

(1) Do you _____ live at the same address?
(2) He wanted to _____ his own house.
(3) Can you _____ French?
(4) There's _____ at the door.
(5) Sue will _____ a house with three other students.

04 다음 괄호 안의 단어를 문맥에 맞게 고쳐 쓰시오.

(1) These new shoes are not very _____. (comfort)
(2) You are the reason for my _____. (happy)
(3) He used magic to _____ a thunderstorm. (creator)

05 다음 빈칸에 알맞은 말을 〈보기〉에서 골라 쓰시오. 필요하면 대문자로 쓰시오.

┌── 보기 ──┐
cheer up   at first
keep an eye on   come up with
└────────────┘

(1) _____, I was very interested in acting.
(2) _____! You'll do better next time.
(3) I'll try to _____ some ideas to solve the problem.
(4) _____ my suitcase while I buy a ticket.

06 다음 영영풀이에 해당하는 단어를 주어진 철자로 시작하여 쓰시오.

(1) g_____ : something that you give someone as a present
(2) d_____ : the person who is driving a vehicle

Conultation

교과서

Conversation

1 도움 요청하기

A Can you do me a favor? 부탁 좀 해도 될까?
B Of course. / Sorry, I can't. 물론이지. / 미안하지만, 그럴 수 없어.

도움을 요청하는 다양한 표현들

• Can you do me a favor? / Could you please help me? / Can you give me a hand? /

  May I ask you a favor? / Can you help me? / Help me, please. / Can I ask you to do something?

• Can you help me move my bag? 내 가방을 옮기는 것을 도와줄 수 있니?

• Could you open the door? 문을 좀 열어 주시겠어요?

• Would you bring me a cup of water? 물 한 잔 가져다주시겠어요?

도움 요청을 부탁받았을 때 대답하기

승낙: Sure. / Okay. / No problem. / Of course, I can. / Why not?

거절: I'm sorry, I can't. / Sorry, but I'm busy. / I'm afraid I can't.

• A: Can you do me a favor? 부탁 하나 해도 되니?
  B: Sure. Go ahead. 물론이지. 어서 말해.
  A: I have a headache. Please buy some medicine for me. 머리가 아파. 약 좀 사 줘

• A: Can you do me a favor? 부탁 좀 해도 될까?
  B: Sure. What is it? 물론이지. 뭔데?

• A: Can you help me wash the dog right now? 지금 개를 씻기는 것을 도와줄래?
  B: I'm afraid I can't. I'm busy now. 유감스럽지만, 안 될 것 같아. 난 지금 바쁘거든.

핵심 Check

1. 다음 우리말과 일치하도록 빈칸에 알맞은 말을 쓰시오.

(1) A: Can you _____ me a _____? (부탁 좀 해도 될까?)

   B: Sure. _____ is it? (물론이야. 뭔데?)

(2) A: Can you _____ _____ make lunch right now?

   (지금 내가 점심 만들고 있는 것 좀 도와줄 수 있어?)

   B: Of _____. (물론이지.)

(3) A: Can you _____ _____ _____ my key? (내 열쇠 찾는 것을 도와줄 수 있니?)

   B: Sorry, I _____. I have to go out now. (미안하지만 안 돼. 나는 지금 나가야 돼.)

❷ 감사하기

> **A** Thank you for inviting me tonight. 오늘 밤 저를 초대해 주셔서 감사합니다.
>
> **B** My pleasure. 별말씀을요.

■ 상대방에게 감사를 표현할 때에는 'Thank you for+명사/동명사'의 형태로 나타내며, '~해 주셔서 감사하다'의 의미로 사용된다. for 뒤에는 무엇에 대해 감사한지를 명시해 주면 되며, 동명사나 명사가 온다는 것에 유의한다. 감사 표현에 대한 응답으로는 You're welcome. / No problem. / Not at all. / My pleasure. / Don't mention it. 등을 사용한다.

> • A: Thank you for painting the wall. 벽을 페인트칠해 줘서 고맙습니다.
> B: No problem. 별말씀을요.
> A: You're very kind. 매우 친절하시군요.

감사를 나타내는 다른 표현

• Thanks a million. 대단히 감사합니다.

• I cannot thank you enough. 어떻게 감사 인사를 드려야 할지 모르겠네요.

• I really appreciate it. 정말 감사합니다.

• I'm very grateful. 정말 고맙습니다.

핵심 Check

2. 다음 우리말과 일치하도록 빈칸에 알맞은 말을 쓰시오.

(1) **A:** _____ you for taking care of the children. (아이들을 돌봐 줘서 고맙습니다.)

　　 B: My _____. (별말씀을요.)

(2) **A:** Please call me if you need any help. (도움이 필요하면 전화해요.)

　　 B: I'm very _____. (정말 고맙습니다.)

　　 A: Not _____ _____. (천만에요.)

(3) **A:** I can ride you to that restaurant. (그 식당까지 태워 드릴게요.)

　　 B: I really _____ your kindness. (친절을 베풀어 주셔서 감사합니다.)

　　 A: No _____. (천만에요.)

Listen & Speak 1 A-1

G: ❶Mark, can you do me a favor?

B: Sure. What is it?

G: ❷My family is going on vacation for a week. ❸Can you come to our house and water the plants?

B: Yes, I can.

G: Mark, 부탁 하나 들어줄래?
B: 물론이지. 부탁할게 무엇이지?
G: 우리 가족은 일주일 동안 휴가를 갈 거야. 우리 집에 와서 식물들에게 물을 줄 수 있니?
B: 응, 할 수 있어.

❶ do me a favor: 나의 부탁을 들어주다
❷ go on vacation: 휴가를 가다
❸ water the plants: 식물들에게 물을 주다

Check(√) True or False

(1) The girl's family will go on vacation for a week.　　T ☐ F ☐

(2) The boy can't water the plants.　　T ☐ F ☐

Listen & Speak 1 A-2

G: Kevin, can you do me a favor?

B: O.K. What is it?

G: ❶Can you help me with my science project this afternoon?

B: ❷Sorry, but I can't. I have to visit my grandma with my mom.

G: Kevin, 부탁 하나 들어줄래?
B: 좋아. 뭔데?
G: 오늘 오후에 내 과학 프로젝트 좀 도와줄래?
B: 미안하지만 안 돼. 엄마랑 할머니 댁에 가야 해.

❶ help me with ~: 내가 ~하는 것을 돕다
❷ Sorry, but I can't.: 거절할 때 쓰는 표현

Check(√) True or False

(3) The girl wants to do her science project by herself.　　T ☐ F ☐

(4) The boy must visit his grandma.　　T ☐ F ☐

Listen & Speak 2 A-2

G: ❶What are you doing this weekend, Eric?

B: Nothing special. ❷I'll just stay home and watch TV.

G: Great! ❸I'm having a birthday party this weekend. Can you come?

B: Sure. Thank you for inviting me.

G: Eric, 이번 주말에 뭐 할 거니?
B: 특별한 건 없어. 그냥 집에 있으면서 TV를 볼 거야.
G: 좋아! 이번 주말에 생일 파티를 할 거야. 올 수 있니?
B: 물론이지. 초대해 줘서 고마워.

❶ What are you doing ~?: 현재진행형이 미래를 나타내는 경우이다.
❷ stay home: 집에 머물다
❸ have a birthday party: 생일 파티를 열다

Check(√) True or False

(5) Eric will watch TV at home this weekend.　　T ☐ F ☐

(6) The girl won't invite Eric.　　T ☐ F ☐

Communicate: A. Listen and Answer

Jaden: Can you do me a favor, Yuri?

Yuri: Sure. What is it, Jaden?

Jaden: ❶Can we go shopping together for a baseball cap for a girl?

Yuri: Yes, of course. ❷Who is it for?

Jaden: ❸It's for my little sister Kate.

Yuri: ❹Oh, are you getting her a birthday gift?

Jaden: ❺No, her birthday isn't until October.

Yuri: Then, why are you getting a baseball cap for her?

Jaden: ❻She broke her leg while she was riding her bike last week. ❼I just want to cheer her up.

Yuri: ❽Oh, I see. I can go this Friday afternoon.

Jaden: ❾That sounds perfect. Thank you.

❶ go shopping: 쇼핑하러 가다
❷ Who is it for? = Whom is it for?
❸ It's for ～.: 그것은 ～을 위한 것이다.
❹ get her a birthday gift: 그녀에게 생일 선물을 사 주다
❺ isn't until ～: ～까지는 아니다
❻ She broke her leg: 그녀의 다리가 부러졌다
❼ cheer her up: 그녀를 격려하다
❽ Oh, I see.: 아, 알겠어.
❾ That sounds perfect.: 그거 아주 좋구나.

Progress Check 1

G: Andrew, can you do me a favor?

B: O.K. What is it?

G: ❶My family is going to go to Jejudo this weekend. ❷Can you take care of my cat during the weekend?

B: Sure. ❸Don't worry about her, and enjoy your trip.

❶ is going to go = will go
❷ take care of: ～을 돌보다 / during: ～ 중에
❸ worry about: ～에 대해 걱정하다 / her = your dog

Progress Check 2

G: Hello, Mr. Smith. ❶We haven't had a chance to thank you for being our teacher. Every morning, you welcome us in the classroom. ❷You always teach us important and interesting things. ❸We're lucky to have you, and we're proud to be your students.

❶ haven't had: 계속을 나타내는 현재완료 / to thank: a chance를 수식하는 형용사적 용법의 to부정사 / thank you for -ing(동명사): ～인 것에 대하여 당신에게 감사하다
❷ always: 빈도부사로 일반동사의 앞에 위치한다.
❸ be lucky to ～: ～해서 행운이다 / be proud to ～: ～해서 자랑스럽다

Progress Check 3

G: ❶Do you have any special plans this weekend?

B: No, I'm just going to stay home.

G: ❷Oh, then can you come over to my house for dinner?

❶ any: (의문문에서) 어떤, 무슨
❷ come over to: ～에 오다 / for dinner: 저녁을 먹으러

Listen & Speak 1-3

A: Can you do me a favor?

B: Sure. What is it?

A: ❶Can you move this table with me? It's too heavy.

B: Sure. ❷No problem.

A: ❸Thank you for helping me.

❶ move this table: 이 식탁을 옮기다
❷ No problem.: 문제없어., 걱정 마.
❸ Thank A for B: B에 대하여 A에게 감사하다

Conversation **65**

다음 우리말과 일치하도록 빈칸에 알맞은 말을 쓰시오.

Listen & Speak 1 A. Listen and Check

1. **G:** Mark, can you _____ me a _____?
   B: Sure. _____ is it?
   G: My _____ is going on _____ for a week. Can you _____ to our house and _____ the plants?
   B: Yes, I _____.

2. **G:** Kevin, _____ you do me a _____?
   B: O.K. What is _____?
   G: Can you _____ me _____ my science _____ this afternoon?
   B: _____, but I _____. I _____ to visit my grandma with my mom.

Listen & Speak 2 A. Listen and Check

1. **G:** _____, Mom! Hi, Dad! As you _____, today is my 15th _____. I _____ had a chance _____ thank you for _____ my parents. You've truly _____ my friends _____ my teachers. Thank you for _____ me and always _____ to understand me. I'm really _____ to be your _____.

2. **G:** What are you _____ this _____, Eric?
   B: Nothing _____. I'll just _____ home and _____ TV.
   G: Great! I'm _____ a birthday _____ this weekend. Can you come?
   B: Sure. Thank you for _____ me.

Listen & Speak 1-B

A: Can you do me a _____?
B: Sure. _____ is it?
A: Can you _____ this table _____ me? It's too _____.
B: Sure. No _____.
A: _____ you for _____ me.

해석

1. G: Mark, 부탁 하나 들어줄래?
   B: 물론이지. 부탁할게 무엇이지?
   G: 우리 가족은 일주일 동안 휴가를 갈 거야. 우리 집에 와서 식물들에게 물을 줄 수 있니?
   B: 응, 할 수 있어.

2. G: Kevin, 부탁 하나 들어줄래?
   B: 좋아. 뭔데?
   G: 오늘 오후에 내 과학 프로젝트 좀 도와줄래?
   B: 미안하지만 안 돼. 엄마랑 할머니 댁에 가야 해.

1. G: 안녕, 엄마! 안녕, 아빠! 엄마, 아빠도 아시다시피, 오늘은 제 15번째 생일이에요. 제 부모님이 되어주신 것에 대해 감사할 기회가 없었어요. 두 분께서는 정말 제 친구이자 선생님이셨어요. 저를 지지해 주시고 항상 저를 이해하려고 노력해 주셔서 감사해요. 저는 두 분의 딸이 되어서 정말 자랑스러워요.

2. G: Eric, 이번 주말에 뭐 할 거니?
   B: 특별한 건 없어. 그냥 집에 있으면서 TV를 볼 거야.
   G: 좋아! 이번 주말에 생일 파티를 할 거야. 올 수 있니?
   B: 물론이지. 초대해 줘서 고마워.

A: 부탁 하나 들어줄래?
B: 그래. 뭔데?
A: 이 테이블 좀 옮겨줄래? 너무 무거워.
B: 물론이지. 문제없어.
A: 도와줘서 고마워.

Communicate A. Listen and Answer

Jaden: _____ you _____ me a favor, Yuri?

Yuri: Sure. _____ is it, Jaden?

Jaden: Can we go _____ together _____ a baseball cap for a girl?

Yuri: Yes, of _____. Who is it _____?

Jaden: It's _____ my little sister Kate.

Yuri: Oh, are you _____ her a birthday _____?

Jaden: No, her birthday isn't _____ October.

Yuri: Then, _____ are you getting a baseball _____ for her?

Jaden: She _____ her leg _____ she was riding her bike _____ week. I _____ want to _____ her up.

Yuri: Oh, I _____. I can _____ this Friday afternoon.

Jaden: That sounds _____. Thank you.

Progress Check

1. **G:** Andrew, can you _____ me a _____?

   B: O.K. What is _____?

   G: My family is _____ to go to Jejudo _____ weekend. Can you take _____ of my cat _____ the weekend?

   B: Sure. Don't _____ about her. And _____ your trip.

2. **G:** _____, Mr. Smith. We _____ had a chance to thank you for _____ our teacher. _____ morning, you _____ us in the classroom. You always _____ us important and interesting _____. We're _____ to have you, and we're _____ to be your _____.

3. **G:** Do you have _____ special _____ this weekend?

   B: No, I'm _____ going to _____ home.

   G: Oh, _____ can you come _____ to my house for _____?

해석

Jaden: 유리야, 부탁 하나 들어줄래?
유리: 물론이지. 뭐야, Jaden?
Jaden: 우리 같이 여자용 야구 모자 사러 쇼핑갈 수 있을까?
유리: 응, 물론이지. 누구 주려고?
Jaden: 내 여동생 Kate에게 줄 거야.
유리: 아, 너 그 애에게 생일 선물을 사 주려고 하는 거야?
Jaden: 아니, 그 애의 생일은 10월이 되어야 해.
유리: 그렇다면, 왜 야구 모자를 사 주려고 하는 거야?
Jaden: 그 애는 지난주에 자전거를 타다가 다리가 부러졌어. 난 그저 그 애를 격려하고 싶어
유리: 아, 그렇구나. 이번 주 금요일 오후에 갈 수 있어.
Jaden: 그거 아주 좋아. 고마워.

1. G: Andrew, 부탁 하나 들어줄래?
   B: 좋아. 뭔데?
   G: 우리 가족은 이번 주말에 제주도에 갈 거야. 주말에 내 고양이 좀 봐줄래?
   B: 물론이지. 고양이 걱정은 하지 말고, 여행을 즐겨.

2. G: 안녕하세요, Smith 선생님. 우리의 선생님이 되어주신 것에 대해 감사할 기회가 없었습니다. 매일 아침, 선생님은 교실에서 우리를 맞이하십니다. 선생님은 항상 우리에게 중요하고 흥미로운 것들을 가르쳐주십니다. 우리는 선생님이 계셔서 행운이고, 선생님의 학생이라는 것이 자랑스럽습니다.

3. G: 이번 주말에 무슨 특별한 계획 있니?
   B: 아니, 그냥 집에 있을 거야.
   G: 아, 그럼 우리 집에 저녁 먹으러 올 수 있어?

01 다음 중 의도하는 바가 나머지 넷과 다른 것은?

① Can I ask you a favor?
② Can you do me a favor?
③ Can you help me, please?
④ What can I do for you?
⑤ Could you give me a hand?

invite 초대하다

02 다음 대화의 밑줄 친 부분과 바꿔 쓸 수 있는 것은?

> A: Thank you for inviting me tonight.
> B: My pleasure.

① Sure.   ② Not at all.
③ I don't know.   ④ Of course.
⑤ I'm sorry I can't.

03 다음 대화의 빈칸에 알맞은 말은?

> A: Can you do me a _____?
> B: Sure. What is it?

① favor   ② help   ③ work
④ share   ⑤ pleasure

04 다음 대화의 밑줄 친 말과 바꾸어 쓸 수 있는 것은?

> A: I came here to help you with your homework.
> B: I appreciate your help.

① Thank you.   ② You're welcome.
③ That's right.   ④ You're right.
⑤ My pleasure.

01 다음 대화를 의미가 통하도록 알맞게 배열한 것은?

> (A) Can you help me with my science project this afternoon?
> (B) Kevin, can you do me a favor?
> (C) O.K. What is it?
> (D) Sorry, but I can't. I have to visit my grandma with my mom.

① (A) – (D) – (B) – (C)
② (B) – (C) – (A) – (D)
③ (C) – (D) – (B) – (A)
④ (D) – (B) – (C) – (A)
⑤ (D) – (C) – (B) – (A)

02 다음 대화의 빈칸에 알맞은 것은?

> A: Happy birthday! This is for you.
> B: Oh, thank you for your present.
> A: _____

① Go ahead.   ② Thanks a lot.
③ Okay.   ④ It's my pleasure.
⑤ I'm very grateful.

서답형

03 다음 대화의 빈칸에 알맞은 말을 쓰시오.

> A: I can ride you to the bus station.
> B: I really _____ your kindness.
> A: No _____.

서답형

04 다음 우리말과 같도록 빈칸에 알맞은 말을 쓰시오.

> 이 상자들을 날라 주셔서 감사해요.
> ➡ _____ you _____ carrying these boxes.

05 다음 밑줄 친 말과 바꾸어 쓸 수 있는 것은?

> A: Can you give me a hand?
> B: Sure. What is it?

① Show me your hand.
② I am left-handed.
③ Please hand me that book.
④ Can you help me?
⑤ Put your right hand up.

06 다음 중 짝지어진 대화가 어색한 것은?

① A: May I ask you a favor?
   B: No problem. What is it?
② A: Can you turn down TV?
   B: You're welcome.
③ A: Help me, please.
   B: Okay. What's the matter?
④ A: Can you help me?
   B: Of course.
⑤ A: Can you help me with something?
   B: Sure. What is it?

[07~11] 다음 대화를 읽고, 물음에 답하시오.

Jaden: ⓐCan you do me a favor, Yuri?

Yuri: Sure. What is it, Jaden?

Jaden: Can we go ⓑshop together for a baseball cap for a girl?

Yuri: Yes, of course. Who is it for?

Jaden: It's for my little sister Kate.

Yuri: Oh, are you getting her a birthday gift?

Jaden: No, her birthday isn't until October.

Yuri: Then, ____ⓒ____ are you getting a baseball cap for her?

Jaden: She broke her leg while she was riding her bike last week. I just want to cheer her ____ⓓ____.

Yuri: Oh, I see. I can go this Friday afternoon.

Jaden: That sounds perfect. Thank you.

서답형

07 위 대화의 밑줄 친 ⓐ와 같은 뜻이 되도록 다음 빈칸에 알맞은 말을 쓰시오.

> Can you _____ me a _____, Yuri?

서답형

08 위 대화의 밑줄 친 ⓑ를 알맞은 어형으로 고치시오.

➡ _____

09 위 대화의 빈칸 ⓒ에 알맞은 것은?

① why ② when ③ how
④ what ⑤ where

10 위 대화의 빈칸 ⓓ에 알맞은 것은?

① on ② to ③ up
④ for ⑤ over

11 위 대화의 내용과 일치하지 <u>않는</u> 것은?

① Jaden은 유리에게 도움을 청한다.
② Jaden은 여동생의 생일 선물을 사기를 원한다.
③ Jaden의 여동생 생일은 10월이다.
④ Jaden의 여동생은 다리가 부러졌다.
⑤ 유리는 Jaden과 함께 모자를 사러 갈 것이다.

[12~14] 다음 대화를 읽고, 물음에 답하시오.

G: What are you doing this weekend, Eric?

B: ⓐ특별히 할 일은 없어. I'll just stay home and watch TV.

G: Great! I'm having a birthday party this weekend. Can you come?

B: Sure. Thank you ____ⓑ____ inviting me.

G: You're ____ⓒ____.

서답형

12 위 대화의 밑줄 친 ⓐ와 같은 뜻이 되도록 다음 문장의 빈칸에 알맞은 말을 쓰시오.

> _____ special.

중요

13 위 대화의 빈칸 ⓑ에 알맞은 것은?

① to ② at
③ in ④ for
⑤ with

서답형

14 위 대화의 빈칸 ⓒ에 알맞은 말을 쓰시오.

➡ _____

01 다음 우리말과 같도록 빈칸에 알맞은 말을 쓰시오.

> 우리의 프로젝트를 도와 주서서 감사해요.
> ➡ Thank you _____ _____ with our project.

[02~03] 다음 대화의 빈칸에 알맞은 말을 쓰시오.

02 중요
A: Can you give me a _____?
B: Sure. What is it?

03
A: Can you _____ me a favor?
B: Sure. Go _____.
A: I have a headache. Please buy some medicine _____ me.

04 중요 다음 대화를 의미가 통하도록 알맞게 배열하시오.

> (A) I have no special plans. Why?
> (B) Sure. Thank you for inviting me.
> (C) I'm going to have my birthday party. Would you like to come?
> (D) Sora, what are you going to do this Friday?

➡ _____

[05~08] 다음 담화문을 읽고, 물음에 답하시오.

> G: Hi, Mom! Hi, Dad! As you know, today is my 15th birthday. I ⓐ(have / haven't) had a chance to thank you for being my parents. You've truly been my friends and my teachers. Thank you for supporting me and always ⓑtry to understand me. ⓒI'm really proud to be your daughter.

05 위 글의 괄호 ⓐ에서 알맞은 말을 골라 쓰시오.

➡ _____

06 위 글에서 다음 정의에 해당하는 단어를 찾아 쓰시오.

> a suitable time or situation when you have the opportunity to do someting

➡ _____

07 중요 위 글의 밑줄 친 ⓑ를 알맞은 어형으로 고치시오.

➡ _____

08 위 글의 밑줄 친 ⓒ를 우리말로 옮기시오.

➡ _____

Grammar

① 목적격 관계대명사

- He was the person **(who/whom/that)** Kenneth respected the most in the world.
  그는 Kenneth가 세상에서 가장 존경하는 사람이었다.

- There were many things **(that/which)** Kenneth had to do.
  Kenneth가 해야 할 많은 일들이 있었다.

- The snack **(that/which)** I ate at night was Hawaiian pizza.
  내가 밤에 먹은 간식은 하와이안 피자였다.

■ 관계대명사는 선행사와 뒤에 이어지는 문장을 연결해 주는 역할을 하며, 문장 내에서의 역할에 따라 주격, 목적격, 소유격으로 나뉜다.

	사람	사물/동물	사람/사물/동물
주격	who	which	that
목적격	who(m)	which	that

■ 목적격 관계대명사는 선행사가 뒤에 이어지는 문장(관계대명사절)에서 목적어 역할을 할 때 쓰며, 생략할 수 있다. 선행사가 사람이면 who(m) 또는 that을, 사물이나 동물이면 which 또는 that을 쓴다. 일반적으로 선행사가 사람일 때 whom보다는 who를 더 많이 쓴다.

- Ann was the person. I met her on the way home.
  → Ann was the person **who[whom, that]** I met on the way home.
  Ann은 내가 집에 오는 길에 만난 사람이었다.

■ 선행사가 최상급이거나 서수, -thing으로 끝나는 경우, 또는 the very, the only가 선행사를 수식하는 경우에는 whom이나 which 대신 that을 쓸 때가 많다.

- This is the biggest dog **that** I have ever seen. 이것은 지금까지 내가 본 가장 큰 개다.

■ 관계대명사가 전치사의 목적어로 쓰일 때는 who(m)이나 which 대신 that을 전치사와 함께 사용할 수 없다.

- The bed in **which** I slept was comfortable. (○) 내가 잔 침대는 편안했다.
  The bed in that I slept was comfortable. (✗)

핵심 Check

1. 다음 괄호 안에서 알맞은 것을 고르시오.

(1) I know the doctor (which / that) everyone likes.

(2) That is the very problem (that / what) I wanted to solve.

(3) The man to (whom / that) you spoke is my homeroom teacher.

(4) This is the book (who / which) I read yesterday.

(5) Police found the knife with (which / that) the man killed her.

2 so ... that ~

- He was **so** happy **that** he jumped for joy. 그는 아주 행복해 기뻐서 펄쩍 뛰었다.
- He wandered off at night **so** often **that** someone had to keep an eye on him.
  그는 밤에 아주 종종 여기저기 쏘다녔기 때문에 누군가가 그를 지켜보아야만 했다.
- Shirley became **so** busy **that** she began to use her father's garage as her office. Shirley는 아주 바빠져서 아버지의 차고를 사무실로 사용하기 시작했다.

■ 'so+형용사+that절'의 구문은 '너무 ~해서 …하다'의 의미로 결과를 나타내는 구문이다. so 다음에는 원인에 해당하는 형용사나 부사가 오고, that절에는 결과를 나타내는 절이 온다. 이유를 나타내는 접속사 because나 결과를 나타내는 접속사를 이용해서 문장을 바꿔 쓸 수도 있다.
  - Nick woke up **so** late **that** he missed the bus. Nick은 너무 늦게 일어나서 버스를 놓쳤다.
    = Nick missed the bus because[as] he woke up too late.
    = Nick woke up too late, so he missed the bus.
  - My grandma is **so** wise **that** everyone respects her.
    나의 할머니는 아주 현명하셔서 모든 사람들이 그녀를 존경한다.
    = Everyone respects my grandma because[as] she is so wise.
    = My grandma is very wise, so everyone respects her.

■ '너무 ~해서 …할 수 없다'의 의미를 나타낼 경우에는 'so ~ that … can't' 구문을 이용한다. 이 구문은 'too ~ to부정사' 구문으로 바꿔 쓸 수 있다.
  - I am **so** tired **that I can't** do it right now. 나는 너무 피곤해서 지금 바로 그 일을 할 수 없다.
    = I am **too** tired **to** do it right now.

■ '형용사/부사+enough to+동사원형'은 '…할 만큼 충분히 ~한/하게'의 뜻을 나타내며, 'so+형용사/부사+that+주어+can+동사원형'의 형태로 바꿔 쓸 수 있다.
  - He is rich **enough to** buy the house. 그는 그 집을 살 만큼 충분히 부유하다.
    = He is **so** rich **that** he can buy the house.

핵심 Check

2. 다음 괄호 안에서 알맞은 것을 고르시오.
   (1) She got up early _____ _____ catch the first train.
   (2) Sam was _____ strong _____ he could move the rock.
   (3) I am _____ busy with my homework _____ play computer games.
   (4) The girl is _____ young _____ she can't ride a bike.
   (5) This book is _____ difficult for me _____ read.

01 다음 괄호 안에서 알맞은 것을 고르시오.

heavy 무거운
carry 나르다, 가지고 가다

(1) The bags are (so / very) heavy that I can't carry them.

(2) Emma is (too / so) young to go to school.

(3) This is the boy (whom / which) I play basketball with every weekend.

(4) I am reading the letter (whom / which) you gave me yesterday.

02 다음 두 문장이 의미가 같도록 빈칸에 알맞은 말을 쓰시오.

(1) She got up early enough to catch the first train.
  ➡ She got up _____ early _____ she _____ catch the first train.

(2) He is too poor to buy the house.
  ➡ He is _____ _____ that he _____ buy the house.

(3) My grandma is so old that she cannot run fast.
  ➡ My grandma is _____ old _____ run fast.

03 다음 빈칸에 알맞은 말을 <보기>에서 골라 쓰시오. (한 단어를 중복해서 쓸 수 없음.)

┌─ 보기 ─
│　　　that　　which　　whom　　who
└──

(1) Look at the boy _____ is watering a flower.

(2) You are the only friend with _____ I can talk.

(3) I need a knife with _____ I can cut the rope.

(4) Money is the only thing _____ he wants.

01 다음 문장의 빈칸에 알맞은 것은?

> The gentleman _____ I met yesterday was a teacher.

① which
② who
③ at which
④ with who
⑤ with that

02 다음 빈칸에 들어갈 말이 바르게 짝지어진 것은?

> The box was _____ heavy that I _____ move it by myself.

① so – couldn't
② too – couldn't
③ so – could
④ enough – could
⑤ such – could

03 다음 두 문장이 같은 뜻이 되도록 빈칸에 알맞은 말을 쓰시오.

> The library is too far for me to go to on foot.
> = The library is _____ far that I _____ go there on foot.

04 다음 문장에서 어법상 어색한 곳을 찾아 바르게 고쳐 쓰시오.

(1) He is an engineer which my father knows very well.

_____ ➡ _____

(2) The village in that I live is very small.

_____ ➡ _____

05 다음 빈칸에 들어갈 말이 바르게 짝지어진 것은?

> We have to go now. We are _____ busy _____ wait for her.

① so – that
② so – to
③ enough – to
④ as – too
⑤ too – to

[06~07] 다음 중 어법상 어색한 것을 고르시오.

06 ① This is the pen I lost yesterday.
② I will give you everything that you need.
③ I forgot to bring the homework which I did yesterday.
④ The music which we listened is by Mozart.
⑤ The car which I bought last month already has engine problems.

07 ① You are too young to drive a car.
② I ran fast enough to catch the bus.
③ My father is too busy to play with me.
④ She was too strong that she could carry the boxes.
⑤ My sister is so tall that she can play basketball well.

08 다음 밑줄 친 부분을 바르게 고쳐 쓰시오.

> Dami is <u>very</u> tired that she can't do her homework.

➡ _____

09 다음 두 문장에서 생략된 것이 바르게 짝지어진 것은?

> • He ate the food everyone hated.
> • The tree I cut yesterday was very big.

① who – who ② who – that
③ that – who ④ who – which
⑤ that – which

서답형

10 다음 빈칸에 공통으로 알맞은 말을 쓰시오.

> • The building _____ I visited yesterday is a museum.
> • The man _____ everyone knows well built his house for himself.

---

11 다음 빈칸에 공통으로 알맞은 것은?

> • I got up early _____ that I could catch the train.
> • The ice cream is _____ cold that I can't eat it.

① so ② as
③ too ④ never
⑤ rarely

서답형

12 다음 우리말과 일치하도록 주어진 단어를 바르게 배열하시오.

> 그 남자는 자기가 갖고 있는 모든 돈을 내게 주었다.
> (he / gave / had / the / man / me / money / all / that / the)

➡ _____

---

13 다음 우리말을 영어로 바르게 옮긴 것은?

> 음식이 너무 짜서 나는 그것을 먹을 수 없었다.

① The food was too salty that I could eat it.
② The food was so salty that I couldn't eat.
③ I couldn't eat it so that the food was salty.
④ The food was salty enough for me to eat.
⑤ The food was so salty that I couldn't eat it.

---

14 다음 중 밑줄 친 부분의 쓰임이 옳은 것은?

① The man which I met yesterday will call me this afternoon.
② I can give you the textbook what I bought last week.
③ The rumor who Jeff told me was very interesting.
④ This is the pen with which he wrote the novel.
⑤ Thanks to the textbooks whom you gave me, I could pass the exam.

---

15 다음 주어진 문장과 의미가 같은 것은?

> It was too hot for him to go out.

① It was not so hot for him to go out.
② It was so hot, but he went out.
③ It was so hot that he couldn't go out.
④ It was hot enough for him to go out.
⑤ It was so hot that he wanted to go out.

서답형

16 다음 두 문장이 같은 뜻이 되도록 빈칸에 알맞은 말을 쓰시오.

> These books are so heavy that I can't carry them.
> = These books are _____ heavy for me _____ _____.

서답형

17 다음 문장에서 어법상 어색한 부분을 찾아 바르게 고쳐 쓰시오.

(1) The girl which I like will leave this town.

_____ ➡ _____

(2) The knife with which I cut these apples were very sharp.

_____ ➡ _____

18 다음 밑줄 친 부분 중 생략할 수 없는 것은?

① This is the piano <u>which</u> Mozart played.
② The boy <u>who</u> is throwing a ball is my brother.
③ Rome is the place <u>that</u> I really want to visit again.
④ These are the gifts <u>which</u> she gave me on my birthday.
⑤ I'm going to return the book <u>that</u> I borrowed last week.

19 다음 중 어법상 올바른 문장을 <u>모두</u> 고른 것은?

> ⓐ This book is so easy that I can read it.
> ⓑ My sister is enough old to ride a bike.
> ⓒ This problem is so difficult that I can't solve.
> ⓓ The bag was too expensive for her to buy.
> ⓔ Jane was so hungry that she had some cake.

① ⓐ, ⓒ, ⓔ ② ⓐ, ⓑ
③ ⓐ, ⓓ, ⓔ ④ ⓐ, ⓑ, ⓒ, ⓓ
⑤ ⓐ, ⓑ, ⓒ, ⓔ

20 다음 중 밑줄 친 that의 쓰임이 나머지와 <u>다른</u> 하나는?

① It is true <u>that</u> we were a little late.
② This is a bag <u>that</u> I bought yesterday.
③ This is the hotel <u>that</u> I stayed at last time.
④ Do you know the boy <u>that</u> I met yesterday?
⑤ This is the tree <u>that</u> I planted five years ago.

21 다음 중 우리말을 알맞게 옮긴 것은? (2개)

> 나는 너무 화가 나서 말을 하지 못했다.

① I was too angry to speak.
② I was too angry not to speak.
③ I was so angry that I can't speak.
④ I was so angry that I could speak.
⑤ I was so angry that I couldn't speak.

01 다음 두 문장을 관계대명사를 써서 한 문장으로 바꿔 쓰시오.

(1) I know the man. You are looking for the man.

➡ _____

_____

(2) This is the bag. I got it from Nancy.

➡ _____

_____

(3) He is the boy. I meet him at the bus stop every morning.

➡ _____

_____

02 다음 빈칸에 알맞은 말을 〈보기〉에서 골라 쓰시오.

┌─ 보기 ─┐
too   so   enough   that
└────────┘

(1) He was _____ kind that he helped me.

(2) Mike is wise _____ to control himself.

(3) My father was _____ sleepy to drive.

(4) This English book is so easy _____ I can read it.

03 다음 빈칸에 공통으로 알맞은 말을 쓰시오.

┌────────────────────────────┐
│ • This is the hat _____ Ann bought yesterday. │
│ • I know the girl _____ is playing the drums. │
└────────────────────────────┘

04 다음 문장에서 어법상 틀린 부분을 찾아 바르게 고쳐 쓰시오.

(1) The test was too difficult that I failed it.

_____ ➡ _____

(2) The bag is too heavy for me to carry it.

_____ ➡ _____

(3) It's enough warm for the children to play outside.

_____ ➡ _____

(4) Nick woke up so late what he missed the bus.

_____ ➡ _____

05 다음 우리말과 같은 뜻이 되도록 빈칸에 알맞은 말을 쓰시오.

┌────────────────────────────┐
│ 그가 너무 빨리 말을 해서 우리는 알아들을 수 없었다. │
│ ➡ He spoke _____ fast _____ we couldn't understand him. │
└────────────────────────────┘

06 다음 주어진 문장을 어법에 맞게 고쳐 쓰시오.

(1) I bought my sister a blouse who was made in France.

➡ _____

_____

(2) Do you know the boy whom I met him on the street yesterday?

➡ _____

_____

(3) This is the city that are famous for its beautiful buildings.

➡ _____

_____

07 다음 우리말과 일치하도록 빈칸에 알맞은 말을 쓰시오.

(1) 이 문제는 너무 어려워서 내가 풀 수 없다.

➡ This problem is _____ difficult _____ I _____ solve it.

(2) 그녀는 다행히도 그 화재를 모면했다.

➡ She was _____ _____ _____ escape the fire.

08 다음 주어진 어구들을 바르게 배열하시오.

(1) (easy / the question / everyone / that / the answer / knows / so / is).

➡ _____

(2) (right now / I / tired / I / can't / it / do / am / so / that).

➡ _____

09 다음 두 문장의 의미가 같도록 빈칸에 알맞은 말을 쓰시오.

(1) This book is too difficult for me _____ read.

➡ This book is _____ difficult _____ I _____ read it.

(2) The wind was strong _____ to blow down trees.

➡ The wind was _____ strong that it _____ _____ down trees.

(3) Dad walked _____ fast that I _____ catch up with him.

➡ Dad walked _____ fast for me _____ catch up with.

10 다음 두 문장을 관계대명사를 이용하여 한 문장으로 쓰시오.

(1) The girl saw a man and his dog. They looked very tired.

➡ _____
_____

(2) John is the best player in this town. I played tennis with him yesterday.

➡ _____
_____

(3) This bike is my treasure. My father bought it for me last year.

➡ _____
_____

(4) My sister ate the only ice cream. My mother bought it for me.

➡ _____
_____

(5) The house was in Incheon. We lived in it two years ago.

➡ _____
_____

11 다음 우리말과 일치하도록 빈칸에 알맞은 말을 쓰시오.

(1) 이 아이가 내 남동생이 지난밤에 만난 소년이다.

➡ This is the boy _____ my brother met last night.

(2) 이것이 나의 부모님이 사 주신 자전거이다.

➡ This is the bike _____ my parents bought for me.

Reading

Socks for Grandpa

Kenneth Shinozuka grew up in a big happy family of three
generations. Since he was little, he has always been very close to his
grandfather. He was Kenneth's first friend, his trusty driver, and his
cook. He also taught him many life lessons. He was the person who
Kenneth respected the most in the world.

When Kenneth was four, his grandfather went out for a walk one
day and got lost. He had Alzheimer's disease. Everyone in Kenneth's
family was in shock. His condition became worse over the next 10
years. He wandered off at night so often that someone had to keep an
eye on him all night long. One night, Kenneth's grandfather got out
of bed, and Kenneth saw it. At that moment, he said to himself, "Why
don't I put pressure sensors on the heels of his socks?"

grow up 자라다, 성장하다

generation 대, 세대

close 가까운, 친한

trusty 신뢰할 수 있는

lesson 교훈

respect 존경하다

get lost 길을 잃다

disease 병

shock 충격

condition 상태

worse 더 나쁜

wander off 여기저기 돌아다니다

all night long 밤새

moment 순간

pressure 압력

censor 센서, 감지기

heel 발뒤꿈치, 뒤꿈치

 **확인문제**

● 다음 문장이 본문의 내용과 일치하면 T, 일치하지 않으면 F를 쓰시오.

1 Kenneth Shinozuka had a small family. ☐

2 Kenneth Shinozuka and his grandfather were very close. ☐

3 Kenneth Shinozuka respected his grandfather. ☐

4 Kenneth Shinozuka and his grandfather often took a walk at night. ☐

5 Kenneth Shinozuka's grandfather got ill. ☐

There were many things that Kenneth had to do. He first had to
= which: 관계대명사 목적격
create a pressure sensor and then find a way to send a signal to his
그러고 나서   to부정사의 형용사적 용법
smart phone. Kenneth also tried many different materials to make
시도해 보았다   to부정사의 목적을 나타내는 부사적 용법
comfortable socks for his elderly grandfather.

When he felt like giving up, he thought about his grandfather's safety.
feel like+-ing: ~하고 싶은 생각이 들다   safe의 명사형
After much trial and error, he finally succeeded in making his device.
~을 만드는 데 성공했다
When it first worked, he was so happy that he jumped for joy. He could
work: 작동하다   기뻐서
not believe that his invention actually worked. For his grandfather,
명사절을 이끄는 접속사
Kenneth is the best inventor in the world. For Kenneth, his grandfather
good의 최상급
is still his best friend.
아직도, 여전히

create 창조하다, 만들어 내다

signal 신호

material 재료

comfortable 편한, 편안한

elderly 연로한

give up 포기하다

safety 안전

trial and error 시행착오

succeed 성공하다

device 장치, 도구

actually 사실

inventor 발명가

still 여전히

확인문제

● 다음 문장이 본문의 내용과 일치하면 T, 일치하지 않으면 F를 쓰시오.

1   Kenneth created a pressure sensor. ☐

2   Kenneth bought comfortable socks for his grandfather. ☐

3   Kenneth gave up making things for his grandfather. ☐

4   Kenneth created his device at last. ☐

5   Kenneth is famous for his invention. ☐

● 우리말을 참고하여 빈칸에 알맞은 말을 쓰시오.

1 Kenneth Shinozuka grew _____ in a big happy _____ of three generations.

2 _____ he was little, he has always _____ very close to his grandfather.

3 He was Kenneth's first _____, his trusty _____, and his _____.

4 He also _____ him many life _____.

5 He was the person _____ Kenneth respected the _____ in the world.

6 _____ Kenneth was four, his grandfather _____ out for a walk one day and _____ lost.

7 He had Alzheimer's _____.

8 _____ in Kenneth's family was in _____.

9 His condition _____ worse _____ the next 10 years.

10 He wandered _____ at night so often _____ someone had to keep an eye on him _____ night long.

11 One night, Kenneth's grandfather _____ out of bed, and Kenneth _____ it.

12 At that _____, he said to _____, "Why _____ I put pressure sensors on the _____ of his socks?"

1	Kenneth Shinozuka는 3대의 행복한 대가족에서 자랐다.
2	그는 어렸을 때부터 항상 할아버지와 매우 친했다.
3	그는 Kenneth의 첫 친구이자, 신뢰할 수 있는 운전기사이자, 요리사였다.
4	그는 또한 그에게 많은 인생 교훈을 가르쳐 주었다.
5	그는 Kenneth가 세상에서 가장 존경하는 사람이었다.
6	Kenneth가 네 살이었을 때, 그의 할아버지는 어느 날 산책을 나갔다가 길을 잃었다.
7	그는 알츠하이머병에 걸렸다.
8	Kenneth의 가족 모두는 충격에 빠졌다.
9	그의 상태는 10년 동안 더 악화되었다.
10	그는 자주 밤에 여기저기 돌아다니기 때문에 누군가가 그를 밤새 감시해야 했다.
11	어느 날 밤, Kenneth의 할아버지가 침대에서 일어났는데, Kenneth가 그것을 보았다.
12	그 순간, 그는 혼잣말을 했다. "내가 할아버지의 양말 뒤꿈치에 압력 감지기를 설치하는 게 어떨까?"

13 There were many things _____ Kenneth had to _____.

14 He first had to _____ a pressure sensor and _____ find a way to send a _____ to his smart phone.

15 Kenneth also _____ many different _____ to make comfortable _____ for his elderly grandfather.

16 When he felt _____ giving up, he thought about his grandfather's _____.

17 _____ much trial and error, he finally _____ in making his device.

18 When it first _____, he was so happy _____ he jumped for _____.

19 He could not _____ that his invention _____ worked.

20 _____ his grandfather, Kenneth is the best _____ in the world.

21 For Kenneth, his grandfather is still his best _____.

13 Kenneth가 해야 할 많은 일들이 있었다.

14 그는 처음에 압력 감지기를 만들고 나서 그의 스마트폰으로 신호를 보낼 방법을 찾아야 했다.

15 Kenneth는 또한 그의 연로한 할아버지에게 편안한 양말을 만들어 주기 위해 많은 다양한 재료들을 가지고 만들어 보았다.

16 그는 포기하고 싶은 생각이 들 때 할아버지의 안전에 대해 생각했다.

17 많은 시행착오 끝에 그는 마침내 자신의 장치를 만드는 데 성공했다.

18 그것이 처음 작동했을 때, 그는 너무 행복해 기뻐서 펄쩍 뛰었다.

19 그는 자신의 발명품이 실제로 작동했다는 것을 믿을 수 없었다.

20 그의 할아버지에게 Kenneth는 세계 최고의 발명가이다.

21 Kenneth에게 그의 할아버지는 여전히 그의 가장 친한 친구이다.

● 우리말을 참고하여 본문을 영작하시오.

1 Kenneth Shinozuka는 3대의 행복한 대가족에서 자랐다.

➡ _____

2 그는 어렸을 때부터 항상 할아버지와 매우 친했다.

➡ _____

3 그는 Kenneth의 첫 친구이자, 신뢰할 수 있는 운전기사이자, 요리사였다.

➡ _____

4 그는 또한 그에게 많은 인생 교훈을 가르쳐 주었다.

➡ _____

5 그는 Kenneth가 세상에서 가장 존경하는 사람이었다.

➡ _____

6 Kenneth가 네 살이었을 때, 그의 할아버지는 어느 날 산책을 나갔다가 길을 잃었다.

➡ _____

7 그는 알츠하이머병에 걸렸다.

➡ _____

8 Kenneth의 가족 모두는 충격에 빠졌다.

➡ _____

9 그의 상태는 10년 동안 더 악화되었다.

➡ _____

10 그는 자주 밤에 여기저기 돌아다니기 때문에 누군가가 그를 밤새 감시해야 했다.

➡ _____

11 어느 날 밤, Kenneth의 할아버지가 침대에서 일어났는데, Kenneth가 그것을 보았다.

➡ _____

12 그 순간, 그는 혼잣말을 했다. "내가 할아버지의 양말 뒤꿈치에 압력 감지기를 설치하는 게 어떨까?"

➡ _____

13 Kenneth가 해야 할 많은 일들이 있었다.

➡ _____

14 그는 처음에 압력 감지기를 만들고 나서 그의 스마트폰으로 신호를 보낼 방법을 찾아야 했다.

➡ _____

15 Kenneth는 또한 그의 연로한 할아버지에게 편안한 양말을 만들어 주기 위해 많은 다양한 재료들을 가지고 만들어 보았다.

➡ _____

16 그는 포기하고 싶은 생각이 들 때 할아버지의 안전에 대해 생각했다.

➡ _____

17 많은 시행착오 끝에 그는 마침내 자신의 장치를 만드는 데 성공했다.

➡ _____

18 그것이 처음 작동했을 때, 그는 너무 행복해 기뻐서 펄쩍 뛰었다.

➡ _____

19 그는 자신의 발명품이 실제로 작동했다는 것을 믿을 수 없었다.

➡ _____

20 그의 할아버지에게 Kenneth는 세계 최고의 발명가이다.

➡ _____

21 Kenneth에게 그의 할아버지는 여전히 그의 가장 친한 친구이다.

➡ _____

[01~05] 다음 글을 읽고, 물음에 답하시오.

(①) Kenneth Shinozuka grew up in a big happy family of three generations. (②) ____ⓐ____ he was little, he has always been very close to his grandfather. (③) He was Kenneth's first friend, his trusty ⓑdrive, and his cook. (④) He was the person ____ⓒ____ Kenneth respected the most in the world. (⑤)

01 위 글의 ①~⑤ 중 다음 주어진 문장이 들어갈 알맞은 곳은?

> He also taught him many life lessons.

①   ②   ③   ④   ⑤

02 위 글의 빈칸 ⓐ에 알맞은 것은?

① If   ② For
③ Since   ④ When
⑤ After

서답형
03 위 글의 밑줄 친 ⓑ를 알맞은 형으로 고치시오.

➡ _____

04 위 글의 빈칸 ⓒ에 알맞은 것은? (3개)

① who   ② whom
③ which   ④ whose
⑤ that

05 위 글의 내용으로 보아 알 수 없는 것은?

① Kenneth의 가족은 대가족이다.
② Kenneth는 할아버지와 아주 친하게 지내 왔다.
③ Kenneth의 할아버지는 운전을 잘하였다.
④ Kenneth의 할아버지는 Kenneth에게 음식을 요리해 주었다.
⑤ Kenneth는 할아버지를 세상에서 가장 존경했다.

[06~10] 다음 글을 읽고, 물음에 답하시오.

When Kenneth was four, his grandfather went out for a walk one day and got ⓐlose. ①He had Alzheimer's disease. Everyone in Kenneth's family was in shock. ②His condition became worse over the next 10 years. ③He wandered off at night ____ⓑ____ often that someone had to keep an eye on ④him all night long. One night, Kenneth's grandfather got out of bed, and Kenneth saw ⓒit. At that moment, ⑤he said to himself, "Why don't I put pressure sensors on the heels of his socks?"

06 위 글의 밑줄 친 ①~⑤ 중 가리키는 대상이 다른 것은?

①   ②   ③   ④   ⑤

서답형
07 위 글의 밑줄 친 ⓐ를 알맞은 형으로 고치시오.

➡ _____

08 위 글의 빈칸 ⓑ에 알맞은 것은?

① too   ② so
③ very   ④ such
⑤ also

서답형

09 위 글의 밑줄 친 ⓒ가 가리키는 것을 우리말로 쓰시오.

➡ _____

중요

10 Kenneth의 할아버지에 관해 위 글의 내용과 일치하지 않는 것은?

① 길을 잃은 적이 있다.
② 알츠하이머병에 걸렸다.
③ 밤에 돌아다녔다.
④ Kenneth를 보살펴 주었다.
⑤ 10년간 건강이 악화되었다.

[11~13] 다음 글을 읽고, 물음에 답하시오.

There were many things ⓐthat Kenneth had to do. He first had to create a pressure sensor and then find a way ⓑto send a signal to his smart phone. Kenneth also tried many different materials to make ⓒcomfort socks for his elderly grandfather.

11 위 글의 밑줄 친 ⓐ와 바꿔 쓸 수 있는 것은?

① who   ② how
③ what   ④ when
⑤ which

12 위 글의 밑줄 친 ⓑ와 용법이 같은 것은?

① We wished to reach the North Pole.
② I was sad to hear the music.
③ Please give me something to drink.
④ Kate wanted to go to Paris again.
⑤ He must study hard to pass the math exam.

서답형

13 위 글의 밑줄 친 ⓒ를 알맞은 형으로 바꿔 쓰시오.

➡ _____

[14~18] 다음 글을 읽고, 물음에 답하시오.

When he felt like giving ___ⓐ___, he thought about his grandfather's safety. (①) After much ⓑtry and error, he finally succeeded in making his device. (②) When it first worked, he was so happy that he jumped ⓒfor joy. (③) For his grandfather, Kenneth is the best inventor in the world. (④) For Kenneth, his grandfather is still his best friend. (⑤)

14 위 글의 ①~⑤ 중 다음 주어진 문장이 들어갈 알맞은 곳은?

He could not believe that his invention actually worked.

①   ②   ③   ④   ⑤

15 위 글의 빈칸 ⓐ에 알맞은 것은?

① up   ② on
③ to   ④ over
⑤ with

16 위 글의 밑줄 친 ⓑ를 알맞은 형으로 고치시오.

➡ _____

17 위 글의 밑줄 친 ⓒ 대신 쓸 수 있는 것은?

① at   ② in

③ over   ④ with

⑤ from

18 Kenneth가 장비를 만드는 것을 포기하지 않은 이유를 우리말로 쓰시오.

➡ _____

[19~22] 다음 글을 읽고, 물음에 답하시오.

Kenneth Shinozuka grew ___ⓐ___ in a big happy family of three generations. Since he was little, he has always ⓑbe very close to his grandfather. He was Kenneth's first friend, his trusty driver, and his cook. ⓒHe also taught him many life lessons. He was the person ⓓwho Kenneth respected the most in the world.

중요

19 위 글의 빈칸 ⓐ에 알맞은 것은?

① on   ② up

③ to   ④ over

⑤ into

20 위 글의 밑줄 친 ⓑ를 알맞은 형으로 고치시오.

➡ _____

21 위 글의 밑줄 친 ⓒ를 우리말로 옮기시오.

➡ _____

중요

22 위 글의 밑줄 친 ⓓ 대신 쓸 수 있는 것은? (2개)

① that   ② whom

③ what   ④ whose

⑤ which

[23~25] 다음 글을 읽고, 물음에 답하시오.

___ⓐ___ Kenneth was four, his grandfather went out for a walk one day and ___ⓑ___ lost. He had Alzheimer's ___ⓒ___. Everyone in Kenneth's family was in shock. His condition became worse over the next 10 years.

23 위 글의 빈칸 ⓐ에 알맞은 것은?

① When   ② If

③ Because   ④ Though

⑤ While

중요

24 위 글의 빈칸 ⓑ에 알맞은 것은?

① made   ② fell

③ got   ④ turned

⑤ became

서답형

25 위 글의 빈칸 ⓒ에 다음 정의에 해당하는 단어를 쓰시오.

> an illness which affects people, animals, or plants, for example one which is caused by bacteria or infection

➡ _____

29 위 글의 빈칸 ⓓ에 알맞은 것은?

① How ② Why
③ What ④ When
⑤ Which

[26~29] 다음 글을 읽고, 물음에 답하시오.

He wandered off ___ⓐ___ night so often that someone had to keep an eye on him all night long. ⓑOne night, Kenneth's grandfather got out of bed, and Kenneth saw it. ⓒAt that moment, he said to him, "___ⓓ___ don't I put pressure sensors on the heels of his socks?"

[30~32] 다음 글을 읽고, 물음에 답하시오.

There ①were many things ___ⓐ___ Kenneth had to do. He ②first had to create a pressure sensor and then find a way to send a signal ③to his smart phone. Kenneth ④also tried many different materials ⓑto make comfortable socks ⑤to his elderly grandfather.

30 위 글의 밑줄 친 ①~⑤ 중 어법상 어색한 것은?

① ② ③ ④ ⑤

26 위 글의 빈칸 ⓐ에 알맞은 것은?

① at ② in
③ on ④ to
⑤ from

중요

31 위 글의 빈칸 ⓐ에 알맞은 것은? (2개)

① who ② that
③ whom ④ which
⑤ what

서답형

27 위 글의 밑줄 친 ⓑ를 우리말로 옮기시오.

➡ _____

_____

32 위 글의 밑줄 친 ⓑ와 용법이 같은 것은?

① My hope is to work as a doctor in Africa.
② It's time to go to bed now.
③ My job is to report the news.
④ The boys hoped to win the baseball game.
⑤ Kate went to a bookstore to buy a book.

서답형

28 위 글의 밑줄 친 ⓒ에서 어법상 어색한 것을 고치시오.

_____ ➡ _____

[01~06] 다음 글을 읽고, 물음에 답하시오.

When he felt like ⓐgive up, he thought about his grandfather's ⓑ . After much trial and error, he finally succeeded ⓒ making his device. When it first worked, ⓓhe was so happy that he jumped for joy. He could not believe that his invention actually worked. For his grandfather, Kenneth is the best ⓔinvent in the world. For Kenneth, his grandfather is still his best friend.

01 위 글의 밑줄 친 ⓐ를 알맞은 형으로 고치시오.

➡ _____

02 위 글의 빈칸 ⓑ에 다음 정의에 해당하는 말을 쓰시오.

> the state of being safe from harm or danger

➡ _____

03 위 글의 빈칸 ⓒ에 알맞은 말을 쓰시오.

➡ _____

04 위 글의 밑줄 친 ⓓ와 같은 뜻이 되도록 다음 문장의 빈칸에 알맞은 말을 쓰시오.

> he jumped for joy _____ he was very happy.

05 위 글의 밑줄 친 ⓔ를 알맞은 형으로 고치시오.

➡ _____

06 Why was Kenneth happy? Answer in English.

➡ _____

[07~09] 다음 글을 읽고, 물음에 답하시오.

Do you want to help children? Join our Child Care Project in Laos. You'll teach local children. You'll also build a school for them. The work is ⓐ(so, too) hard that you'll want to go home at first, but you'll find ⓑhappy in helping these children.

07 위 글의 괄호 ⓐ에서 알맞은 것을 고르시오.

➡ _____

08 위 글의 밑줄 친 ⓑ를 알맞은 형으로 고치시오.

➡ _____

09 라오스의 Child Care Project가 하고 있는 일 두 가지를 우리말로 쓰시오.

① _____
② _____

[10~14] 다음 글을 읽고, 물음에 답하시오.

Hello, I am Kim Doha, and I would like to join your volunteer project. One day, I saw some poor dogs ⓐ TV. ⓑThey looked so sad that I wanted to help them. I like dogs, and there are many things ⓒthat I can do for them. I can walk the dogs, give them a bath, and play with them. I am the person who you are looking ⓓ !

10 위 글의 밑줄 친 ⓐ에 알맞은 말을 쓰시오.

➡ _____

11 위 글의 밑줄 친 ⓑ와 같은 뜻이 되도록 다음 문장의 빈칸에 알맞은 말을 쓰시오.

> They looked very sad, _____ I wanted to help them.

12 위 글의 밑줄 친 ⓒ와 바꿔 쓸 수 있는 것을 쓰시오.

➡ _____

13 위 글의 빈칸 ⓓ에 알맞은 말을 쓰시오.

➡ _____

14 What can Kim Doha do for dogs? Answer in Korean.

➡ _____
_____

[15~19] 다음 글을 읽고, 물음에 답하시오.

Kenneth Shinozuka grew ⓐ in a big happy family of three generations. ⓑSince he was little, he is always been very close to his grandfather. ⓒHe was Kenneth's first friend, his trusty driver, and his cook. ⓓHe also taught him many life lessons. He was the person who Kenneth respected the most in the world.

15 위 글의 빈칸 ⓐ에 알맞은 부사를 쓰시오.

➡ _____

16 위 글의 밑줄 친 ⓑ에서 어법상 어색한 것을 고치시오.

_____ ➡ _____

17 위 글의 밑줄 친 ⓒ에서 Kenneth의 할아버지가 Kenneth에게 한 일 두 가지를 우리말로 쓰시오.

① _____
② _____

18 위 글의 밑줄 친 ⓓ와 같은 뜻이 되도록 다음 문장의 빈칸에 알맞은 말을 쓰시오.

> He also taught many life lessons _____ him.

19 Who did Kenneth respect the most in the world? Answer in English.

➡ _____

구석구석

Link - Share

I'd like to talk about the volunteer work that we're planning to do for the
관계대명사 목적격(=which) ~할 계획이다
elderly people in our city. We came up with three activities. One of them is to
~을 생각해 냈다 ~ 중 하나 = three activities
make patbingsu for them and eat it together.
= the elderly people = patbingsu

구문해설 · volunteer work: 자원봉사 · elderly: 연세가 드신; 어르신들 · acticity: 활동
· together: 함께

나는 우리가 우리 도시의 노인들을 위해 계획하고 있는 자원봉사에 대해 이야기하고 싶다. 우리는 세 가지 활동을 생각해 냈다. 그 중 하나는 그들을 위해 팥빙수를 만들어 함께 먹는 것이다.

Write - Write

Hello, I am Kim Doha, and I would like to join your volunteer project. One
would like to+동사원형: ~하고 싶다 어느 날
day, I saw some poor dogs on TV. They looked so sad that I wanted to help
텔레비전에서 so ~ that … 구문: 너무 ~해서 …하다
them. I like dogs, and there are many things that I can do for them. I can walk
= some poor dogs there are + 복수명사: ~이 있다 관계대명사 목적격(=which)
the dogs, give them a bath, and play with them. I am the person who you are
= give a bath to them 관계대명사 목적격(=that)
looking for!
look for: ~을 찾다

구문해설 · poor: 불쌍한 · sad: 슬픈 · walk: 산책시키다 · bath: 목욕 · person: 사람

안녕, 나는 김도하야, 그리고 나는 너의 자원봉사 프로젝트에 참가하고 싶어. 어느 날, 나는 TV에서 몇 마리의 불쌍한 개들을 보았어. 그들은 너무 슬퍼 보여서 나는 그들을 돕고 싶었어. 나는 개를 좋아하고, 그들을 위해 내가 할 수 있는 많은 것들이 있어. 나는 개들을 산책시키고, 목욕시키고 그들과 함께 놀 수 있어. 네가 찾는 사람이 바로 나야!

Culture Project

Do you want to help children? Join our Child Care Project in Laos. You'll
동사원형 ~: ~해라 in + 국가명
teach local children. You'll also build a school for them. The work is so hard
= local children
that you'll want to go home at first, but you'll find happiness in helping these
so ~ that … 구문: 너무 ~해서 …하다 처음에 전치사 in+동명사
children.

구문해설 · care: 보호 · local: 지역의, 현지의 · build: 짓다, 건설하다 · hard: 어려운, 힘든
· happiness: 행복

여러분은 아이들을 돕고 싶나요? 라오스에 있는 우리의 아동 보호 프로젝트에 참여하십시오. 여러분은 지역 아이들을 가르칠 겁니다. 여러분은 또한 그들을 위해 학교를 지을 겁니다. 일이 너무 힘들어 처음에는 집에 가고 싶지만, 이 아이들을 돕는 데서 행복을 찾을 수 있을 겁니다.

01 다음 중 짝지어진 두 단어의 관계가 나머지 넷과 다른 것은?

① true – truly
② real – really
③ slow – slowly
④ love – lovely
⑤ actual – actually

02 다음 빈칸에 들어갈 말로 적절하지 <u>않은</u> 것은?

- It's raining _____ than ever.
- He was at the door to _____ us.
- I don't _____ what he's saying.
- The _____ time is 10:50 in the morning.

① local
② understand
③ still
④ worse
⑤ welcome

03 다음 짝지어진 두 단어의 관계가 같도록 빈칸에 알맞은 말을 쓰시오.

warm : cool = light : _____

04 다음 문장의 빈칸에 알맞은 것은?

Kate, take this boy and keep an eye _____ him.

① in
② on
③ to
④ for
⑤ with

05 다음 영영풀이에 해당하는 단어는?

to agree with someone, and perhaps help them because you want them to succeed

① advise
② fail
③ praise
④ share
⑤ support

06 다음 문장의 빈칸에 공통으로 들어갈 말을 쓰시오.

- Andy grew _____ in Paris.
- I hope you can come _____ with a better idea than this.

07 다음 우리말에 맞게 빈칸에 알맞은 말을 쓰시오.

그것은 단지 시행착오의 과정일 뿐이다.
➡ It's just a process of _____ and _____.

08 다음 대화의 빈칸에 알맞지 <u>않은</u> 것은?

A: Can you do me a favor?
B: _____

① Sure.
② Of course.
③ Sorry, I can't.
④ I'm afraid I can't.
⑤ I cannot thank too much.

[09~13] 다음 대화를 읽고, 물음에 답하시오.

Jaden: Can you ___ⓐ___ me a favor, Yuri?

Yuri: Sure. What is it, Jaden?

Jaden: Can we go shopping together for a baseball cap for a girl?

Yuri: Yes, of course. Who is it for?

Jaden: It's for my little sister Kate.

Yuri: Oh, are you getting her a birthday gift? (①)

Jaden: No, her birthday isn't ___ⓑ___ October. (②)

Yuri: ⓒThen, why are you getting a baseball cap to her? (③)

Jaden: She broke her leg while she was riding her bike last week. (④)

Yuri: Oh, I see. I can go this Friday afternoon. (⑤)

Jaden: That sounds perfect. Thank you.

09 위 대화의 ①~⑤ 중 다음 주어진 문장이 들어갈 알맞은 곳은?

> I just want to cheer her up.

①   ②   ③   ④   ⑤

10 위 대화의 빈칸 ⓐ에 알맞은 것은?

① do
② help
③ give
④ make
⑤ take

11 위 대화의 빈칸 ⓑ에 알맞은 것은?

① on
② to
③ as
④ when
⑤ until

12 위 대화의 밑줄 친 ⓒ에서 어법상 어색한 것을 고치시오.

_____ ➡ _____

13 위 대화의 내용으로 보아 대답할 수 없는 질문은?

① What does Jaden want to buy?
② Will Yuri help Jaden buy a baseball cap?
③ Who is Kate?
④ When is Kate's birthday?
⑤ Why did Kate break her leg?

14 다음 대화의 빈칸에 알맞은 것은?

> A: Thank you for helping me with my homework.
> B:

① Yes, I got it.
② That's great.
③ No problem.
④ You're right.
⑤ I appreciate your help.

15 다음 문장의 빈칸에 알맞은 것은?

> I lost the ring _____ my best friend Yujin gave me.

① who
② how
③ what
④ which
⑤ where

16 다음 빈칸에 알맞은 말이 바르게 짝지어진 것은?

> Vicky was _____ tired _____ she went to bed early last night.

① so – as
② so – that
③ as – to
④ too – to
⑤ such – to

17 다음 두 문장을 한 문장으로 만들 때 빈칸에 알맞은 말을 쓰시오.

> You are the only friend. I can look to you for advice.
> = You are the only friend to _____ I can look for advice.

18 다음 문장의 빈칸에 알맞은 것은?

> The man was brave enough to save the boy from the fire.
> = The man was _____ brave that he _____ the boy from the fire.

① such – save
② so – save
③ too – saved
④ as – saved
⑤ so – could save

[19~20] 다음 중 어법상 <u>어색한</u> 것을 고르시오.

19 ① The woman with whom I went there is my aunt.
② The man with whom she is talking is Mr. Allen.
③ I have no friends with whom I can talk about it.
④ The people whom I work are all very kind.
⑤ Those whom he lived with respected him.

20 ① My brother is old enough to drive a car.
② I didn't have enough money to buy the sneakers.
③ The policeman was enough fast to catch the pickpocket.
④ I like the doll that Ann gave to me the other day.
⑤ The girl whom you are looking at is my cousin.

21 다음 〈보기〉의 밑줄 친 부분과 쓰임이 <u>다른</u> 하나는?

> ┤ 보기 ├
> Do you know the boy <u>that</u> you saw at the library?

① Meryl Streep is a famous actress <u>that</u> I like a lot.
② He is the smartest boy <u>that</u> I've ever met.
③ The tomato pasta <u>that</u> we ate for lunch was a little spicy.
④ I thought <u>that</u> I had to finish my homework.
⑤ The pants <u>that</u> I'm wearing are very comfortable.

22 다음 문장을 같은 뜻으로 바꿔 쓴 것은?

> My dad is very sick, so he can't go to work.

① My dad is so sick not to go to work.
② My dad is too sick not to go to work.
③ My dad is so sick that he can't go to work.
④ My dad is such sick that he can't go to work.
⑤ My dad is very sick that he can't go to work.

23 다음 밑줄 친 부분의 쓰임이 바르지 <u>않은</u> 것은?

① I know the girl <u>whom</u> you met at the store.

② The woman <u>whom</u> we saw on the street is a famous singer.

③ This is the house in <u>that</u> she was born.

④ Do you know the doctor <u>who</u> I visited last night?

⑤ I cannot find the watch <u>which</u> I bought last week.

Reading

[24~28] 다음 글을 읽고, 물음에 답하시오.

When Kenneth was four, his grandfather went out ____ⓐ____ a walk one day and got lost. He had Alzheimer's disease. ⓑEveryone in Kenneth's family were in shock. His condition became worse over the next 10 years. He wandered off at night so often that someone had to keep an eye ____ⓒ____ him all night long. One night, Kenneth's grandfather got out of bed, and Kenneth saw it. At that moment, he said to himself, "____ⓓ____ don't I put pressure sensors on the heels of his socks?"

24 위 글의 빈칸 ⓐ에 알맞은 것은?

① to   ② in
③ at   ④ for
⑤ along

25 위 글의 밑줄 친 ⓑ에서 어법상 어색한 것을 고치시오.

_____ ➡ _____

26 위 글의 빈칸 ⓒ에 알맞은 것은?

① at   ② on
③ to   ④ in
⑤ with

27 위 글의 빈칸 ⓓ에 알맞은 것은?

① Why   ② How
③ When   ④ What
⑤ Which

28 위 글의 내용으로 보아 대답할 수 <u>없는</u> 질문은?

① How old was Kenneth when his grandfather got lost?

② What disease did Kenneth's grandfather have?

③ Did Kenneth's grandfather get well?

④ What did Kenneth see one night?

⑤ Did Kenneth put pressure sensors on the heels of his grandfather's socks?

[29~32] 다음 글을 읽고, 물음에 답하시오.

I'd like to talk about the volunteer work ⓐthat we're planning to do for the elderly people in our city. We came ____ⓑ____ with three activities. One of them is to make *patbingsu* ____ⓒ____ them and eat it together.

29 위 글의 밑줄 친 ⓐ와 바꿔 쓸 수 있는 것은?

① who　　② whom　　③ what
④ whose　　⑤ which

30 위 글의 빈칸 ⓑ에 알맞은 것은?

① on　　② to　　③ in
④ up　　⑤ over

31 위 글의 빈칸 ⓒ에 알맞은 것은?

① of　　② to　　③ for
④ at　　⑤ over

32 What is one of three activities? Answer in Korean.

➡ _____

[33~37] 다음 글을 읽고, 물음에 답하시오.

　Hello, I am Kim Doha, and I would like to join your ___ⓐ___ project. (①) One day, I saw some poor dogs on TV. (②) ⓑThey looked so sad that I wanted to help them. (③) I can walk the dogs, give them a bath, and play with them. (④) I am the person ⓒwho you are looking for! (⑤)

33 위 대화의 ①~⑤ 중 다음 주어진 문장이 들어갈 알맞은 곳은?

I like dogs, and there are many things that I can do for them.

①　　②　　③　　④　　⑤

34 위 글의 빈칸 ⓐ에 다음 정의에 해당하는 단어를 쓰시오.

someone who does work without being paid for it, because they want to do it

➡ _____

35 위 글의 밑줄 친 ⓑ와 같은 뜻이 되도록 다음 문장의 빈칸에 알맞은 말을 쓰시오.

They looked very sad, _____ I wanted to help them.

36 위 글의 밑줄 친 ⓒ와 바꿔 쓸 수 있는 것은? (2개)

① whom　　② what
③ whose　　④ that
⑤ which

37 위 글의 내용으로 보아 대답할 수 없는 질문은?

① What is the writer's name?
② What is Kim Doha's hobby?
③ What did Kim Doha see on TV?
④ How did the dogs look?
⑤ What can Kim Doha do for dogs?

출제율 95%

01 다음 중 짝지어진 단어의 관계가 나머지 넷과 <u>다른</u> 것은?

① wrong : right   ② heavy : light
③ clean : dirty   ④ near : close
⑤ succeed : fail

출제율 100%

02 다음 빈칸에 공통으로 알맞은 것은?

> • Mike is looking _____ his hat.
> • You should be thankful _____ your health.

① at   ② for
③ to   ④ with
⑤ from

출제율 90%

03 다음 중 영영풀이가 <u>잘못된</u> 것은?

① safety: the state of being safe from harm or danger
② always: at all times
③ praise: to agree with someone, and perhaps help them because you want them to succeed
④ inventor: a person who has invented something, or whose job is to invent things
⑤ heel: the back part of your foot, just below your ankle

출제율 90%

04 다음 짝지어진 두 단어의 관계가 같도록 빈칸에 알맞은 말을 쓰시오.

> son : daughter = king : _____

출제율 95%

05 다음 우리말에 맞게 빈칸에 알맞은 말을 쓰시오.

> 낮 동안에 날씨가 더 나빠졌다.
> ➡ The weather got _____ during the day.

출제율 90%

06 다음 대화의 밑줄 친 부분의 의도로 알맞은 것은?

> A: <u>Thank you for taking care of the children.</u>
> B: My pleasure.
> A: You're very kind.

① 제안하기   ② 동의하기
③ 초대하기   ④ 감사하기
⑤ 화남 표현하기

출제율 100%

07 다음 대화의 빈칸에 알맞은 것은?

> A: Can you return this book for me?
> B: _____

① It's a very famous story.
② Sorry, but I'm busy now.
③ No, I will return it for you.
④ It's very kind of you to help me.
⑤ Where should we meet tomorrow?

08 다음 중 짝지어진 대화가 <u>어색한</u> 것은?

① A: Can you do me a favor?

B: Sure. What is it?

② A: Can you help me do my homework?

B: I'm afraid I can't. I'm busy now.

③ A: Thank you for cleaning the refrigerator.

B: My pleasure.

④ A: Thank you for making cookies.

B: I'm sorry I can't.

⑤ A: Could you open the door?

B: No problem.

[09~11] 다음 대화를 읽고, 물음에 답하시오.

G: Andrew, can you do me a ____ⓐ____ ?

B: O.K. What is it?

G: My family is going to go to Jejudo this ____ⓑ____. Can you ©take care of my cat during the weekend?

B: Sure. Don't worry about her. And enjoy your trip.

09 위 대화의 빈칸 ⓐ에 알맞은 말을 쓰시오.

➡ _____

10 위 대화의 빈칸 ⓑ에 다음 정의에 해당하는 단어를 쓰시오.

Saturday and Sunday

➡ _____

11 위 대화의 밑줄 친 ©와 바꿔 쓸 수 있는 것은?

① wait for ② look for

③ look after ④ watch out

⑤ watch on

12 다음 빈칸에 공통으로 알맞은 말은?

• I like the doll _____ my mom made.

• Do you know the man _____ Jane wants to meet?

① how ② who

③ whom ④ which

⑤ that

13 다음 빈칸에 알맞은 말이 바르게 짝지어진 것은?

그녀의 노래들은 너무 좋아서 나는 마치 꿈속에 있는 것 같다.

➡ Her songs are _____ nice _____ I feel like I'm in dream.

① so — as ② as — as

③ so — that ④ such — as

⑤ such — that

14 다음 문장에서 어법상 어색한 부분을 찾아 고치시오.

When you read, you will often find words you don't know them.

_____ ➡ _____

15 출제율 95%

다음 문장에서 어법상 어색한 부분을 찾아 바르게 고쳐 쓰시오

> The cookie was too hard that Shirley almost broke her tooth.

_____ ➡ _____

16 출제율 95%

다음 우리말과 일치하도록 괄호 안에 주어진 어구를 배열하시오.

> 이것은 내가 Paul에게 빌렸던 책이다.
> (the book / which / this is / I / from Paul / borrowed)

➡ _____

17 출제율 100%

다음 중 밑줄 친 관계대명사가 잘못 쓰인 것은?

① Jack needs a car which he can drive.
② I need a man that can speak English.
③ I know the girl which you are looking for.
④ This is the book which I bought two days ago.
⑤ They saw the old man and his cat that were running in the park.

18 출제율 95%

다음 우리말을 참고하여 빈칸에 알맞은 말을 쓰시오.

> 시험이 너무 어려워서 그는 잘 보지 못했다.
> = The test was _____ difficult _____ he didn't do well.

19 출제율 85%

다음 문장의 밑줄 친 부분 중 생략할 수 없는 것은?

① This is the story that Kevin wrote.
② The dress which she is wearing is pink.
③ This is the table which his father made.
④ The man whom I saw yesterday was Mr. Brown.
⑤ The man who lives in Seoul will come tomorrow.

[20~23] 다음 글을 읽고, 물음에 답하시오.

> (①) Join our Child Care Project in Laos. You'll teach local children. (②) You'll also build a school for them. (③) The work is so hard that you'll want to go home ⓐ_____ first. (④) But you'll find happiness in ⓑhelp these children. (⑤)

20 출제율 95%

위 글의 ①~⑤ 중 다음 주어진 문장이 들어갈 알맞은 곳은?

> Do you want to help children?

①　　②　　③　　④　　⑤

21 출제율 90%

위 글의 빈칸 ⓐ에 알맞은 것은?

① to ② in
③ at ④ on
⑤ for

22 출제율 85%

위 글의 밑줄 친 ⓑ를 알맞은 형으로 고치시오.

➡ _____

23 라오스에서 행해지는 Child Care Project의 목적이 무엇인지 우리말로 간단히 쓰시오.

➡ _____

[24~27] 다음 글을 읽고, 물음에 답하시오.

ⓐThere were many things Kenneth had to do. He first had to create a pressure sensor and then find a way ___ⓑ___ a signal to his smart phone. Kenneth also tried many different materials to make comfortable socks ___ⓒ___ his elderly grandfather.

24 위 글의 밑줄 친 ⓐ를 생략된 관계대명사를 보충하여 다시 쓰시오.

➡ _____

_____

25 위 글의 빈칸 ⓑ에 알맞은 것은?

① send   ② sending

③ for send   ④ to send

⑤ to sending

26 위 글의 빈칸 ⓒ에 알맞은 것은?

① at   ② of

③ for   ④ to

⑤ with

27 What did Kenneth do to make comfortable socks? Answer in Korean.

➡ _____

[28~31] 다음 글을 읽고, 물음에 답하시오.

When he felt ___ⓐ___ giving up, he thought about his grandfather's safety. After much trial and ___ⓑ___, he finally succeeded in making his device. When it first ⓒworked, he was so happy that he jumped for joy. He could not believe that his invention actually worked. For his grandfather, Kenneth is the best inventor in the world. For Kenneth, his grandfather is still his best friend.

28 위 글의 빈칸 ⓐ에 알맞은 말을 쓰시오.

➡ _____

29 위 글의 빈칸 ⓑ에 알맞은 것은?

① error   ② fault

③ lie   ④ blame

⑤ mistake

30 위 글의 밑줄 친 ⓒ와 같은 의미로 쓰인 것은?

① I can't work if it is cold.

② Mary worked at mathematics last night.

③ Can you work this computer?

④ Mr. Jackson worked for an oil company.

⑤ The brakes on this car don't work.

31 Why was Kenneth happy? Answer in English.

➡ _____

[01~03] 다음 글을 읽고, 물음에 답하시오.

A: Can you ___ⓐ___ me a favor?
B: Sure. What is it?
A: Can you move this table with me? It's too ___ⓑ___.
B: Sure. No problem.
A: Thank you for ⓒhelp me.

01 위 대화의 빈칸 ⓐ에 알맞은 말을 쓰시오.

➡ _____

02 위 대화의 빈칸 ⓑ에 다음 정의에 해당하는 말을 쓰시오.

weighing a lot

➡ _____

03 위 대화의 밑줄 친 ⓒ를 알맞은 형으로 고치시오.

➡ _____

04 다음 대화의 순서를 바르게 배열하시오.

(A) Yes, I can.
(B) Sure. What is it?
(C) Mark, can you do me a favor?
(D) My family is going on vacation for a week. Can you come to our house and water the plants?

➡ _____

05 다음 괄호 안에 주어진 단어를 배열하여 문장을 완성하시오.

(1) Mr. Brown is a teacher (everyone, class, my, whom, in) respects.
➡ Mr. Brown is a teacher _____
_____ respects.

(2) The movie (I, to, watch, want, which) is *Shrek*.
➡ The movie _____ is *Shrek*.

06 다음 〈조건〉에 맞게 괄호 안의 단어를 이용하여 우리말을 영어로 옮기시오.

┌─ 조건 ─┐
1. 주어진 단어를 모두 이용할 것.
2. 필요시 관사를 붙이거나 단어를 추가하고 동사의 어형 변화를 할 것.
3. 대·소문자 및 구두점에 유의할 것.

(1) 음식이 너무 매워서 Chris는 많이 먹을 수 없었다. (spicy, that, can, eat, much)
➡ _____

(2) 날씨가 너무 추워서 우리는 소풍을 갈 수가 없었다. (it, too, for, go, picnic)
➡ _____

(3) 그는 저 자동차를 살 수 있을 만큼 부자이다. (rich, enough, buy)
➡ _____

07 다음 문장에서 어법상 어색한 부분을 찾아 바르게 고쳐 쓰시오.

I have a pen what my father gave me.

_____ ➡ _____

[08~12] 다음 글을 읽고, 물음에 답하시오.

When Kenneth was four, his grandfather went out for a walk one day and ⓐgot lost. He had Alzheimer's disease. Everyone in Kenneth's family was in shock. His condition became ⓑbad over the next 10 years. He wandered off at night so often ___ⓒ___ someone had to keep an eye on him all night long. One night, Kenneth's grandfather got out of bed, and Kenneth saw it. At that moment, he said to ⓓ(him, himself), "Why don't I put pressure sensors on the heels of his socks?"

08 위 글의 밑줄 친 ⓐ를 우리말로 옮기시오.

➡ ______________________

09 위 글의 밑줄 친 ⓑ를 알맞은 어형으로 고치시오.

➡ ______________________

10 중요 위 글의 빈칸 ⓒ에 알맞은 말을 쓰시오.

➡ ______________________

11 위 글의 괄호 ⓓ에서 알맞은 것을 고르시오.

➡ ______________________

12 중요 Why was everyone in Kenneth's family in shock? Answer in English.

➡ ______________________________________

____

[13~16] 다음 글을 읽고, 물음에 답하시오.

There were many things ⓐthat Kenneth had to do. He first had to ___ⓑ___ a pressure sensor and then find a way to send a signal to his smart phone. Kenneth also tried many different materials ⓒmake comfortable socks for his elderly grandfather.

13 위 글의 밑줄 친 ⓐ와 바꿔 쓸 수 있는 것을 쓰시오.

➡ ______________________

14 위 글의 빈칸 ⓑ에 다음 정의에 해당하는 단어를 주어진 철자로 시작하여 쓰시오.

to cause something to happen or exist

➡ c______________________

15 중요 위 글의 밑줄 친 ⓒ를 알맞은 형으로 고치시오.

➡ ______________________

16 위 글에서 Kenneth가 할아버지를 위해 한 일을 우리말로 쓰시오.

➡ ______________________________________

____

____

01 다음 주어진 어구를 이용하여 예시와 같이 쓰시오.

Teacher	teach, students, school	ex) A teacher is someone who teaches students at a school.
Waiter	serve, food, restaurant	(1)
Zookeeper	look after, animals, zoo	(2)
Dessert	sweet food, serve, after meal	(3)

the woman	I, met	ex) She is the woman whom I met in the park yesterday.
the sport	Ann, play, table tennis	(4)
the camera	you, got	(5)
the woman	I, talk about	(6)

(1) _____

(2) _____

(3) _____

(4) _____

(5) _____

(6) _____

02 다음 어구를 이용하여 〈보기〉와 같이 여러분의 상황에 맞게 영어 문장을 쓰시오. (3개 이상)

enough ... to   too ... to   so ... that
last year   last month   this year   yesterday   now
old   young   tall   short   strong   weak   early   late   noisy   quiet   light   heavy   busy

보기

Last year, I was too short to play basketball, but now I'm tall enough to play it.

(1) _____

(2) _____

(3) _____

단원별 모의고사

01 다음 중 우리말 뜻이 잘못된 것은?

① wander off: 여기저기 쏘다니다
② feel like -ing: ~하고 싶은 기분이다
③ at first: 마침내
④ for joy: 기뻐서
⑤ take care of: ~을 돌보다

02 다음 영영풀이에 해당하는 단어로 알맞은 것은?

> an illness which affects people, animals, or plants, for example one which is caused by bacteria or infection

① disease
② death
③ treat
④ health
⑤ hospital

03 다음 빈칸에 알맞은 말이 바르게 짝지어진 것은?

> • Will you do me a _____?
> • The car won't start, can you _____ it?

① favor – fix
② pardon – mend
③ excuse – fix
④ service – mend
⑤ favor – attend

04 다음 짝지어진 두 단어의 관계가 같도록 빈칸에 알맞은 말을 쓰시오.

> rain : rainy = luck : _____

05 다음 빈칸에 공통으로 들어갈 말을 쓰시오.

> • I want to become a minister when I grow _____.
> • They gave _____ without a fight.

06 다음 대화를 의미가 통하도록 알맞게 배열한 것은?

> (A) Great! I'm having a birthday party this weekend. Can you come?
> (B) Sure. Thank you for inviting me.
> (C) Nothing special. I'll just stay home and watch TV.
> (D) What are you doing this weekend, Eric?

① (A) – (D) – (B) – (C)
② (B) – (C) – (A) – (D)
③ (C) – (D) – (B) – (A)
④ (D) – (B) – (C) – (A)
⑤ (D) – (C) – (A) – (B)

07 다음 중 짝지어진 대화가 어색한 것은?

① A: May I ask you a favor?
　 B: No problem. What is it?
② A: Can you bring me a cup of coffee?
　 B: You're welcome.
③ A: Can you help me find my key?
　 B: Sorry, I can't. I have to go out now.
④ A: Thank you for taking care of my dog.
　 B: My pleasure.
⑤ A: Can you help me with something?
　 B: Sure. What's up?

08 다음 대화에서 밑줄 친 부분의 의도로 알맞은 것은?

> A: Can you do me a favor?
> B: Sure. What is it?
> A: Can you help me clean the board?
> B: No problem.

① 충고하기　　　　② 초대하기
③ 위치 확인하기　　④ 도움 요청하기
⑤ 음식 주문하기

[09~13] 다음 대화를 읽고, 물음에 답하시오.

> Jaden: Can you do me a favor, Yuri?
> Yuri: Sure. What is it, Jaden? (①)
> Jaden: Can we go shopping together ⓐ a baseball cap for a girl? (②)
> Yuri: Yes, of course. (③)
> Jaden: It's for my little sister Kate. (④)
> Yuri: ⓑOh, are you getting her a birthday gift? (⑤)
> Jaden: No, her birthday isn't until October.
> Yuri: Then, why are you getting a baseball cap ⓒ her?
> Jaden: She broke her leg while she was riding her bike last week. I just want to cheer her up.
> Yuri: Oh, I see. I can go this Friday afternoon.
> Jaden: That sounds perfect. Thank you.

09 위 대화의 ①~⑤ 중 다음 주어진 문장이 들어갈 알맞은 곳은?

> Who is it for?

①　　②　　③　　④　　⑤

10 위 대화의 빈칸 ⓐ에 알맞은 전치사를 쓰시오.

➡ _____

11 위 대화의 밑줄 친 ⓑ를 우리말로 옮기시오.

➡ _____

12 위 대화의 빈칸 ⓒ에 알맞은 것은?

① to　　　　② for
③ in　　　　④ of
⑤ with

13 위 대화의 내용과 일치하지 <u>않는</u> 것은?

① Jaden wants to go shopping with Yuri.
② Jaden will buy a baseball cap for Yuri.
③ Jaden's little sister's name is Kathy.
④ Kathy broke her leg last week.
⑤ Yuri will go shopping with Jaden this Friday afternoon.

14 다음 빈칸에 공통으로 알맞은 것은?

> • My dad bought me a bag _____ was black.
> • I know the man _____ you are looking for.

① how　　　　② who
③ that　　　　④ whom
⑤ which

15 다음 두 문장의 의미가 같도록 할 때 빈칸에 알맞은 것은?

> The bags are so heavy that I can't carry them.
> = The bags are _____ heavy _____ carry.

① so – as　　　　② too – to
③ as – that　　　④ very – to
⑤ such – that

16 다음 밑줄 친 that의 쓰임이 나머지와 다른 하나는?

① He is the man that I can trust.
② That is the dog that I really love.
③ I know the man that is singing a song.
④ I like the car that you bought yesterday.
⑤ She is wearing a sweater that she bought yesterday.

17 다음 문장 중 어법상 어색한 것은? (2개)

① You are too young to go swimming alone.
② Kate didn't have enough money to buy the smart phone.
③ She was enough kind to help the old woman.
④ This puzzle is so difficult that I can't solve.
⑤ Dad walked too fast for me to catch up with.

18 다음 문장의 빈칸에 알맞은 것은? (2개)

Javlon's father got a new job in Korea, so his family moved to Seoul three months ago. Let's look at the writings _____ Javlon posted on his blog.

① who
② whom
③ what
④ that
⑤ which

19 다음 두 문장이 같은 의미가 되도록 빈칸에 알맞은 말을 쓰시오.

The chair is so small that I can't sit on it.
= The chair is _____ small for me _____ sit on.

20 다음 밑줄 친 부분 중 생략할 수 있는 것은?

① I know a boy whose name is Mark.
② He bought me a bag which was red.
③ I don't like the boy who makes a noise.
④ The cake that he baked was very nice.
⑤ Do you know the man who is playing with a ball?

[21~26] 다음 글을 읽고, 물음에 답하시오.

Hello, I am Kim Doha, and I would like to ___ⓐ___ your volunteer project. One day, I saw some poor dogs ⓑ___ TV. They looked so sad ⓒthat I wanted to help them. ⓓI like dogs, and there are many things I can do for them. I can walk the dogs, give them a bath, and play with them. I am the person ⓔwho you are looking for!

21 위 글의 빈칸 ⓐ에 알맞은 것은?

① agree
② pass
③ join
④ belong
⑤ share

22 위 글의 빈칸 ⓑ에 알맞은 것은?

① on
② in
③ at
④ with
⑤ from

23 위 글의 밑줄 친 ⓒ와 용법이 같은 것은?

① It is strange that she doesn't come.
② It was such a big noise that we were awakened.
③ Look at the trees that stand on the hill.
④ It was here that she first met Mike.
⑤ This is the doll that my mother made for me.

24 위 글의 밑줄 친 ⓓ를 생략된 관계대명사를 보충하여 다시 쓰시오.

➡ _____

_____

25 위 글의 밑줄 친 ⓔ와 바꿔 쓸 수 있는 것은? (2개)

① that   ② what
③ whose   ④ whom
⑤ which

26 위 글의 내용과 일치하지 <u>않는</u> 것은?

① 김도하는 자원봉사 프로젝트에 가입하기를 원한다.
② 김도하는 텔레비전에서 불쌍한 개들을 보았다.
③ 김도하는 개를 좋아한다.
④ 김도하는 개를 목욕시킬 수 있다.
⑤ 김도하는 자원봉사 프로젝트에 적합하지 않다.

[27~30] 다음 글을 읽고, 물음에 답하시오.

_____ ⓐ _____ he felt like giving up, he thought about his grandfather's safety. (①) After much trial and error, he finally succeeded in making his device. (②) When it first worked, he was so happy _____ ⓑ _____ he jumped for joy. (③) He could not believe _____ ⓒ _____ his invention ⓓ<u>actual</u> worked. (④) For Kenneth, his grandfather is still his best friend. (⑤)

27 위 글의 ①~⑤ 중 다음 주어진 문장이 들어갈 알맞은 곳은?

For his grandfather, Kenneth is the best inventor in the world.

①   ②   ③   ④   ⑤

28 위 글의 빈칸 ⓐ에 알맞은 것은? (2개)

① If   ② As
③ When   ④ Though
⑤ Because

29 위 글의 빈칸 ⓑ와 ⓒ에 공통으로 알맞은 것은?

① what   ② whether
③ that   ④ which
⑤ though

30 위 글의 밑줄 친 ⓓ를 알맞은 어형으로 고치시오.

➡ _____

Lesson 5

Bravo! Brava!

 의사소통 기능

- 제안하기
  Why don't we see a magic show?

- 약속 정하기
  A: What time shall we meet?
  B: How about 10 o'clock on Saturday?

언어 형식

- 접속사 if
  You will appreciate it better **if** you know the story.

- as + 형용사/부사의 원급 + as
  Turandot is **as cold as** ice.

교과서
Words & Expressions

Key Words

☐ **actually** [ǽktʃuəli] 부 실은, 사실은, 실제로
☐ **add** [æd] 동 (말을) 덧붙이다, 더하다
☐ **agree** [əgríː] 동 동의하다
☐ **already** [ɔːlrédi] 부 이미, 벌써
☐ **amazing** [əméiziŋ] 형 놀라운
☐ **anniversary** [ænəvə́ːrsəri] 명 기념일
☐ **answer** [ǽnsər] 동 대답하다(= reply)
☐ **appreciate** [əpríːʃièit] 동 감상하다, 감사하다, 진가를 알아보다
☐ **aria** [ɛ́əriə] 명 아리아, 영창
☐ **beauty** [bjúːti] 명 아름다움, 미
☐ **brave** [breiv] 형 용감한
☐ **celebrate** [séləbrèit] 동 기념하다
☐ **century** [séntʃəri] 명 세기
☐ **Chinese** [tʃàiníːz] 형 중국의 명 중국인
☐ **correctly** [kəréktli] 부 정확하게, 바르게
☐ **dawn** [dɔːn] 명 새벽
☐ **difficult** [dífikʌlt] 형 어려운
☐ **discount** [dískaunt] 명 할인
☐ **fail** [feil] 동 실패하다
☐ **famous** [féiməs] 형 유명한
☐ **find** [faind] 동 찾다, 알아내다, 발견하다
☐ **guess** [ges] 동 추측하다
☐ **incorrectly** [ìnkəréktli] 부 정확하지 않게, 틀리게
☐ **Italian** [itǽljən] 명 이탈리아어, 이탈리아인 형 이탈리아의

☐ **like** [laik] 전 ~처럼
☐ **marry** [mǽri] 동 ~와 결혼하다
☐ **mean** [miːn] 동 의미하다
☐ **moving** [múːviŋ] 형 감동적인
☐ **ostrich** [ɔ́ːstritʃ] 명 타조
☐ **part** [paːrt] 명 역할, 배역, 부분
☐ **perform** [pərfɔ́ːrm] 동 공연하다, 수행하다
☐ **performance** [pərfɔ́ːrməns] 명 공연
☐ **place** [pleis] 명 장소
☐ **play** [plei] 명 연극, 극, 희곡
☐ **practice** [prǽktis] 동 연습하다
☐ **princess** [prínsis] 명 공주
☐ **riddle** [rídl] 명 수수께끼
☐ **right** [rait] 부 즉시, 곧바로
☐ **safe** [seif] 형 안전한
☐ **secret** [síːkrit] 명 비밀
☐ **stranger** [stréindʒər] 명 낯선 사람, 이방인
☐ **storyline** [stɔ́ːrilàin] 명 줄거리
☐ **subway** [sʌ́bwèi] 명 지하철
☐ **suggestion** [səgdʒéstʃən] 명 제안
☐ **theater** [θíːətər] 명 극장
☐ **tonight** [tənáit] 부 오늘밤에
☐ **until** [əntíl] 접 ~할 때까지
☐ **whole** [houl] 명 전체 형 모든, 전부의

Key Expressions

☐ **as+형용사+as** ~ …만큼 ~한
☐ **at first sight** 첫눈에
☐ **be able to+동사원형** ~할 수 있다
☐ **be going to+동사원형** ~할 예정이다
☐ **be late for** ~ ~에 늦다, 지각하다
☐ **fall in love with** ~ ~와 사랑에 빠지다
☐ **find out** 알아내다, 발견하다
☐ **Guess what!** 있잖아.
☐ **have to+동사원형** ~해야 한다
☐ **How about+명사** ~? ~은 어때?

☐ **hurry up** 서두르다
☐ **in time** 제시간에, 늦지 않게
☐ **Let's+동사원형** ~. ~하자.
☐ **nothing more than** ~ ~에 지나지 않는
☐ **of beauty** 아름다운
☐ **one day** 어느 날
☐ **take off** (일을) 쉬다
☐ **take the subway** 지하철을 타다
☐ **Why don't you+동사원형** ~? ~하는 게 어때?
☐ **would like to+동사원형** ~하고 싶다

Word Power

※ 서로 반대되는 뜻을 가진 단어

☐ **brave**(용감한) ↔ **cowardly**(겁이 많은)

☐ **correctly**(정확하게) ↔ **incorrectly**(정확하지 않게)

☐ **difficult**(어려운) ↔ **easy**(쉬운)

☐ **safe**(안전한) ↔ **dangerous**(위험한)

☐ **fail**(실패하다) ↔ **succeed**(성공하다)

☐ **famous**(유명한) ↔ **unknown**(알려지지 않은)

※ 서로 비슷한 뜻을 가진 단어

☐ **answer : reply to** (~에 대답하다)

☐ **moving : touching** (감동적인)

☐ **suggestion : proposal** (제안)

☐ **amazing : surprising** (놀라운)

☐ **famous : well-known** (유명한)

☐ **agree : assent** (동의하다)

English Dictionary

☐ **already** 이미
→ earlier than the time expected
예상된 시간보다 더 이르게

☐ **amazing** 놀라운
→ very surprising
매우 놀라운

☐ **anniversary** 기념일
→ a day on which you remember or celebrate something that happened on that day in the past
과거의 그 날에 일어난 일을 기억하거나 축하하는 날

☐ **appreciate** 진가를 알아보다
→ to understand how good something or someone is
어떤 것이나 어떤 사람이 얼마나 좋은지 이해하다

☐ **aria** 아리아, 영창
→ a piece of music in an opera sung by one person
한 사람이 부른 오페라의 음악

☐ **brave** 용감한
→ showing no fear of dangerous or difficult things
위험하거나 어려운 일에 두려움을 보이지 않는

☐ **celebrate** 축하하다, 기념하다
→ to do something enjoyable on a special occasion
특별한 경우에 즐거운 어떤 것을 하다

☐ **century** 세기
→ a period of 100 years
100년

☐ **discount** 할인
→ a reduction in the normal price
정상 가격에서의 감소

☐ **guess** 추측하다
→ to give an answer to a particular question when you do not have all the facts and so cannot be certain if you are correct
모든 사실을 가지고 있지 않아서 당신이 옳은지 확신할 수 없을 때 특정한 질문에 답을 하다

☐ **marry** 결혼하다
→ to become the legally accepted husband or wife of someone in an official or religious ceremony
공식적 또는 종교적 의식에서 합법적으로 인정된 남편이나 아내가 되다

☐ **moving** 감동적인
→ causing strong feelings of sadness or sympathy
슬픔이나 공감의 강한 감정을 불러일으키는

☐ **perform** 수행하다, 공연하다
→ to do an action or piece of work
행동이나 작품을 하다

☐ **riddle** 수수께끼
→ a type of question that describes something in a difficult and confusing way and has a clever or funny answer
어렵고 혼란스러운 방식으로 무언가를 묘사하고 교묘하거나 재미있는 답을 가지는 질문 유형

☐ **secret** 비밀
→ a piece of information that is only known by one person or a few people and should not be told to others
한 사람이나 몇 사람만 알고 다른 사람에게는 말하지 말아야 하는 정보

☐ **storyline** 줄거리
→ the series of events that happen in a book, film, play, etc.
책, 영화, 희곡 등에서 일어나는 일련의 사건

서답형

01 다음 짝지어진 두 단어의 관계가 같도록 빈칸에 알맞은 단어를 쓰시오.

unknown : famous = cowardly : _____

[02~03] 다음 빈칸에 들어갈 말로 가장 적절한 것은?

02

It's _____. The sun is rising.

① dawn   ② crowd   ③ drought

④ discount   ⑤ aria

중요

03

Background knowledge will help you to _____ the musical.

① mean   ② discount

③ guess   ④ appreciate

⑤ celebrate

[04~05] 다음 영영 풀이에 해당하는 단어를 고르시오.

04

a piece of music in an opera sung by one person

① musical   ② century

③ storyline   ④ touch

⑤ aria

05

causing strong feelings of sadness or sympathy

① riddle   ② moving

③ brave   ④ cowardly

⑤ difficult

중요

06 밑줄 친 부분의 의미가 잘못된 것은?

① Tonight, we are going to perform a musical. (공연하다)

② Why don't we go out to celebrate the New Year? (축하하다)

③ It's our school's 75th anniversary. (기념일)

④ A brave prince falls in love with her at first sight. (사랑에 빠지다)

⑤ He is nothing more than a stranger to her. (결코 ~가 아닌)

서답형

07 다음 밑줄 친 부분과 의미가 비슷한 것을 주어진 철자로 시작하여 쓰시오.

He becomes the first man to answer all three puzzles.

➡ r_____

서답형

08 다음 두 문장이 같은 뜻이 되도록 빈칸에 알맞은 말을 쓰시오.

Turandot is a woman of great beauty.
= Turandot is a very _____ woman.

➡ _____

서답형

09 다음 주어진 우리말에 맞게 빈칸을 채우시오.

(1) 이런, 영화 시간에 늦을 거야.
    ➡ Oh, we're going to _____ _____ _____ the movie.

(2) 나는 오후에 일을 쉴 수 있을 것 같구나.
    ➡ I guess I can _____ the afternoon _____.

01 다음 우리말에 맞게 빈칸에 알맞은 단어를 쓰시오.

(1) 학교 끝나고 바로, 네 시에 어때?

➡ How about 4 o'clock, _____ _____ school?

(2) 당신이 맞게 대답한다면 나는 죽는 것에 동의하겠습니다.

➡ If you answer _____, I will _____ _____ die.

(3) 그녀와 결혼하길 원하는 왕자는 누구든지 반드시 세 가지 수수께끼에 답해야 합니다.

➡ Any prince who wants to _____ her must answer three _____.

02 영어 설명을 읽고, 문장의 빈칸에 들어갈 알맞은 단어를 쓰시오.

> to understand how good something or someone is

(1) Her family doesn't _____ her.

> the series of events that happen in a book, film, play, etc.

(2) Having a clear _____ is very important to movies and novels.

03 다음 〈보기〉에서 빈칸에 공통으로 들어갈 단어를 골라 쓰시오.

┌─ 보기 ─┐
take   be   care   look
└───────┘

• Can I _____ the afternoon off?

• Why don't we _____ the bus?

04 다음 빈칸에 알맞은 단어를 〈보기〉에서 골라 쓰시오. (형태 변화 가능)

┌─ 보기 ─┐
like   famous   celebrate   perform
└───────┘

(1) The prince then sings the _____ _____ aria of the whole opera, "Nessun Dorma."

(2) _____ many other famous operas, *Turandot* is in Italian.

(3) She _____ my birthday last year.

(4) How was our _____?

05 다음 주어진 우리말에 맞게 빈칸을 채우시오. (필요하면 변형하여 쓰시오.)

(1) 수요일에 가면 할인을 받을 수 있어요.

➡ We can get a _____ if we go on a Wednesday.

(2) 그는 그녀에게 단지 낯선 사람일 뿐입니다.

➡ He is _____ _____ _____ a stranger to her.

(3) 만약 실패하면 그는 죽어야 합니다.

➡ If he _____, he must die.

(4) 누군가 그의 이름을 알아낼 때까지 그 누구도 잠들 수 없을 것이다.

➡ No one will go to sleep _____ someone finds out his name.

1 제안하기

> **Why don't we see a magic show?** 마술 쇼 보는 게 어때?

- 상대방에게 '함께 ~하자'라고 제안이나 권유할 때에는 'Why don't we ~?'를 사용할 수 있다. 'Why don't you ~?'는 함께 하는 것이 아니고 상대방에게만 권유하는 것이다.

- **제안하는 다양한 표현**

  Why don't we+동사원형 ~? = Let's+동사원형 ~. = Shall we+동사원형 ~? = How[What] about+동사원형+-ing ~? = What do you say to+동사원형+-ing ~?

제안하기와 답하기

- A: Why don't we go on a bike ride? 함께 자전거 타러 가자.
  B: Yes, let's go. 좋아. 가자.

- A: Why don't you get some sleep? 잠을 좀 자렴.
  B: Yes, I think I should. 네. 그래야겠어요.

- A: What shall we do at the park? 우리 공원에서 뭘 할까?
  B: Why don't we see a magic show? 마술 쇼 보는 게 어때?
  A: That's a good idea. 좋은 생각이야.

핵심 Check

1. 다음 대화의 빈칸에 들어갈 말로 알맞은 것은?

M: _____ The subway will be faster than the bus at this time of day.

W: That's a good idea.

① How do I get to the subway station?
② Let's keep our fingers crossed for him.
③ Shall we take the subway?
④ What happened to the subway?
⑤ What's the matter?

2. 다음 대화의 밑줄 친 부분의 의도로 적절한 것은?

B: Mom, I got only one question wrong on the Korean history exam!

W: Great! I was sure you would do well. <u>Why don't we go out to celebrate tonight?</u>

① 화남 표현하기　② 제안하기　③ 설명하기　④ 의도 표현하기　⑤ 금지하기

2 약속 정하기

A What time shall we meet? 우리 몇 시에 만날까?

B How about 10 o'clock on Saturday? 토요일 10시는 어때?

■ 약속을 정할 때는 What time shall we meet?, 또는 What time should we meet?, Where shall we meet?, Where should we meet? 등의 표현을 써서 몇 시에[어디서] 만날지를 묻고, 시간 및 장소를 제안할 때는 How about ~? What about ~? 등의 표현을 사용한다.

■ 시간과 장소 등의 약속을 정할 때 조동사 'should'를 사용하여 '~할까요?'라는 의미를 전달한다.

• A: What time should we meet? 우리 몇 시에 만날까?
  B: How about 6 o'clock? 6시 어때?
  A: OK. Where should we meet? 좋아. 어디서 만날까?
  B: Let's meet at the subway station. 지하철역에서 만나자.

• A: Let's go on a picnic this weekend. 이번 주말에 소풍가자.
  B: Good idea! What time shall we meet? 좋은 생각이야. 몇 시에 만날래?
  A: How about 10 o'clock on Saturday? 토요일 10시는 어때?
  B: O.K. Let's meet at the subway station. 좋아. 지하철역에서 만나자.

핵심 Check

3. 다음 빈칸에 들어갈 말로 알맞은 것을 <u>모두</u> 고르시오.

M: Karen, let's practice our parts for the school play today.

G: O.K. _____

B: How about 4 o'clock, right after school?

G: Sounds good.

① Where should we meet?
② How about at the park near your place?
③ What time shall we meet?
④ Please tell me where I should go.
⑤ When should we meet?

4. 다음 밑줄 친 문장과 같은 표현을 주어진 철자로 쓰시오.

Sue: What time shall we meet?

Dan: <u>How about 12?</u>

➡ W_____

Listen & Speak 1-A-1

> M: Liz, hurry up. ❶It's already 6 o'clock.
> W: Oh, ❷we're going to be late for the concert.
> M: ❸Why don't we take the subway? The subway will be ❹faster than the bus at this time of day.
> W: ❺That's a good idea.

> M: Liz, 서둘러. 벌써 여섯 시야.
> W: 이런, 우린 콘서트에 늦을 거야.
> M: 지하철을 타는 게 어때? 지하철은 지금 이 시간에 버스보다 빠를 거야.
> W: 좋은 생각이야.

❶ It은 시간을 나타낼 때 사용하는 비인칭 주어다.
❷ 'be going to+동사원형'은 '~할 것 같다'는 의미고, 'be late for'는 '~에 늦다'는 뜻이다.
❸ 'Why don't we+동사원형?'은 상대방에게 제안을 할 때 사용하는 표현으로 'Shall we+동사원형?'으로 바꾸어 쓸 수 있다.
❹ '비교급+than' 구문으로 '~보다 더 …한'의 의미이다.
❺ 상대가 제안한 말에 대해 동의하는 표현이다.

Check(√) True or False

(1) Liz and her friend are going to take the bus.　　　　T ☐ F ☐

(2) Liz is going to go to the concert.　　　　T ☐ F ☐

 Listen & Speak 1-A-2

> B: Mom, I got only one question wrong on the Korean history exam!
> W: Great! ❶I was sure you would do well. ❷Why don't we go out to celebrate tonight?
> B: Yes! Can we ❸have pizza for dinner?
> W: Of course, Joe. I'll call your dad.

> B: 엄마, 제가 한국사 시험에서 겨우 한 문제만 틀렸어요!
> W: 대단해! 네가 잘할 거라고 확신했단다. 오늘밤 축하하러 나가는 건 어때?
> B: 좋아요! 저녁으로 피자를 먹어도 되나요?
> W: 물론이지, Joe. 아빠에게 전화걸게.

❶ be sure (that) 주어+동사 ~: ~을 확신하다
❷ 'Why don't we+동사원형?'은 상대방에게 제안을 할 때 사용하는 표현으로 'Shall we+동사원형?'으로 바꾸어 쓸 수 있다.
❸ have는 eat의 의미로 사용되었다.

Check(√) True or False

(3) The boy did well on the Korean history exam.　　　　T ☐ F ☐

(4) The boy's family are going to go out for dinner.　　　　T ☐ F ☐

 Listen & Speak 1-B

> A: ❶What shall we do at the park?
> B: ❷Why don't we see a magic show?
> A: That's a good idea.

> A: 우리 공원에서 뭘 할까?
> B: 마술 쇼를 보는 건 어때?
> A: 좋은 생각이야.

❶ What shall we do ~?: 우리 뭘 할까?
❷ 상대방에게 제안을 할 때 사용하는 표현으로 'Shall we+동사원형?', 'Let's+동사원형' 등으로 바꾸어 쓸 수 있다.

Listen & Speak 2-A-1

B: Karen, ❶let's practice our parts for the school play today.
G: O.K. ❷What time shall we meet?
B: ❸How about 4 o'clock, right after school?
G: Sounds good.

❶ Let's+동사원형: '~하자'라는 제안이나 권유의 표현이다.
❷ 시간을 정하는 표현으로 '몇 시에 만날래?'의 뜻이다.
❸ 시간 및 장소를 제안할 때는 'How about ~?', 'What about ~?' 등의 표현을 사용한다.

Listen & Speak 2-A-2

G: Do you want to play badminton together this afternoon, Mark?
B: Sure. ❶Where shall we play?
G: ❷How about at the park near your place?
B: O.K. See you there at 3 o'clock.

❶ 어디서 만날지 장소를 제안하는 표현이다.
❷ 장소를 제안할 때는 'How about ~?', 'What about ~?' 등의 표현을 사용한다.

Listen & Speak 2-B

A: ❶Let's go on a picnic this weekend.
B: Good idea. ❷What time shall we meet?
A: How about 10 o'clock on Saturday?
B: O.K. Let's meet at the subway station. See you there.

❶ Let's+동사원형: '~하자'라는 제안이나 권유의 표현이다.
❷ 몇 시에 만날지 시간을 제안하는 표현이다.

Communicate A

Anna: Dad, ❶guess what! I have no school next Wednesday.
Dad: Really? ❷Why not?
Anna: It's our school's 75th anniversary.
Dad: Oh, I see.
Anna: Can we do something together that day?
Dad: ❸I guess I can take the afternoon off. What do you want to do?
Anna: ❹Why don't we go see a musical at Bravo Theater near your work? We can get a discount if we go on a Wednesday.

Dad: Good idea, Anna! Then, let's just meet at the theater.
Anna: O.K. ❺What time shall we meet?
Dad: How about 12? Then, we can have lunch together, too.
Anna: You're the best, Dad!

❶ 'Guess what!'은 '있잖아'라는 의미로 상대방의 주의를 끌 때 사용하는 표현이다.
❷ 'Why not?'은 Why do you have no school?의 줄임말이다.
❸ 'I guess ~'는 '~할 것 같아'라는 의미다.
❹ 상대방에게 제안을 할 때 사용하는 표현으로 'Shall we+동사원형?', 'Let's+동사원형' 등으로 바꾸어 쓸 수 있다.
❺ 시간을 정하는 표현으로 '몇 시에 만날래?'의 뜻이다.

Communicate B

A: ❶What shall we do this afternoon?
B: ❷Why don't we go see *Wonder Woman*?
A: Good idea! What time shall we meet?
B: How about 4 o'clock?
A: O.K. Let's meet at Moon Theater.

❶ What shall we do ~?: 우리 뭘 할까?
❷ 'Why don't we+동사원형?'은 '~하는 게 어때?'라는 뜻으로 어떤 활동을 함께 하자고 제안할 경우에 사용하는 표현으로 'Let's+동사원형' 등으로 바꾸어 쓸 수 있다.

Progress Check

1. G: Jim, hurry up. It's already 10 o'clock.
   B: Oh, ❶we're going to be late for the movie.
   G: ❷Why don't we take the bus? The bus will be faster than the subway at this time of day.
   B: That's a good idea.
2. B: ❸It's very hot today. ❹Let's go swimming, Julie.
   G: Good idea! Where shall we meet?
   B: ❺How about at the subway station near my place?
   G: O.K. See you there at 11 o'clock.

❶ 'be going to+동사원형'은 '~할 것 같다'는 의미이고, 'be late for'는 '~에 늦다'는 뜻이다.
❷ 'Why don't we+동사원형?'은 '~하는 게 어때?'라는 뜻으로 어떤 활동을 함께 하자고 제안할 경우에 사용한다.
❸ 날씨를 나타내는 비인칭 주어 It이다.
❹ 'Let's+동사원형'은 '~하자'라고 제안을 할 때 사용한다.
❺ 'How about ~?'은 '~는 어때?'라는 표현으로 제안할 때 사용한다.

● 다음 우리말과 일치하도록 빈칸에 알맞은 말을 쓰시오.

Listen & Speak 1-A

1. **M:** Liz, _____ _____. It's _____ 6 o'clock.

   W: Oh, we're going to _____ _____ _____ the concert.

   M: _____ _____ _____ _____ the subway? The subway will be _____ _____ the bus at this time of day.

   W: That's a good idea.

2. **B:** Mom, I got only one question _____ on the Korean history exam!

   W: Great! I was _____ you would do _____. _____ _____ _____ go out to _____ tonight?

   B: Yes! Can we have pizza _____ dinner?

   W: _____ _____, Joe. I'll call your dad.

Listen & Speak 1-B

A: What _____ _____ do at the park?

B: _____ _____ _____ see a magic show?

A: That's a _____ _____.

Listen & Speak 2-A

1. **B:** Karen, _____ practice our _____ for the school _____ today.

   G: O.K. _____ _____ _____ _____ _____ _____?

   B: _____ _____ 4 o'clock, _____ after school?

   G: _____ good.

2. **G:** Do you want to play badminton together this afternoon, Mark?

   B: Sure. _____ _____ _____ play?

   G: How _____ at the park _____ your place?

   B: O.K. See you there _____ 3 o'clock.

Listen & Speak 2-B

A: _____ go on a picnic this weekend.

B: Good idea. What time _____ we meet?

A: _____ _____ 10 o'clock on Saturday?

B: O.K. _____ _____ at the subway station. See you there.

해석

1. M: Liz, 서둘러. 벌써 여섯 시야.
   W: 이런, 우린 콘서트에 늦을 거야.
   M: 지하철을 타는 게 어때? 지하철은 지금 이 시간에 버스보다 빠를 거야.
   W: 좋은 생각이야.

2. B: 엄마, 제가 한국사 시험에서 겨우 한 문제만 틀렸어요!
   W: 대단해! 네가 잘할 거라고 확신했단다. 오늘 축하하러 나가는 건 어때?
   B: 좋아요! 저녁으로 피자를 먹어도 되나요?
   W: 물론이지, Joe. 아빠에게 전화하마.

A: 우리 공원에서 뭘 할까?
B: 마술 쇼를 보는 건 어때?
A: 좋은 생각이야.

1. B: Karen, 오늘 학교 연극에서 우리 부분을 연습하자.
   G: 좋아. 몇 시에 만날까?
   B: 학교 끝나고 바로, 네 시 어때?
   G: 좋아.

2. G: Mark, 오후에 같이 배드민턴 하지 않을래?
   B: 물론이지. 어디서 할까?
   G: 너희 집 근처 공원은 어때?
   B: 좋아. 세 시에 거기서 보자.

A: 주말에 소풍가자.
B: 좋은 생각이야. 몇 시에 만날래?
A: 토요일 10시는 어때?
B: 좋아. 지하철역에서 만나자. 거기서 봐.

Communicate A

Anna: Dad, _____ what! I have no school next Wednesday.

Dad: Really? _____ _____?

Anna: It's our school's 75th _____.

Dad: Oh, I see.

Anna: Can we do something _____ that day?

Dad: I guess I can _____ the afternoon _____. What do you want to do?

Anna: _____ _____ _____ go see a musical at Bravo Theater near your work? We can _____ a _____ _____ we go on a Wednesday.

Dad: Good idea, Anna! Then, _____ just meet at the theater.

Anna: O.K. What time _____ _____ meet?

Dad: _____ _____ 12? Then, we can have lunch together, too.

Anna: You're the _____, Dad!

Communicate B

A: _____ _____ _____ do this afternoon?

B: _____ _____ _____ go see _Wonder Woman_?

A: Good idea! What _____ _____ _____ meet?

B: _____ about 4 o'clock?

A: O.K. _____ meet at Moon Theater.

Progress Check

1. **G:** Jim, hurry up. It's already 10 o'clock.

   B: Oh, we're going to be late for the movie.

   G: _____ _____ _____ _____ the bus? The bus will be _____ than the subway _____ _____ _____ _____ _____.

   B: That's a good idea.

2. **B:** It's very hot today. _____ _____ _____, Julie.

   G: Good idea! _____ shall we meet?

   B: _____ _____ at the subway station near my place?

   G: O.K. See you there at 11 o'clock.

Anna: 아빠, 있잖아요! 저는 다음 주 수요일에 수업이 없어요.

아빠: 정말? 왜 없니?

Anna: 75주년 개교 기념일이에요.

아빠: 그렇구나.

Anna: 그날 오후에 같이 뭔가 할 수 있을까요?

아빠: 나는 오후에 휴무를 할 수 있을 것 같구나. 뭘 하고 싶니?

Anna: 아빠 직장 근처 Bravo 극장에서 뮤지컬을 보는 건 어때요? 수요일에 가면 할인을 받을 수 있어요.

아빠: 좋은 생각이구나, Anna! 그럼 바로 극장에서 만나자.

Anna: 좋아요. 몇 시에 만날까요?

아빠: 12시는 어떠니? 그럼 점심도 같이 먹을 수 있단다.

Anna: 최고예요, 아빠!

A: 오늘 오후에 뭘 할까?

B: 원더 우먼을 보러 가는 건 어때?

A: 좋은 생각이야! 몇 시에 만날까?

B: 4시는 어때?

A: 좋아. Moon 극장에서 보자.

1. G: Jim, 서둘러. 벌써 10시야.
   B: 이런, 영화 시간에 늦을 거야.
   G: 버스를 타는 게 어때? 지금 이 시간에는 버스가 지하철보다 빠를 거야.
   B: 좋은 생각이야.

2. B: 오늘 굉장히 덥네. 수영하러 가자, Julie.
   G: 좋은 생각이야! 어디서 만날래?
   B: 우리 집 근처 지하철역에서 만나는 게 어때?
   G: 좋아. 11시에 거기서 보자.

[01~03] 다음 대화의 빈칸에 알맞은 말은?

01

> B: It's very hot today. Let's go swimming, Julie.
>
> G: Good idea! _____
>
> B: How about at the subway station near my place?
>
> G: O.K. See you there at 11 o'clock.

① Why don't we take the bus?　　② What time shall we meet?

③ Let's go there.　　④ Where shall we meet?

⑤ Oh, I see.

02

> A: Let's go on a picnic this weekend.
>
> B: Good idea. _____
>
> A: How about 10 o'clock on Saturday?
>
> B: O.K. Let's meet at the subway station. See you there.

① Where shall we meet?

② How about at the park near your place?

③ What time shall we meet?

④ What shall we do at the park?

⑤ Why don't we take the subway?

03

> M: Liz, hurry up. It's already 6 o'clock.
>
> W: Oh, we're going to be late for the concert.
>
> M: Why don't we take the subway? The subway will be _____ the bus at this time of day.
>
> W: That's a good idea.

① faster than　　② more fast than　　③ fast than

④ the fastest than　　⑤ the faster than

04 자연스러운 대화가 되도록 순서대로 배열하시오.

> (A) O.K. See you there at 3 o'clock.
>
> (B) Sure. Where shall we play?
>
> (C) Do you want to play badminton together this afternoon, Mark?
>
> (D) How about at the park near your place?

➡ _____

[01~03] 다음 대화를 읽고 물음에 답하시오.

> A: _____(A)_____ this afternoon?
> B: Why don't we go see *Wonder Woman*?
> A: Good idea! _____(B)_____
> B: How ___(C)___ 4 o'clock?
> A: O.K. Let's meet at Moon Theater.

01 빈칸 (A)에 알맞은 말을 고르시오.

① What do you do
② What did you do
③ Where shall we meet
④ What shall we do
⑤ What will you make

02 빈칸 (B)에 알맞은 말을 고르시오.

① Shall we make it at 4?
② What time shall we meet?
③ I'm sorry but I can't.
④ Where shall we meet?
⑤ Why don't we go see a musical?

03 빈칸 (C)에 알맞은 말은?

① about   ② at   ③ for
④ of   ⑤ in

04 밑줄 친 부분과 바꾸어 쓸 수 있는 문장을 <u>모두</u> 고르시오.

> B: It's very hot today. <u>Let's go swimming.</u>
> G: Good idea!

① Why don't we go swimming?
② Are you planning to go swimming?
③ Are you going to go swimming?
④ Shall we go swimming?
⑤ What about going swimming?

05 다음 중 짝지어진 대화가 <u>어색한</u> 것은?

① A: Where shall we play?
   B: How about at the park near your place?
② A: Let's go on a picnic this weekend.
   B: Good idea.
③ A: I have no school next Wednesday.
   B: Really? Why not?
④ A: What time shall we meet?
   B: How about 1 o'clock?
⑤ A: Jim, hurry up. It's already 10 o'clock.
   B: What shall we try first?

[06~07] 다음 대화를 읽고 물음에 답하시오.

> B: It's very hot today. ___ⓐ___ go swimming, Julie.
> G: Good idea! ___ⓑ___ shall we meet?
> B: How about at the subway station near my place?
> G: O.K. See you there at 11 o'clock.

06 빈칸 ⓐ, ⓑ에 들어갈 말로 알맞은 것은?

① Let us – What
② Let us – When
③ Let's – What time
④ Let's – Where
⑤ Let's – Whom

서답형
07 다음 영영풀이에 해당하는 단어를 대화에서 찾아 쓰시오.

> a building and the surrounding area where buses or trains stop for people to get on or off

➡ _____

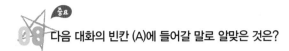

08 다음 대화의 빈칸 (A)에 들어갈 말로 알맞은 것은?

> G: Do you want to play badminton together this afternoon, Mark?
> B: Sure. Where shall we play?
> G: _____ (A)
> B: O.K. See you there at 3 o'clock.

① How about at the park near your place?
② Let's meet at 3 o'clock.
③ What time shall we meet?
④ I'm playing badminton at the park.
⑤ I'd like to play badminton with you at the park.

[09~12] 다음 대화를 읽고 물음에 답하시오.

> Anna: Dad, guess what! I have no school next Wednesday.
> Dad: Really? Why not?
> Anna: It's our school's 75th anniversary.
> Dad: Oh, I see. (①)
> Anna: Can we do something together that day? (②)
> Dad: ⓐ나는 오후에 휴무를 할 수 있을 것 같구나. What do you want to do?
> Anna: (③) We can get a discount if we go on a Wednesday.
> Dad: Good idea, Anna! Then, let's just meet at the theater. (④)
> Anna: O.K. What time shall we meet?
> Dad: How about 12? Then, we can have lunch together, too. (⑤)
> Anna: You're the best, Dad!

09 위 대화의 ①~⑤ 중 다음 주어진 말이 들어갈 알맞은 곳은?

> Why don't we go see a musical at Bravo Theater near your work?

①   ②   ③   ④   ⑤

10 다음 영영풀이에 해당하는 단어를 대화에서 찾아 쓰시오.

> a day on which you remember or celebrate something that happened on that day in the past

➡ _____

11 밑줄 친 ⓐ의 우리말에 맞게 주어진 단어를 알맞게 배열하시오.

> I, guess, take, off, I, can, the afternoon

➡ _____

12 대화의 내용과 일치하지 <u>않는</u> 것은?

① Anna has no school next Wednesday.
② They are talking about getting a discount for a movie.
③ Bravo Theater provides a discount for people on a Wednesday.
④ They will meet at Bravo Theater.
⑤ They will also have lunch together.

13 대화의 흐름상 빈칸 (A)와 (B)에 들어갈 말로 알맞은 것을 〈보기〉에서 골라 쓰시오.

> ┌─ 보기 ─┐
> right   guess   appreciate   perform
> wrong   suggest   celebrate

> Boy: Mom, I got only one question ___(A)___ on the Korean history exam!
> Woman: Great! I was sure you would do well. Why don't we go out to ___(B)___ tonight?
> Boy: Yes! Can we have pizza for dinner?
> Woman: Of course, Joe. I'll call your dad.

➡ (A) _____ (B) _____

[01~02] 다음 대화를 읽고 물음에 답하시오.

M: Liz, hurry up. It's already 6 o'clock.

W: Oh, we're going to be late for the concert.

M: Why don't we take the subway? (A)지하철은 지금 이 시간에 버스보다 빠를 거야.

W: That's a good idea.

01 What are the speakers going to take?

➡ They _____.

02 밑줄 친 (A)의 우리말에 맞게 주어진 어구를 이용하여 영작하시오.

this time, day, the subway, the bus, be, will, than, fast, at, of

➡ _____

_____

03 다음 대화의 밑줄 친 부분을 같은 말로 바꾸어 쓸 때, 주어진 철자로 시작하여 쓰시오.

A: What shall we do at the park?

B: Why don't we see a magic show?

A: That's a good idea.

➡ L_____

➡ S_____

➡ W_____

04 다음 대화에서 괄호 안의 단어를 바르게 배열하시오.

A: (shall, what, meet, time, we)?

B: How about 4 o'clock?

➡ _____

[05~07] 다음 대화를 읽고 물음에 답하시오.

Anna: Dad, guess what! I have no school next Wednesday.

Dad: Really? Why not?

Anna: It's our school's 75th anniversary.

Dad: Oh, I see.

Anna: Can we do something together that day?

Dad: I guess I can ___(A)___ the afternoon off. What do you want to do?

Anna: Why don't we go see a musical at Bravo Theater near your work? We can get a discount if we go on a Wednesday.

Dad: Good idea, Anna! Then, let's just meet at the theater.

Anna: O.K. What time shall we meet?

Dad: How ___(B)___ 12? Then, (C) we can have a lunch together, too.

Anna: You're the best, Dad!

05 빈칸 (A)와 (B)에 알맞은 단어를 쓰시오.

➡ (A) _____ (B) _____

06 위 대화의 밑줄 친 (C)에서 어법상 틀린 것을 고치시오.

_____ ➡ _____

07 위 대화를 읽고 아래의 표의 빈칸을 완성하시오.

Anna's Next Week Plan		
What: see _____ _____ with _____		
When: _____ Wednesday at _____		
Where: at _____		

Grammar

1 접속사 if

> • You will appreciate it better **if** you know the story.
> 네가 그 이야기를 안다면 더 잘 감상할 것이다.
>
> • **If** he fails, he must die. 만약 실패한다면, 그는 죽어야만 한다.

■ 접속사 if는 '만약 ~한다면'이라는 뜻으로, 조건의 부사절을 이끌며, 'if + 주어 + 동사 ~'의 형태로 쓴다. if절이 주절 앞에 오면 if절 뒤에 콤마(,)를 사용하고, 주절 뒤에 오면 콤마(,)를 사용하지 않는다.

　• **If** you miss the bus, you'll be late for school.

　= You'll be late for school **if** you miss the bus. 네가 버스를 놓친다면, 너는 학교에 늦을 것이다.

■ 조건 부사절인 if절에서는 현재시제가 미래시제를 대신한다.

　• **If** it **rains** tomorrow, I will stay at home. (○) 내일 비가 온다면, 나는 집에 머물 것이다.

　If it will rain tomorrow, I will stay at home. (✕)

cf. 시간을 나타내는 부사절도 현재시제가 미래시제를 대신한다. 시간을 나타내는 부사절 접속사는 when(~할 때), until(~까지), before, after, as soon as(~하자마자) 등이 있다.

　• No one will go to sleep **until** someone **finds** out his name. (○)

　No one will go to sleep until someone will find out his name. (✕)

cf. if절이 동사의 목적어 자리에 사용되는 명사절일 경우는 미래시제를 사용할 수 있다.

　• I don't know **if** he **will come** tomorrow. 나는 그가 내일 올지 안 올지 모른다.

　• I wonder **if** she **will tell** you the secret. 그녀가 너에게 그 비밀을 말해 줄지 궁금하다.

핵심 Check

1. 괄호 안에서 알맞은 것을 고르시오.

　(1) If it is fine tomorrow, we (will go / go) on a picnic.

　(2) If you (miss / will miss) the bus, you will be late for the movie.

　(3) If you (will be / are) late for the movie, your friend will be very angry!

2. 다음 문장에서 어법상 틀린 곳이 있다면 바르게 고치오.

　(1) If you will exercise every day, you'll stay healthy.

　➡ _____

　(2) I don't know if he will come to my house tonight.

　➡ _____

2 as + 형용사/부사의 원급 + as

- Turandot is **as** cold **as** ice. Turandot는 얼음처럼 차갑다.
- I can jump **as** high **as** Michael Jordan. 나는 Michael Jordan만큼 높이 점프할 수 있다.

■ 형태: as + 형용사/부사의 원급 + as

■ 의미: ~만큼 …한/하게 (두 대상의 정도가 같음을 나타냄)

e.g. She is **as** tall **as** you. 그녀는 너만큼 키가 크다.

Jane is **as** old **as** Tom. (= Jane and Tom are the same age.)

■ 부정문: not as[so] + 형용사/부사의 원급 + as (~만큼 …하지 않은/않게)

e.g. Tom is **not as** tall **as** Amy. Tom은 Amy만큼 키가 크지 않다.

My bike is **not so** old **as** his bike. 나의 자전거는 그의 자전거만큼 오래되지 않았다.

Tom is **not as** old **as** Peter. Tom은 Peter만큼 나이가 많지 않다.

= Tom is **younger than** Peter. Tom은 Peter보다 어리다.

= Peter is **older than** Tom. Peter는 Tom보다 나이가 많다.

cf. ■ 비교급을 이용한 비교

두 대상 중 하나가 우위에 있음을 나타낼 때 사용한다.

형태: 형용사/부사의 비교급 + than ~: ~보다 더 …한/하게

- Fred is **taller than** I am. Fred는 나보다 더 크다.
- Cathy is **smarter than** I am. Cathy는 나보다 더 똑똑하다.

■ 최상급을 이용한 비교급

세 개 이상의 대상 중 어느 하나의 정도가 가장 높을 때 사용한다.

형태: the + 형용사/부사의 최상급: 가장 ~한/ 하게

- Sujin is **the tallest** of the three. Sujin은 셋 중에서 가장 크다.
- Here is **the most interesting** place in Busan. 부산에서 가장 흥미로운 장소가 여기에 있다.

핵심 Check

3. 괄호 안에서 알맞은 것을 고르시오.

(1) A dog is as [cleverer / clever] as a cat.

(2) Science is as [interestingly / interesting] as history.

4. 다음 빈칸에 공통으로 들어갈 말로 알맞은 것은?

This car is _____ cheap _____ that one.

① so   ② as   ③ too   ④ such   ⑤ to

Grammar 시험대비 기본평가

01 다음 문장에서 어법상 <u>어색한</u> 부분을 바르게 고치시오.

(1) This new smartphone is as more expensive as a computer.

_____ ➡ _____

(2) This turtle is as small than a coin.

_____ ➡ _____

(3) If you will answer incorrectly, you will have to marry me.

_____ ➡ _____

(4) If you won't run now, you will miss the bus.

_____ ➡ _____

> expensive 비싼
> turtle 거북
> marry 결혼하다
> miss 놓치다

02 다음 빈칸에 공통으로 들어갈 말로 알맞은 것은? (대·소문자 무시)

> • I asked him _____ he could study with me.
> • _____ you watch it, you'll enter a fantasy world.

① whether   ② who   ③ which
④ though   ⑤ if

> enter 들어가다
> fantasy 상상, 공상

03 두 문장을 한 문장으로 만들 때 빈칸에 알맞은 말을 고르시오.

> • Sue is 168 cm tall.
> • Sam is 168 cm tall, too.
> ➡ Sue is _____ Sam.

① tall   ② taller than   ③ tall as
④ as tall as   ⑤ as taller as

04 다음 빈칸에 들어갈 말로 알맞은 것은?

> • They do not work _____ we do.

① as hard than   ② as hardly as   ③ as hard as
④ hard than   ⑤ as harder as

> hard 열심히
> hardly 거의 ~ 않다

01 다음 중 어법상 어색한 문장은?

① His riddle is as difficult as her.
② This shirt isn't so large as that one.
③ Jenny can speak English as fluently as Maria.
④ Sandra is as heavy as Tom.
⑤ This river is as long as the Han River.

서답형

02 다음 대화를 읽고, 빈칸에 알맞은 말을 쓰시오.

> M: Liz, hurry up. It's already 6 o'clock.
> W: Oh, we're going to be late for the concert.
> M: Why don't we take the subway? The subway will be _____ than the bus at this time of day.
> W: That's a good idea.

➡ _____

03 다음 우리말과 일치하도록 알맞게 영작한 것은?

> 네가 약속을 어긴다면, 아무도 너를 믿지 않을 거야.

① Though you break your promises, nobody will trust you.
② Because you will break your promises, nobody will trust you.
③ If you will break your promises, nobody will trust you.
④ If you break your promises, nobody won't trust you.
⑤ If you break your promises, nobody will trust you.

서답형

04 다음 괄호 안에서 알맞은 단어를 고르시오.

(1) Suji is as pretty (so / as) her sister.
(2) Minji is as (taller / tall) as I.
(3) My room is as big as (yours / you).

서답형

05 다음 우리말에 맞게 주어진 어구를 알맞은 순서로 배열하시오. ((1)과 (2)는 if로 문장을 시작하시오.)

(1) 만약 당신이 이어폰을 사용해야 한다면 음악을 크게 틀지 마시오.
(If / play / have to / do / earphones / use / you / your music / not / loud)
➡ _____

(2) 지하철을 놓친다면, 모임에 늦을 거야.
(If / you / you / will be / miss / late / the subway / the meeting / for)
➡ _____

(3) 내 목소리는 너만큼 크다.
(my voice / as / as / yours / loud / is)
➡ _____

(4) Nick은 Peter만큼 빨리 달릴 수 있다.
(Nick / Peter / run / as / as / can / fast)
➡ _____

중요

06 다음 빈칸에 들어갈 알맞은 것은?

> If your friend _____ very angry, you will have to buy her ice cream.

① will be   ② is
③ won't be   ④ will is
⑤ are

07 〈보기〉의 밑줄 친 부분과 쓰임이 같은 것을 <u>모두</u> 고르시오.

보기

Tom will be happy <u>if</u> you visit him.

① He asked me <u>if</u> I could play with him.
② I don't know <u>if</u> it will rain tomorrow.
③ I wonder <u>if</u> he will buy a new car.
④ We will play baseball <u>if</u> it doesn't rain tomorrow.
⑤ <u>If</u> he comes back tomorrow, I'll talk to him about the problem.

08 다음 중 어법상 <u>어색한</u> 것은?

① My eyes are as dark as chocolate.
② Fred is as tall as I am.
③ My bike is as old as Tom's bike.
④ Minho speaks English as good as a native speaker.
⑤ Dora is not as fast as I am.

09 다음 우리말을 바르게 영작한 것은?

내일 날씨가 맑으면 그들은 바다에 갈 것이다.

① They will go to the sea if it is sunny tomorrow.
② They go to the sea if it will be sunny tomorrow.
③ They go to the sea if it is sunny tomorrow.
④ If it will be sunny tomorrow, they will go to the sea.
⑤ If it was sunny tomorrow, they went to the sea.

서답형

10 어법상 <u>틀린</u> 부분을 찾아 바르게 고치시오.

(1) Juho doesn't study so hard than Dora.
_____ ➡ _____

(2) This song sounds as more beautiful as a poem.
_____ ➡ _____

(3) I can jump as highly as Michael Jordan.
_____ ➡ _____

(4) If she will miss the bus, she won't get here on time.
_____ ➡ _____

서답형

11 다음 문장에서 <u>틀린</u> 부분을 찾아 바르게 고치시오.

(1) Your sister is as friend as his.
_____ ➡ _____

(2) She can't run as faster as Billy.
_____ ➡ _____

12 다음 중 어법상 <u>어색한</u> 것은?

① If he fails, he must die.
② If you answer correctly, I will agree to die.
③ If you answer incorrectly, you will have to marry me.
④ You will appreciate it better if you know the story.
⑤ If you get up early tomorrow morning, you see the sunrise.

13 다음 두 문장을 한 문장으로 바르게 바꾼 것은?

> • Jomin reads many books.
> • Sumin reads many books, too.

① Jomin reads as much books as Sumin.
② Jomin reads as much as Sumin.
③ Jomin reads as many as Sumin's books.
④ Jomin reads as many books as Sumin.
⑤ Jomin reads more books than Sumin does.

서답형

14 다음 괄호 안에서 알맞은 것을 고르시오.

(1) Anne is not (too / as) tall as Judy.
(2) Sumi speaks English as (well / better) as Minsu.
(3) Your house is as small as (I / mine).

서답형

[15~16] 다음 우리말에 맞게 주어진 어구를 이용하여 영작하시오.

15
> 그녀는 깃털만큼 가볍다.
> (light, a feather)

➡ _____

16
> 호랑이는 코끼리만큼 크지 않다.
> (a tiger, so, big, an elephant)

➡ _____

서답형

17 다음 밑줄 친 부분과 바꿔 쓸 수 있는 말을 한 단어로 쓰시오.

> The bus is not <u>as</u> fast as the subway at this time of day.

➡ _____

[18~19] 주어진 어구들을 사용하여 원급 비교 문장으로 바르게 나타낸 것을 <u>모두</u> 고르시오.

18
> This soldier, brave, a lion

① This soldier is so braver as a lion.
② This soldier isn't as brave as a lion.
③ This soldier is as brave as a lion.
④ This soldier is so brave than a lion.
⑤ This soldier is too brave as a lion.

19
> My father, strong, an ox

① My father isn't so strong as an ox.
② My father is stronger than an ox.
③ My father isn't so stronger as an ox.
④ My father is as stronger as an ox.
⑤ My father is as strong as an ox.

서답형

20 우리말에 맞게 괄호 안에서 알맞은 것을 고르시오.

> • 내가 이탈리아에 간다면 나는 피자와 스파게티를 먹을 것이다.
> • 우리가 내일 만나면 무엇을 할 거니?

➡ If I (will go / go) to Italy, I (will eat / eat) pizza and spaghetti.
➡ When we (will meet / meet) tomorrow, what (will / do) you do?

01 다음 두 문장의 의미가 같도록 빈칸을 완성하시오.

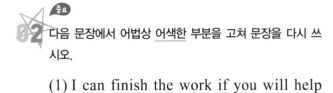

Mina is bigger than Jenny.
= Jenny _____ Mina.

02 다음 문장에서 어법상 어색한 부분을 고쳐 문장을 다시 쓰시오.

(1) I can finish the work if you will help me.

➡ _____

_____

(2) If school will finish early tomorrow, I will go see a movie.

➡ _____

_____

(3) If my mom will catch a cold, I will do the dishes for her.

➡ _____

_____

03 다음 그림을 보고 주어진 문장을 완성하시오.

(1)

➡ The dog can _____ the ostrich.

(2)

➡ This turtle is _____ small _____ a coin.

04 다음 문장에서 어색한 부분을 찾아 바르게 고치시오.

(1) Your car is as expensive as me.

_____ ➡ _____

(2) Soccer isn't as more popular as baseball in Korea.

_____ ➡ _____

(3) If it won't rain tomorrow, we'll go on a picnic.

_____ ➡ _____

(4) You will fail if you won't study harder from now on.

_____ ➡ _____

05 두 문장을 'as ~ as'를 이용하여 한 문장으로 쓰시오.

(1) • John is 170cm tall.
• Susan is 170cm tall, too.

➡ _____

(2) • This apple is sweet.
• That pineapple is also sweet.

➡ _____

(3) • My bike is old.
• But his bike is older than mine.

➡ _____

(4) • I watch 5 movies every month.
• Kate also watches 5 movies every month.

➡ _____

06 다음 표를 보고 원급 비교를 이용하여 다음 빈칸을 완성하시오.

Name	Tom	Eric	Amy
Age	15	14	15
Height	167cm	167cm	163cm
Weight	58kg	52kg	52kg

(1) Eric is _____ Amy.

(2) Tom is _____ Amy.

(3) Tom is _____ Eric.

07 우리말과 일치하도록 주어진 어구를 알맞은 순서로 배열하시오. (부사절로 문장을 시작하시오.)

(1) 만약 당신이 초콜릿을 너무 많이 먹는다면 당신의 치아가 상할 것이다.

(if / too much / you / eat / your / will / teeth / go / bad / chocolate)

➡ _____

_____

(2) 만약 Fred가 학교에 걸어간다면 40분이 걸릴 것이다.

(Fred / to / if / walks / it / take / school / will / 40 minutes)

➡ _____

_____

(3) 만약 네가 지도를 따라간다면 너는 나의 할머니의 집에 도착할 것이다.

(the / follow / you / get / you'll / if / map / to / my grandma's house)

➡ _____

_____

08 다음 주어진 문장에서 어법상 틀린 부분을 찾아 바르게 고쳐 쓰시오.

Turandot must find the answer before dawn, but his riddle is as difficult than her. She says to everyone, "No one will go to sleep until someone will find out his name."

➡ _____

➡ _____

09 다음 표를 보고 수지와 민지를 비교하는 글을 완성하시오. (동등비교 구문을 이용할 것.)

이름	나이	키	100m 기록
Suji	14	167 cm	15초
Minji	14	164 cm	12초

(1) Minji is _____ Suji. (나이)

(2) Minji is _____ Suji. (키)

(3) Suji is _____ Minji. (100m 기록)

10 다음 우리말에 맞게 주어진 어구를 이용하여 영작하시오.

(1) 그녀의 여동생은 새끼 고양이만큼 장난꾸러기다. (playful, a kitten)

➡ _____

(2) 우리 집은 묘지만큼이나 조용하다. (home, quiet, a grave)

➡ _____

(3) 나는 내 남동생만큼 키가 크지 않다. (tall, my brother)

➡ _____

Reading

교과서

Turandot

The Most Dangerous Love in the World!

Welcome, everyone! Tonight, we are going to perform Giacomo
Puccini's opera *Turandot*. Like many other famous operas, *Turandot* is
in Italian because opera started in Italy in the 16th century. Before we
begin, I'd like to tell you the storyline of the opera *Turandot*. You will
appreciate it better if you know the story.

Turandot, a Chinese princess, is a woman of great beauty, but she is
as cold as ice. Any prince who wants to marry her must answer three
riddles. If he fails, he must die. No one has ever been able to answer
them. One day, a brave prince falls in love with her at first sight. He
becomes the first man to answer all three riddles.

perform 공연하다, 수행하다
Italian 이탈리아어, 이탈리아인; 이탈리아의
century 100년, 세기
storyline (소설·연극·영화 등의) 줄거리
appreciate 감상하다, 감사하다, 알아주다
riddle 수수께끼
fall in love 사랑에 빠지다, 반하다

 확인문제

● 다음 문장이 본문의 내용과 일치하면 T, 일치하지 않으면 F를 쓰시오.

1 Giacomo Puccini composed the opera *Turandot*. ☐

2 *Turandot* is in Italian because Puccini was born in Italy. ☐

3 Many famous operas are in Italian because opera started in Italy. ☐

4 You must appreciate the opera before you know the story. ☐

5 Turandot is a very beautiful Chinese princess. ☐

6 Any prince who wants to marry her must answer four riddles. ☐

7 If the prince fails to answer the riddles, he must die. ☐

8 One day, a brave prince falls in love with her at first sight, but he fails to answer the
   riddles. ☐

However, Turandot does not want to marry the prince. He is nothing more than a stranger to her. He then gives her a riddle of his own. He asks her, "What is my name?" He adds, "If you answer correctly, I will agree to die. If you answer incorrectly, you will have to marry me."

Turandot must find the answer before dawn, but his riddle is as difficult as hers. She says to everyone, "No one will go to sleep until someone finds out his name." The prince then sings the most famous aria of the whole opera, "Nessun Dorma." It means no one sleeps.

No one sleeps.

No one sleeps, not even you, Princess.

…

My secret is safe.

No one will know my name.

…

At dawn, I will win! I will win!

The prince's name is Calaf. Will the princess learn his name in time?

Let's watch the opera and find out.
= How about watching the opera and finding out?

dawn 새벽, 동틀 녘
aria 아리아, 영창
whole 전체; 모든, 전부의
secret 비밀
safe 안전한
in time 제시간에, 늦지 않게
find out 알아내다, 발견하다

확인문제

● 다음 문장이 본문의 내용과 일치하면 T, 일치하지 않으면 F를 쓰시오.

1 Turandot wants to marry the prince. ☐

2 The prince is only a stranger to her. ☐

3 The prince gives Turandot a riddle of his own. ☐

4 If Turandot answers correctly, the prince will marry her. ☐

5 The prince's riddle is as difficult as Turandot's. ☐

6 Turandot will learn the prince's name in time. ☐

● 우리말을 참고하여 빈칸에 알맞은 말을 쓰시오.

1 Turandot _____ _____ _____ Love in the World

2 _____, everyone!

3 Tonight, we are going to _____ Giacomo Puccini's opera *Turandot*.

4 _____ many other famous operas, *Turandot* is _____ _____ because opera started _____ _____ in the 16th century.

5 Before we begin, _____ _____ _____ _____ you the storyline of the opera *Turandot*.

6 You will _____ it better _____ you know the story.

7 Turandot, a Chinese princess, is a woman _____ _____ _____, but she is _____ _____ _____ _____.

8 Any prince _____ wants to _____ _____ must answer three riddles.

9 If he _____, he must die.

10 No one _____ _____ _____ able to answer them.

11 One day, a brave prince _____ _____ her at first sight.

12 He becomes _____ _____ _____ to answer all three riddles.

13 _____, Turandot does not want _____ _____ the prince.

14 He is _____ _____ _____ a stranger to her.

15 He then gives her a riddle _____ _____ _____.

---

1 투란도트, 세상에서 가장 위험한 사랑

2 여러분, 환영합니다!

3 오늘 밤, 우리는 지아코모 푸치니의 오페라 《투란도트》를 공연할 것입니다.

4 다른 많은 유명한 오페라들처럼 《투란도트》는 이탈리아어로 되어 있는데, 오페라가 16세기 이탈리아에서 시작되었기 때문입니다.

5 시작하기 전에 오페라 《투란도트》의 줄거리를 알려 드리려고 합니다.

6 여러분이 줄거리를 알면 이 오페라를 더 잘 감상하게 될 것입니다.

7 중국의 공주 Turandot는 굉장히 아름다운 여인이지만, 그녀는 얼음처럼 차갑습니다.

8 그녀와 결혼길 원하는 왕자는 누구든지 반드시 세 가지 수수께끼에 답해야 합니다.

9 만약 실패하면 그는 죽어야 합니다.

10 그 누구도 수수께끼에 답할 수 없었습니다.

11 어느 날, 어떤 용감한 왕자가 그녀에게 첫눈에 반합니다.

12 그는 세 수수께끼를 모두 맞힌 첫 번째 사람이 됩니다.

13 그러나 Turandot는 그 왕자와 결혼하길 원하지 않습니다.

14 그는 그녀에게 단지 낯선 사람일 뿐입니다.

15 그러자 그는 그녀에게 자신의 수수께끼를 냅니다.

16 He asks her, "_____ is my name?"

17 He _____, "If you answer correctly, I will agree _____ _____. If you answer _____, you will have to marry me."

18 Turandot must find the answer _____ _____, but his riddle is _____ _____ _____ _____.

19 She says to everyone, "No one will go to sleep _____ someone _____ _____ his name."

20 The prince then sings _____ _____ _____ _____ of the whole opera, "Nessun Dorma."

21 It _____ no one sleeps.

22 No one _____.

23 No one sleeps, _____ _____ _____, Princess.

24 My secret is _____.

25 No one _____ _____ my name.

26 _____ _____, I will win! I will win!

27 The _____ name is Calaf.

28 Will the princess learn his name _____ _____?

29 _____ _____ the opera and find out.

16 그는 그녀에게 "제 이름이 무엇 입니까?"라고 묻습니다.

17 그는 "당신이 맞게 대답한다면 나는 죽는 것에 동의하겠습니 다. 만약 답이 틀리면 당신은 저 와 결혼해야 할 것입니다."라고 덧붙입니다.

18 Turandot는 동이 트기 전에 답 을 찾아야 하지만 그의 수수께 끼는 그녀의 것만큼 어렵습니 다.

19 그녀는 모두에게 "누군가 그의 이름을 알아낼 때까지 그 누구 도 잠들 수 없다."라고 말합니 다.

20 그리고 왕자는 이 오페라 전 체에서 가장 유명한 아리아, Nessun Dorma를 부릅니다.

21 그것은 누구도 잠들지 못한다는 뜻입니다.

22 누구도 잠들지 못하네.

23 누구도 잠들지 못하네, 당신조 차도, 공주여.

24 나의 비밀은 안전하다네.

25 누구도 나의 이름을 알지 못할 것이네.

26 동틀 녘에, 내가 이길 것이라네! 내가 승리할 것이라네!

27 왕자의 이름은 Calaf입니다.

28 공주는 그의 이름을 제때 알아 낼 수 있을까요?

29 오페라를 보고 알아봅시다.

● 우리말을 참고하여 본문을 영작하시오.

1 투란도트, 세상에서 가장 위험한 사랑

➡ _____

2 여러분, 환영합니다!

➡ _____

3 오늘 밤, 우리는 지아코모 푸치니의 오페라 《투란도트》를 공연할 것입니다.

➡ _____

4 다른 많은 유명한 오페라들처럼 《투란도트》는 이탈리아어로 되어 있는데, 오페라가 16세기 이탈리아에서 시작되었기 때문입니다.

➡ _____

5 시작하기 전에 오페라 《투란도트》의 줄거리를 알려 드리려고 합니다.

➡ _____

6 여러분이 줄거리를 알면 이 오페라를 더 잘 감상하게 될 것입니다.

➡ _____

7 중국의 공주 Turandot는 굉장히 아름다운 여인이지만, 그녀는 얼음처럼 차갑습니다.

➡ _____

8 그녀와 결혼하길 원하는 왕자는 누구든지 반드시 세 가지 수수께끼에 답해야 합니다.

➡ _____

9 만약 실패하면 그는 죽어야 합니다.

➡ _____

10 그 누구도 수수께끼에 답할 수 없었습니다.

➡ _____

11 어느 날, 어떤 용감한 왕자가 그녀에게 첫눈에 반합니다.

➡ _____

12 그는 세 수수께끼를 모두 맞힌 첫 번째 사람이 됩니다.

➡ _____

13 그러나 Turandot는 그 왕자와 결혼하길 원하지 않습니다.

➡ _____

14 그는 그녀에게 단지 낯선 사람일 뿐입니다.

➡ _____

15 그러자 그는 그녀에게 자신의 수수께끼를 냅니다.

➡ _____

16 그는 그녀에게 "제 이름이 무엇입니까?"라고 묻습니다.

➡ _____

17 그는 "당신이 맞게 대답한다면 나는 죽는 것에 동의하겠습니다. 만약 답이 틀리면 당신은 저와 결혼해야 할 것입니다."라고 덧붙입니다.

➡ _____

18 Turandot는 동이 트기 전에 답을 찾아야 하지만 그의 수수께끼는 그녀의 것만큼 어렵습니다.

➡ _____

19 그녀는 모두에게 "누군가 그의 이름을 알아낼 때까지 그 누구도 잠들 수 없다."라고 말합니다.

➡ _____

20 그리고 왕자는 이 오페라 전체에서 가장 유명한 아리아, Nessun Dorma를 부릅니다.

➡ _____

21 그것은 누구도 잠들지 못한다는 뜻입니다.

➡ _____

22 누구도 잠들지 못하네.

➡ _____

23 누구도 잠들지 못하네, 당신조차도, 공주여.

➡ _____

24 나의 비밀은 안전하다네.

➡ _____

25 누구도 나의 이름을 알지 못할 것이네.

➡ _____

26 동틀 녘에, 내가 이길 것이라네! 내가 승리할 것이라네!

➡ _____

27 왕자의 이름은 Calaf입니다.

➡ _____

28 공주는 그의 이름을 제때 알아낼 수 있을까요?

➡ _____

29 오페라를 보고 알아봅시다.

➡ _____

[01~03] 다음 글을 읽고 물음에 답하시오.

Welcome, everyone! Tonight, we are going to perform Giacomo Puccini's opera *Turandot*. Like many other famous operas, *Turandot* is in (A)[Italy / Italian] because opera started in Italy in the 16th century. Before we begin, I'd like (B)[to tell / telling] you the storyline of the opera *Turandot*. You will appreciate it better if you (C)[know / will know] the story.

01 위 글의 괄호 (A)~(C)에서 문맥이나 어법상 알맞은 낱말을 골라 쓰시오.

➡ (A) _____ (B) _____ (C) _____

02 위 글의 뒤에 올 내용으로 가장 알맞은 것을 고르시오.

① 오페라 《투란도트》의 작곡가 소개
② 오페라에 나오는 이탈리아어 이해하기
③ 이탈리아의 유명한 오페라들 소개
④ 오페라 《투란도트》의 줄거리 소개
⑤ 오페라 《투란도트》의 공연 관람 후기

03 위 글의 내용과 일치하지 <u>않는</u> 것은?

① 오늘 밤, 오페라 《투란도트》를 공연할 것이다.
② 오페라 《투란도트》의 작곡가는 지아코모 푸치니이다.
③ 《투란도트》는 이탈리아어로 되어 있다.
④ 오페라는 16세기 이탈리아에서 시작되었다.
⑤ 이탈리아어를 알면 오페라를 더 잘 감상하게 될 것이다.

[04~06] 다음 글을 읽고 물음에 답하시오.

One day, a brave prince falls in love with her at first sight. He becomes the first man to answer all three riddles.

_____ⓐ_____, Turandot does not want to marry the prince. (①) He is nothing more than a stranger to ⓐher. (②) He asks her, "What is ⓑmy name?" (③) He adds, "If ⓒyou answer correctly, I will agree to die. (④) If you answer incorrectly, you will have to marry ⓓme." (⑤)

Turandot must find the answer before dawn, but ⓔhis riddle is as difficult as hers. She says to everyone, "No one will go to sleep until someone finds out his name."

04 위 글의 빈칸 ⓐ에 들어갈 알맞은 말을 고르시오.

① However   ② Therefore
③ In other words   ④ For example
⑤ As a result

05 위 글의 흐름으로 보아, 주어진 문장이 들어가기에 가장 적절한 곳은?

| He then gives her a riddle of his own. |

①   ②   ③   ④   ⑤

06 위 글의 밑줄 친 ⓐ~ⓔ 중 가리키는 대상이 같은 것끼리 짝 지어진 것은?

① ⓐ – ⓑ   ② ⓐ – ⓓ
③ ⓑ – ⓔ   ④ ⓒ – ⓓ
⑤ ⓒ – ⓔ

[07~09] 다음 글을 읽고 물음에 답하시오.

Turandot, a Chinese princess, is a woman of great beauty, but she is ⓐas cold as ice. Any prince who wants to marry her must answer three riddles. If he fails, he must die. No one has ever been able to answer them. One day, a brave prince falls in love with her at first sight. He becomes the first man to answer all three riddles.

07 위 글에서 알 수 있는 Turandot의 성격으로 가장 알맞은 것을 고르시오.

① considerate   ② warm-hearted
③ heartless   ④ friendly
⑤ careless

08 위 글의 밑줄 친 ⓐas와 같은 용법으로 쓰인 것은?

① Do as you are told.
② Run as fast as you can.
③ As we go up, the air grows colder.
④ I regarded them as kind helpers.
⑤ As she was tired, she soon fell asleep.

09 위 글을 읽고 대답할 수 없는 질문은?

① Who is Turandot?
② What does Turandot look like?
③ What does the prince who wants to marry Turandot have to do?
④ What are the three riddles that Turandot asks?
⑤ Who becomes the first man to answer all three riddles?

[10~13] 다음 글을 읽고 물음에 답하시오.

Turandot must find the answer ___ⓐ___ dawn, but his riddle is as difficult as hers. She says to everyone, "No one will go to sleep until someone finds out his name."
The prince then sings the most famous aria of the whole opera, "Nessun Dorma." It means no one ___ⓑ___.
No one ___ⓑ___.
No one ___ⓑ___, not even you, Princess.
…
My secret is safe.
No one will know my name.
…
___ⓒ___ dawn, I will win! I will win!
The prince's name is Calaf. Will the princess learn his name in time? Let's watch the opera and ⓓfind out.

10 위 글의 빈칸 ⓐ와 ⓒ에 들어갈 전치사가 바르게 짝지어진 것은?

① at – In   ② before – To
③ before – At   ④ at – To
⑤ on – At

11 위 글의 빈칸 ⓑ에 공통으로 들어갈 알맞은 단어를 고르시오.

① mustn't sleep   ② sleep
③ slept   ④ can't sleep
서답형 ⑤ sleeps

12 다음 질문에 대한 알맞은 대답을 주어진 단어로 시작하여 쓰시오. (6 단어)

> Q: Why does the prince say "My secret is safe"?
> A: Because _____.

➡ _____

서답형

13 위 글의 밑줄 친 ⓐfind out과 바꿔 쓸 수 있는 단어를 본문에서 찾아 쓰시오.

➡ _____

[14~16] 다음 글을 읽고 물음에 답하시오.

I saw *Beauty and the Beast* last Saturday. It is about a beautiful girl and a beast. I enjoyed it a lot. The songs were great, and the love story was as beautiful as a gem. If you like heart-warming stories about love, you will like it, too.

by Lee Minsu on Aug. 12

14 위 글의 종류로 알맞은 것을 고르시오.

① book report   ② essay
③ article   ④ review
⑤ biography

중요

15 위 글의 내용을 다음과 같이 정리하고자 한다. 다음 빈칸에 들어갈 알맞은 말을 고르시오.

Minsu _____ *Beauty and the Beast* to people who like heart-warming stories about love.

① demands   ② recommends
③ expresses   ④ reports
⑤ advises

16 위 글의 영화에 대해 알 수 없는 것은?

① What's the title of it?
② When did Minsu see it?
③ What is the story about?
④ How did Minsu like it?
⑤ With whom did Minsu see it?

[17~19] 다음 글을 읽고 물음에 답하시오.

ⓐ중국의 공주 Turandot는 굉장히 아름다운 여인이지만, 그녀는 얼음처럼 차갑습니다. Any prince who wants to marry her must answer three riddles. If he fails, he must die. No one has ever been able to answer ⓑthem. One day, a brave prince falls in love with her at first sight. He becomes the first man ⓒto answer all three riddles.

서답형

17 위 글의 밑줄 친 ⓐ의 우리말에 맞게 한 단어를 보충하여, 주어진 어휘를 알맞게 배열하시오. (콤마를 사용할 것.)

beauty / Turandot / she / as / is / but / a Chinese princess / ice / as / a woman / cold / is / great

➡ _____
_____

서답형

18 위 글의 밑줄 친 ⓑthem이 가리키는 것을 본문에서 찾아 쓰시오.

➡ _____

19 위 글의 밑줄 친 ⓒto answer와 to부정사의 용법이 다른 것을 모두 고르시오.

① I want a pen to write it with.
② She was pleased to meet her friend.
③ It was easy for me to do the work.
④ There's not a moment to lose.
⑤ How lucky you are to win the first prize!

[20~23] 다음 글을 읽고 물음에 답하시오.

However, Turandot does not want to marry the prince. He is nothing more than a ⓐ_____ to her. He then gives her ⓑa riddle of his own. He asks her, "What is my name?" He adds, "If you answer correctly, I will agree (A)[dying / to die]. If you answer incorrectly, you will have to marry me."

Turandot must find the answer before dawn, but his riddle is as difficult as (B)[her / hers]. She says to everyone, "No one will go to sleep until someone (C)[finds / will find] out his name."

20 위 글의 빈칸 ⓐ에 들어갈 알맞은 말을 고르시오.

① neighbor ② friend
③ husband ④ stranger
⑤ co-worker

서답형
21 위 글의 괄호 (A)~(C)에서 어법상 알맞은 낱말을 골라 쓰시오.

➡ (A) _____ (B) _____ (C) _____

서답형
22 위 글의 밑줄 친 ⓑ가 가리키는 것을 본문에서 찾아 쓰시오.

➡ _____

23 위 글의 마지막 부분에서 알 수 있는 'Turandot'의 심경으로 가장 알맞은 것을 고르시오.

① desperate ② satisfied
③ bored ④ ashamed
⑤ excited

[24~26] 다음 글을 읽고 물음에 답하시오.

Review of *La La Land*　★★★★☆
　I saw *La La Land* last Friday. It is about the dreams and love of Mia and Sebastian. I enjoyed its beautiful and ⓐmoving songs. ⓑ The story was also as good as the songs. If you are looking for a good musical movie, you should see this movie.

by Kim Jisu on Aug. 11

24 위 글의 밑줄 친 ⓐmoving과 바꿔 쓸 수 있는 말을 고르시오.

① lively ② cheerful
③ touching ④ energetic
⑤ depressing

서답형
25 To whom does Jisu recommend *La La Land*? Fill in the blank with the suitable words.

➡ To people who _____
_____.

26 위 글의 밑줄 친 ⓑ와 같은 의미의 문장을 모두 고르시오.

① Not only the story but also the songs were good.
② Not the story but the songs were good.
③ Both the story and the songs were good.
④ Either the story or the songs were good.
⑤ Neither the story nor the songs were good.

[01~03] 다음 글을 읽고 물음에 답하시오.

Welcome, everyone! Tonight, we are going to perform Giacomo Puccini's opera *Turandot*. Like many other famous operas, *Turandot* is in Italian because opera started in Italy in the 16th century. Before we begin, ⓐ I'd like to tell you the storyline of the opera *Turandot*. You will appreciate ⓑit better if you know the story.

01 위 글의 밑줄 친 ⓐ를 우리말로 옮기시오.

➡ _____

02 위 글의 밑줄 친 ⓑ가 가리키는 것을 본문에서 찾아 쓰시오.

➡ _____

03 Why is *Turandot* in Italian? Fill in the blank with the suitable words.

➡ It's because _____
_____.

[04~06] 다음 글을 읽고 물음에 답하시오.

However, Turandot does not want to marry the prince. He is ⓐnothing more than a stranger to her. He then gives her a riddle of his own. He asks her, "What is my name?" He adds, "ⓑIf you answer incorrectly, I will agree to die. If you answer correctly, you will have to marry me."

Turandot must find the answer before dawn, but his riddle is as difficult as hers. She says to everyone, "ⓒNo one will go to sleep until someone finds out his name."

04 위 글의 밑줄 친 ⓐnothing more than과 바꿔 쓸 수 있는 한 단어를 쓰시오.

➡ _____

05 위 글의 밑줄 친 ⓑ에서 흐름상 어색한 부분을 고치시오. (두 군데)

➡ _____, _____

06 위 글의 밑줄 친 ⓒ를 다음과 같이 바꿔 쓸 때 빈칸에 들어갈 알맞은 말을 쓰시오. (5 단어)

➡ People will go to sleep only after
_____.

[07~09] 다음 글을 읽고 물음에 답하시오.

ⓐTurandot, a Chinese princess, is a woman of great beauty, but she is as cold as ice. Any prince ___ⓑ___ wants to marry her must answer three riddles. If he fails, he must die. No one has ever been able to answer them. One day, a brave prince falls in love with her at first sight. He becomes the first man to answer all three riddles.

07 위 글의 밑줄 친 ⓐ를 다음과 같이 바꿔 쓸 때 빈칸에 들어갈 알맞은 말을 쓰시오.

➡ Turandot, a Chinese princess, is a
_____ woman.

08 위 글의 빈칸 ⓑ에 들어갈 알맞은 말을 쓰시오.

➡ _____

09 다음 문장에서 위 글의 내용과 <u>다른</u> 부분을 찾아서 고치시오.

> • Before a brave prince gives answers to all three riddles, a few princes have been able to give correct answers.

_____ ➡ _____

[10~12] 다음 글을 읽고 물음에 답하시오.

Turandot, a Chinese princess, (A)[is / are] a woman of great beauty, but she is as cold as ice. Any prince who wants to (B)[marry / marry with] her must answer three riddles. If he fails, he must die. No one has ever been able to answer them. One day, a brave prince falls in love with her ⓐ첫눈에. He becomes the first man to (C)[answer / answer to] all three riddles.

10 위 글의 괄호 (A)~(C)에서 어법상 알맞은 낱말을 골라 쓰시오.

➡ (A) _____ (B) _____ (C) _____

11 위 글의 밑줄 친 ⓐ의 우리말을 세 단어로 쓰시오.

➡ _____

12 본문의 내용과 일치하도록 다음 빈칸 (A)와 (B)에 알맞은 단어를 쓰시오.

> Turandot, the Chinese princess, gives (A) _____ to any prince who wants to get married to her. If he doesn't reply to them correctly, he (B)_____ _____.

[13~14] 다음 글을 읽고 물음에 답하시오.

Turandot must find the answer before dawn, but his riddle is as difficult as ___ⓐ___. She says to everyone, "No one will go to sleep until someone finds out his name."

The prince's name is Calaf. Will the princess learn his name ⓑ<u>in time</u>? Let's watch the opera and find out.

13 위 글의 빈칸 ⓐ에 she를 알맞은 형태로 쓰시오.

➡ _____

14 위 글의 밑줄 친 ⓑ<u>in time</u>과 바꿔 쓸 수 있는 단어를 본문에서 찾아 쓰시오.

➡ _____

[15~16] 다음 글을 읽고 물음에 답하시오.

The prince then gives her a riddle of his own. He asks her, "What is my name?" He adds, "ⓐ<u>당신이 맞게 대답한다면 나는 죽는 것에 동의하겠습니다.</u> If you answer incorrectly, you will have to marry me."

ⓑ<u>Turandot must find the answer before dawn, but his riddle is so difficult as hers.</u> She says to everyone, "No one will go to sleep until someone finds out his name."

15 위 글의 밑줄 친 ⓐ의 우리말에 맞게 한 단어를 보충하여, 주어진 어휘를 알맞게 배열하시오.

> die / answer / if / I / correctly / to / you / agree / ,

➡ _____

16 위 글의 밑줄 친 ⓑ에서 어법상 틀린 부분을 고치시오.

➡ _____ ➡ _____

Link

A: How was our performance?
~은 어땠니?

B: It was amazing! Actually, I've seen the musical *Cats* before, and your song
현재완료(경험)

was as great as the musical's.
~만큼 …한(원급 비교)   = the musical's song

구문해설 • performance 공연   • amazing 놀라운   • actually 사실

A: 우리 공연 어땠어?
B: 굉장했어! 사실, 난 뮤지컬 캣츠를 전에 본 적이 있는데, 너희 노래는 그 뮤지컬의 노래만큼 훌륭했어.

Write

Review of *La La Land* ★★★★☆

I saw *La La Land* last Friday. It is about the dreams and love of Mia and
과거의 일이라 과거시제 사용함   ~에 관한 것이다

Sebastian. I enjoyed its beautiful and moving songs. The story was also

as good as the songs. If you are looking for a good musical movie, you should
as+원급+as: ~만큼 좋은   조건의 부사절 접속사   ~해야 한다

see this movie.

by Kim Jisu on Aug. 11

구문해설 • enjoy 즐기다   • moving 감동적인   • look for ~을 찾다

라라랜드에 대한 감상

나는 지난 금요일에 라라랜드를 보았어. 그건 Mia와 Sebastian의 꿈과 사랑에 대한 이야기야. 나는 그것의 아름답고 감동적인 노래를 즐겼어. 이야기도 노래만큼이나 좋았지. 좋은 뮤지컬 영화를 찾고 있다면, 이 영화를 봐야 할 거야.

8월 11일, 김지수 씀

Write

Review of *Beauty and the Beast* ★★★★★

I saw *Beauty and the Beast* last Saturday. It is about a beautiful girl and a beast.
on last Saturday(×)   *Beauty and the Beast*

I enjoyed it a lot. The songs were great, and the love story was as beautiful as
Beauty and the Beast   as+원급+as: 동등비교 표현으로, 두 대상의 동등한 가치를 나타낸다.

a gem. If you like heart-warming stories about love, you will like it, too.
조건의 부사절에서 미래시제 대신 현재시제를 사용   *Beauty and the Beast*

by Lee Minsu on Aug. 12

구문해설 • beauty 아름다움, 미녀   • beast 짐승, 야수   • gem 보석
• heart-warming 마음이 따뜻해지는

미녀와 야수에 대한 감상

나는 지난 토요일에 미녀와 야수를 봤어. 그건 예쁜 여자 아이와 야수에 대한 이야기야. 나는 그것을 매우 즐겼어. 노래들은 아주 좋았고, 사랑 이야기는 보석만큼 아름다웠어. 마음이 따뜻해지는 사랑 이야기를 좋아한다면, 너도 이걸 좋아할 거야.

8월 12일, 이민수 씀

01 두 단어의 관계가 나머지 넷과 다른 것은?

① brave – cowardly

② safe – dangerous

③ difficult – easy

④ fail – succeed

⑤ moving – touching

02 밑줄 친 단어와 의미가 같은 것을 고르시오.

> A: How was our performance?
> B: It was very surprising!

① amazing   ② interesting

③ famous   ④ moving

⑤ popular

03 다음 제시된 단어를 사용하여 자연스러운 문장을 만들 수 없는 것은? (형태 변화 가능)

> ┌ 보기 ┐
> brave   century   mean   dawn   practice

① One day, a _____ prince falls in love with her at first sight.

② Opera started in Italy in the 16th _____.

③ Why don't we _____ the subway?

④ She must find the answer before _____.

⑤ "Nessun Dorma" _____ no one sleeps.

04 사진을 보고 대화의 빈칸에 어울리는 단어를 고르시오.

> B: Mom, I got only one question wrong on the Korean history exam!
> W: Great! I was sure you would do well. Why don't we go out to _____ tonight?
> B: Yes!

① marry   ② appreciate

③ celebrate   ④ leave

⑤ finish

05 우리말에 맞게 빈칸에 알맞은 단어를 쓰시오.

> 학교 끝나고 바로, 네 시 어때?
> How about 4 o'clock, _____ after school?

[06~07] 다음 대화를 읽고 물음에 답하시오.

> G: Do you want to play badminton together this afternoon, Mark?
> B: Sure. ___(A)___ shall we play?
> G: ___(B)___ about at the park near your place?
> B: O.K. See you there at 3 o'clock.

06 빈칸 (A)와 (B)에 들어갈 말을 쓰시오.

➡ (A) _____   (B) _____

07 위 대화의 목적으로 알맞은 것은?

① to advise
② to inform
③ to recommend
④ to make plans
⑤ to appreciate

[08~09] 다음 대화를 읽고 물음에 답하시오.

A: (A)Why don't we eat pizza after school?
B: Good idea. (B)몇 시에 만날까?
A: How about 5 o'clock at the restaurant?
B: O.K. See you then.

08 밑줄 친 (A)와 바꾸어 쓸 수 <u>없는</u> 표현은?

① Let's eat pizza after school.
② Shall we eat pizza after school?
③ Why are we going to eat pizza after school?
④ How about eating pizza after school?
⑤ What about eating pizza after school?

09 밑줄 친 (B)의 우리말에 맞게 주어진 단어를 이용하여 영어로 쓰시오.

what, shall, meet

➡ _____

10 주어진 문장 뒤에 이어질 대화의 순서를 바르게 배열하시오.

What shall we do this afternoon?

(A) Good idea! What time shall we meet?
(B) Why don't we go to the art museum?
(C) How about 2 o'clock?
(D) O.K. Let's meet in front of the museum.

➡ _____

[11~12] 다음 대화를 읽고 물음에 답하시오.

Anna: Dad, guess what! I have no school next Wednesday.
Dad: Really? Why not?
Anna: It's our school's 75th anniversary.
Dad: Oh, I see.
Anna: Can we do something together that day?
Dad: I guess I can take the afternoon ___(A)___. What do you want to do?
Anna: Why don't we go see a musical at Bravo Theater near your work? We can get a discount ___(B)___ we go on a Wednesday.
Dad: Good idea, Anna! Then, let's just meet at the theater.
Anna: O.K. What time ___(C)___ meet?
Dad: How about 12? Then, we can have lunch together, too.
Anna: You're the best, Dad!

11 위 대화의 빈칸 (A)~(C)에 알맞은 말을 쓰시오.

➡ (A) _____ (B) _____ (C) _____

12 위 대화를 읽고 다음 물음에 대해 영어로 답하시오.

Q: Why does Anna have no school next Wednesday?

➡ Because it's _____.

13 우리말에 맞게 주어진 어구를 이용하여 영어로 쓰시오.

세상을 위해 뭔가 특별한 일을 한다면, 세상은 변할 것이다. (if / something / the world / do / change / special / for)

➡ _____

_____

14 다음 우리말을 올바르게 영작한 것은?

> 나는 내가 여배우만큼 예쁘다고 생각해.

① I think I am prettier than an actress.
② I think I am so pretty as an actress.
③ I think I am as pretty as an actress.
④ I think I am the prettiest actress.
⑤ I think I am as pretty than an actress.

15 다음 우리말을 주어진 〈조건〉에 맞게 영작하시오.

┌─── 조건 ───┐
• 부정어 'not'을 사용할 것.
• 'as+원급+as' 구문을 사용할 것.

> 그는 나만큼 TV를 많이 보지 않는다.

➡ _____ I do.

16 다음 빈칸에 공통으로 들어갈 말은? (대·소문자 무시)

> (1) You should check _____ it will rain during the trip.
> (2) _____ your bag is too heavy, I'll help you to carry it.

① that   ② whether   ③ if
④ when   ⑤ which

17 다음 중 밑줄 친 부분의 쓰임이 다른 것은?

① Do you know if he is a tailor?
② I am not sure if she is Korean or not.
③ They want to know if the answer is right.
④ He wonders if she likes James.
⑤ We will go swimming if the weather is good.

18 다음 중 주어진 문장을 어법상 바르게 고친 것이 아닌 것은?

① My room is as not large as yours.
  → My room is not as large as yours.
② This donkey is as bigger as that horse.
  → This donkey is so big as that horse.
③ I'll join the club if you will teach me how to snowboard.
  → I'll join the club if you teach me how to snowboard.
④ If you will find something valuable, you should keep it in the safe.
  → If you find something valuable, you should keep it in the safe. *safe: 금고
⑤ Her dress looks as love as mine.
  → Her dress looks as lovely as mine.

19 다음 중 어법상 어색한 문장을 고르시오.

① If my mom catches a cold, I will do the dishes for her.
② I can finish the work if you help me.
③ If you want to succeed in life, you will have to study harder.
④ Bills are not so heavy so coins.
⑤ He kicks the ball as hard as he can.

*bill: 지폐

20 다음 중 어법상 바르지 않은 문장은 몇 개인가?

> • This tool is not so useful as that one.
> • I read as many books as she does.
> • The subway is as faster as the train.
> • We will go swimming if the weather will be fine tomorrow.
> • My mother is as tall as my father.

① 1개   ② 2개   ③ 3개   ④ 4개   ⑤ 5개

21 다음 빈칸에 들어갈 형태로 알맞은 것은?

> • If my friends _____ their promises, I will talk to them about it.

① breaks   ② will break

③ broken   ④ break

⑤ won't break

22 다음 교통수단에 관한 표를 보고 as ~ as를 이용하여 비교하는 문장을 완성하시오.

Transportation	Subway	Bus	Taxi
Speed	60km	80km	80km
Fare	1,200 won	1,200 won	3,000 won

(1) The subway cannot go _____ the bus. (speed)

(2) The bus is _____ the taxi. (speed)

(3) The subway is _____ the bus. (fare)

23 다음 중 의미가 <u>다른</u> 하나는?

① I'm not as old as you.

② You are older than I.

③ I'm younger than you.

④ I am as young as you.

⑤ You are not as young as I.

24 다음 우리말에 맞게 주어진 단어를 이용하여 빈칸을 채우시오.

(1) 그녀의 얼굴은 CD만큼이나 작다. (small)

➡ Her face is _____ a CD.

(2) 나는 그녀만큼 빨리 달릴 수 있다. (fast)

➡ I can _____ she can.

(3) 나는 너만큼 키가 크고 싶어.

➡ I want to be _____ you.

25 다음 문장에서 틀린 것을 바르게 고치시오.

> • Justin will not go if Judy won't go.

_____ ➡ _____

26 다음 문장에서 어법상 틀린 부분을 찾아 바르게 고치시오.

(1) I won't wash my car if it will rain.

_____ ➡ _____

(2) I'm not sure if my grandma comes tomorrow.

_____ ➡ _____

Reading

[27~28] 다음 글을 읽고 물음에 답하시오.

Welcome, everyone! Tonight, we are going to ____ⓐ____ Giacomo Puccini's opera *Turandot*. ⓑLike many other famous operas, *Turandot* is in Italian because opera started in Italy in the 16th century. Before we begin, I'd like to tell you the storyline of the opera *Turandot*. You will appreciate it better if you know the story.

27 위 글의 빈칸 ⓐ에 들어갈 알맞은 말을 고르시오.

① practice   ② perform

③ work   ④ achieve

⑤ complete

28 위 글의 밑줄 친 ⓑLike와 같은 의미로 쓰인 것을 고르시오.

① Do you like vegetables?

② I like playing tennis.

③ Which pen do you like best?

④ I, like everyone else, make mistakes.

⑤ I like my coffee strong.

[29~31] 다음 글을 읽고 물음에 답하시오.

Turandot, a Chinese princess, is a woman of great beauty, but she is as cold as ice. (①) Any prince who wants to marry her must answer three riddles. (②) If he fails, he must die. (③) No one ⓐhas ever been able to answer them. (④) He becomes the first man to answer all three riddles. (⑤)

29 위 글의 흐름으로 보아, 주어진 문장이 들어가기에 가장 적절한 곳은?

> One day, a brave prince falls in love with her at first sight.

①   ②   ③   ④   ⑤

30 위 글의 밑줄 친 ⓐ와 현재완료의 용법이 같은 것을 모두 고르시오.

① I have seen a tiger before.

② He has lost his camera.

③ How many times have you read it?

④ She has just arrived here.

⑤ I have known him for five years.

31 위 글의 내용과 일치하지 않는 것은?

① Turandot는 중국의 공주이다.

② Turandot와 결혼하기를 원하는 왕자는 반드시 세 가지 수수께끼에 답해야 한다.

③ 수수께끼에 답하지 못하는 왕자는 죽어야 한다.

④ 지금까지 수수께끼에 답하지 못해 죽은 왕자는 없다.

⑤ 어느 날, 어떤 용감한 왕자가 Turandot에게 첫눈에 반한다.

[32~33] 다음 글을 읽고 물음에 답하시오.

However, Turandot does not want to marry the prince. He is nothing (A)[more / less] than a stranger to her. ⓐHe then gives her a riddle of his own. He asks her, "What is my name?" He adds, "If you answer correctly, I will (B)[agree / refuse] to die. If you answer incorrectly, you will have to marry me."

Turandot must find the answer before dawn, but his riddle is as (C)[different / difficult] as hers. She says to everyone, "No one will go to sleep until someone finds out his name."

32 위 글의 괄호 (A)~(C)에서 문맥이나 어법상 알맞은 낱말을 골라 쓰시오.

➡ (A) _____ (B) _____ (C) _____

33 다음 중 3형식 문장으로 바꿀 때 필요한 전치사가 밑줄 친 ⓐ와 같은 문장을 모두 고르시오.

① Did he buy you the present?

② She sent Tom an email.

③ Mom made me a birthday cake.

④ He asked me a question.

⑤ Who wrote you the thank-you note?

출제율 95%

01 다음 짝지어진 단어의 관계가 같도록 빈칸에 알맞은 말을 쓰시오.

> proposal : suggestion = reply to : _____

출제율 90%

02 우리말에 맞게 빈칸에 세 단어의 알맞은 말을 쓰시오.

> 금은 단지 돌에 지나지 않는다.
> Gold is _____ a stone.

출제율 95%

03 다음 우리말 해석에 맞게 빈칸을 완성하시오. (철자가 주어진 경우 그 철자로 시작할 것)

(1) 중국의 공주 Turandot는 굉장히 아름다운 여인이지만, 그녀는 얼음처럼 차갑습니다.
   ➡ Turandot, a Chinese princess, is a woman of great _____, but she is as _____ as ice.

(2) 우리는 지아코모 푸치니의 오페라 《투란도트》를 공연할 것입니다.
   ➡ We are going to _____ Giacomo Puccini's opera *Turandot*.

(3) 만약 답이 틀리면 당신은 저와 결혼해야 할 것입니다.
   ➡ If you answer _____, you will have to _____ me.

(4) 어느 날, 어떤 용감한 왕자가 그녀에게 첫눈에 반합니다.
   ➡ One day, a brave prince _____ _____ _____ with her at first _____.

출제율 90%

04 다음 영영풀이에 해당하는 단어는?

> earlier than the time expected

① tomorrow   ② already
③ near   ④ hardly
⑤ still

[05~07] 다음 대화를 읽고 물음에 답하시오.

A: ⓐLet's go on a picnic this weekend. ①
B: Good idea. ② What time shall we meet? ③
A: ⓑHow about 10 o'clock on Saturday?
B: ④ O.K. ⑤ See you there.

출제율 100%

05 위 대화의 ①~⑤ 중 주어진 문장이 들어갈 알맞은 곳은?

> Let's meet at the subway station.

①   ②   ③   ④   ⑤

출제율 85%

06 밑줄 친 ⓐ와 같은 의미를 가진 문장을 쓰고자 한다. 괄호 안에 주어진 어구를 알맞게 배열하시오

(1) (go / why / we / on / don't / a picnic / this weekend / ?)
   ➡ _____

(2) (going / what / on / this weekend / a picnic / about / ?)
   ➡ _____

출제율 95%

07 밑줄 친 ⓑ의 목적으로 알맞은 것은?

① 시간 묻기   ② 비교하며 말하기
③ 수정하기   ④ 약속 정하기
⑤ 의도 표현하기

Anna: Dad, _____(A)_____ I have no school next Wednesday.

Dad: Really? Why not?

Anna: It's our school's 75th anniversary.

Dad: Oh, I see.

Anna: Can we do something together that day?

Dad: I guess I can take the afternoon off. What do you want to do?

Anna: Why don't we go see a musical at Bravo Theater near your work? (B)수요일에 가면 할인을 받을 수 있어요.

Dad: Good idea, Anna! Then, let's just meet at the theater.

Anna: O.K. (C)몇 시에 만날까요?

Dad: How about 12? Then, we can have lunch together, too.

Anna: (D)You're the best, Dad!

08 출제율 95%

다음 영어 설명을 참고하여, 위 대화의 빈칸 (A)에 들어갈 말을 고르시오.

> used before telling someone something interesting or surprising

① you know why?　② what did it say?
③ of course.　　　④ well done.
⑤ guess what!

09 출제율 90%

밑줄 친 (B)의 우리말과 같도록 다음 문장의 빈칸을 완성하시오.

➡ We can _____ a _____ _____ we go on a Wednesday.

10 출제율 85%

밑줄 친 (C)의 우리말을 괄호 안의 단어를 이용하여 영어로 쓰시오.

➡ _____ (shall, meet)

11 출제율 90%

밑줄 친 (D)에서 추측할 수 있는 Anna의 기분으로 가장 알맞은 것은?

① sad　　　　② lonely
③ happy　　　④ relaxed
⑤ ashamed

12 출제율 95%

대화의 빈칸에 들어갈 표현으로 적절하지 <u>않은</u> 것은?

> A: Oh, we're going to be late for the concert.
> B: _____ The subway will be faster than the bus at this time of the day.

① Let's take the subway.
② How about taking the subway?
③ Are you taking the subway?
④ Why don't we take the subway?
⑤ What about taking the subway?

13 출제율 100%

대화의 흐름상 <u>어색한</u> 곳을 고르시오.

> B: Mom, I got only one question ① <u>wrong</u> on the Korean history exam!
> W: ②<u>Great</u>! I was sure you would do ③<u>well</u>. Why don't we go out to ④ <u>appreciate</u> tonight?
> B: Yes! Can we have pizza for dinner?
> W: ⑤<u>Of course</u>, Joe. I'll call your dad.

①　　②　　③　　④　　⑤

14 다음 문장의 빈칸에 공통으로 들어갈 말은?

> • You will be late for the class _____ you miss the subway.
> • _____ the weather is bad, I won't go hiking.

① as[As]　　　　　　② if[If]
③ because[Because]　④ which[Which]
⑤ though[Though]

15 다음 표를 보고 틀린 문장을 고르시오.

	Tom	Jane	Mike
나이	15	14	15
키	163	170	170
성적	90	90	70

① Tom is as old as Mike.
② Tom isn't as tall as Jane.
③ Tom is as smart as Jane.
④ Jane is as tall as Mike.
⑤ Jane isn't as smart as Mike.

16 다음 〈보기〉에서 알맞은 단어를 골라 빈칸에 쓰시오. (필요하면 단어를 변형하시오.)

> ┤ 보기 ├
> study　finish　rain　give
> leave　change　meet　hurry

(1) Can I watch TV if I _____ my homework?
(2) If you _____ this book to him, he will be glad.
(3) If your mom _____ her mind, let me know.

17 다음 중 어법상 어색한 것은?

① The prince then sings the most famous aria of the whole opera.
② No one will go to sleep until someone will find out his name.
③ My sister is as tall as my father.
④ If you don't give me candy, I will cry!
⑤ If you want to experience something special, come and enjoy the festival.

18 다음 중 어법상 어색한 것은?

① I can run as fast as Junsu.
② This flower is as pretty as that one.
③ His backpack is as bigger as mine.
④ You are not as smart as I.
⑤ His cell phone is as good as mine.

19 밑줄 친 부분의 쓰임이 나머지와 다른 것은?

① If he is honest, I'll employ him.
② You can be successful in life if you work hard.
③ I will meet him if he visits you.
④ If you do the work, your parents will be happy.
⑤ Can you tell me if he will come?

20 다음 〈보기〉의 단어를 이용하여 빈칸에 알맞은 말을 쓰시오.

> ┤ 보기 ├
> well　tall　kind　good　big　heavy

(1) Jinhee is 150cm tall and I am 170cm tall. Jinhee is _____ me.
(2) Katy doesn't sing as _____ as Jessica.
(3) Subin is 65kg and Jongmin is 65kg, too. Subin is _____ Jongmin.

[21~23] 다음 글을 읽고 물음에 답하시오.

Welcome, everyone! Tonight, we are going to perform Giacomo Puccini's opera *Turandot*. Like many other famous operas, *Turandot* is ___ⓐ___ Italian because opera started ___ⓑ___ Italy ___ⓒ___ the 16th century. Before we begin, I'd like to tell you the storyline of the opera *Turandot*. You will ⓓappreciate it better if you know the story.

✏️ 출제율 95%
21 위 글의 빈칸 ⓐ~ⓒ에 공통으로 들어갈 전치사를 고르시오.

① for   ② from   ③ in
④ at   ⑤ on

✏️ 출제율 85%
22 위 글의 밑줄 친 ⓓappreciate와 같은 의미로 쓰인 것을 고르시오.

① This is a great chance to appreciate the architecture of Korea.
② I'd appreciate your help.
③ You won't appreciate how expensive it is.
④ Thanks for coming. I appreciate it.
⑤ I failed to appreciate the distance between the two cities.

✏️ 출제율 90%
23 다음 질문에 대한 알맞은 대답을 주어진 단어로 시작하여 쓰시오. (3 단어)

Q: How will you be able to appreciate the opera *Turandot* better?
A: By _____.

➡️ _____

[24~26] 다음 글을 읽고 물음에 답하시오.

ⓐTurandot, a Chinese princess, is a woman of great beauty, but she is as sweet as honey. Any prince who wants to marry her must answer three ___ⓑ___. If he fails, he must die. No one has ever been able to answer them. One day, a brave prince falls in love with her at first sight. He becomes the first man to answer all three ___ⓑ___.

✏️ 출제율 95%
24 위 글의 밑줄 친 ⓐ에서 흐름상 어색한 부분을 고치시오.

_____ ➡️ _____

✏️ 출제율 90%
25 주어진 영영풀이를 참고하여 빈칸 ⓑ에 철자 r로 시작하는 단어를 쓰시오.

puzzles or jokes in which you ask a question that seems to be nonsense but which has a clever or amusing answer

➡️ _____

✏️ 출제율 100%
26 위 글을 읽고 알 수 없는 것을 고르시오.

① Turandot의 신분
② Turandot의 외모
③ Turandot와 결혼하려는 왕자들이 통과해야만 하는 절차
④ 절차를 통과하지 못한 왕자들이 감수해야 하는 위험
⑤ 절차를 통과하지 못한 왕자들의 숫자

01 주어진 단어를 이용하여 대화의 빈칸을 완성하시오.

> A: Let's go on a picnic this weekend.
> B: Good idea. _____(A)_____ (time, shall, meet)
> A: How about 10 o'clock on Saturday?
> B: O.K. _____(B)_____ (shall, meet)
> A: Let's meet at the subway station. See you there.

➡ (A) _____

　　(B) _____

02 대화의 빈칸에 제안을 하는 표현을 이용하여 6 단어로 문장을 완성하시오.

> M: _____? The subway will be faster than the bus at this time of day.
> W: That's a good idea.

➡ _____

03 대화의 빈칸 (A)~(C)에 알맞은 표현을 〈보기〉에서 찾아 쓰시오.

> ┤ 보기 ├
> • Why don't we go see *Wonder Woman*?
> • What shall we do this afternoon?
> • How about 4 o'clock?

> A: (A) _____
> B: (B) _____
> A: Good idea! What time shall we meet?
> B: (C) _____
> A: O.K. Let's meet at Moon Theater.

➡ (A) _____

　　(B) _____

　　(C) _____

04 다음 우리말에 맞게 주어진 단어를 이용하여 빈칸에 알맞은 말을 쓰시오.

(1) 그녀의 반지는 나의 것만큼 비싸다.
　➡ Her ring is _____. (expensive)

(2) Cathy는 Juliet만큼 친절하지 않다.
　➡ Cathy is _____ Juliet. (so, kind)

(3) 그가 내일 여기로 오면, 나에게 데려와.
　➡ If he _____ here tomorrow, _____ him _____ me. (come, take)

05 다음 문장에서 어법상 틀린 부분을 찾아 바르게 고치시오.

(1) If it will rain tomorrow, we won't go on a picnic.
　_____ ➡ _____

(2) I'll call you if I will need your help.
　_____ ➡ _____

06 다음 표를 보고 문장의 빈칸을 채우시오.

조건 1: 번호에 해당하는 표현을 찾아 주어, 동사를 포함한 완전한 문장으로 쓰시오.

조건 2: 동등 비교 표현을 이용하여 쓰시오.

	Minho	Mike	Jane
(1) Age	14	13	14
(2) Height	160	160	165
(3) Weight	50	40	50

(1) Minho is _____ Jane.
　But Mike is _____ Minho.

(2) Minho is _____ Mike.
　But _____ Jane.

(3) Minho is _____ Jane.
　But Mike _____ Minho.

07 다음 문장에서 어법상 틀린 부분을 찾아 바르게 고치시오.

> I'll stop talking about it if you won't pay attention to me.

_____ ➡ _____

[08~10] 다음 글을 읽고 물음에 답하시오.

Turandot, a Chinese princess, is a woman of great beauty, but she is _____ⓐ_____ . (A) [Some / Any] prince who wants to marry her must answer three riddles. If he fails, he must die. No one has (B)[ever / never] been able to answer them. One day, a brave prince falls in love with her at first (C)[see / sight]. He becomes the first man to answer all three riddles.

08 다음과 같은 뜻이 되도록 위 글의 빈칸 ⓐ에 들어갈 알맞은 말을 as와 ice를 포함하여 쓰시오.

> very cold

➡ _____

09 위 글의 괄호 (A)~(C)에서 문맥이나 어법상 알맞은 낱말을 골라 쓰시오.

➡ (A) _____ (B) _____ (C) _____

10 본문의 내용과 일치하도록 다음 빈칸에 알맞은 단어를 쓰시오. (본문의 단어를 변형하여 쓰시오.)

> All the princes who tried to answer three riddles at the risk of their lives have _____ to answer them except one prince.

[11~13] 다음 글을 읽고 물음에 답하시오.

However, Turandot does not want to marry the prince. ⓐ그는 그녀에게 단지 낯선 사람일 뿐입니다. He then gives her a riddle of his own. He asks her, "What is my name?" He adds, "If you answer correctly, I will agree to die. If you answer incorrectly, you will have to marry me."

Turandot must find the answer before dawn, but his riddle is as difficult as ⓑhers. She says to everyone, "No one will go to sleep until someone finds out his name."

11 위 글의 밑줄 친 ⓐ의 우리말에 맞게 주어진 어휘를 이용하여 9 단어로 영작하시오.

> nothing

➡ _____

12 위 글의 밑줄 친 ⓑhers가 가리키는 것을 영어로 쓰시오.

➡ _____

13 본문의 내용과 일치하도록 다음 빈칸 (A)와 (B)에 알맞은 단어를 쓰시오.

> If Turandot answers the prince's riddle incorrectly, she will have to (A)_____ _____ . If Turandot answers correctly, he will agree (B)_____ _____ .

01 다음 그림을 보고 놀이동산에서 해야 할 일을 제안하는 대화를 〈보기〉를 참고하여 완성하시오.

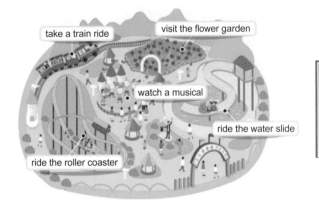

take a train ride
visit the flower garden
watch a musical
ride the water slide
ride the roller coaster

━━ 보기 ━━

A: What shall we do at the park?
B: Why don't we see a magic show?
A: That's a good idea.

02 다음 그림을 보고 지하철과 버스의 속도와 요금을 비교하는 문장을 'as ~ as'를 이용하여 완성하시오. (fast, expensive를 사용할 것)

Transportation	Subway	Bus
Speed	60km	80km
Fare	1,200 won	1,200 won

(1) _____

(2) _____

03 다음 내용을 바탕으로 영화의 감상문을 쓰시오.

• What is the title?
  La La Land
• What is it about?
  the dreams and love of Mia and Sebastian

• What did you think about it?
  – beautiful and moving songs
  – a good story

_____(A)_____ of *La La Land* ★★★★☆
I saw *La La Land* last Friday. It is about _____(B)_____ of Mia and Sebastian. I enjoyed its _____(C)_____ songs. The _____(D)_____ was also as good as the songs. If you are looking for a good musical movie, you should see this movie.

by Kim Jisu on Aug. 11

단원별 모의고사

01 다음 단어에 대한 영어 설명이 <u>어색한</u> 것은?

① moving: causing strong feelings of sadness or sympathy

② storyline: the series of events that happen in a book, film, play, etc.

③ marry: to become the legally accepted husband or wife of someone in an official or religious ceremony

④ riddle: a type of question that describes something in a difficult and confusing way and has a clever or funny answer

⑤ appreciate: to do something enjoyable on a special occasion

02 다음 우리말 해석에 맞게 알맞은 단어를 쓰시오.

(1) 나는 오후에 휴무를 할 수 있을 것 같구나.

➡ I guess I can _____ the afternoon _____.

(2) Karen, 오늘 학교 연극의 우리 역할을 연습하자.

➡ Karen, let's _____ our parts for the school _____ today.

(3) 오늘 축하하러 나가는 건 어때?

➡ Why _____ we go out to _____ tonight?

[03~04] 다음 글을 읽고 물음에 답하시오.

I saw *La La Land* last Friday. It is about the dreams and love of Mia and Sebastian. (A)<u>나는 그것의 아름답고 감동적인 이야기가 좋았어.</u> The story was also _____ ⓐ _____ the songs. If you are looking for a good musical movie, you should see this movie.

03 위 글의 빈칸 ⓐ에 들어갈 말로 알맞은 것은?

① as well as
② as better as
③ as good as
④ good as
⑤ the best

04 위 글의 밑줄 친 (A)의 우리말에 맞게 빈칸에 알맞은 단어를 쓰시오. (m으로 시작할 것)

➡ I enjoyed its beautiful and _____ songs.

[05~06] 다음 대화를 읽고 물음에 답하시오.

M: Liz, hurry up. It's already 6 o'clock.

W: Oh, we're going to be late for the concert.

M: Why don't we take the subway? The subway will be faster than the bus at this time of day.

W: That's a good idea.

05 다음 영영풀이에 해당하는 단어를 대화에서 찾아 쓰시오.

happening or arriving after the planned, expected, usual, or necessary time

➡ _____

06 위 대화를 읽고 답할 수 <u>없는</u> 질문을 고르시오.

① What time is it now?
② Where are they going to go?
③ When does the concert begin?
④ What will they take to go to the concert?
⑤ Which is faster, the subway or the bus?

[07~08] 다음 대화를 읽고 물음에 답하시오.

Joe: Mom, I got only one question ①wrong on the Korean history exam!

Mom: Great! I was sure you would ②do poorly. ③Why don't we go out to ④celebrate tonight?

Joe: Yes! Can we ⑤have pizza for dinner?

Mom: Of course, Joe. I'll call your dad.

07 위 대화의 ①~⑤ 중 어휘의 쓰임이 어색한 것은?

①   ②   ③   ④   ⑤

08 위 대화의 내용과 일치하지 않는 것은?

① Joe took the Korean history exam.
② Joe's mom suggests going out tonight.
③ Joe got only one question wrong on the exam.
④ Joe's mom did well on the exam.
⑤ Joe's family will go out for dinner.

09 다음 중 짝지어진 대화가 어색한 것은?

① A: Why don't we see a magic show?
   B: That's a good idea.
② A: Karen, let's practice our parts for the school play today.
   B: O.K. What time shall we meet?
③ A: Where shall we play?
   B: How about at the park near your place?
④ A: What time shall we meet?
   B: How about at the bus stop?
⑤ A: What shall we do this afternoon?
   B: Why don't we go see *Wonder Woman*?

[10~12] 다음 대화를 읽고 물음에 답하시오.

Anna: Dad, guess what! I have no school next Wednesday.

Dad: Really? _____(A)_____

Anna: It's our school's 75th anniversary.

Dad: Oh, I see.

Anna: Can we do something together that day?

Dad: I guess I can take the afternoon off. (B)뭘 하고 싶니?

Anna: Why don't we go see a musical at Bravo Theater near your work? We can get a discount if we go on a Wednesday.

Dad: Good idea, Anna! Then, let's just meet at the theater.

Anna: O.K. What time shall we meet?

Dad: How about 12? Then, we can have lunch together, too.

Anna: You're the best, Dad!

10 빈칸 (A)에 알맞은 말은?

① You know what?   ② I know.
③ Why not?   ④ Excuse me?
⑤ What are you going to do?

11 밑줄 친 (B)의 우리말에 맞게 주어진 단어를 이용하여 영작하시오.

➡ _____ (what / want / do)

12 위 대화의 내용과 일치하지 않는 것은?

① Next Wednesday is Anna's school's 75th anniversary.
② Anna won't go to school next Wednesday.
③ Anna and her dad will go see a movie next Wednesday.
④ Anna and her dad will meet at the theater.
⑤ Anna and her dad will have lunch together.

13 다음 괄호 안의 단어를 알맞은 곳에 넣어 문장을 다시 쓰시오.

(1) Anna is as as Julie. (beautiful)

➡ _____

(2) I will let you go out you do finish your job. (if)

➡ _____

14 다음 주어진 문장은 어법상 틀린 문장이다. 바르게 고친 것이 아닌 것은?

① I am not as braver as Jack.

→ I am not as brave as Jack.

② He drove so fast as I.

→ He drove as fast as I

③ Her hair is as long as I.

→ Her hair is as long as me.

④ This bicycle is as not expensive as that one.

→ This bicycle is not as expensive as that one.

⑤ If she will go to the island, she will spend all day swimming.

→ If she goes to the island, she will spend all day swimming.

15 다음 문장에서 어법상 어색한 곳을 찾아 바르게 고치시오.

(1) My room is as not larger as yours.

_____ ➡ _____

(2) This donkey is as bigger as that horse.

_____ ➡ _____

16 다음 그림과 같은 의미가 되도록 'as ~ as'를 이용하여 알맞은 단어를 쓰시오.

Tom
Ann

➡ Ann is _____ Tom.

17 다음 두 문장을 한 문장으로 알맞게 바꾼 것은?

• I will go swimming.
• It will not rain tomorrow.

① I will go swimming if it didn't rain tomorrow.

② I will go swimming if it will not rain tomorrow.

③ I go swimming if it will not rain tomorrow.

④ I will go swimming if it does not rain tomorrow.

⑤ I go swimming if it do not rain tomorrow.

18 다음 중 어법상 어색한 것은?

① If it is sunny tomorrow, how about playing soccer?

② If I'm not busy tomorrow, I will go with you.

③ That tower is as high as this tower.

④ This dog is as big as that dog.

⑤ Tennis is as less popular as soccer.

[19~20] 다음 글을 읽고 물음에 답하시오.

Welcome, everyone! Tonight, we are going to perform Giacomo Puccini's opera *Turandot*. Like many other famous operas, *Turandot* is in _____ⓐ_____ because opera started in Italy in the 16th century. Before we begin, I'd like to tell you the ⓑstoryline of the opera *Turandot*. You will appreciate it better if you know the story.

19 본문의 한 단어를 변형하여 위 글의 빈칸 ⓐ에 들어갈 알맞은 말을 쓰시오.

➡ _____

20 위 글의 밑줄 친 ⓑstoryline과 바꿔 쓸 수 있는 말을 고르시오.

① theme   ② setting   ③ plot
④ concept   ⑤ subject

[21~22] 다음 글을 읽고 물음에 답하시오.

Turandot, a Chinese princess, is a woman _____ⓐ_____ great beauty, but she is as cold as ice. ⓑAny prince who wants to marry her must ask three riddles. If he fails, he must die. No one has ever been able to answer them. One day, a brave prince falls in love _____ⓒ_____ her at first sight. He becomes the first man to answer all three riddles.

21 위 글의 빈칸 ⓐ와 ⓒ에 들어갈 전치사가 바르게 짝지어진 것은?

① for – from   ② of – at
③ of – with   ④ for – at
⑤ on – with

22 위 글의 밑줄 친 ⓑ에서 흐름상 어색한 부분을 찾아 고치시오.

_____ ➡ _____

[23~24] 다음 글을 읽고 물음에 답하시오.

However, Turandot does not want to marry the prince. He is nothing more than a stranger to her. He then gives her a riddle of his own. He asks her, "What is my name?" He adds, "If you answer correctly, I will agree ⓐto die. If you answer incorrectly, you will have to marry me."

Turandot must find the answer before dawn, but his riddle is as difficult as hers. She says to everyone, "No one will go to sleep until someone finds out his name."

23 아래 〈보기〉에서 위 글의 밑줄 친 ⓐto die와 문법적 쓰임이 같은 문장의 개수를 고르시오.

┌─── 보기 ───┐
① I would be happy to be helpful to you.
② She learned to play the piano.
③ This book is too difficult to read.
④ He has a few friends to play with.
⑤ Her plan is to go to the movies tonight.
└─────────────┘

① 1개   ② 2개   ③ 3개   ④ 4개   ⑤ 5개

24 위 글의 내용과 일치하지 않는 것은?

① Turandot는 그 왕자와 결혼하기를 원하지 않는다.
② 왕자는 Turandot에게 단지 낯선 사람일 뿐이다.
③ 왕자는 Turandot에게 자신의 수수께끼를 낸다.
④ 만약 Turandot의 답이 틀리면 왕자는 죽는 것에 동의할 것이다.
⑤ Turandot는 동이 트기 전에 수수께끼의 답을 찾아야 한다.

INSIGHT
on the textbook

교과서 파헤치기

Lesson **3** **My Travel, My Way**

Lesson **4** **Giving a Hand**

Lesson **5** **Bravo! Brava!**

※ 다음 영어를 우리말로 쓰시오.

01	perfect	22	market
02	amazing	23	foreign
03	become	24	mystery
04	capture	25	freezing
05	seafood	26	actually
06	travel	27	expect
07	simple	28	journal
08	bungee jumping	29	scary
09	forecast	30	indoors
10	earth	31	create
11	else	32	university
12	famous	33	vacation
13	portrait	34	appear
14	finally	35	get to
15	food	36	be full of
16	graduate	37	get into
17	chance	38	right now
18	island	39	a lot of
19	remain	40	such as
20	weather	41	set foot at[in]
21	guess	42	a little
		43	show up

※ 다음 우리말을 영어로 쓰시오.

01 만지다 _____

02 접시, 그릇 _____

03 살피다, 점검하다 _____

04 흐린 _____

05 (짐을) 싸다 _____

06 결정하다 _____

07 ~ 동안[내내] _____

08 외국의 _____

09 ~ 둘레에, ~ 주위에 _____

10 (차량을) 몰다 _____

11 바람이 많이 부는 _____

12 초대하다 _____

13 큰, 거대한 _____

14 화신 _____

15 현장 학습 _____

16 물건, 물체 _____

17 전문학교 _____

18 날씨 _____

19 잠깐, 잠시 _____

20 휴식을 취하다 _____

21 그림, 소묘 _____

22 여행 _____

23 거북 _____

24 시장 _____

25 존경하다, 감탄하며 바라보다 _____

26 수첩, 일기 _____

27 완전한 _____

28 예상[기대]하다 _____

29 포착하다, 담아내다 _____

30 졸업하다 _____

31 꽁꽁 얼게[너무나] 추운 _____

32 무서운, 겁나는 _____

33 간단한 _____

34 섬 _____

35 소수의, 약간의 _____

36 지금, 당장 _____

37 ~에 도착하다 _____

38 ~으로 가득 차다 _____

39 마침내 _____

40 나타나다 _____

41 ~에 발을 들여놓다 _____

42 ~에 들어가다, ~에 타다 _____

43 ~와 같은 _____

※ 다음 영영풀이에 알맞은 단어를 <보기>에서 골라 쓴 후, 우리말 뜻을 쓰시오.

1 _____ : what people and animals eat: _____

2 _____ : the possibility that something will happen: _____

3 _____ : a piece of land that is completely surrounded by water: _____

4 _____ : a place where goods are bought and sold, usually outdoors: _____

5 _____ : to like and respect someone or something very much: _____

6 _____ : a picture made with a pencil or pen: _____

7 _____ : very surprising and making you feel pleasure, approval, or wonder:
_____

8 _____ : an area of sand or stones beside the sea: _____

9 _____ : to cause something to happen or exist: _____

10 _____ : to ask someone to come to something such as a party: _____

11 _____ : something that is not understood or known about: _____

12 _____ : unusual or unexpected, and making you feel slightly nervous or afraid:
_____

13 _____ : to go from one place to another, often to a place that is far away:
_____

14 _____ : to choose to do something, usually after you have thought carefully
about the other possibilities: _____

15 _____ : to spend time resting or doing something enjoyable especially after you
have been doing work: _____

16 _____ : to put clothes and other things into a bag, because you are leaving a
place: _____

보기			
create	chance	mystery	market
admire	invite	travel	pack
island	decide	food	drawing
amazing	strange	relax	beach

※ 다음 우리말과 일치하도록 빈칸에 알맞은 말을 쓰시오.

Listen & Speak 1 A. Listen and Check

1. G: _____ you ever _____ Indian food?

   B: Yes, I _____, but I've _____ _____ Indian curry.

   G: _____ was _____?

   B: It was really _____, _____ I loved it.

2. G: Bill, _____ you ever _____ bungee jumping?

   B: _____, I _____. _____ _____ you, Katie?

   G: _____ I _____ New Zealand, I _____ bungee jumping

   _____.

   B: _____ it _____?

   G: No, I liked it. I _____ _____ do it _____.

Listen & Speak 2 A. Listen and Answer

1. B: Mom, _____ the _____ today? Do I _____ an umbrella?

   W: It's quite _____ _____. I'll _____ the weather _____.

   B: _____ you, Mom.

   W: Well, it's not _____ _____ _____ today.

   B: Good! Then, I _____ _____ an umbrella today.

2. W: Good morning, and ____ _____ the weather forecast.

   It's _____ _____, but we're _____ some rain in the

   afternoon. _____ _____ home _____ your umbrella.

   That's the _____ _____ for today. _____ a nice day.

해석

1. G: 너 인도 음식을 먹어 본 적이 있니?
   B: 응, 있어. 하지만 인도 카레만 먹어 봤어.
   G: 어땠어?
   B: 정말 매웠지만, 아주 좋았어.

2. G: Bill, 번지 점프하러 가 본 적 있니?
   B: 아니, 없어. Katie, 넌 어때?
   G: 뉴질랜드를 방문했을 때, 번지 점프를 한 번 해봤어.
   B: 무섭지 않았어?
   G: 아니, 좋았어. 또 하고 싶어.

1. B: 엄마, 오늘 날씨 어때요? 우산이 필요한가요?
   W: 바깥 날씨가 아주 흐려. 일기예보를 확인해 볼게.
   B: 고마워요, 엄마.
   W: 음, 오늘은 비가 안 올 거야.
   B: 좋아요! 그럼, 오늘은 우산이 필요 없어요.

2. W: 좋은 아침입니다. 일기예보에 오신 것을 환영합니다. 밖은 화창하지만 오후에는 약간의 비가 예상됩니다. 우산 없이 집을 나서지 마세요. 오늘의 일기예보입니다. 좋은 하루 되세요.

Communicate A~B

A. **Suho** Anna, _____ you _____ _____ Australia before?

    Anna: Yes, I _____. Actually, I _____ in Sydney _____ a year.

    Suho: Great! _____ the weather _____ in April? I'm _____ _____ visit Sydney _____ _____ next week.

    Anna: April is a great time _____ _____ Sydney. In April, it's _____ in Australia.

    Suho: Good. I'm _____ _____ _____ some time on the beach and _____ in the sun.

    Anna: Well, it _____ _____ in April, but you _____ have some _____ _____.

    Suho: I'll _____ my hat and _____ an umbrella, _____.

    Anna: That's a _____ _____. _____ a great time.

B. **A:** _____ you _____ _____ any special _____ in Korea?

    B: Yes, I _____. I _____ _____ Ulleungdo _____ summer _____ my family.

    A: _____ was the _____ there?

    B: It was _____ _____, but the weather _____ often.

Progress Check

1. **G:** _____ you ever _____ a horse?

    B: Yes, I _____. _____ _____ you?

    G: No, I _____. _____ was it?

    B: It was _____, but it was _____ _____ scary, _____.

2. **B:** Mom, how's the _____ today?

    W: It's quite _____ _____. I'll _____ the weather _____.

    B: Thanks, Mom.

    W: Well, it's _____ _____ _____ in the afternoon.

3. **M:** Good evening, and _____ _____ the weather forecast. It's _____ _____ _____, but we're _____ a sunny day tomorrow. Don't _____ home tomorrow _____ your hat.

A. 수호: Anna, 너 전에 호주에 가본 적 있어?

  Anna: 응, 있어. 사실, 나는 시드니에서 1년 동안 살았어.

  수호: 멋지다! 그곳의 4월 날씨는 어때? 난 다음 주 방학 때 시드니에 갈 거야.

  Anna: 4월은 시드니를 방문하기에 좋은 시기야. 4월에, 호주는 가을이야.

  수호: 좋아. 나는 해변에서 시간을 좀 보내고 햇빛을 쬐며 휴식을 취할 계획이야.

  Anna: 음, 4월에는 종종 비가 오지만, 맑은 날도 좀 있을 거야.

  수호: 나도 모자를 가져가고 우산도 챙길 거야.

  Anna: 좋은 생각이야. 좋은 시간 보내.

B. A: 넌 한국의 어느 특별한 장소들을 가본 적이 있니?

  B: 응, 있어. 나는 작년 여름에 가족과 울릉도에 갔어.

  A: 거기 날씨는 어땠어?

  B: 대체로 맑았지만, 날씨가 자주 바뀌었어.

1. G: 너 말을 타본 적 있니?

  B: 응, 있어. 너는 어때?

  G: 아니, 난 없어. 말 타는 거 어땠어?

  B: 재미있었지만, 조금 무섭기도 했어.

2. B: 엄마, 오늘 날씨 어때요?

  W: 바깥 날씨가 꽤 흐려. 일기예보를 확인해 볼게.

  B: 고마워요, 엄마.

  W: 음, 오후에 비가 올 거야.

3. M: 안녕하세요, 일기예보에 오신 것을 환영합니다. 지금은 비가 오지만 내일은 화창한 날씨가 예상됩니다. 내일 모자를 쓰지 않고 집을 나서지 마세요.

※ 다음 우리말에 맞도록 대화를 영어로 쓰시오.

Listen & Speak 1 A. Listen and Check

1. G: _____

   B: _____

   G: _____

   B: _____

2. G: _____

   B: _____

   G: _____

   B: _____

   G: _____

Listen & Speak 2 A. Listen and Answer

1. B: _____

   W: _____

   B: _____

   W: _____

   B: _____

2. W: _____

   _____

해석

1. G: 너 인도 음식을 먹어 본 적이 있니?
   B: 응, 있어. 하지만 인도 카레만 먹어봤어.
   G: 어땠어?
   B: 정말 매웠지만, 아주 좋았어.

2. G: Bill, 번지 점프하러 가 본 적 있니?
   B: 아니, 없어. Katie, 넌 어때?
   G: 뉴질랜드를 방문했을 때, 번지 점프를 한 번 해봤어.
   B: 무섭지 않았어?
   G: 아니, 좋았어. 또 하고 싶어.

1. B: 엄마, 오늘 날씨 어때요? 우산이 필요한가요?
   W: 바깥 날씨가 아주 흐려. 일기예보를 확인해 볼게.
   B: 고마워요, 엄마.
   W: 음, 오늘은 비가 안 올 거야.
   B: 좋아요! 그럼, 오늘은 우산이 필요 없어요.

2. W: 좋은 아침입니다, 일기예보에 오신 것을 환영합니다. 밖은 화창하지만 오후에는 약간의 비가 예상됩니다. 우산 없이 집을 나서지 마세요. 오늘의 일기예보입니다. 좋은 하루 되세요.

Communicate A~B

A. Suho _____

   Anna: _____

   Suho: _____

         _____

   Anna: _____

   Suho: _____

   Anna: _____

   Suho: _____

   Anna: _____

B. A: _____

   B: _____

   A: _____

   B: _____

Progress Check

1. G: _____

   B: _____

   G: _____

   B: _____

2. B: _____

   W: _____

   B: _____

   W: _____

3. M: _____

         _____

A. 수호: Anna, 너 전에 호주에 가본 적 있어?

   Anna: 응, 있어. 사실, 나는 시드니에서 1년 동안 살았어.

   수호: 멋지다! 그곳의 4월 날씨는 어때? 난 다음 주 방학 때 시드니에 갈 거야.

   Anna: 4월은 시드니를 방문하기에 좋은 시기야. 4월에, 호주는 가을이야.

   수호: 좋아. 나는 해변에서 시간을 좀 보내고 햇빛을 쐬며 휴식을 취할 계획이야.

   Anna: 음, 4월에는 종종 비가 오지만, 맑은 날도 좀 있을 거야.

   수호: 나도 모자를 가져가고 우산도 챙길 거야.

   Anna: 좋은 생각이야. 좋은 시간 보내.

B. A: 넌 한국의 어느 특별한 장소들을 가본 적이 있니?

   B: 응, 있어. 나는 작년 여름에 가족과 울릉도에 갔어.

   A: 거기 날씨는 어땠어?

   B: 대체로 맑았지만, 날씨가 자주 바뀌었어.

1. G: 너 말을 타본 적 있니?

   B: 응, 있어. 너는 어때?

   G: 아니, 난 없어. 말 타는 거 어땠어?

   B: 재미있었지만, 조금 무섭기도 했어.

2. B: 엄마, 오늘 날씨 어때요?

   W: 바깥 날씨가 꽤 흐려. 일기예보를 확인해 볼게.

   B: 고마워요, 엄마.

   W: 음, 오후에 비가 올 거야.

3. M: 안녕하세요, 일기예보에 오신 것을 환영합니다. 지금은 비가 오지만 내일은 화창한 날씨가 예상됩니다. 내일 모자를 쓰지 않고 집을 나서지 마세요.

※ 다음 우리말과 일치하도록 빈칸에 알맞은 것을 골라 쓰시오.

1 Hi, I _____ Lucy Hunter, and I _____ _____ London.
A. in   B. am   C. live

2 _____ week, my family went _____ a vacation _____ three days.
A. for   B. last   C. on

3 _____ our trip, I made _____ drawings in my _____.
A. journal   B. simple   C. during

4 That was a great _____ to _____ all the _____ moments.
A. special   B. capture   C. way

5 At _____, we _____ foot at Stonehenge, one of the most _____ places on Earth.
A. mysterious   B. set   C. last

6 _____ a two-hour _____ from our home in London, we _____ got to Stonehenge.
A. finally   B. drive   C. after

7 It was just _____ to see the _____ of _____ stones.
A. huge   B. ring   C. amazing

8 How did those huge _____ get there _____ of years _____?
A. ago   B. thousands   C. stones

9 _____ were they _____?
A. for   B. what

10 I _____ Stonehenge will _____ a _____ for a long time.
A. remain   B. guess   C. mystery

11 Don't _____ to make a _____ drawing.
A. perfect   B. try

12 A _____ colors will be _____.
A. enough   B. few

13 _____ the morning, we walked _____ the Cotswolds.
A. around   B. in

14 It _____ to rain in the afternoon, _____ we _____ to stay indoors at our B&B.
A. decided   B. started   C. so

15 A B&B is a _____ place to _____ in England.
A. stay   B. popular

1 안녕, 나는 Lucy Hunter이고 런던에 살아요.

2 지난주에 우리 가족은 3일 동안 휴가를 갔습니다.

3 여행 중에 나는 일기에 간단한 그림을 그렸어요.

4 그것은 모든 특별한 순간을 포착하는 훌륭한 방법이었어요.

5 마침내, 우리는 지구에서 가장 불가사의한 장소 중 하나인 스톤헨지에 발을 디뎠다.

6 런던에 있는 집에서 차로 두 시간을 달려서 우리는 마침내 스톤헨지에 도착했다.

7 원형으로 둘러서 있는 거대한 돌들을 보는 것은 정말 놀라웠다.

8 어떻게 그 거대한 돌들이 수천 년 전에 그곳에 도착했을까?

9 그것들은 무엇을 위한 것이었을까?

10 스톤헨지는 오랫동안 미스터리로 남을 것 같다.

11 완벽한 그림을 그리려고 하지 마세요.

12 몇 가지 색깔이면 충분할 것입니다.

13 아침에 우리는 코츠월드 언덕을 돌아다녔다.

14 오후에 비가 오기 시작해서, 우리는 B&B의 실내에서 머물기로 결정했다.

15 B&B는 영국에서 체류하는 곳으로 인기가 있다.

16 It feels more _____ a home _____ a hotel.
A. than   B. like

17 The owner _____ us _____ afternoon tea today.
A. for   B. invited

18 The _____ table was _____ of cookies, cake, bread, _____ cheese.
A. and   B. full   C. dining

19 While I was _____ eating, Mom was _____ the beautiful cups and _____.
A. plates   B. admiring   C. busy

20 I ate too _____, so I couldn't eat _____ for dinner.
A. anything   B. much

21 It is O.K. to _____ everyday objects _____ cups and plates in your _____.
A. journal   B. like   C. draw

22 _____ last _____ was Oxford.
A. stop   B. our

23 We first _____ Christ Church _____.
A. College   B. visited

24 It has _____ a world famous place to visit _____ it in the *Harry Potter* movies.
A. appeared   B. since   C. become

25 In the _____, Harry and everyone _____ eat _____ at the Hall of Christ Church.
A. dinner   B. else   C. movies

26 We _____ saw _____ of famous people who _____ from the college.
A. graduated   B. portraits   C. also

27 When we were _____ the building, I _____ to the famous olive tree and _____ it.
A. touched   B. outside   C. walked

28 "_____ I _____ this tree," I said, "I will _____ into Oxford University!"
A. get   B. touched   C. because

29 Then, my brother _____ to me with a _____, "I can't _____ to see your portrait on the wall."
A. wait   B. smile   C. said

30 _____ your _____ avatar.
A. own   B. create

31 Your _____ journal will become _____ more _____.
A. interesting   B. much   C. drawing

| | |
16 그것은 호텔이라기보다는 집처럼 느껴진다.

17 주인은 오늘 오후의 다과회에 우리를 초대했다.

18 식탁에는 쿠키, 케이크, 빵, 그리고 치즈가 가득했다.

19 내가 먹느라고 바쁠 때, 엄마는 아름다운 컵과 접시를 감탄하며 바라보고 계셨다.

20 나는 너무 많이 먹어서 저녁으로 아무것도 먹을 수 없었다.

21 당신의 일기에 컵과 접시 같은 일상적인 물건들을 그려도 괜찮습니다.

22 우리가 마지막으로 머문 곳은 옥스퍼드였다.

23 우리는 먼저 Christ Church College를 방문했다.

24 이곳은 해리포터 영화에 등장한 이후 방문해야 할 세계적으로 유명한 장소가 되었다.

25 영화에서 Harry와 다른 모든 사람들이 Christ Church의 회관에서 저녁을 먹는다.

26 우리는 또한 그 대학을 졸업한 유명한 사람들의 초상화를 보았다.

27 우리가 건물 밖으로 나왔을 때, 나는 유명한 올리브 나무로 걸어가서 그것을 만졌다.

28 "이 나무를 만졌기 때문에, 난 옥스퍼드 대학교에 들어갈 거야!"라고 말했다.

29 그러자 오빠가 웃으면서 "벽에 걸린 네 초상화가 빨리 보고 싶어."라고 내게 말했다.

30 여러분 자신의 아바타를 만드세요.

31 그림일기가 훨씬 더 재미있을 거예요.

※ 다음 우리말과 일치하도록 빈칸에 알맞은 말을 쓰시오.

1 Hi, I _____ Lucy Hunter, and I _____ _____ London.

2 _____ _____, my family _____ _____ a vacation _____ three days.

3 _____ our trip, I made simple _____ in my _____.

4 That was a great way _____ all the _____ _____.

5 At last, we _____ _____ _____ Stonehenge, _____ _____ the most mysterious _____ on Earth.

6 _____ a two-hour _____ _____ our home in London, we finally _____ _____ Stonehenge.

7 It was just _____ to see the _____ of huge stones.

8 How did those _____ _____ get there _____ of years _____?

9 _____ were they _____?

10 I _____ Stonehenge will _____ a mystery _____ a long time.

11 _____ _____ to make a _____ drawing.

12 _____ _____ colors will be _____.

13 _____ the morning, we _____ _____ the Cotswolds.

14 It started _____ _____ in the afternoon, so we _____ _____ _____ indoors at our B&B.

15 A B&B is a _____ place to _____ _____ England.

1 안녕, 나는 Lucy Hunter이고 런던에 살아요.

2 지난주에 우리 가족은 3일 동안 휴가를 갔습니다.

3 여행 중에 나는 일기에 간단한 그림을 그렸어요.

4 그것은 모든 특별한 순간을 포착하는 훌륭한 방법이었어요.

5 마침내, 우리는 지구에서 가장 불가사의한 장소 중 하나인 스톤헨지에 발을 디뎠다.

6 런던에 있는 집에서 차로 두 시간을 달려서 우리는 마침내 스톤헨지에 도착했다.

7 원형으로 둘러서 있는 거대한 돌들을 보는 것은 정말 놀라웠다.

8 어떻게 그 거대한 돌들이 수천 년 전에 그곳에 도착했을까?

9 그것들은 무엇을 위한 것이었을까?

10 스톤헨지는 오랫동안 미스터리로 남을 것 같다.

11 완벽한 그림을 그리려고 하지 마세요.

12 몇 가지 색깔이면 충분할 것입니다.

13 아침에 우리는 코츠월드 언덕을 돌아다녔다.

14 오후에 비가 오기 시작해서, 우리는 B&B의 실내에서 머물기로 결정했다.

15 B&B는 영국에서 체류하는 곳으로 인기가 있다.

16 It _____ more _____ a home _____ a hotel.

17 The _____ _____ us for afternoon tea today.

18 The _____ table _____ _____ _____ cookies, cake, bread, and cheese.

19 While I was _____ _____, Mom was _____ the beautiful cups and _____.

20 I _____ too much, _____ I _____ _____ anything for dinner.

21 It is O.K. _____ _____ everyday objects _____ cups and plates in your _____.

22 Our _____ _____ was Oxford.

23 We _____ _____ Christ Church College.

24 It _____ _____ a world _____ _____ to visit _____ it appeared in the *Harry Potter* movies.

25 In the movies, Harry and _____ else _____ _____ at the Hall of Christ Church.

26 We also _____ _____ of famous people who _____ _____ the college.

27 _____ we were _____ the building, I _____ _____ the famous olive tree and _____ it.

28 "_____ I _____ this tree," I said, "I will _____ _____ Oxford University!"

29 Then, my brother said to me _____ _____ _____, "I _____ _____ _____ see your portrait on the wall."

30 _____ your own _____.

31 Your _____ _____ will become _____ _____ interesting.

16 그것은 호텔이라기보다는 집처럼 느껴진다.

17 주인은 오늘 오후의 다과회에 우리를 초대했다.

18 식탁에는 쿠키, 케이크, 빵, 그리고 치즈가 가득했다.

19 내가 먹느라고 바쁠 때, 엄마는 아름다운 컵과 접시를 감탄하며 바라보고 계셨다.

20 나는 너무 많이 먹어서 저녁으로 아무것도 먹을 수 없었다.

21 당신의 일기에 컵과 접시 같은 일상적인 물건들을 그려도 괜찮습니다.

22 우리가 마지막으로 머문 곳은 옥스퍼드였다.

23 우리는 먼저 Christ Church College를 방문했다.

24 이곳은 해리포터 영화에 등장한 이후 방문해야 할 세계적으로 유명한 장소가 되었다.

25 영화에서 Harry와 다른 모든 사람들이 Christ Church의 회관에서 저녁을 먹는다.

26 우리는 또한 그 대학을 졸업한 유명한 사람들의 초상화를 보았다.

27 우리가 건물 밖으로 나왔을 때, 나는 유명한 올리브 나무로 걸어가서 그것을 만졌다.

28 "이 나무를 만졌기 때문에, 난 옥스퍼드 대학교에 들어갈 거야!"라고 말했다.

29 그러자 오빠가 웃으면서 "벽에 걸린 네 초상화가 빨리 보고 싶어."라고 내게 말했다.

30 여러분 자신의 아바타를 만드세요.

31 그림일기가 훨씬 더 재미있을 거예요.

※ 다음 문장을 우리말로 쓰시오.

1 ▶ Hi, I am Lucy Hunter, and I live in London.

➡ _____

2 ▶ Last week, my family went on a vacation for three days.

➡ _____

3 ▶ During our trip, I made simple drawings in my journal.

➡ _____

4 ▶ That was a great way to capture all the special moments.

➡ _____

5 ▶ At last, we set foot at Stonehenge, one of the most mysterious places on Earth.

➡ _____

6 ▶ After a two-hour drive from our home in London, we finally got to Stonehenge.

➡ _____

7 ▶ It was just amazing to see the ring of huge stones.

➡ _____

8 ▶ How did those huge stones get there thousands of years ago?

➡ _____

9 ▶ What were they for?

➡ _____

10 ▶ Don't try to make a perfect drawing.

➡ _____

11 ▶ A few colors will be enough.

➡ _____

12 ▶ I guess Stonehenge will remain a mystery for a long time.

➡ _____

13 ▶ In the morning, we walked around the Cotswolds.

➡ _____

14 ▶ It started to rain in the afternoon, so we decided to stay indoors at our B&B.

➡ _____

15 ▶ A B&B is a popular place to stay in England.

➡ _____

16 It feels more like a home than a hotel.

➡ _____

17 The owner invited us for afternoon tea today.

➡ _____

18 The dining table was full of cookies, cake, bread, and cheese.

➡ _____

19 While I was busy eating, Mom was admiring the beautiful cups and plates.

➡ _____

20 I ate too much, so I couldn't eat anything for dinner.

➡ _____

21 It is O.K. to draw everyday objects like cups and plates in your journal.

➡ _____

22 Our last stop was Oxford.

➡ _____

23 We first visited Christ Church College.

➡ _____

24 It has become a world famous place to visit since it appeared in the *Harry Potter* movies.

➡ _____

25 In the movies, Harry and everyone else eat dinner at the Hall of Christ Church.

➡ _____

26 We also saw portraits of famous people who graduated from the college.

➡ _____

27 When we were outside the building, I walked to the famous olive tree and touched it.

➡ _____

28 "Because I touched this tree," I said, "I will get into Oxford University!"

➡ _____

29 Then, my brother said to me with a smile, "I can't wait to see your portrait on the wall."

➡ _____

30 Create your own avatar.

➡ _____

31 Your drawing journal will become much more interesting.

➡ _____

※ 다음 괄호 안의 단어들을 우리말에 맞도록 바르게 배열하시오.

1 (am / hi, / Hunter, / I / Lucy / and / London. / live / I / in)
➡ _____

2 (week, / last / went / family / my / a / on / days. / three / for / vacation)
➡ _____

3 (our / during / trip, / made / I / drawings / in / journal. / simple / my)
➡ _____

4 (was / a / that / great / way / capture / to / moments. / the / all / special)
➡ _____

5 (last, / at / foot / set / we / Stonehenge, / at / of / one / places / Earth. / most / the / on / mysterious)
➡ _____

6 (a / drive / after / two-hour / our / from / home / London, / in / we / Stonehenge. / to / finally / got)
➡ _____

7 (just / it / amazing / was / see / to / the / stones. / of / huge / ring)
➡ _____

8 (did / how / stones / huge / those / there / get / ago? / years / of / thousands)
➡ _____

9 (were / they / for? / what)
➡ _____

10 (try / don't / make / to / drawing. / perfect / a)
➡ _____

11 (few / a / colors / enough. / be / will)
➡ _____

12 (guess / I / Stonehenge / remain / will / a / time. / a / mystery / long / for)
➡ _____

13 (the / morning, / in / walked / the / we / Cotswolds. / around)
➡ _____

14 (to / started / rain / the / it / in / afternoon, / so / decided / we / to / at / indoors / B&B. / stay / our)
➡ _____

15 (a / is / B&B / place / popular / a / stay / England. / to / in)
➡ _____

1 안녕, 나는 Lucy Hunter이고 런던에 살아요.

2 지난주에 우리 가족은 3일 동안 휴가를 갔습니다.

3 여행 중에 나는 일기에 간단한 그림을 그렸어요.

4 그것은 모든 특별한 순간을 포착하는 훌륭한 방법이었어요.

5 마침내, 우리는 지구에서 가장 불가사의한 장소 중 하나인 스톤헨지에 발을 디뎠다.

6 런던에 있는 집에서 차로 두 시간을 달려서 우리는 마침내 스톤헨지에 도착했다.

7 원형으로 둘러서 있는 거대한 돌들을 보는 것은 정말 놀라웠다.

8 어떻게 그 거대한 돌들이 수천 년 전에 그곳에 도착했을까?

9 그것들은 무엇을 위한 것이었을까?

10 스톤헨지는 오랫동안 미스터리로 남을 것 같다.

11 완벽한 그림을 그리려고 하지 마세요.

12 몇 가지 색깔이면 충분할 것입니다.

13 아침에 우리는 코츠월드 언덕을 돌아다녔다.

14 오후에 비가 오기 시작해서, 우리는 B&B의 실내에서 머물기로 결정했다.

15 B&B는 영국에서 체류하는 곳으로 인기가 있다.

16 (feels / it / like / a / more / hotel. / than / home / a)
➡ _____

17 (owner / the / us / invited / today. / for / tea / afternoon)
➡ _____

18 (dining / the / table / of / was / full / cookies, / bread, / and / cheese. / cake,)
➡ _____

19 (was / eating, / while / I / busy / was / Mom / admiring / the / plates. / cups / and / beautiful)
➡ _____

20 (ate / much, / I / too / so / I / eat / anything / couldn't / dinner. / for)
➡ _____

21 (is / to / O.K. / it / draw / objects / eveyday / cups / like / in / and / journal. / your / plates)
➡ _____

22 (last / our / was / Oxford. / stop)
➡ _____

23 (first / we / visited / College. / Church / Christ)
➡ _____

24 (it / become / has / a / place / famous / world / visit / to / in / since / appeared / it / movies. / the / Potter / Harry)
➡ _____
_____

25 (the / in / movies, / and / everyone / Harry / eat / else / dinner / Church. / of / Hall / at / the / Christ)
➡ _____
_____

26 (also / saw / we / portraits / people / of / famous / who / college. / the / from / graduated)
➡ _____

27 (were / we / when / the / building, / the / outside / I / walked / tree / the / olive / to / famous / and / it. / touched)
➡ _____
_____

28 (I / tree," / touched / "because / this / I / said, / will / "I / into / University!" / get / Oxford)
➡ _____

29 (then, / brother / my / said / me / to / smile, / a / with / "I / wait / see / can't / to / on / wall." / the / portrait / your)
➡ _____
_____

30 (your / avatar. / own / create)
➡ _____

31 (drawing / your / journal / become / will / more / interesting. / much)
➡ _____

16 그것은 호텔이라기보다는 집처럼 느껴진다.

17 주인은 오늘 오후의 다과회에 우리를 초대했다.

18 식탁에는 쿠키, 케이크, 빵, 그리고 치즈가 가득했다.

19 내가 먹느라고 바쁠 때, 엄마는 아름다운 컵과 접시를 감탄하며 바라보고 계셨다.

20 나는 너무 많이 먹어서 저녁으로 아무것도 먹을 수 없었다.

21 당신의 일기에 컵과 접시 같은 일상적인 물건들을 그려도 괜찮습니다.

22 우리가 마지막으로 머문 곳은 옥스퍼드였다.

23 우리는 먼저 Christ Church College를 방문했다.

24 이곳은 해리포터 영화에 등장한 이후 방문해야 할 세계적으로 유명한 장소가 되었다.

25 영화에서 Harry와 다른 모든 사람들이 Christ Church의 회관에서 저녁을 먹는다.

26 우리는 또한 그 대학을 졸업한 유명한 사람들의 초상화를 보았다.

27 우리가 건물 밖으로 나왔을 때, 나는 유명한 올리브 나무로 걸어가서 그것을 만졌다.

28 "이 나무를 만졌기 때문에, 난 옥스퍼드 대학교에 들어갈 거야!"라고 말했다.

29 그러자 오빠가 웃으면서 "벽에 걸린 네 초상화가 빨리 보고 싶어."라고 내게 말했다.

30 여러분 자신의 아바타를 만드세요.

31 그림일기가 훨씬 더 재미있을 거예요.

※ 다음 우리말을 영어로 쓰시오.

1 안녕, 나는 Lucy Hunter이고 런던에 살아요.

➡ _____

2 지난주에 우리 가족은 3일 동안 휴가를 갔습니다.

➡ _____

3 여행 중에 나는 일기에 간단한 그림을 그렸어요.

➡ _____

4 그것은 모든 특별한 순간을 포착하는 훌륭한 방법이었어요.

➡ _____

5 마침내, 우리는 지구에서 가장 불가사의한 장소 중 하나인 스톤헨지에 발을 디뎠다.

➡ _____

6 런던에 있는 집에서 차로 두 시간을 달려서 우리는 마침내 스톤헨지에 도착했다.

➡ _____

7 원형으로 둘러서 있는 거대한 돌들을 보는 것은 정말 놀라웠다.

➡ _____

8 어떻게 그 거대한 돌들이 수천 년 전에 그곳에 도착했을까?

➡ _____

9 그것들은 무엇을 위한 것이었을까?

➡ _____

10 완벽한 그림을 그리려고 하지 마세요.

➡ _____

11 몇 가지 색깔이면 충분할 것입니다.

➡ _____

12 스톤헨지는 오랫동안 미스터리로 남을 것 같다.

➡ _____

13 아침에 우리는 코츠월드 언덕을 돌아다녔다.

➡ _____

14 오후에 비가 오기 시작해서, 우리는 B&B의 실내에서 머물기로 결정했다.

➡ _____

15 B&B는 영국에서 체류하는 곳으로 인기가 있다.

➡ _____

16 그것은 호텔이라기보다는 집처럼 느껴진다.

➡ _____

17 주인은 오늘 오후의 다과회에 우리를 초대했다.

➡ _____

18 식탁에는 쿠키, 케이크, 빵, 그리고 치즈가 가득했다.

➡ _____

19 내가 먹느라 바쁠 때, 엄마는 아름다운 컵과 접시를 감탄하며 바라보고 계셨다.

➡ _____

20 나는 너무 많이 먹어서 저녁으로 아무것도 먹을 수 없었다.

➡ _____

21 당신의 일기에 컵과 접시 같은 일상적인 물건들을 그려도 괜찮습니다.

➡ _____

22 우리가 마지막으로 머문 곳은 옥스퍼드였다.

➡ _____

23 우리는 먼저 Christ Church College를 방문했다.

➡ _____

24 이곳은 해리포터 영화에 등장한 이후 방문해야 할 세계적으로 유명한 장소가 되었다.

➡ _____

25 영화에서 Harry와 다른 모든 사람들이 Christ Church의 회관에서 저녁을 먹는다.

➡ _____

26 우리는 또한 그 대학을 졸업한 유명한 사람들의 초상화를 보았다.

➡ _____

27 우리가 건물 밖으로 나왔을 때, 나는 유명한 올리브 나무로 걸어가서 그것을 만졌다.

➡ _____

28 "이 나무를 만졌기 때문에, 난 옥스퍼드 대학교에 들어갈 거야!"라고 말했다.

➡ _____

29 그러자 오빠가 웃으면서 "벽에 걸린 네 초상화가 빨리 보고 싶어."라고 말했다.

➡ _____

30 여러분 자신의 아바타를 만드세요.

➡ _____

31 그림일기가 훨씬 더 재미있을 거예요.

➡ _____

※ 다음 우리말과 일치하도록 빈칸에 알맞은 말을 쓰시오.

Link - Share

1. We _____ _____ a field trip to Namhae _____ month.

2. _____ was just _____ to see so many beautiful _____.

3. We _____ _____ Namhae German _____.

4. We'll _____ _____ that trip.

1. 우리는 지난달에 남해로 현장 학습을 갔다.
2. 그토록 아름다운 많은 섬들을 보는 것은 아주 놀라웠다.
3. 우리는 남해 독일 마을도 방문했다.
4. 우리는 그 여행을 절대 잊지 못할 것이다.

Write

1. _____ _____, I _____ to Laos _____ my family.

2. We visited a _____ of beautiful _____ and went to the night _____ in Vientiane.

3. Then, we _____ _____ Vang Vieng and _____ river tubing.

4. We also _____ their _____ food.

5. It was a _____ _____ fun _____ _____ new things in a _____ country.

6. I hope I will have a _____ _____ _____ Laos again.

1. 지난 겨울, 나는 가족과 함께 라오스에 갔다.
2. 우리는 아름다운 절들을 많이 방문했고 Vientiane의 야시장에 갔다.
3. 그러고 나서, 우리는 Vang Vieng으로 옮겨서 강에 튜브를 타러 갔다.
4. 우리는 또한 그들의 전통 음식을 즐겼다.
5. 외국에서 새로운 것을 시도하는 것은 매우 재미있었다.
6. 나는 라오스를 다시 방문할 기회가 있기를 바란다.

Culture Project

1. _____ 15, 1835

2. We finally _____ _____ this island.

3. There _____ many animals _____ here.

4. Today, I _____ some _____ turtles.

5. It was _____ to _____ them.

1. 1835년 9월 15일
2. 우리는 마침내 이 섬에 도착했다.
3. 여기는 조사할 동물들이 많다.
4. 오늘, 나는 몇몇 이상한 거북들을 보았다.
5. 그들을 보는 것은 놀라웠다.

※ 다음 우리말을 영어로 쓰시오.

Link - Share

1. 우리는 지난달에 남해로 현장 학습을 갔다.
   ➡ _____

2. 그토록 아름다운 많은 섬들을 보는 것은 아주 놀라웠다.
   ➡ _____

3. 우리는 남해 독일 마을도 방문했다.
   ➡ _____

4. 우리는 그 여행을 절대 잊지 못할 것이다.
   ➡ _____

Write

1. 지난 겨울, 나는 가족과 함께 라오스에 갔다.
   ➡ _____

2. 우리는 아름다운 절들을 많이 방문했고 Vientiane의 야시장에 갔다.
   ➡ _____

3. 그리고 나서, 우리는 Vang Vieng으로 옮겨서 강에 튜브를 타러 갔다.
   ➡ _____

4. 우리는 또한 그들의 전통 음식을 즐겼다.
   ➡ _____

5. 외국에서 새로운 것을 시도하는 것은 매우 재미있었다.
   ➡ _____

6. 나는 라오스를 다시 방문할 기회가 있기를 바란다.
   ➡ _____

Culture Project

1. 1835년 9월 15일
   ➡ _____

2. 우리는 마침내 이 섬에 도착했다.
   ➡ _____

3. 여기는 조사할 동물들이 많다.
   ➡ _____

4. 오늘, 나는 몇몇 이상한 거북들을 보았다.
   ➡ _____

5. 그들을 보는 것은 놀라웠다.
   ➡ _____

※ 다음 영어를 우리말로 쓰시오.

01 inventor _____

02 pressure _____

03 activity _____

04 support _____

05 bath _____

06 shopping _____

07 childhood _____

08 purpose _____

09 trial _____

10 truly _____

11 driver _____

12 shock _____

13 project _____

14 favor _____

15 fix _____

16 gift _____

17 close _____

18 homeless _____

19 invention _____

20 joy _____

21 local _____

22 comfortable _____

23 perfect _____

24 still _____

25 board _____

26 person _____

27 plant _____

28 succeed _____

29 lucky _____

30 safety _____

31 always _____

32 sensor _____

33 condition _____

34 understand _____

35 give up _____

36 grow up _____

37 be thankful for _____

38 feel like -ing _____

39 for[with] joy _____

40 wander off _____

41 come up with _____

42 come over to _____

43 take care of _____

※ 다음 우리말을 영어로 쓰시오.

01	걱정하다	
02	믿다	
03	딸	
04	질병	
05	자랑스러워하는	
06	오류	
07	함께 쓰다, 공유하다	
08	깨끗한; 청소하다	
09	세대	
10	행복	
11	더 나쁜; 더 심하게	
12	기쁨, 즐거움	
13	그저, 단지	
14	(물건의) 재료	
15	발뒤꿈치	
16	신호	
17	이해하다	
18	거닐다, 돌아다니다	
19	목욕, 욕조	
20	존경하다; 존경	
21	실제로	

22	무거운	
23	신뢰할 수 있는	
24	상태	
25	~할 때까지	
26	자원 봉사자	
27	안전	
28	노숙자의	
29	성공하다	
30	지지하다	
31	편안한	
32	압력, 압박	
33	발명, 발명품	
34	기쁨, 환희	
35	~을 돌보다	
36	~에 오다	
37	~을 찾다	
38	A에게 B에 대해 감사하다	
39	(해답 등을) 찾아내다	
40	처음에는	
41	여기저기 쏘다니다	
42	~을 격려하다	
43	~을 계속 지켜보다	

※ 다음 영영풀이에 알맞은 단어를 <보기>에서 골라 쓴 후, 우리말 뜻을 쓰시오.

1 _____ : weighing a lot: _____

2 _____ : at all times: _____

3 _____ : a feeling of great happiness: _____

4 _____ : the back part of your foot, just below your ankle: _____

5 _____ : cause something to happen or exist: _____

6 _____ : the person who is driving a vehicle: _____

7 _____ : as good as something could possibly be: _____

8 _____ : to accept or regard something as true: _____

9 _____ : something that you give someone as a present: _____

10 _____ : force that you produce when you press hard on something: _____

11 _____ : the state of being safe from harm or danger: _____

12 _____ : the period of a person's life when they are a child: _____

13 _____ : a person who has invented something, or whose job is to invent things:

_____

14 _____ : making you feel physically relaxed when you use something: _____

15 _____ : to agree with someone, and perhaps help them because you want them to

succeed: _____

16 _____ : to keep thinking about problems that you have or about unpleasant

things that might happen _____

보기			
create	perfect	worry	inventor
heavy	joy	believe	heel
pressure	comfortable	gift	childhood
support	driver	safety	always

※ 다음 우리말과 일치하도록 빈칸에 알맞은 말을 쓰시오.

Listen & Speak 1 A. Listen and Check

1. **G:** Mark, can you _____ _____ _____ _____?

   B: Sure. _____ is it?

   G: My _____ is _____ _____ _____ for a week. Can

   you _____ to our house and _____ the plants?

   B: Yes, I _____.

2. **G:** Kevin, _____ you do me a _____?

   B: O.K. What is _____?

   G: Can you _____ _____ _____ my science _____ this

   afternoon?

   B: _____, but I _____. I _____ _____ _____ my

   grandma _____ my mom.

Listen & Speak 2 A. Listen and Check

1. **G:** _____, Mom! Hi, Dad! _____ _____ _____, today

   is my 15th _____. I _____ _____ a chance _____

   thank you for _____ my parents. You've truly _____ my

   friends _____ my teachers. Thank you _____ _____ me

   and always _____ to understand me. I'm really _____ to be

   your _____.

2. **G:** What _____ you _____ this _____, Eric?

   B: _____ _____. I'll just _____ home and _____ TV.

   G: Great! I'm _____ a birthday _____ this weekend. Can

   you come?

   B: Sure. Thank you _____ _____ me.

Listen & Speak 1-B

A: _____ you _____ me a _____?

B: Sure. _____ is it?

A: Can you _____ this table _____ me? It's too _____.

B: Sure. _____ _____.

A: _____ you _____ _____ me.

해석

1. G: Mark, 부탁 하나 들어줄래?
   B: 물론이지. 부탁할게 무엇이지?
   G: 우리 가족은 일주일 동안 휴가를 갈 거야. 우리 집에 와서 식물들에게 물을 줄 수 있니?
   B: 응, 할 수 있어.

2. G: Kevin, 부탁 하나 들어줄래?
   B: 좋아. 뭔데?
   G: 오늘 오후에 내 과학 프로젝트 좀 도와줄래?
   B: 미안하지만 안 돼. 엄마랑 할머니 댁에 가야 해.

1. G: 안녕, 엄마! 안녕, 아빠! 엄마, 아빠도 아시다시피, 오늘은 제 15번째 생일이에요. 제 부모님이 되어주신 것에 대해 감사할 기회가 없었어요. 두 분께서는 정말 제 친구이자 선생님이셨어요. 저를 지지해 주시고 항상 저를 이해하려고 노력해 주셔서 감사해요. 저는 두 분의 딸이 되어서 정말 자랑스러워요.

2. G: Eric, 이번 주말에 뭐 할 거니?
   B: 특별한 건 없어. 그냥 집에 있으면서 TV를 볼 거야.
   G: 좋아! 이번 주말에 생일 파티를 할 거야. 올 수 있니?
   B: 물론이지. 초대해 줘서 고마워.

A: 부탁 하나 들어줄래?
B: 그래. 뭔데?
A: 이 테이블 좀 옮겨줄래? 너무 무거워.
B: 물론이지. 문제없어.
A: 도와줘서 고마워.

Communicate A. Listen and Answer

Jaden: _____ you _____ _____ _____ _____, Yuri?

Yuri: Sure. _____ is it, Jaden?

Jaden: Can we _____ _____ together _____ a baseball cap for a girl?

Yuri: Yes, _____ _____. _____ is it _____?

Jaden: It's _____ _____ _____ _____ Kate.

Yuri: Oh, are you _____ her _____ _____ _____?

Jaden: No, her birthday _____ _____ _____.

Yuri: Then, _____ _____ you _____ a baseball _____ for her?

Jaden: She _____ her leg _____ _____ _____ _____ her bike _____ week. I _____ want to _____ _____ _____.

Yuri: Oh, I _____. I _____ _____ this Friday afternoon.

Jaden: That _____ _____. Thank you.

Progress Check

1. **G:** Andrew, _____ _____ _____ _____ me a _____?

   B: O.K. _____ is _____?

   G: My family is _____ _____ _____ to Jejudo _____ _____. Can you _____ _____ _____ my cat _____ the weekend?

   B: Sure. Don't _____ about her. And _____ your trip.

2. **G:** _____, Mr. Smith. We _____ had _____ _____ _____ you _____ _____ our teacher. _____ morning, you _____ us in the classroom. You _____ _____ us important and interesting _____. We're _____ _____ _____ you, and we're _____ _____ _____ your _____.

3. **G:** Do you have _____ _____ _____ this weekend?

   B: No, I'm _____ _____ _____ _____ home.

   G: Oh, _____ can you _____ _____ to my house _____ _____?

Jaden: 유리야, 부탁 하나 들어줄래?
유리: 물론이지. 뭐야, Jaden?
Jaden: 우리 같이 여자용 야구 모자 사러 쇼핑갈 수 있을까?
유리: 응, 물론이지. 누구 주려고?
Jaden: 내 여동생 Kate에게 줄 거야.
유리: 아, 너 그 애에게 생일 선물을 사 주려고 하는 거야?
Jaden: 아니, 그 애의 생일은 10월이 되어야 해.
유리: 그렇다면, 왜 야구 모자를 사 주려고 하는 거야?
Jaden: 그 애는 지난주에 자전거를 타다가 다리가 부러졌어. 난 그저 그 애를 격려하고 싶어
유리: 아, 그렇구나. 이번 주 금요일 오후에 갈 수 있어.
Jaden: 그거 아주 좋아. 고마워.

1. G: Andrew, 부탁 하나 들어줄래?
   B: 좋아. 뭔데?
   G: 우리 가족은 이번 주말에 제주도에 갈 거야. 주말에 내 고양이 좀 봐줄래?
   B: 물론이지. 고양이 걱정은 하지 말고, 여행을 즐겨.

2. G: 안녕하세요, Smith 선생님. 우리의 선생님이 되어주신 것에 대해 감사할 기회가 없었습니다. 매일 아침, 선생님은 교실에서 우리를 맞이하십니다. 선생님은 항상 우리에게 중요하고 흥미로운 것들을 가르쳐주십니다. 우리는 선생님이 계셔서 행운이고, 선생님의 학생이라는 것이 자랑스럽습니다.

3. G: 이번 주말에 무슨 특별한 계획 있니?
   B: 아니, 그냥 집에 있을 거야.
   G: 아, 그럼 우리 집에 저녁 먹으러 올 수 있어?

대화문 Test **25**

※ 다음 우리말에 맞도록 대화를 영어로 쓰시오.

Listen & Speak 1 A. Listen and Check

1. G: _____

   B: _____

   G: _____

   _____

   B: _____

2. G: _____

   B: _____

   G: _____

   B: _____

Listen & Speak 2 A. Listen and Check

1. G: _____

   _____

   _____

   _____

2. G: _____

   B: _____

   G: _____

   B: _____

Listen & Speak 1-B

A: _____

B: _____

A: _____

B: _____

A: _____

해석

1. G: Mark, 부탁 하나 들어줄래?
   B: 물론이지. 부탁할게 무엇이지?
   G: 우리 가족은 일주일 동안 휴가를 갈 거야. 우리 집에 와서 식물들에게 물을 줄 수 있니?
   B: 응, 할 수 있어.

2. G: Kevin, 부탁 하나 들어줄래?
   B: 좋아. 뭔데?
   G: 오늘 오후에 내 과학 프로젝트 좀 도와줄래?
   B: 미안하지만 안 돼. 엄마랑 할머니 댁에 가야 해.

1. G: 안녕, 엄마! 안녕, 아빠! 엄마, 아빠도 아시다시피, 오늘은 제 15번째 생일이에요. 제 부모님이 되어주신 것에 대해 감사할 기회가 없었어요. 두 분께서는 정말 제 친구이자 선생님이셨어요. 저를 지지해 주시고 항상 저를 이해하려고 노력해 주셔서 감사해요. 저는 두 분의 딸이 되어서 정말 자랑스러워요.

2. G: Eric, 이번 주말에 뭐 할 거니?
   B: 특별한 건 없어. 그냥 집에 있으면서 TV를 볼 거야.
   G: 좋아! 이번 주말에 생일 파티를 할 거야. 올 수 있니?
   B: 물론이지. 초대해 줘서 고마워.

A: 부탁 하나 들어줄래?
B: 그래. 뭔데?
A: 이 테이블 좀 옮겨줄래? 너무 무거워.
B: 물론이지. 문제없어.
A: 도와줘서 고마워.

Communicate A. Listen and Answer

Jaden: _____

Yuri: _____

Jaden: _____

Yuri: _____

Jaden: _____

Yuri: _____

Jaden: _____

Yuri: _____

Jaden: _____

_____

Yuri: _____

Jaden: _____

Jaden: 유리야, 부탁 하나 들어줄래?

유리: 물론이지. 뭐야, Jaden?

Jaden: 우리 같이 여자용 야구 모자 사러 쇼핑갈 수 있을까?

유리: 응, 물론이지. 누구 주려고?

Jaden: 내 여동생 Kate에게 줄 거야.

유리: 아, 너 그 애에게 생일 선물을 사주려고 하는 거야?

Jaden: 아니, 그 애의 생일은 10월이 되어야 해.

유리: 그렇다면, 왜 야구 모자를 사 주려고 하는 거야?

Jaden: 그 애는 지난주에 자전거를 타다가 다리가 부러졌어. 난 그저 그 애를 격려하고 싶어

유리: 아, 그렇구나. 이번 주 금요일 오후에 갈 수 있어.

Jaden: 그거 아주 좋아. 고마워.

Progress Check

1. G: _____

B: _____

G: _____

_____

B: _____

2. G: _____

_____

_____

3. G: _____

B: _____

G: _____

1. G: Andrew, 부탁 하나 들어줄래?
   B: 좋아. 뭔데?
   G: 우리 가족은 이번 주말에 제주도에 갈 거야. 주말에 내 고양이 좀 봐줄래?
   B: 물론이지. 고양이 걱정은 하지 말고, 여행을 즐겨.

2. G: 안녕하세요, Smith 선생님. 우리의 선생님이 되어주신 것에 대해 감사할 기회가 없었습니다. 매일 아침, 선생님은 교실에서 우리를 맞이하십니다. 선생님은 항상 우리에게 중요하고 흥미로운 것들을 가르쳐주십니다. 우리는 선생님이 계셔서 행운이고, 선생님의 학생이라는 것이 자랑스럽습니다.

3. G: 이번 주말에 무슨 특별한 계획 있니?
   B: 아니, 그냥 집에 있을 거야.
   G: 아, 그럼 우리 집에 저녁 먹으러 올 수 있어?

※ 다음 우리말과 일치하도록 빈칸에 알맞은 것을 골라 쓰시오.

1 Kenneth Shinozuka grew _____ in a big happy _____ of three _____.

A. generations B. family C. up

2 Since he was _____, he has always _____ very _____ to his grandfather.

A. close B. been C. little

3 He was Kenneth's _____ friend, his _____ driver, and his _____.

A. cook B. first C. trusty

4 He also _____ him many life _____.

A. lessons B. taught

5 He was the _____ who Kenneth _____ the _____ in the world.

A. most B. respected C. person

6 When Kenneth was four, his grandfather _____ out _____ a walk one day and _____ lost.

A. got B. for C. went

7 He _____ Alzheimer's _____.

A. disease B. had

8 _____ in Kenneth's family _____ in _____.

A. was B. everyone C. shock

9 His condition _____ worse _____ the next 10 years.

A. became B. over

10 He _____ _____ at night so often that someone had to _____ an eye on him _____ night long.

A. keep B. off C. all D. wandered

11 _____ night, Kenneth's grandfather _____ out of bed, and Kenneth _____ it.

A. saw B. got C. one

12 At that _____, he said to _____, "Why _____ I put pressure sensors on the _____ of his socks?"

A. heels B. himself C. don't D. moment

1 Kenneth Shinozuka는 3대의 행복한 대가족에서 자랐다.

2 그는 어렸을 때부터 항상 할아버지와 매우 친했다.

3 그는 Kenneth의 첫 친구이자, 신뢰할 수 있는 운전기사이자, 요리사였다.

4 그는 또한 그에게 많은 인생 교훈을 가르쳐 주었다.

5 그는 Kenneth가 세상에서 가장 존경하는 사람이었다.

6 Kenneth가 네 살이었을 때, 그의 할아버지는 어느 날 산책을 나갔다가 길을 잃었다.

7 그는 알츠하이머병에 걸렸다.

8 Kenneth의 가족 모두는 충격에 빠졌다.

9 그의 상태는 10년 동안 더 악화되었다.

10 그는 자주 밤에 여기저기 돌아다니기 때문에 누군가가 그를 밤새 감시해야 했다.

11 어느 날 밤, Kenneth의 할아버지가 침대에서 일어났는데, Kenneth가 그것을 보았다.

12 그 순간, 그는 혼잣말을 했다. "내가 할아버지의 양말 뒤꿈치에 압력 감지기를 설치하는 게 어떨까?"

13 There _____ many things _____ Kenneth had to _____.

A. do   B. that   C. were

14 He first had to create a pressure _____ and then find a _____ to send a _____ to his smart phone.

A. signal   B. sensor   C. way

15 Kenneth also _____ many different _____ to make _____ socks for his _____ grandfather.

A. comfortable   B. tried   C. elderly   D. materials

16 When he felt _____ giving _____, he thought about his grandfather's _____.

A. safety   B. up   C. like

17 After much _____ and _____, he finally _____ in making his device.

A. succeeded   B. error   C. trial

18 When it first _____, he was _____ happy _____ he jumped for joy.

A. that   B. so   C. worked

19 He could not _____ that his _____ actually _____.

A. worked   B. invention   C. believe

20 _____ his grandfather, Kenneth is the best _____ in the _____.

A. world   B. for   C. inventor

21 For Kenneth, _____ grandfather is _____ his _____ friend.

A. best   B. his   C. still

13 Kenneth가 해야 할 많은 일들이 있었다.

14 그는 처음에 압력 감지기를 만들고 나서 그의 스마트폰으로 신호를 보낼 방법을 찾아야 했다.

15 Kenneth는 또한 그의 연로한 할아버지에게 편안한 양말을 만들어 주기 위해 많은 다양한 재료들을 가지고 만들어 보았다.

16 그는 포기하고 싶은 생각이 들 때 할아버지의 안전에 대해 생각했다.

17 많은 시행착오 끝에 그는 마침내 자신의 장치를 만드는 데 성공했다.

18 그것이 처음 작동했을 때, 그는 너무 행복해 기뻐서 펄쩍 뛰었다.

19 그는 자신의 발명품이 실제로 작동했다는 것을 믿을 수 없었다.

20 그의 할아버지에게 Kenneth는 세계 최고의 발명가이다.

21 Kenneth에게 그의 할아버지는 여전히 그의 가장 친한 친구이다.

※ 다음 우리말과 일치하도록 빈칸에 알맞은 말을 쓰시오.

1 Kenneth Shinozuka _____ _____ in a big happy _____ of _____ _____ .

2 _____ he _____ _____ , he has always _____ very _____ _____ his grandfather.

3 He was Kenneth's _____ _____ , his _____ _____ , and his _____ .

4 He _____ _____ him many _____ _____ .

5 He was the person _____ Kenneth _____ _____ _____ in the world.

6 _____ Kenneth was four, his grandfather _____ _____ _____ _____ one day and _____ _____ .

7 He _____ Alzheimer's _____ .

8 _____ in Kenneth's family _____ _____ _____ .

9 His condition _____ _____ _____ the next 10 years.

10 He _____ _____ at night _____ often _____ someone had to _____ _____ _____ on him _____ night long.

11 One night, Kenneth's grandfather _____ _____ _____ bed, and Kenneth _____ it.

12 At that _____ , he _____ _____ _____ , "Why _____ I put pressure sensors on the _____ of his socks?"

1 Kenneth Shinozuka는 3대의 행복한 대가족에서 자랐다.

2 그는 어렸을 때부터 항상 할아버지와 매우 친했다.

3 그는 Kenneth의 첫 친구이자, 신뢰할 수 있는 운전기사이자, 요리사였다.

4 그는 또한 그에게 많은 인생 교훈을 가르쳐 주었다.

5 그는 Kenneth가 세상에서 가장 존경하는 사람이었다.

6 Kenneth가 네 살이었을 때, 그의 할아버지는 어느 날 산책을 나갔다가 길을 잃었다.

7 그는 알츠하이머병에 걸렸다.

8 Kenneth의 가족 모두는 충격에 빠졌다.

9 그의 상태는 10년 동안 더 악화되었다.

10 그는 자주 밤에 여기저기 돌아다니기 때문에 누군가가 그를 밤새 감시해야 했다.

11 어느 날 밤, Kenneth의 할아버지가 침대에서 일어났는데, Kenneth가 그것을 보았다.

12 그 순간, 그는 혼잣말을 했다. "내가 할아버지의 양말 뒤꿈치에 압력 감지기를 설치하는 게 어떨까?"

13 There _____ many things _____ Kenneth _____

_____ _____ .

14 He first _____ _____ _____ a pressure sensor and

_____ find _____ _____ _____ _____ a _____

to his smart phone.

15 Kenneth also _____ many different _____ to make

comfortable _____ for his elderly grandfather.

16 When he _____ _____ _____ _____ , he thought about

his grandfather's _____ .

17 _____ much _____ and _____ , he finally _____

_____ _____ his device.

18 When it first _____ , he was so happy _____ he _____

_____ _____ .

19 He _____ _____ _____ that his invention _____ _____ .

20 _____ his grandfather, Kenneth is _____ _____ _____

in the world.

21 For Kenneth, his grandfather _____ _____ his _____

_____ .

13 Kenneth가 해야 할 많은 일들이 있었다.

14 그는 처음에 압력 감지기를 만들고 나서 그의 스마트폰으로 신호를 보낼 방법을 찾아야 했다.

15 Kenneth는 또한 그의 연로한 할아버지에게 편안한 양말을 만들어 주기 위해 많은 다양한 재료들을 가지고 만들어 보았다.

16 그는 포기하고 싶은 생각이 들 때 할아버지의 안전에 대해 생각했다.

17 많은 시행착오 끝에 그는 마침내 자신의 장치를 만드는 데 성공했다.

18 그것이 처음 작동했을 때, 그는 너무 행복해 기뻐서 펄쩍 뛰었다.

19 그는 자신의 발명품이 실제로 작동했다는 것을 믿을 수 없었다.

20 그의 할아버지에게 Kenneth는 세계 최고의 발명가이다.

21 Kenneth에게 그의 할아버지는 여전히 그의 가장 친한 친구이다.

※ 다음 문장을 우리말로 쓰시오.

1 ▶ Kenneth Shinozuka grew up in a big happy family of three generations.

➡ _____

2 ▶ Since he was little, he has always been very close to his grandfather.

➡ _____

3 ▶ He was Kenneth's first friend, his trusty driver, and his cook.

➡ _____

4 ▶ He also taught him many life lessons.

➡ _____

5 ▶ He was the person who Kenneth respected the most in the world.

➡ _____

6 ▶ When Kenneth was four, his grandfather went out for a walk one day and got lost.

➡ _____

7 ▶ He had Alzheimer's disease.

➡ _____

8 ▶ Everyone in Kenneth's family was in shock.

➡ _____

9 ▶ His condition became worse over the next 10 years.

➡ _____

10 ▶ He wandered off at night so often that someone had to keep an eye on him all night long.

➡ _____

11 ▶ One night, Kenneth's grandfather got out of bed, and Kenneth saw it.

➡ _____

12 ▶ At that moment, he said to himself, "Why don't I put pressure sensors on the heels of his socks?"

➡ _____

13 There were many things that Kenneth had to do.

➡ _____

14 He first had to create a pressure sensor and then find a way to send a signal to his smart phone.

➡ _____

15 Kenneth also tried many different materials to make comfortable socks for his elderly grandfather.

➡ _____

16 When he felt like giving up, he thought about his grandfather's safety.

➡ _____

17 After much trial and error, he finally succeeded in making his device.

➡ _____

18 When it first worked, he was so happy that he jumped for joy.

➡ _____

19 He could not believe that his invention actually worked.

➡ _____

20 For his grandfather, Kenneth is the best inventor in the world.

➡ _____

21 For Kenneth, his grandfather is still his best friend.

➡ _____

※ 다음 괄호 안의 단어들을 우리말에 맞도록 바르게 배열하시오.

1 (Shinozuka / Kenneth / up / grew / in / happy / a / family / big / generations. / three / of)

➡ _____

2 (he / little, / since / was / has / he / been / always / to / grandfather. / close / very / his)

➡ _____

3 (was / he / friend, / Kenneth's / first / his / driver, / and / trusty / cook. / his)

➡ _____

4 (also / he / taught / many / him / lessons. / life)

➡ _____

5 (was / the / he / person / Kenneth / who / the / respected / in / world. / the / most)

➡ _____

6 (Kenneth / when / four, / was / grandfather / his / for / went / out / one / a / day / walk / lost. / and / got)

➡ _____
_____

7 (had / disease. / he / Alzheimer's)

➡ _____

8 (Kenneth's / in / family / everyone / shock. / in / was)

➡ _____

9 (condition / his / worse / became / the / years. / over / 10 / next)

➡ _____

10 (wondered / he / off / night / at / often / that / so / someone / to / had / keep / night / an / long. / all / eye / him / on)

➡ _____
_____

11 (night, / one / grandfather / Kenneth's / out / bed, / got / of / and / it. / saw / Kenneth)

➡ _____

12 (moment, / that / at / he / to / said / himself, / "why / put / I / don't / sensors / pressure / socks?" / of / on / heels / the / his)

➡ _____
_____

1 Kenneth Shinozuka는 3대의 행복한 대가족에서 자랐다.

2 그는 어렸을 때부터 항상 할아버지와 매우 친했다.

3 그는 Kenneth의 첫 친구이자, 신뢰할 수 있는 운전기사이자, 요리사였다.

4 그는 또한 그에게 많은 인생 교훈을 가르쳐 주었다.

5 그는 Kenneth가 세상에서 가장 존경하는 사람이었다.

6 Kenneth가 네 살이었을 때, 그의 할아버지는 어느 날 산책을 나갔다가 길을 잃었다.

7 그는 알츠하이머병에 걸렸다.

8 Kenneth의 가족 모두는 충격에 빠졌다.

9 그의 상태는 10년 동안 더 악화되었다.

10 그는 자주 밤에 여기저기 돌아다니기 때문에 누군가가 그를 밤새 감시해야 했다.

11 어느 날 밤, Kenneth의 할아버지가 침대에서 일어났는데, Kenneth가 그것을 보았다.

12 그 순간, 그는 혼잣말을 했다. "내가 할아버지의 양말 뒤꿈치에 압력 감지기를 설치하는 게 어떨까?"

13 (were / things / there / many / that / do. / Kenneth / to / had)

➡ _____

14 (first / he / to / had / create / sensor / pressure / a / and / then / a / find / way / send / to / his / signal / to / a / phone. / smart)

➡ _____
_____

15 (also / Kenneth / many / tried / materials / different / socks / to / comfortable / make / grandfather. / his / for / elderly)

➡ _____
_____

16 (he / like / when / up, / felt / giving / he / about / thought / safety. / grandfather's / his)

➡ _____

17 (error, / much / and / after / trial / he / succeeded / finally / device. / his / making / in)

➡ _____

18 (first / it / worked, / when / he / so / was / happy / that / joy. / he / for / jumped)

➡ _____

19 (could / he / believe / not / that / worked. / his / invention / actually)

➡ _____

20 (his / for / grandfather, / is / Kenneth / inventor / best / the / world. / the / in)

➡ _____

21 (Kenneth, / for / grandfather / his / still / his / is / friend. / best)

➡ _____

13 Kenneth가 해야 할 많은 일들이 있었다.

14 그는 처음에 압력 감지기를 만들고 나서 그의 스마트폰으로 신호를 보낼 방법을 찾아야 했다.

15 Kenneth는 또한 그의 연로한 할아버지에게 편안한 양말을 만들어 주기 위해 많은 다양한 재료들을 가지고 만들어 보았다.

16 그는 포기하고 싶은 생각이 들때 할아버지의 안전에 대해 생각했다.

17 많은 시행착오 끝에 그는 마침내 자신의 장치를 만드는 데 성공했다.

18 그것이 처음 작동했을 때. 그는 너무 행복해 기뻐서 펄쩍 뛰었다.

19 그는 자신의 발명품이 실제로 작동했다는 것을 믿을 수 없었다.

20 그의 할아버지에게 Kenneth는 세계 최고의 발명가이다.

21 Kenneth에게 그의 할아버지는 여전히 그의 가장 친한 친구이다.

※ 다음 우리말을 영어로 쓰시오.

1 Kenneth Shinozuka는 3대의 행복한 대가족에서 자랐다.

➡ _____

2 그는 어렸을 때부터 항상 할아버지와 매우 친했다.

➡ _____

3 그는 Kenneth의 첫 친구이자, 신뢰할 수 있는 운전기사이자, 요리사였다.

➡ _____

4 그는 또한 그에게 많은 인생 교훈을 가르쳐 주었다.

➡ _____

5 그는 Kenneth가 세상에서 가장 존경하는 사람이었다.

➡ _____

6 Kenneth가 네 살이었을 때, 그의 할아버지는 어느 날 산책을 나갔다가 길을 잃었다.

➡ _____

7 그는 알츠하이머병에 걸렸다.

➡ _____

8 Kenneth의 가족 모두는 충격에 빠졌다.

➡ _____

9 그의 상태는 10년 동안 더 악화되었다.

➡ _____

10 그는 자주 밤에 여기저기 돌아다니기 때문에 누군가가 그를 밤새 감시해야 했다.

➡ _____

11 어느 날 밤, Kenneth의 할아버지가 침대에서 일어났는데, Kenneth가 그것을 보았다.

➡ _____

12 그 순간, 그는 혼잣말을 했다. "내가 할아버지의 양말 뒤꿈치에 압력 감지기를 설치하는 게 어떨까?"

➡ _____

13 Kenneth가 해야 할 많은 일들이 있었다.

➡ _____

14 그는 처음에 압력 감지기를 만들고 나서 그의 스마트폰으로 신호를 보낼 방법을 찾아야 했다.

➡ _____

15 Kenneth는 또한 그의 연로한 할아버지에게 편안한 양말을 만들어 주기 위해 많은 다양한 재료들을 가지고 만들어 보았다.

➡ _____

16 그는 포기하고 싶은 생각이 들 때 할아버지의 안전에 대해 생각했다.

➡ _____

17 많은 시행착오 끝에 그는 마침내 자신의 장치를 만드는 데 성공했다.

➡ _____

18 그것이 처음 작동했을 때, 그는 너무 행복해 기뻐서 펄쩍 뛰었다.

➡ _____

19 그는 자신의 발명품이 실제로 작동했다는 것을 믿을 수 없었다.

➡ _____

20 그의 할아버지에게 Kenneth는 세계 최고의 발명가이다.

➡ _____

21 Kenneth에게 그의 할아버지는 여전히 그의 가장 친한 친구이다.

➡ _____

※ 다음 우리말과 일치하도록 빈칸에 알맞은 말을 쓰시오.

Link - Share

1. I'd like to talk about the _____ _____ that we're _____ to do for the _____ people in our city.

2. We _____ _____ _____ three activities.

3. _____ _____ them is to make *patbingsu* _____ them and eat it together.

1. 나는 우리가 우리 도시의 노인들을 위해 계획하고 있는 자원봉사에 대해 이야기하고 싶다.
2. 우리는 세 가지 활동을 생각해 냈다.
3. 그 중 하나는 그들을 위해 팥빙수를 만들어 함께 먹는 것이다.

Write - Write

1. Hello, I am Kim Doha, and I _____ _____ to join your _____ project.

2. _____ day, I saw some poor dogs _____ TV.

3. They looked _____ sad _____ I wanted _____ _____ them.

4. I like dogs, and _____ _____ many things _____ I can do for them.

5. I can _____ the dogs, give them a _____, and play _____ them.

6. I am the person _____ you are _____ _____!

1. 안녕, 나는 김도하야, 그리고 나는 너의 자원봉사 프로젝트에 참가하고 싶어.
2. 어느 날, 나는 TV에서 몇 마리의 불쌍한 개들을 보았어.
3. 그들은 너무 슬퍼 보여서 나는 그들을 돕고 싶었어.
4. 나는 개를 좋아하고, 그들을 위해 내가 할 수 있는 많은 것들이 있어.
5. 나는 개들을 산책시키고, 목욕시키고 그들과 함께 놀 수 있어.
6. 네가 찾는 사람이 바로 나야!

Culture Project

1. Do you want _____ _____ children?

2. _____ our Child _____ Project in Laos.

3. You'll teach _____ children.

4. You'll also _____ a school _____ them.

5. The work is _____ hard _____ you'll want to go home _____ first, but you'll find _____ in _____ these children.

1. 여러분은 아이들을 돕고 싶나요?
2. 라오스에 있는 우리의 아동 보호 프로젝트에 참여하십시오.
3. 여러분은 지역 아이들을 가르칠 겁니다.
4. 여러분은 또한 그들을 위해 학교를 지을 겁니다.
5. 일이 너무 힘들어 처음에는 집에 가고 싶지만, 이 아이들을 돕는 데서 행복을 찾을 수 있을 겁니다.

※ 다음 우리말을 영어로 쓰시오.

Link - Share

1. 나는 우리가 우리 도시의 노인들을 위해 계획하고 있는 자원봉사에 대해 이야기하고 싶다.

   ➡ _____

2. 우리는 세 가지 활동을 생각해 냈다.

   ➡ _____

3. 그 중 하나는 그들을 위해 팥빙수를 만들어 함께 먹는 것이다.

   ➡ _____

Write - Write

1. 안녕, 나는 김도하야, 그리고 나는 너의 자원봉사 프로젝트에 참가하고 싶어.

   ➡ _____

2. 어느 날, 나는 TV에서 몇 마리의 불쌍한 개들을 보았어.

   ➡ _____

3. 그들은 너무 슬퍼 보여서 나는 그들을 돕고 싶었어.

   ➡ _____

4. 나는 개를 좋아하고, 그들을 위해 내가 할 수 있는 많은 것들이 있어.

   ➡ _____

5. 나는 개들을 산책시키고, 목욕시키고 그들과 함께 놀 수 있어.

   ➡ _____

6. 네가 찾는 사람이 바로 나야!

   ➡ _____

Culture Project

1. 여러분은 아이들을 돕고 싶나요?

   ➡ _____

2. 라오스에 있는 우리의 아동 보호 프로젝트에 참여하십시오.

   ➡ _____

3. 여러분은 지역 아이들을 가르칠 겁니다.

   ➡ _____

4. 여러분은 또한 그들을 위해 학교를 지을 겁니다.

   ➡ _____

5. 일이 너무 힘들어 처음에는 집에 가고 싶지만, 이 아이들을 돕는 데서 행복을 찾을 수 있을 겁니다.

   ➡ _____

   _____

※ 다음 영어를 우리말로 쓰시오.

01	practice	
02	subway	
03	appreciate	
04	brave	
05	century	
06	actually	
07	marry	
08	dawn	
09	perform	
10	fail	
11	storyline	
12	riddle	
13	princess	
14	celebrate	
15	already	
16	performance	
17	secret	
18	correctly	
19	suggestion	
20	famous	
21	guess	

22	incorrectly	
23	stranger	
24	discount	
25	difficult	
26	mean	
27	amazing	
28	ostrich	
29	add	
30	anniversary	
31	right	
32	safe	
33	theater	
34	whole	
35	hurry up	
36	be late for ~	
37	Why don't you+동사원형 ~?	
38	would like to+동사원형	
39	as+형용사+as ~	
40	fall in love with ~	
41	nothing more than ~	
42	in time	
43	find out	

※ 다음 우리말을 영어로 쓰시오.

01 비밀 _____

02 추측하다 _____

03 세기 _____

04 정확하지 않게 _____

05 실은, 사실은 _____

06 공주 _____

07 용감한 _____

08 타조 _____

09 할인 _____

10 감상하다, 감사하다 _____

11 낯선 사람, 이방인 _____

12 정확하게, 바르게 _____

13 동의하다 _____

14 연극, 극, 희곡 _____

15 줄거리 _____

16 이미, 벌써 _____

17 기념일 _____

18 ~와 결혼하다 _____

19 공연하다, 수행하다 _____

20 실패하다 _____

21 전체, 모든, 전부의 _____

22 지하철 _____

23 (말을) 덧붙이다, 더하다 _____

24 기념하다 _____

25 유명한 _____

26 안전한 _____

27 공연 _____

28 제안 _____

29 연습하다 _____

30 감동적인 _____

31 어려운 _____

32 놀라운 _____

33 수수께끼 _____

34 아름다움, 미 _____

35 ~에 늦다, 지각하다 _____

36 제시간에, 늦지 않게 _____

37 알아내다, 발견하다 _____

38 서두르다 _____

39 ~와 사랑에 빠지다 _____

40 (일을) 쉬다 _____

41 어느 날 _____

42 첫눈에 _____

43 ~하고 싶다 _____

※ 다음 영영풀이에 알맞은 단어를 <보기>에서 골라 쓴 후, 우리말 뜻을 쓰시오.

1 _____ : a period of 100 years: _____

2 _____ : earlier than the time expected: _____

3 _____ : to do an action or piece of work: _____

4 _____ : very surprising: _____

5 _____ : the series of events that happen in a book, film, play, etc.: _____

6 _____ : a piece of music in an opera sung by one person: _____

7 _____ : showing no fear of dangerous or difficult things: _____

8 _____ : a reduction in the normal price: _____

9 _____ : to understand how good something or someone is: _____

10 _____ : to do something enjoyable on a special occasion: _____

11 _____ : causing strong feelings of sadness or sympathy: _____

12 _____ : to give an answer to a particular question when you do not have all the facts and so cannot be certain if you are correct: _____

13 _____ : a piece of information that is only known by one person or a few people and should not be told to others: _____

14 _____ : to become the legally accepted husband or wife of someone in an official or religious ceremony: _____

15 _____ : a day on which you remember or celebrate something that happened on that day in the past: _____

16 _____ : a type of question that describes something in a difficult and confusing way and has a clever or funny answer: _____

보기			
marry	celebrate	secret	moving
amazing	discount	century	aria
guess	anniversary	appreciate	perform
riddle	storyline	already	brave

※ 다음 우리말과 일치하도록 빈칸에 알맞은 말을 쓰시오.

해석

Listen & Speak 1-A

1. **M:** Liz, _____ _____. It's _____ 6 o'clock.

   W: Oh, we're _____ _____ _____ _____ _____ _____ the concert.

   M: _____ _____ _____ _____ the subway? The subway will be _____ _____ the bus at this time of day.

   W: That's a _____ _____.

2. **B:** Mom, I _____ _____ one question _____ on the Korean history exam!

   W: Great! I was _____ you would do _____. _____ _____ _____ _____ _____ _____ _____ tonight?

   B: Yes! Can we _____ _____ _____ dinner?

   W: _____ _____, Joe. I'll call your dad.

1. M: Liz, 서둘러. 벌써 여섯 시야.
   W: 이런, 우린 콘서트에 늦을 거야.
   M: 지하철을 타는 게 어때? 지하철은 지금 이 시간에 버스보다 빠를 거야.
   W: 좋은 생각이야.

2. B: 엄마, 제가 한국사 시험에서 겨우 한 문제만 틀렸어요!
   W: 대단해! 네가 잘할 거라고 확신했단다. 오늘 축하하러 나가는 건 어때?
   B: 좋아요! 저녁으로 피자를 먹어도 되나요?
   W: 물론이지, Joe. 아빠에게 전화하마.

Listen & Speak 1-B

A: _____ _____ _____ _____ at the park?

B: _____ _____ _____ _____ a magic show?

A: That's _____ _____ _____.

A: 우리 공원에서 뭘 할까?
B: 마술 쇼를 보는 건 어때?
A: 좋은 생각이야.

Listen & Speak 2-A

1. **B:** Karen, _____ _____ our _____ for the _____ _____ today.

   G: O.K. _____ _____ _____ _____ _____?

   B: _____ _____ 4 o'clock, _____ _____ _____?

   G: _____ good.

2. **G:** Do you want to _____ _____ together this afternoon, Mark?

   B: Sure. _____ _____ _____ play?

   G: _____ _____ at the park _____ your place?

   B: O.K. _____ _____ _____ _____ 3 o'clock.

1. B: Karen, 오늘 학교 연극에서 우리 부분을 연습하자.
   G: 좋아. 몇 시에 만날까?
   B: 학교 끝나고 바로, 네 시 어때?
   G: 좋아.

2. G: Mark, 오후에 같이 배드민턴 하지 않을래?
   B: 물론이지. 어디서 할까?
   G: 너희 집 근처 공원은 어때?
   B: 좋아. 세 시에 거기서 보자.

Listen & Speak 2-B

A: _____ _____ _____ _____ _____ _____ this weekend.

B: Good idea. _____ _____ _____ _____ _____ _____?

A: _____ _____ 10 o'clock _____ Saturday?

B: O.K. _____ _____ at the subway station. See you there.

A: 주말에 소풍가자.
B: 좋은 생각이야. 몇 시에 만닐래?
A: 토요일 10시는 어때?
B: 좋아. 지하철역에서 만나자. 거기서 봐.

Communicate A

Anna: Dad, _____ _____! I _____ _____ _____ next Wednesday.

Dad: Really? _____ _____?

Anna: It's our school's 75th _____.

Dad: Oh, I see.

Anna: Can we do something _____ that day?

Dad: I guess I can _____ the afternoon _____. _____ do you _____ _____ do?

Anna: _____ _____ _____ _____ _____ _____ a musical at Bravo Theater _____ _____ _____? We can _____ a _____ _____ we _____ _____ _____ _____.

Dad: Good idea, Anna! Then, _____ _____ _____ at the theater.

Anna: O.K. What time _____ _____ meet?

Dad: _____ _____ 12? Then, we can _____ _____ together, too.

Anna: You're the _____, Dad!

Communicate B

A: _____ _____ _____ do this afternoon?

B: _____ _____ _____ go see *Wonder Woman*?

A: Good idea! What _____ _____ _____ _____?

B: _____ _____ 4 o'clock?

A: O.K. _____ _____ at Moon Theater.

Progress Check

1. **G:** Jim, _____ _____. It's _____ 10 o'clock.

   B: Oh, we're going to _____ _____ _____ the movie.

   G: _____ _____ _____ _____ the bus? The bus will be _____ _____ the subway _____ _____ _____ _____ _____.

   B: That's a _____ _____.

2. **B:** It's very _____ _____. _____ _____ _____ _____, Julie.

   G: Good idea! _____ _____ _____ we _____?

   B: _____ _____ at the subway station near my place?

   G: O.K. _____ you _____ at 11 o'clock.

Anna: 아빠, 있잖아요! 저는 다음 주 수요일에 수업이 없어요.

아빠: 정말? 왜 없니?

Anna: 75주년 개교 기념일이에요.

아빠: 그렇구나.

Anna: 그날 오후에 같이 뭔가 할 수 있을까요?

아빠: 나는 오후에 휴무를 할 수 있을 것 같구나. 뭘 하고 싶니?

Anna: 아빠 직장 근처 Bravo 극장에서 뮤지컬을 보는 건 어때요? 수요일에 가면 할인을 받을 수 있어요.

아빠: 좋은 생각이구나, Anna! 그럼 바로 극장에서 만나자.

Anna: 좋아요. 몇 시에 만날까요?

아빠: 12시는 어떠니? 그럼 점심도 같이 먹을 수 있단다.

Anna: 최고예요, 아빠!

A: 오늘 오후에 뭘 할까?

B: 원더 우먼을 보러 가는 건 어때?

A: 좋은 생각이야! 몇 시에 만날까?

B: 4시는 어때?

A: 좋아. Moon 극장에서 보자.

---

1. **G:** Jim, 서둘러. 벌써 10시야.

   B: 이런, 영화 시간에 늦을 거야.

   G: 버스를 타는 게 어때? 지금 이 시간에는 버스가 지하철보다 빠를 거야.

   B: 좋은 생각이야.

2. **B:** 오늘 굉장히 덥네. 수영하러 가자, Julie.

   G: 좋은 생각이야! 어디서 만날래?

   B: 우리 집 근처 지하철역에서 만나는 게 어때?

   G: 좋아. 11시에 거기서 보자.

※ 다음 우리말에 맞도록 대화를 영어로 쓰시오.

Listen & Speak 1-A

1. M: _____

   W: _____

   M: _____

   _____

   W: _____

2. B: _____

   W: _____

   _____

   B: _____

   W: _____

Listen & Speak 1-B

A: _____

B: _____

A: _____

Listen & Speak 2-A

1. B: _____

   G: _____

   B: _____

   G: _____

2. G: _____

   B: _____

   G: _____

   B: _____

Listen & Speak 2-B

A: _____

B: _____

A: _____

B: _____

해석

1. M: Liz, 서둘러. 벌써 여섯 시야.
   W: 이런, 우린 콘서트에 늦을 거야.
   M: 지하철을 타는 게 어때? 지하철은 지금 이 시간에 버스보다 빠를 거야.
   W: 좋은 생각이야.

2. B: 엄마, 제가 한국사 시험에서 겨우 한 문제만 틀렸어요!
   W: 대단해! 네가 잘할 거라고 확신했단다. 오늘 축하하러 나가는 건 어때?
   B: 좋아요! 저녁으로 피자를 먹어도 되나요?
   W: 물론이지, Joe. 아빠에게 전화하마.

A: 우리 공원에서 뭘 할까?
B: 마술 쇼를 보는 건 어때?
A: 좋은 생각이야.

1. B: Karen, 오늘 학교 연극에서 우리 부분을 연습하자.
   G: 좋아. 몇 시에 만날까?
   B: 학교 끝나고 바로, 네 시 어때?
   G: 좋아.

2. G: Mark, 오후에 같이 배드민턴 하지 않을래?
   B: 물론이지. 어디서 할까?
   G: 너희 집 근처 공원은 어때?
   B: 좋아. 세 시에 거기서 보자.

A: 주말에 소풍가자.
B: 좋은 생각이야. 몇 시에 만날래?
A: 토요일 10시는 어때?
B: 좋아. 지하철역에서 만나자. 거기서 봐.

Communicate A

Anna: _____

Dad: _____

Anna: _____

Dad: _____

Anna: _____

Dad: _____

Anna: _____

_____

Dad: _____

Anna: _____

Dad: _____

Anna: _____

Anna: 아빠, 있잖아요! 저는 다음 주 수요일에 수업이 없어요.

아빠: 정말? 왜 없니?

Anna: 75주년 개교 기념일이에요.

아빠: 그렇구나.

Anna: 그날 오후에 같이 뭔가 할 수 있을까요?

아빠: 나는 오후에 휴무를 할 수 있을 것 같구나. 뭘 하고 싶니?

Anna: 아빠 직장 근처 Bravo 극장에서 뮤지컬을 보는 건 어때요? 수요일에 가면 할인을 받을 수 있어요.

아빠: 좋은 생각이구나, Anna! 그럼 바로 극장에서 만나자.

Anna: 좋아요. 몇 시에 만날까요?

아빠: 12시는 어떠니? 그럼 점심도 같이 먹을 수 있단다.

Anna: 최고예요, 아빠!

Communicate B

A: _____

B: _____

A: _____

B: _____

A: _____

A: 오늘 오후에 뭘 할까?

B: 원더 우먼을 보러 가는 건 어때?

A: 좋은 생각이야! 몇 시에 만날까?

B: 4시는 어때?

A: 좋아. Moon 극장에서 보자.

Progress Check

1. G: _____

B: _____

G: _____

_____

B: _____

2. B: _____

G: _____

B: _____

G: _____

1. G: Jim, 서둘러. 벌써 10시야.
   B: 이런, 영화 시간에 늦을 거야.
   G: 버스를 타는 게 어때? 지금 이 시간에는 버스가 지하철보다 빠를 거야.
   B: 좋은 생각이야.

2. B: 오늘 굉장히 덥네. 수영하러 가자, Julie.
   G: 좋은 생각이야! 어디서 만날래?
   B: 우리 집 근처 지하철역에서 만나는 게 어때?
   G: 좋아. 11시에 거기서 보자.

※ 다음 우리말과 일치하도록 빈칸에 알맞은 것을 골라 쓰시오.

1 Turandot The _____ _____ Love in the _____

    A. Dangerous   B. Most   C. World

2 _____, _____!

    A. everyone   B. welcome

3 Tonight, we are _____ to _____ Giacomo Puccini's _____ *Turandot*.

    A. perform   B. going   C. opera

4 _____ many _____ famous operas, *Turandot* is in _____ _____ opera started in Italy in the 16th century.

    A. because   B. like   C. Italian   D. other

5 _____ we begin, I'd _____ to tell you the _____ of the opera *Turandot*.

    A. like   B. before   C. storyline

6 You will _____ it _____ _____ you know the story.

    A. better   B. if   C. appreciate

7 Turandot, a Chinese princess, is a woman _____ great _____, but she is as _____ _____ ice.

    A. of   B. cold   C. beauty   D. as

8 Any prince _____ wants to _____ her _____ answer three riddles.

    A. marry   B. who   C. must

9 If he _____, he must _____.

    A. die   B. fails

10 No one _____ ever _____ _____ to answer them.

    A. able   B. been   C. has

11 _____ day, a brave prince _____ in love with her _____ first _____.

    A. falls   B. sight   C. one   D. at

12 He _____ the first man to _____ all three _____.

    A. answer   B. becomes   C. riddles

13 _____, Turandot does not want to _____ the _____.

    A. marry   B. however   C. prince

14 He is _____ _____ _____ a stranger to her.

    A. than   B. nothing   C. more

15 He _____ gives her a riddle _____ his _____.

    A. of   B. then   C. own

1 투란도트, 세상에서 가장 위험한 사랑

2 여러분, 환영합니다!

3 오늘 밤, 우리는 지아코모 푸치니의 오페라 《투란도트》를 공연할 것입니다.

4 다른 많은 유명한 오페라들처럼 《투란도트》는 이탈리아어로 되어 있는데, 오페라가 16세기 이탈리아에서 시작되었기 때문입니다.

5 시작하기 전에 오페라 《투란도트》의 줄거리를 알려 드리려고 합니다.

6 여러분이 줄거리를 알면 이 오페라를 더 잘 감상하게 될 것입니다.

7 중국의 공주 Turandot는 굉장히 아름다운 여인이지만, 그녀는 얼음처럼 차갑습니다.

8 그녀와 결혼하길 원하는 왕자는 누구든지 반드시 세 가지 수수께끼에 답해야 합니다.

9 만약 실패하면 그는 죽어야 합니다.

10 그 누구도 수수께끼에 답할 수 없었습니다.

11 어느 날, 어떤 용감한 왕자가 그녀에게 첫눈에 반합니다.

12 그는 세 수수께끼를 모두 맞힌 첫 번째 사람이 됩니다.

13 그러나 Turandot는 그 왕자와 결혼하길 원하지 않습니다.

14 그는 그녀에게 단지 낯선 사람일 뿐입니다.

15 그러자 그는 그녀에게 자신의 수수께끼를 냅니다.

16 He _____ her, "_____ is my name?"

A. what   B. asks

17 He _____, "If you answer _____, I will agree to _____. If you answer _____, you will have to marry me."

A. correctly   B. die   C. adds   B. incorrectly

18 Turandot must find the answer _____ _____, but his riddle is _____ difficult as _____.

A. dawn   B. hers   C. as   D. before

19 She says to everyone, "No one will go _____ sleep _____ someone _____ _____ his name."

A. out   B. finds   C. until   D. to

20 The prince then sings the _____ _____ _____ of the _____ opera, "Nessun Dorma."

A. most   B. whole   C. famous   D. aria

21 It _____ no one _____.

A. sleeps   B. means

22 _____ one _____.

A. sleeps   B. no

23 No _____ sleeps, _____ _____ you, Princess.

A. even   B. one   C. not

24 My _____ is _____.

A. safe   B. secret

25 _____ one _____ _____ my name.

A. know   B. will   C. no

26 _____ _____, I _____ win! I will win!

A. will   B. at   C. dawn

27 The _____ name _____ Calaf.

A. is   B. prince's

28 Will the princess _____ his name _____ _____?

A. time   B. learn   C. in

29 Let's _____ the opera and _____ _____.

A. out   B. watch   C. find

---

16 그는 그녀에게 "제 이름이 무엇입니까?"라고 묻습니다.

17 그는 "당신이 맞게 대답한다면 나는 죽는 것에 동의하겠습니다. 만약 답이 틀리면 당신은 저와 결혼해야 할 것입니다."라고 덧붙입니다.

18 Turandot는 동이 트기 전에 답을 찾아야 하지만 그의 수수께끼는 그녀의 것만큼 어렵습니다.

19 그녀는 모두에게 "누군가 그의 이름을 알아낼 때까지 그 누구도 잠들 수 없다."라고 말합니다.

20 그리고 왕자는 이 오페라 전체에서 가장 유명한 아리아, Nessun Dorma를 부릅니다.

21 그것은 누구도 잠들지 못한다는 뜻입니다.

22 누구도 잠들지 못하네.

23 누구도 잠들지 못하네, 당신조차도, 공주여.

24 나의 비밀은 안전하다네.

25 누구도 나의 이름을 알지 못할 것이네.

26 동틀 녘에, 내가 이길 것이라네! 내가 승리할 것이라네!

27 왕자의 이름은 Calaf입니다.

28 공주는 그의 이름을 제때 알아낼 수 있을까요?

29 오페라를 보고 알아봅시다.

※ 다음 우리말과 일치하도록 빈칸에 알맞은 말을 쓰시오.

1 Turandot _____ _____ _____ Love in the _____

2 _____, _____!

3 Tonight, we _____ _____ _____ _____ Giacomo Puccini's opera *Turandot*.

4 _____ many _____ _____ _____, *Turandot* is _____ _____ _____ opera started _____ _____ in the _____ _____.

5 Before we begin, _____ _____ _____ _____ you the _____ _____ _____ _____ *Turandot*.

6 You will _____ it _____ _____ you know the story.

7 Turandot, a Chinese princess, is a woman _____ _____ _____, but she is _____ _____ _____ _____.

8 Any prince _____ wants to _____ _____ must answer _____ _____.

9 If he _____, he _____ _____.

10 No one _____ _____ _____ _____ _____ answer them.

11 One day, a brave prince _____ _____ _____ _____ her _____ _____ _____.

12 He becomes _____ _____ _____ _____ _____ _____ all three riddles.

13 _____, Turandot does not want _____ _____ the prince.

14 He is _____ _____ a stranger to her.

15 He then gives _____ _____ _____ _____ _____ _____.

1 투란도트, 세상에서 가장 위험한 사랑
2 여러분, 환영합니다!
3 오늘 밤, 우리는 지아코모 푸치니의 오페라 《투란도트》를 공연할 것입니다.
4 다른 많은 유명한 오페라들처럼 《투란도트》는 이탈리아어로 되어 있는데, 오페라가 16세기 이탈리아에서 시작되었기 때문입니다.
5 시작하기 전에 오페라 《투란도트》의 줄거리를 알려 드리려고 합니다.
6 여러분이 줄거리를 알면 이 오페라를 더 잘 감상하게 될 것입니다.
7 중국의 공주 Turandot는 굉장히 아름다운 여인이지만, 그녀는 얼음처럼 차갑습니다.
8 그녀와 결혼하길 원하는 왕자는 누구든지 반드시 세 가지 수수께끼에 답해야 합니다.
9 만약 실패하면 그는 죽어야 합니다.
10 그 누구도 수수께끼에 답할 수 없었습니다.
11 어느 날, 어떤 용감한 왕자가 그녀에게 첫눈에 반합니다.
12 그는 세 수수께끼를 모두 맞힌 첫 번째 사람이 됩니다.
13 그러나 Turandot는 그 왕자와 결혼하길 원하지 않습니다.
14 그는 그녀에게 단지 낯선 사람일 뿐입니다.
15 그러자 그는 그녀에게 자신의 수수께끼를 냅니다.

16 He _____ _____, "_____ is my name?"

17 He _____, "If you answer _____, I will _____ _____

_____. If you answer _____, you will _____ _____

_____ me."

18 Turandot must find the answer _____ _____, but his riddle is

_____ _____ _____ _____.

19 She says to everyone, "No one will _____ _____ _____

_____ someone _____ _____ his name."

20 The prince then sings _____ _____ _____ _____ of the

_____ _____, "Nessun Dorma."

21 It _____ no one _____.

22 _____ one _____.

23 No one sleeps, _____ _____ _____, Princess.

24 _____ _____ is _____.

24 _____ _____ _____ _____ my name.

26 _____ _____, I _____ _____! I will win!

27 The _____ _____ is Calaf.

28 _____ the princess _____ his name _____ _____?

29 _____ _____ the opera and _____ _____.

16 그는 그녀에게 "제 이름이 무엇입니까?"라고 묻습니다.

17 그는 "당신이 맞게 대답한다면 나는 죽는 것에 동의하겠습니다. 만약 답이 틀리면 당신은 저와 결혼해야 할 것입니다."라고 덧붙입니다.

18 Turandot는 동이 트기 전에 답을 찾아야 하지만 그의 수수께끼는 그녀의 것만큼 어렵습니다.

19 그녀는 모두에게 "누군가 그의 이름을 알아낼 때까지 그 누구도 잠들 수 없다."라고 말합니다.

20 그리고 왕자는 이 오페라 전체에서 가장 유명한 아리아, Nessun Dorma를 부릅니다.

21 그것은 누구도 잠들지 못한다는 뜻입니다.

22 누구도 잠들지 못하네.

23 누구도 잠들지 못하네, 당신조차도, 공주여.

24 나의 비밀은 안전하다네.

25 누구도 나의 이름을 알지 못할 것이네.

26 동틀 녘에, 내가 이길 것이라네! 내가 승리할 것이라네!

27 왕자의 이름은 Calaf입니다.

28 공주는 그의 이름을 제때 알아낼 수 있을까요?

29 오페라를 보고 알아봅시다.

※ 다음 문장을 우리말로 쓰시오.

1 Turandot The Most Dangerous Love in the World

➡ _____

2 Welcome, everyone!

➡ _____

3 Tonight, we are going to perform Giacomo Puccini's opera *Turandot*.

➡ _____

4 Like many other famous operas, *Turandot* is in Italian because opera started in Italy in the 16th century.

➡ _____

5 Before we begin, I'd like to tell you the storyline of the opera *Turandot*.

➡ _____

6 You will appreciate it better if you know the story.

➡ _____

7 Turandot, a Chinese princess, is a woman of great beauty, but she is as cold as ice.

➡ _____

8 Any prince who wants to marry her must answer three riddles.

➡ _____

9 If he fails, he must die.

➡ _____

10 No one has ever been able to answer them.

➡ _____

11 One day, a brave prince falls in love with her at first sight.

➡ _____

12 He becomes the first man to answer all three riddles.

➡ _____

13 However, Turandot does not want to marry the prince.

➡ _____

14 He is nothing more than a stranger to her.

➡ _____

15 He then gives her a riddle of his own.

➡ _____

16 He asks her, "What is my name?"

➡ _____

17 He adds, "If you answer correctly, I will agree to die. If you answer incorrectly, you will have to marry me."

➡ _____

_____

18 Turandot must find the answer before dawn, but his riddle is as difficult as hers.

➡ _____

19 She says to everyone, "No one will go to sleep until someone finds out his name."

➡ _____

20 The prince then sings the most famous aria of the whole opera, "Nessun Dorma."

➡ _____

21 It means no one sleeps.

➡ _____

22 No one sleeps.

➡ _____

23 No one sleeps, not even you, Princess.

➡ _____

24 My secret is safe.

➡ _____

25 No one will know my name.

➡ _____

26 At dawn, I will win! I will win!

➡ _____

27 The prince's name is Calaf.

➡ _____

28 Will the princess learn his name in time?

➡ _____

29 Let's watch the opera and find out.

➡ _____

※ 다음 괄호 안의 단어들을 우리말에 맞도록 바르게 배열하시오.

1 (Turandot / Most / The / Love / Dangerous / the / in / World)
➡ _____

2 (everyone! / welcome,)
➡ _____

3 (we / tonight, / going / are / perform / to / Puccini's / Giacomo / *Turandot.* / opera)
➡ _____

4 (many / like / famous / other / operas, / is *Turandot* / Italian / in / opera / because / in / started / Italy / the / century. / 16th / in)
➡ _____
_____

5 (we / before / begin, / like / I'd / tell / to / the / you / of / storyline / *Turandot.* / opera / the)
➡ _____

6 (will / you / it / appreciate / better / you / if / know / story. / the)
➡ _____

7 (a / Turandot, / princess, / Chinese / a / is / woman / great / of / beauty, / but / is / she / cold / as / ice. / as)
➡ _____
_____

8 (prince / any / wants / who / marry / to / her / answer / must / riddles. / three)
➡ _____

9 (he / if / fails, / he / die. / must)
➡ _____

10 (one / no / ever / has / been / to / able / them. / answer)
➡ _____

11 (day, / one / brave / a / prince / falls / love / in / her / with / sight. / first / at)
➡ _____

12 (becomes / he / first / the / to / man / answer / all / riddles. / three)
➡ _____

13 (Turandot / however / not / does / to / want / prince. / the / marry)
➡ _____

14 (is / he / more / nothing / a / than / stranger / her. / to)
➡ _____

15 (then / he / gives / a / her / riddel / own. / his / of)
➡ _____

1 투란도트, 세상에서 가장 위험한 사랑

2 여러분, 환영합니다!

3 오늘 밤, 우리는 지아코모 푸치니의 오페라 《투란도트》를 공연할 것입니다.

4 다른 많은 유명한 오페라들처럼 《투란도트》는 이탈리아어로 되어 있는데, 오페라가 16세기 이탈리아에서 시작되었기 때문입니다.

5 시작하기 전에 오페라 《투란도트》의 줄거리를 알려 드리려고 합니다.

6 여러분이 줄거리를 알면 이 오페라를 더 잘 감상하게 될 것입니다.

7 중국의 공주 Turandot는 굉장히 아름다운 여인이지만, 그녀는 얼음처럼 차갑습니다.

8 그녀와 결혼길 원하는 왕자는 누구든지 반드시 세 가지 수수께끼에 답해야 합니다.

9 만약 실패하면 그는 죽어야 합니다.

10 그 누구도 수수께끼에 답할 수 없었습니다.

11 어느 날, 어떤 용감한 왕자가 그녀에게 첫눈에 반합니다.

12 그는 세 수수께끼를 모두 맞힌 첫 번째 사람이 됩니다.

13 그러나 Turandot는 그 왕자와 결혼하길 원하지 않습니다.

14 그는 그녀에게 단지 낯선 사람일 뿐입니다.

15 그러자 그는 그녀에게 자신의 수수께끼를 냅니다.

16 (asks / he / her, / is / "what / name?" / my)

➡ _____

17 (adds, / he / you / "if / answer / correctly, / will / I / die. / to / agree / you / if / incorrectly, / answer / will / you / to / have / me." / marry)

➡ _____

_____

18 (must / Turandot / find / answer / the / dawn, / before / his / but / as / is / riddle / difficult / hers. / as)

➡ _____

_____

19 (says / she / everyone, / to / one "no / go / will / sleep / to / someone / until / out / finds / name." / his)

➡ _____

_____

20 (prince / the / sings / then / most / the / aria / famous / of / opera, / whole / the / Dorma." / "Nessun)

➡ _____

_____

21 (means / it / one / sleeps. / no)

➡ _____

22 (sleeps. / one / no)

➡ _____

23 (one / no / sleeps, even / not / Princess. / you,)

➡ _____

24 (secret / safe. / is / my)

➡ _____

25 (one / no / know / will / name. / my)

➡ _____

26 (dawn, / at / will / I / win! / will / I / win!)

➡ _____

27 (prince's / the / is / Calaf. / name)

➡ _____

28 (the / will / learn / princess / name / his / time? / in)

➡ _____

29 (watch / let's / opera / the / out. / find / and)

➡ _____

16 그는 그녀에게 "제 이름이 무엇 입니까?"라고 묻습니다.

17 그는 "당신이 맞게 대답한다면 나는 죽는 것에 동의하겠습니 다. 만약 답이 틀리면 당신은 저 와 결혼해야 할 것입니다."라고 덧붙입니다.

18 Turandot는 동이 트기 전에 답 을 찾아야 하지만 그의 수수께 끼는 그녀의 것만큼 어렵습니다.

19 그녀는 모두에게 "누군가 그의 이름을 알아낼 때까지 그 누구 도 잠들 수 없다."라고 말합니다.

20 그리고 왕자는 이 오페라 전 체에서 가장 유명한 아리아, Nessun Dorma를 부릅니다.

21 그것은 누구도 잠들지 못한다는 뜻입니다.

22 누구도 잠들지 못하네.

23 누구도 잠들지 못하네, 당신조 차도, 공주여.

24 나의 비밀은 안전하다네.

25 누구도 나의 이름을 알지 못할 것이네.

26 동틀 녘에, 내가 이길 것이라네! 내가 승리할 것이라네!

27 왕자의 이름은 Calaf입니다.

28 공주는 그의 이름을 제때 알아 낼 수 있을까요?

29 오페라를 보고 알아봅시다.

※ 다음 우리말을 영어로 쓰시오.

1 투란도트, 세상에서 가장 위험한 사랑

➡ _____

2 여러분, 환영합니다!

➡ _____

3 오늘 밤, 우리는 지아코모 푸치니의 오페라 《투란도트》를 공연할 것입니다.

➡ _____

4 다른 많은 유명한 오페라들처럼 《투란도트》는 이탈리아어로 되어 있는데, 오페라가 16세기 이탈리아에서 시작되었기 때문입니다.

➡ _____

5 시작하기 전에 오페라 《투란도트》의 줄거리를 알려 드리려고 합니다.

➡ _____

6 여러분이 줄거리를 알면 이 오페라를 더 잘 감상하게 될 것입니다.

➡ _____

7 중국의 공주 Turandot는 굉장히 아름다운 여인이지만, 그녀는 얼음처럼 차갑습니다.

➡ _____

8 그녀와 결혼하길 원하는 왕자는 누구든지 반드시 세 가지 수수께끼에 답해야 합니다.

➡ _____

9 만약 실패하면 그는 죽어야 합니다.

➡ _____

10 그 누구도 수수께끼에 답할 수 없었습니다.

➡ _____

11 어느 날, 어떤 용감한 왕자가 그녀에게 첫눈에 반합니다.

➡ _____

12 그는 세 수수께끼를 모두 맞힌 첫 번째 사람이 됩니다.

➡ _____

13 그러나 Turandot는 그 왕자와 결혼하길 원하지 않습니다.

➡ _____

14 그는 그녀에게 단지 낯선 사람일 뿐입니다.

➡ _____

15 그러자 그는 그녀에게 자신의 수수께끼를 냅니다.

➡ _____

16 그는 그녀에게 "제 이름이 무엇입니까?"라고 묻습니다.

  ➡ _____

17 그는 "당신이 맞게 대답한다면 나는 죽는 것에 동의하겠습니다. 만약 답이 틀리면 당신은 저와 결혼해야 할 것입니다."라고 덧붙입니다.

  ➡ _____

     _____

18 Turandot는 동이 트기 전에 답을 찾아야 하지만 그의 수수께끼는 그녀의 것만큼 어렵습니다.

  ➡ _____

19 그녀는 모두에게 "누군가 그의 이름을 알아낼 때까지 그 누구도 잠들 수 없다."라고 말합니다.

  ➡ _____

20 그리고 왕자는 이 오페라 전체에서 가장 유명한 아리아, Nessun Dorma를 부릅니다.

  ➡ _____

21 그것은 누구도 잠들지 못한다는 뜻입니다.

  ➡ _____

22 누구도 잠들지 못하네.

  ➡ _____

23 누구도 잠들지 못하네, 당신조차도, 공주여.

  ➡ _____

24 나의 비밀은 안전하다네.

  ➡ _____

25 누구도 나의 이름을 알지 못할 것이네.

  ➡ _____

26 동틀 녘에, 내가 이길 것이라네! 내가 승리할 것이라네!

  ➡ _____

27 왕자의 이름은 Calaf입니다.

  ➡ _____

28 공주는 그의 이름을 제때 알아낼 수 있을까요?

  ➡ _____

29 오페라를 보고 알아봅시다.

  ➡ _____

※ 다음 우리말과 일치하도록 빈칸에 알맞은 말을 쓰시오.

Link

1. A: _____ was _____ _____?

2. B: It was _____! Actually, I've _____ the musical *Cats* before, and your song was _____ _____ _____ the _____.

1. A: 우리 공연 어땠어?
2. B: 굉장했어. 사실, 뮤지컬 캣츠를 전에 본 적이 있는데, 너희 노래는 뮤지컬의 노래만큼 대단했어.

Write

1. _____ _____ *La La Land*

2. I _____ *La La Land* _____ _____.

3. It _____ _____ the _____ and _____ of Mia and Sebastian.

4. I enjoyed _____ _____ and _____ _____.

5. The story _____ _____ _____ _____ _____ the songs.

6. If you _____ _____ _____ a good musical movie, you _____ _____ this movie.

7. _____ Kim Jisu _____ Aug. 11

1. 라라랜드에 대한 감상
2. 나는 지난 금요일에 라라랜드를 보았다.
3. 그건 Mia와 Sebastian의 꿈과 사랑에 대한 이야기야.
4. 나는 그것의 아름답고 감동적인 노래를 즐겼어.
5. 이야기도 노래만큼이나 좋았지.
6. 좋은 뮤지컬 영화를 찾고 있다면, 이 영화를 봐야 할 거야.
7. 8월 11일, 김지수 씀

Write

1. _____ _____ *Beauty and the Beast*

2. I _____ *Beauty and the Beast* _____ _____.

3. It is about a _____ _____ and a _____.

4. I enjoyed _____ _____ _____.

5. The songs were great, and the love story was _____ _____ _____ _____ _____.

6. If you _____ _____ _____ about love, you _____ _____ it, _____.

7. _____ Lee Minsu _____ _____. 12

1. 미녀와 야수에 대한 감상
2. 나는 지난 토요일에 미녀와 야수를 봤어.
3. 그건 예쁜 여자아이와 야수에 대한 이야기야.
4. 나는 그것을 매우 즐겼어.
5. 노래들은 아주 좋았고, 사랑 이야기는 보석만큼 아름다웠어.
6. 마음이 따뜻해지는 사랑 이야기를 좋아한다면, 너도 이걸 좋아할 거야.
7. 8월 12일, 이민수 씀

※ 다음 우리말을 영어로 쓰시오.

Link

1. A: 우리 공연 어땠어?

➡ _____

2. B: 굉장했어. 사실, 뮤지컬 캣츠를 전에 본적이 있는데, 너희 노래는 뮤지컬의 노래만큼 대단했어.

➡ _____

Write

1. 라라랜드에 대한 감상

➡ _____

2. 나는 지난 금요일에 라라랜드를 보았다.

➡ _____

3. 그건 Mla와 Sebastian의 꿈과 사랑에 대한 이야기야.

➡ _____

4. 나는 그것의 아름답고 감동적인 노래를 즐겼어.

➡ _____

5. 이야기도 노래만큼이나 좋았지.

➡ _____

6. 좋은 뮤지컬 영화를 찾고 있다면, 이 영화를 봐야 할 거야.

➡ _____

7. 8월 11일, 김지수 씀

➡ _____

Write

1. 미녀와 야수에 대한 감상

➡ _____

2. 나는 지난 토요일에 미녀와 야수를 봤어.

➡ _____

3. 그건 예쁜 여자아이와 야수에 대한 이야기야.

➡ _____

4. 나는 그것을 매우 즐겼어.

➡ _____

5. 노래들은 아주 좋았고, 사랑 이야기는 보석만큼 아름다웠어.

➡ _____

6. 마음이 따뜻해지는 사랑 이야기를 좋아한다면, 너도 이걸 좋아할 거야.

➡ _____

7. 8월 12일, 이민수 씀

➡ _____

MEMO

적중100

1학기

정답 및 해설

미래 | 최연희

중 2

적중100

영어 기출 문제집

1학기

정답 및 해설

미래 | 최연희

중 2

My Travel, My Way

Conversation

핵심 Check   p.10~11

1 (1) Have, read / have   (2) Have, eaten / haven't
2 (1) How, weather / snowy   (2) What's, like / hot
  (3) How's / raining

시험대비 실력평가   p.08

01 ②   02 ②   03 ④   04 decision
05 ③   06 (c)hance 07 check   08 ②

01 ①, ③, ④, ⑤는 날씨와 관련된 단어이고, ②는 날씨와 관련이
   없다.
02 a lot of: 많은 / get into: ~에 들어가다, ~을 타다
03 보통 옥외에서 물건을 사고파는 장소: 시장(market)
04 동사-명사의 관계이다. 충고하다 : 충고 = 결정하다 : 결정
05 a few: 소수의, 약간의
06 어떤 것이 일어날 가능성: chance(가능성)
07 check: 살피다, 점검하다
08 be full of: ~으로 가득 차다 / think of: ~을 생각하다

교과서 대화문 익히기

Check(√) True or False   p.12

1 F   2 T   3 F   4 T   5 T   6 F

서술형 시험대비   p.09

01 (1) snowy   (2) cool   (3) creator
02 (1) at last   (2) a little   (3) stay indoors
03 (1) anything   (2) mostly   (3) pack   (4) different
04 (1) actually   (2) amazing   (3) mysterious
05 (1) right now   (2) get to
   (3) is full of   (4) catch a cold
06 (1) (a)dmire   (2) (d)rawing   (3) (f)ood

01 (1) 명사 - 형용사 (2) 반의어 관계 (3) 동사 - 행위자 관계
02 (1) at last: 마침내 (2) a little: 조금 (3) stay indoors: 집안
   에 머물러 있다
03 (1) anything: 무엇, 아무것, 무엇이든 (2) mostly: 주로, 일반적
   으로 (3) pack: 짐을 싸다, 챙기다 (4) different: 각각 다른, (각
   양) 각색의
04 (1) actually: 사실, 실제로, 정말로 (2) amazing: 놀라운 (3)
   mysterious: 신비한
05 (1) right now: 지금, 당장 (2) get to: ~에 도착하다 (3) be
   full of: ~으로 가득하다 (4) catch a cold: 감기에 걸 리다
06 (1) admire: 존경하다 (2) drawing: 그림, 데생 (3) food: 음
   식, 식량

교과서 확인학습   p.14~15

Listen & Speak 1 A. Listen and Check
1 Have, tired / have, tried / How / but
2 ever, jumping / haven't, about / When, tried /
  Wasn't / liked, want

Listen & Speak 2 A. Listen and Answer
1 weather, need / outside, check / going / don't
2 Good, welcome, forecast, sunny, but, rain, home,
  forecast, Have

Communicate A~B
A been, before / have, lived, for / weather, going,
  vacation / time, visit, autumn / planning, relax /
  often, may / take, pack / idea, great
B been, places / have, last / How, weather / mostly,
  changed

Progress Check
1 ridden / have, about / haven't, was / fun, little
2 weather / quite, check / Thanks / going
3 Good, welcome, raining, but, sunny, leave, without

시험대비 기본평가   p.16

01 What's, like
02 ③   03 ④   04 ③

01 날씨를 물을 때는 How is[How's] the weather?나 What
   is[What's] the weather like?의 표현을 쓴다.
02 '~에 가 본 적 있니?'라고 경험을 물을 때는 Have you been ~?

표현을 사용한다. '전에'는 before로 쓴다.

03 현재의 바깥 날씨를 묻는데 미래 시제로 답하는 것은 적절하지 않다.

04 현재완료로 경험을 묻는 말에 부정으로 답할 때는 No, I haven't.라고 한다.

시험대비 실력평가 p.17~18

01 ② 02 Have, ever / have 03 ③
04 ④ 05 ① 06 ⑤ 07 ②, ⑤
08 나는 뉴질랜드를 방문했을 때 번지 점프를 한 번 해 보았어.
09 bungee jumping
10 ④ 11 Actually 12 What's, like
13 relax 14 ①

01 What's the weather like outside?(바깥 날씨 어떤가요?)처럼 날씨가 어떤지 물을 때는 비인칭 주어 it을 사용하여 「It's+날씨.」의 형태를 써서 답한다.

02 경험을 묻는 현재완료를 쓴다.

03 엄마, 오늘 날씨 어때요? - 바깥 날씨가 꽤 흐려. 일기예보를 확인해 볼게. - 고마워요, 엄마. - 음, 오후에 비가 올 거야.

04 영화를 본 경험이 있는지 묻는 말에 본 적이 없다고 답하며 '너는 봤어?'라고 상대방에게 되묻는 표현이다. 대화의 흐름상 현재완료형으로 물어야 하므로 Have you (seen it)?의 ④가 적절하다.

05 A가 선글라스를 써야겠다고 했으므로 빈칸에는 날씨가 화창하다는 대답이 와야 한다. ⑤는 특정 지역의 가을 날씨를 묻는 질문에 적절한 대답이다.

06 경험을 묻는 현재완료이므로 'have+과거분사'의 형태가 알맞다.

07 How[What] about you?: 너는 어때?

08 try: 시도해 보다 / once: 한 번

09 it은 인칭대명사로 앞에 나온 단수 명사를 받을 수 있다.

10 have been to: ~에 다녀오다, ~에 가 본 적이 있다 / have gone to: ~에 갔다(그래서 지금 여기 없다)

11 문장 전체를 수식하는 부사가 되어야 한다.

12 날씨를 나타낼 때는 How's the weather?나 What's the weather like?의 표현을 쓴다.

13 특히 일이 끝난 후 쉬거나 즐거운 일을 하면서 시간을 보내다

14 ① Ann이 언제 호주에 가는지는 위 대화를 통해 알 수 없다.

서술형 시험대비 p.19

01 like, It 02 Have, haven't
03 (B) – (C) – (D) – (A) 04 weather
05 cloudy 06 forecast 07 welcome
08 sunny 09 비가 좀 내릴 것으로 예상된다.

---

01 It은 날씨를 나타내는 비인칭 용법이다.

02 경험을 나타내는 현재완료 문장이다.

03 너 인도 음식을 먹어 본 적이 있니? - 응, 있어, 하지만 인도 카레만 먹어 봤어. - 어땠어? - 정말 매웠지만, 아주 좋았어.

04 날씨를 묻는 표현이다.

05 cloud의 형용사형이 와야 한다.

06 특히 특별한 사건이나 상황에 관련하여 미래에 일어날 것으로 기대되는 것에 대한 언급: forecast(예측, 예보)

07 welcome to: ~에 오신 것을 환영합니다

08 sun의 형용사형이 와야 한다.

교과서 Grammar

핵심 Check p.20~21

1 (1) to go (2) to help (3) to write with
  (4) cold to drink
2 (1) to understand (2) It (3) to exercise (4) of (5) for

시험대비 기본평가 p.22

01 (1) to visit (2) to do (3) It (4) of (5) for
02 (1) to exercise (2) to finish (3) It (4) of (5) for
03 (1) to change (2) to visit (3) to read

01 (1), (2) 형용사적 용법의 to부정사가 필요하다. (3) 가주어 It이 필요하다. (4) 형용사가 kind이므로 의미상의 주어는 'of+목적격'을 쓴다. (5) 형용사가 hard이므로 의미상의 주어는 'for+목적격'을 쓴다.

02 (1), (2) 가주어 It이 있는 구문이므로 밑줄 친 부분을 to부정사로 바꾼다. (3) 가주어는 It으로 나타낸다. (4) 형용사가 brave이므로 의미상의 주어는 'of+목적격'을 쓴다. (5) 형용사가 easy이므로 의미상의 주어는 'for+목적격'을 쓴다.

시험대비 실력평가 p.23~25

01 ③ 02 ④ 03 ③ 04 to write
05 It, to 06 ① 07 ① 08 Do you want anything to eat? [Do you want to eat anything?]
09 ④ 10 ④ 11 It is difficult to fix the machine. 12 ② 13 ① 14 to
15 ① 16 ⑤ 17 sit → sit on[in]
18 ③ 19 ① 20 ③ 21 It is

pleasant to listen to music. 22 ⑤   23 going
→ to go

01 가주어 It의 진주어로 to부정사가 필요하다.

02 부정대명사 anything을 수식하는 형용사적 용법의 to부정사가
   와야 한다.

03 ③은 부사적 용법의 to부정사이다. '~하기 위해'로 해석한다. 나
   머지는 모두 형용사적 용법이다.

04 '써야 할 편지들'이라는 뜻으로 명사 letters를 수식하는 to 부정
   사의 형용사적 용법이다.

05 주어로 쓰인 to부정사가 긴 경우, 이를 뒤로 보내고 그 자리에 가
   주어 it을 쓴다.

06 가주어 – 진주어 구문으로 「It is+형용사+to부정사」 형태가 적
   절하다.

07 <보기>의 to read는 앞에 나온 명사 books를 수식하는 형용사적
   용법의 to부정사이다. ① 형용사적 용법 ② 명사적 용법 ③ 부사
   적 용법 ④ 명사적 용법 ⑤ 부사적 용법

08 부정대명사를 수식하는 to부정사의 형용사적 용법을 쓴다.

09 ④ to going 대신 time을 수식하는 형용사적 용법의 to부정사
   가 필요하다.

10 ④의 it은 인칭대명사이고 나머지는 가주어 it[It]이다.

11 '그 기계를 고치는 것은'은 to fix the machine으로 나타낸다.

12 첫 문장은 형용사가 kind이므로 의미상의 주어는 'of+목적격'
   을 쓴다. 두 번째 문장은 형용사가 natural이므로 의미상의 주
   어는 'for+목적격'을 쓴다.

13 honest와 wise는 의미상의 주어로 'of+목적격'을 쓴다.

14 don't have to: ~할 필요가 없다 / reason to be angry at: ~
   에게 화낸 이유

15 It이 가주어이므로 진주어인 to부정사가 와야 한다.

16 ①, ④ 진주어로 쓰인 to부정사 ② hopes는 to부정사를 목적어
   로 취한다. ③ enough to+동사원형: ~하기에 충분히 …한 ⑤
   사역동사의 목적격보어는 동사원형이 와야 한다.

17 to부정사의 수식을 받는 명사가 전치사의 목적어일 경우 뒤에
   전치사가 온다.

18 to부정사의 수식을 받는 명사가 전치사의 목적어일 경우 to부정
   사 뒤에 전치사를 쓴다. ③은 to talk with라고 해야 옳다.

19 ①은 '때'를 나타내는 비인칭 주어이다. 나머지는 가주어 it으로
   쓰였다.

20 ③은 앞의 명사 house를 꾸며주는 형용사적 용법의 to부정사이
   고, 나머지는 모두 명사적 용법으로 쓰였다.

21 to부정사로 쓰인 주어가 길거나 의미를 강조하고 싶을 때 가주어
   it을 주어 자리에 쓰고 진주어인 to부정사를 문장 뒤로 보낸다.

22 time을 수식하는 to부정사와 「don't have to+동사원형」의 형
   태가 필요하다.

23 진주어로 to부정사가 와야 한다.

---

01 It, to   02 to

03 (1) It is easy to bake cookies.
   (2) He bought a magazine to read on the train.

04 to receive

05 (1) It wasn't easy to visit him every weekend.
   (2) It is an exciting experience to live in another
       country.

06 (1) She has a strong desire to be a singer.
   (2) I will make every effort to solve this problem.
   (3) We had something to talk about.
   (4) I want a sheet[piece] of papeer to write on.
   (5) Please give me something hot to drink.

07 (1) It   (2) on   (3) with   (4) to

08 (1) play → to play
   (2) of → for

09 to visit   10 for you   11 It, to learn 12 to

13 (1) for → of
   (2) of → for

14 It's a place to sell many things for 24 hours.

01 가주어 it을 문장 앞에 두고 진주어 to부정사구를 뒤로 보낸다.

02 앞의 명사를 수식하는 형용사적 용법의 to부정사가 필요하다.

03 (1) 가주어-진주어 구문으로 「It is + 형용사 + to부정사」 어순이
   되어야 한다. (2) '읽을 잡지'이므로 to부정사의 형용사적 용법을
   쓴다.

04 가주어인 It의 진주어에 해당하는 to부정사구가 되어야 하므로
   to receive로 쓴다.

05 (1) '주말마다 그를 방문하는 것은'는 to visit him every
   weekend로 나타낸다. (2) '다른 나라에서 사는 것은'는 to
   live in another country로 나타낸다.

06 (1), (2), (3) to부정사의 형용사적 용법을 이용해 「명사+to부정
   사」의 형태로 쓴다. (4) to부정사의 목적어가 있고 to부정사의 동
   사가 자동사일 때는 전치사가 필요하다. (5) -thing으로 끝나는
   부정대명사는 「-thing+형용사+to부정사」의 어순을 따른다.

07 (1) 가주어 it이 필요하다. (2) '~ 위에' 쓰는 것이므로 전치사
   on이 필요하다. (3) '칼을 가지고 로프를 자르는' 것이므로 전치
   사 with가 필요하다. (4) 형용사적 용법의 to부정사가 온다.

08 (1) time을 수식하는 to부정사로 바꾼다. (2) important는 의
   미상의 주어로 'for+목적격'을 쓴다.

09 명사 places를 수식하는 to부정사의 형용사적 용법이다.

10 important는 의미상 주어로 「for+목적격」을 쓴다.

11 to learn to ride a bike가 주어인 문장으로, 가주어 it이 앞에
   온다. to ride는 learn의 목적어로 쓰인 to부정사이다.

12 가주어인 It의 진주어에 해당하는 to부정사와 「don't have
   to+동사원형」의 형태가 필요하다.

13 (1) 형용사가 stupid이므로 의미상의 주어는 'of+목적격'을 쓴다. (2) 형용사가 necessary이므로 의미상의 주어는 'for+목적격'을 쓴다.

14 to부정사의 형용사적 용법(a place to sell ~)을 이용한다.

Reading

확인문제 p.28

1 T 2 F 3 T 4 F 5 T

확인문제 p.29

1 F 2 T 3 T 4 F

교과서 확인학습 A p.30~31

01 live	02 week, vacation	
03 trip, journal	04 way, special	
05 set, mysterious, Earth	06 drive, finally	
07 amazing, ring	08 stones, thousands	
09 for	10 guess, mystery	
11 perfect	12 colors	13 In, around
14 started, so	15 popular, stay	16 like
17 invited	18 full, and	
19 busy, admiring		
20 much, anything	21 draw, like	
22 stop	23 visited	24 become, since
25 movies, else, dinner	26 also, who	
27 When, outside, walked	28 touched, get	
29 said, smile, portrait	30 Create	
31 journal, much		

교과서 확인학습 B p.32~33

1 Hi, I am Lucy Hunter, and I live in London.

2 Last week, my family went on a vacation for three days.

3 During our trip, I made simple drawings in my journal.

4 That was a great way to capture all the special moments.

5 At last, we set foot at Stonehenge, one of the most mysterious places on Earth.

6 After a two-hour drive from our home in London, we finally got to Stonehenge.

7 It was just amazing to see the ring of huge stones.

8 How did those huge stones get there thousands of years ago?

9 What were they for?

10 Don't try to make a perfect drawing.

11 A few colors will be enough.

12 I guess Stonehenge will remain a mystery for a long time.

13 In the morning, we walked around the Cotswolds.

14 It started to rain in the afternoon, so we decided to stay indoors at our B&B.

15 A B&B is a popular place to stay in England.

16 It feels more like a home than a hotel.

17 The owner invited us for afternoon tea today.

18 The dining table was full of cookies, cake, bread, and cheese.

19 While I was busy eating, Mom was admiring the beautiful cups and plates.

20 I ate too much, so I couldn't eat anything for dinner.

21 It is O.K. to draw everyday objects like cups and plates in your journal.

22 Our last stop was Oxford.

23 We first visited Christ Church College.

24 It has become a world famous place to visit since it appeared in the Harry Potter movies.

25 In the movies, Harry and everyone else eat dinner at the Hall of Christ Church.

26 We also saw portraits of famous people who graduated from the college.

27 When we were outside the building, I walked to the famous olive tree and touched it.

28 "Because I touched this tree," I said, "I will get into Oxford University!"

29 Then, my brother said to me with a smile, "I can't wait to see your portrait on the wall."

30 Create your own avatar.

31 Your drawing journal will become much more interesting.

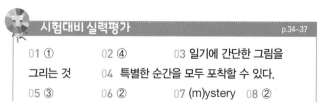

시험대비 실력평가 p.34~37

01 ①   02 ④   03 일기에 간단한 그림을 그리는 것   04 특별한 순간을 모두 포착할 수 있다.

05 ③   06 ②   07 (m)ystery   08 ②

5

09 ④	10 ③	11 ⑤	12 ②
13 ④	14 because[as]		15 ④
16 ④	17 Christ Church College		18 ⑤

19 We also saw portraits of famous people who graduated from the college.

20 ③	21 ①	22 famous	23 ①, ③
24 ④	25 ②	26 ②	27 market

28 traditional 29 외국에서 새로운 일들을 해 보는 것

30 ②

01 go on a vacation: 휴가를 가다

02 for+수사가 붙은 기간을 나타내는 명사 / during+특정 기간을 나타내는 명사

03 That은 지시대명사로 앞에 나온 문장을 받는다.

05 What were they for?의 they는 those huge stones를 받으므로 이 문장 앞에 와야 한다.

06 get to: ~에 도착하다

07 이해되거나 알려지지 않은 어떤 것

08 colors가 복수형이고 문맥상 '약간의, 몇 개의'라는 뜻이 필요하므로 A few가 알맞다.

09 거대한 돌의 고리가 무슨 용도로 쓰였는지는 알 수 없다.

10 주어진 문장의 It은 A B&B를 받으므로 B&B를 설명하는 문장 다음에 와야 한다.

11 ⑤는 '그것'의 뜻으로 특정한 명사를 받는 인칭대명사이고 나머지는 모두 비인칭 용법으로 쓰였다.

12 be full of: ~으로 가득 차다

13 while: ~하는 동안

14 이유를 나타내는 접속사가 와야 하므로 because 외에 as나 since도 올 수 있다.

15 ④ 주인이 왜 그들을 초대했는지는 언급되지 않았다.

16 그 장소가 Harry Potter 영화에 등장해서 유명해졌다는 문장 다음에 와야 한다.

17 It은 인칭대명사로 앞에 나온 단수 명사를 받는다.

18 '~한 이래로'의 뜻으로 현재완료에 쓰이는 접속사는 since이다.

19 graduate는 자동사이기 때문에 목적어 앞에 전치사 from이 필요하다.

20 ③ Christ Church College가 영국에서 가장 인기 있는 관광지 중의 하나인지는 언급되지 않았다.

21 '~했을 때'의 뜻으로 때를 나타내는 접속사 when이 알맞다.

22 아주 잘 알려져 있는: famous(유명한)

23 비교급을 강조할 때는 much, far, even, a lot 등을 쓸 수 있다.

24 ④ Lucy의 초상화는 벽에 걸려 있지 않다.

25 Then이 있으므로 야시장에 갔다는 문장 다음에 와야 한다.

26 temples가 복수 명사이므로 much는 쓸 수 없다.

27 대개는 옥외에서 물건을 사고파는 장소: market(시장)

28 명사 food을 수식하므로 형용사형으로 고쳐야 한다.

29 It은 가주어로 진주어인 to try 이하를 받는다.

30 민수가 왜 절을 방문했는지는 언급되지 않았다.

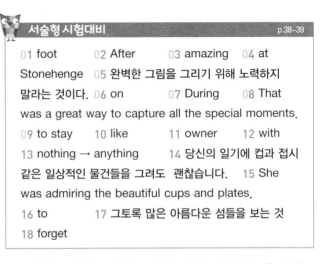

01 foot 02 After 03 amazing 04 at Stonehenge 05 완벽한 그림을 그리기 위해 노력하지 말라는 것이다. 06 on 07 During 08 That was a great way to capture all the special moments. 09 to stay 10 like 11 owner 12 with 13 nothing → anything 14 당신의 일기에 컵과 접시 같은 일상적인 물건들을 그려도 괜찮습니다. 15 She was admiring the beautiful cups and plates. 16 to 17 그토록 많은 아름다운 섬들을 보는 것 18 forget

01 사람이 그 위에 서 있거나 다리 끝에 있는 신체 부분: foot(발)

02 after a two-hour drive from ~: ~에서 두 시간 동안 운전한 후에

03 사물이 사람을 놀라게 하는 것이므로 현재분사형의 형용사를 쓴다.

04 there는 앞에 언급된 장소를 가리키는 부사이다.

06 go on a vacation: 휴가를 가다

07 for+수사가 붙은 일정한 기간 / during+특정 기간

08 'all the+복수 명사'의 어순을 취한다.

09 decide는 to부정사를 목적어로 취한다.

10 feel like+명사: ~처럼 느껴지다

11 own: 소유하다 / owner: 소유자, 주인

12 be full of = be filled with: ~으로 가득 차다

13 앞에 not이 있기 때문에 nothing을 쓸 수 없다.

14 like: ~와 같은

16 go on a field trip to: ~으로 현장 학습을 가다

17 It은 가주어로 진주어인 to see ~의 내용을 나타낸다.

18 문맥상 '잊지 않을 것이다'가 되어야 한다.

01 ④	02 ③	03 different	04 ③
05 ⑤	06 ②	07 guess	08 ③
09 ③	10 ②	11 (B)-(C)-(A)-(D)	
12 ④	13 ②	14 ④	15 won't
16 No, he doesn't.		17 ①	18 ④
19 ②	20 it is	21 ③	22 ②
23 ②	24 write → write with		25 ⑤
26 anything to make myself look slimmer			27 It, to
28 ④	29 ①, ⑤	30 to visit	31 ③
32 ④	33 have	34 ②, ③	35 ①

01 ④는 '명사 - 형용사' 관계인데, 나머지는 '형용사 - 부사'의 관계이다.

02 • 저런 걸 들은 적이 있어요? • 제가 들어갈 만한 충분한 공간이 있나요? • 그가 또 다른 말은 뭐라고 했나요? • 넌 정말 내가 너를 믿으리라고 기대하니?

03 반의어 관계이다. 추운 : 더운 = 같은 : 다른

04 get into: ~에 들어가다 / watch out: 조심하다

05 육지에 완전히 둘러싸인 땅: island(섬)

06 at last: 마침내(=finally)

07 guess: 추측하다

08 ③은 '집에 갔니?'라고 결과를 묻는 표현이고, 나머지는 경험을 묻는 표현이다.

09 B가 비가 오고 있다고 말하고 있고, Yes나 No로 답하지 않았으므로 의문사를 이용한 날씨를 묻는 질문이 와야 알맞다.

10 It was very tasty.(그것은 매우 맛있었어.)라는 말로 보아 긍정의 대답이 들어가야 한다. Have you ever ~?의 긍정의 대답은 Yes, I have.이다.

11 너 말을 타본 적 있니? - 응, 있어. 너는 어때? - 아니, 난 없어. 말 타는 거 어땠어? - 재미있었지만, 조금 무섭기도 했어.

12 How about Seoul?은 서울의 날씨는 어떠냐는 의미이다. ④는 날씨를 묻는 말에 대한 응답으로 적절하지 않다.

13 주어진 문장은 일기예보를 확인해 보겠다는 문장이므로 우산이 필요하냐고 묻는 문장 다음에 와야 한다.

14 날씨를 묻는 표현은 How is the weather?와 What is the weather like?가 있다.

15 be going to는 will을 써서 바꿔 쓸 수 있다.

17 가주어 It을 설명하는 진주어 to부정사가 필요하다.

18 -thing으로 끝나는 부정대명사를 수식하는 to부정사가 필요하다.

19 형용사가 stupid와 clever이므로 의미상의 주어는 'of+목적격'을 쓴다.

20 뒤에 진주어인 to부정사구가 왔으므로 빈칸에는 가주어인 it과 be동사가 와야 한다.

21 -thing으로 끝나는 부정대명사는 「-thing+형용사+to부정사」의 어순을 취한다.

22 <보기>와 나머지는 모두 형용사적 용법이고 ②는 부사적 용법이다.

23 ②는 날씨를 나타내는 비인칭 주어 it이고, 나머지는 to부정사구를 진주어로 하는 가주어 it이다.

24 to부정사의 수식을 받는 명사가 전치사의 목적어일 경우 뒤에 전치사가 온다.

25 형용사적 용법의 to부정사는 명사나 대명사를 뒤에서 수식하여 형용사처럼 쓰인다. 또한, food는 보통 단수로 쓰인다.

26 anything: 어떤 것이든

27 To finish this work이 주어인 문장으로, 가주어 it이 앞에 온다.

28 주어진 문장은 외국에서 새로운 일들을 시도하는 것이 즐거웠다는 뜻이므로 여러 가지 일들을 했다는 문장 다음에 와야 한다.

29 a lot of는 '많은'의 뜻인데 뒤에 복수명사가 오므로 much는 쓸 수 없다.

30 명사 a chance를 꾸며 주는 to부정사의 형용사적 용법이다

31 ③ 민수가 쇼핑을 했다는 말은 언급되지 않았다.

32 부사절 since ~가 있으므로 계속을 나타내는 현재완료가 온다.

33 eat[have] dinner: 저녁을 먹다

34 선행사가 사람이고 주격이므로 who나 that을 쓴다.

35 이유를 나타내는 접속사로 because나 as를 쓸 수 있다.

36 비교급을 강조하는 부사(구)는 much, even, far, a lot 등이다.

37 ③ Christ Church College를 누가 졸업했는지는 언급되지 않았다.

38 final의 부사형은 finally이다.

39 It은 가주어로 진주어인 to watch ~의 내용을 받는다.

단원별 예상문제   p.46~49

01 ④   02 ②   03 creation   04 else
05 ⑤   06 ①, ④   07 ④   08 been
09 나는 해변에서 시간을 좀 보내고 햇빛을 쬐며 휴식을 취할 계획이야.   10 ⑤   11 write → write on
12 ②   13 ④   14 It, to   15 ⑤
16 ①   17 ⑤   18 ④   19 ②
20 ②   21 ⑤   22 ②
23 thousand → thousands   24 ③   25 to make   26 ④, ⑤   27 그토록 아름다운 많은 섬들을 보는 것은 아주 놀라웠다.   28 They went there last month.

01 ④는 유의어 관계이고 나머지는 반의어 관계이다.

02 appear: 나타나다 / show up: 나타나다

03 동사 - 명사의 관계이다.

04 else: 또 다른, 다른

05 ⑤는 pack(짐을 싸다)의 영영풀이이다.

06 날씨를 묻는 표현에는 How's the weather today?, What's the weather like today? 등이 있다

07 No, I haven't.로 답했으므로 현재완료를 이용해서 경험을 묻는 질문이 와야 알맞다.

08 be의 과거분사는 been이다.

09 be planning to: ~할 계획이다

10 4월에는 비가 자주 온다고 언급되었다.

11 to부정사의 수식을 받는 명사가 전치사의 목적어일 경우 뒤에 전치사가 온다.

12 첫 문장은 형용사가 wise이므로 의미상의 주어는 'of+목적격'을 쓴다. 두 번째 문장은 형용사가 impossible이므로 의미상의 주어는 'for+목적격'을 쓴다.

13 It이 가주어이므로 진주어인 to부정사가 와야 한다.

14 To solve this puzzle이 주어인 문장으로, 가주어 it이 앞에 온다.

15 <보기>와 ⑤의 It은 가주어이다. ①, ④ 비인칭 주어, ②, ③ 인칭대명사

16 ①에서 sit은 자동사이므로 chair를 목적어로 취하기 위해서는 전치사 in이나 on이 필요하다.

17 many places to visit(방문할 많은 장소)에서 to visit은 형용사적 용법의 to부정사로 명사인 many places를 수식한다.

18 ④는 to부정사의 형용사적 용법이고, 나머지는 모두 '~하기 위해서'라는 목적을 나타내는 부사적 용법이다.

19 for+수사가 붙은 기간

20 ⓐ, ② 형용사적 용법 ①, ⑤ 명사적 용법 ③, ④ 부사적 용법

21 at last=in the long run: 결국, 마침내

22 get to=arrive at=reach: ~에 도착하다

23 thousand 뒤에 of가 와서 '수천의, 수많은'의 뜻을 나타낼 때는 복수형을 취한다.

24 remain: 계속[여전히] ~이다, 남아 있다

25 try+to부정사: ~하기 위해 애쓰다 / try+-ing: 시험 삼아 ~해 보다

27 It은 to see 이하를 받는 가주어이다.

28 지난달에 남해에 갔다고 언급되었다.

서술형 실전문제 p.50~51

01 gone → been   02 What, like
03 but   04 (A) - (C) - (B) - (D)
05 (1) It isn't easy to keep a diary every day.
   (2) I like the photographs which my little[younger] brother takes.
06 (1) It is difficult for me to park a car.
   (2) It is safe to ride a bike with a helmet.
   (3) It is an exciting experience to live in another country.
07 (1) to go to school
   (2) to have lunch
   (3) to play on the playground
   (4) to do my homework
08 because[as]   09 A B&B
10 of   11 anything
12 They walked around the Cotswolds.   13 many
14 나는 다시 라오스를 방문할 기회를 갖기를 바란다.
15 He or she went to Laos with his or her family.

01 have gone to: ~에 갔다(그래서 여기 없다) / have been to: ~에 가 본 적이 있다, ~에 다녀왔다

02 날씨를 묻는 표현에는 How's the weather today?, What's the weather like today? 등이 있다.

03 상반되는 내용을 연결하는 접속사 but이 알맞다.

04 (A) 엄마, 오늘 날씨 어때요? - (C) 바깥 날씨가 꽤 흐려. 일기 예보를 확인해 볼게. - (B) 고마워요, 엄마. - (D) 음, 오후에 비가 올 거야

05 (1) 「It ~ to부정사」 구문을 이용하여 문장을 완성한다. (2) 관계대명사 which를 이용하여 선행사 the photographs를 수식하도록 한다.

06 to부정사가 이끄는 구가 주어로 오는 경우, to부정사 주어를 문장 뒤로 보내고 그 자리에 It을 쓴다.

07 to부정사의 형용사적 용법을 이용하여 문장을 완성한다.

08 결과의 접속사 so는 이유를 나타내는 접속사를 써서 바꿔 쓸 수 있다. because나 as 대신 since를 쓸 수도 있다.

09 It은 인칭대명사로 앞에 나온 단수 명사를 받는다.

10 be full of: ~으로 가득 차다

11 something은 긍정문, anything은 부정문에서 쓰인다.

12 그들은 코츠월드 언덕을 돌아다녔다고 언급되었다.

13 temples가 복수 명사이기 때문에 much는 쓸 수 없다.

14 to visit는 chance를 수식하는 형용사적 용법이다.

창의사고력 서술형 문제 p.52

|모범답안|
01 (1) I need something to drink.
   (2) I need a chair to sit on[in].
   (3) He needs friends to talk with.
02 (1) It is kind of her to help the poor.
   (2) It is difficult for us to win the game.
   (3) It is stupid of you to agree to the proposal.
   (4) It is possible for you to finish the work on time.
   (5) It is necessary for foreigners to learn Korean.
03 (1) a movie to watch
   (2) a baseball game to watch
   (3) a piano lesson to take
   (4) four comic books to read

01 앞의 명사를 꾸며주는 to부정사의 형용사적 용법을 이용한다.

02 「It is ~ for[of]+목적어+to부정사」의 가주어, 진주어 구문을 이용한다.

03 to부정사의 형용사적 용법을 이용하여 내용에 맞도록 빈칸을 채운다.

01 ④	02 ③	03 ④	
04 decision	05 up	06 ②	07 ③
08 ⑤	09 ①, ③	10 ④	11 ④
12 ③	13 ③	14 to finish	15 ③
16 ⑤	17 ②	18 ⑤	19 ⓐ to find ⓑ to find
22 ①, ②	23 ④	20 ③	21 ④
26 ①	27 그 올리브 나무에 손을 대면 옥스퍼드	24 ③	25 portrait
대학에 들어가기 때문이다.	28 ②		29 many
30 ④			

01 어떤 것이 일어나거나 존재하게 하다: create(창조하다)

02 right now: 지금, 당장

03 be full of: ~으로 가득 차다 / be fond of: ~을 좋아하다

04 '동사 : 명사'의 관계이다.

05 show up: 나타나다 / clean up: ~을 청소하다

06 Have you ever+과거분사 ~?에 대한 응답은 Yes, I have. / No, I haven't.이다. 빈칸 다음의 말로 보아 부정의 대답이 와야 한다.

07 대답이 No, I haven't.이므로 경험을 묻는 표현인 ③ '넌 곰을 본 적이 있니?'가 알맞다.

08 A가 날씨를 물었으므로 춥고 때때로 눈이 많이 내린다는 응답이 가장 적절하다.

09 How[What] about you?: 너는 어때?

10 Bill이 두려워서 번지 점프를 하지 않는다는 말은 언급되지 않았다.

11 명사 things를 수식하는 형용사적 용법의 to부정사가 와야 한다.

12 문맥상 '함께 여행할 친구를 찾고 있다'는 흐름이 자연스러우므로, 빈칸에는 '~와 함께'에 해당하는 with가 알맞다.

13 기숙사에서 사는 것이므로 live 다음에 전치사 in이 필요하다.

14 it은 가주어이고, 진주어는 형용사 뒤에 to부정사 형태로 와야 한다.

15 <보기>의 to eat는 형용사적 용법의 to부정사이다. ①, ②, ⑤ 부사적 용법 ③ 형용사적 용법 ④ 명사적 용법

16 ⑤ -thing이나 -body로 끝나는 부정대명사의 경우 형용사와 to부정사의 수식을 동시에 받으면 「부정대명사+형용사+to부정사」의 순서로 써야 한다. something important to tell

17 ②의 경우, 두 개의 동사(is, skate)가 같이 쓰일 수는 없다. 가주어 it과 진주어 to부정사구(to skate ~)의 구문으로 만든다.

18 to부정사의 형용사적 용법이다.

19 가주어 It의 진주어로 to부정사 형태가 필요하다.

20 other → else

21 현재완료형에서 '~한 이후로'의 뜻으로 부사절을 이끄는 접속사는 since이다.

22 선행사가 사람이고 주격이므로 who나 that을 쓴다.

23 ④ Harry Potter가 Christ Church College의 학생이라는 말은 언급되지 않았다.

24 ⓐ에는 때를 나타내는 접속사, ⓑ에는 이유를 나타내는 접속사가 와야 한다.

25 어떤 특정한 사람을 그린 그림이나 찍은 사진: portrait(초상화)

26 very는 비교급을 수식할 수 없다.

28 Then이 있으므로 Vientiane의 야시장에 갔다는 문장 다음에 와야 한다.

29 a lot of: 많은

30 ④ 그들의 전통 음식이 무엇인지는 언급되지 않았다.

Giving a Hand

시험대비 실력평가 p.60

01 ②	02 ④	03 ③	04 heavy
05 ②	06 create	07 until[till]	08 ③

01 ①, ③, ④, ⑤는 모두 plant(식물)에 속한다.

02 at first: 처음에 / be thankful for: ~에게 감사하다

03 어떤 특정한 방향으로 갈 생각 없이, 종종 아무렇게나 어떤 장소를 거닐다: wander(거닐다, 헤매다)

04 반의어의 관계이다. 낮은 : 높은 = 가벼운 : 무거운

05 look for: ~을 찾다

06 어떤 것이 발생하거나 존재하게 하다 : create(창조하다, 만들어 내다)

07 until: ~할 때까지(=till)

08 grow up: 성장하다 / give up; 포기하다

서술형 시험대비 p.61

01 (1) daughter   (2) activity

02 (1) with[for] joy   (2) come over to   (3) thank, for

03 (1) still   (2) build   (3) understand
   (4) someone   (5) share

04 (1) comfortable   (2) happiness   (3) create

05 (1) Af first   (2) Cheer up   (3) come up with
   (4) Keep an eye on

06 (1) (g)ift   (2) (d)river

01 (1) 남성명사 : 여성명사의 관계이다. (2) 형용사 : 명사의 관계이다.

02 (1) with[for] joy: 기뻐서 (2) come over to: ~으로 오다
   (3) thank A for B: B에 대하여 A에게 감사하다

03 (1) still: 아직(도) (2) build: 짓다, 건설하다 (3) understand: 이해하다, 알아듣다 (4) someone: 어떤 사람 (5) share: 함께 쓰다

04 (1) comfortable: 편안한 (2) happiness: 행복 (3) create: 만들어 내다, 창조하다

05 (1) at first: 처음에는 (2) cheer up: 기운 내다 (3) come up with: ~을 생각해 내다 (4) keep an eye on: ~을 계속 지켜보다

06 (1) gift: 선물 (2) driver: 운전자, 운전기사

교과서 Conversation

핵심 Check p.62~63

1 (1) do, favor / What   (2) help me / course
  (3) help me find / can't

2 (1) Thank / pleasure   (2) grateful / at all
  (3) appreciate / problem

교과서 대화문 익히기

Check(√) True or False p.64

1 T   2 F   3 F   4 T   5 T   6 F

교과서 확인학습 p.66~67

Listen & Speak 1 A. Listen and Check

1 do, favor / What / family, vacation, come, water / can

2 can, favor / it / help, with, project / Sorry, can't, have

Listen & Speak 2 A. Listen and Check

1 Hi, know, birthday, haven't, to, being, been, and, supporting, trying, proud, daughter

2 doing, weekend, special, stay, watch, having, party, inviting

Listen & Speak 1-B

favor / What / move, with, heavy / problem / Thank, helping

Communicate A. Listen and Answer

Can, do / What / shopping, for / course, for / for / getting, gift / until / why, cap / broke, while, last, just, cheer / see, go / perfect

Progress Check

1 do, favor / it / going, this, care, during / worry, enjoy

2 Hello, haven't, being, Every, welcome, teach, things, lucky, proud, students

3 any, plans / just, stay / then, over, dinner

시험대비 기본평가 p.68

01 ④	02 ②	03 ①	04 ①

01 ①, ②, ③, ⑤는 도움을 요청하는 반면, ④ What can I do for you?는 도움을 주겠다고 제안하는 표현이다.

02 감사 표현에 대한 응답은 My pleasure. / Not at all. / Don't mention it. 등을 이용하여 나타낸다.

03 Can you do me a favor?는 '부탁 좀 해도 될까?'의 의미로 상대방에게 도움을 요청할 때 사용하는 표현이다.

04 감사의 의미를 나타내는 말이다.

시험대비 실력평가 p.69~70

01 ②	02 ④	03 appreciate, problem	
04 Thank, for	05 ④	06 ②	07 give, hand
08 shopping	09 ①	10 ③	
11 ②	12 Nothing	13 ④	14 welcome

01 Kevin, 부탁 하나 들어줄래? - 좋아. 뭔데? - 오늘 오후에 내 과학 프로젝트 좀 도와줄래? - 미안하지만 안돼. 엄마랑 할머니 댁에 가야 해.

02 ④ 고맙다는 말에 대한 응답이다.

03 appreciate: 고맙게 여기다 / No problem.: 천만에.

04 thank you for -ing: ~에 감사하다

05 Can you give me a hand?는 상대방에게 도움을 요청하는 표현이다.

06 ② TV 소리를 줄여달라는 요청에 '천만에요.'라고 응답하는 것은 어울리지 않는다.

07 Can you do me a favor?와 Can you give me a hand?는 남에게 도움을 요청할 때 쓰는 표현이다.

08 go shopping: 쇼핑하러 가다

09 문맥상 이유를 묻는 의문부사 why가 알맞다.

10 cheer up: ~을 격려하다

11 ② Jaden은 여동생의 생일 선물을 사는 것이 아니라고 했다.

12 Nothing special.: 특별히 할 일은 없다.

13 thank A for B: B에 대하여 A에게 감사하다

14 You're welcome.: 천만에.

서술형 시험대비 p.71

01 for helping	02 hand	03 do / ahead / for
04 (D)–(A)–(C)–(B)	05 haven't	06 chance
07 trying	08 저는 두 분의 딸인 것을 자랑스럽게 여깁니다.	

01 thank you for -ing: ~에 감사하다 / help with: ~을 돕다

02 Can you give me a hand?: 나를 도와 줄 수 있니?

03 Go ahead.: 어서 그렇게 해라., 어서 말해라. / buy A for B: B에게 A를 사 주다

04 (D) 소라야, 이번 주 금요일에 뭐 할 거니? - (A) 특별한 계획은 없어. 왜? - (C) 나는 내 생일파티를 열 거야. 너도 올래? - (B) 물론이지. 초대해 줘서 고마워.

05 문맥상 현재완료 부정문이 와야 한다.

06 뭔가를 할 기회가 있는 적절한 시간 또는 상황: 기회 (chance)

07 supporting과 함께 전치사 for의 목적어이므로 동명사형이 되어야 한다.

08 be proud to ~: ~해서 자랑스럽게 여기다

교과서
Grammar

핵심 Check p.72~73

1 (1) that (2) that (3) whom (4) which (5) which
2 (1) enough to (2) so, that (3) too, to (4) so, that (5) too, to

시험대비 기본평가 p.74

01 (1) so (2) too (3) whom (4) which
02 (1) so, that, could (2) so poor, can't (3) too, to
03 (1) who (2) whom (3) which (4) that

01 (1) so ~ that+S+can't ... 구문으로 '너무 ~해서 …할 수 없다'의 의미이다. (2) too ~ to부정사 구문으로 '너무 ~해서 …할 수 없다'의 의미이다. (3) 선행사가 사람이고 목적격이므로 관계대명사 whom으로 연결한다. (4) 선행사가 사물이고 목적격이므로 관계대명사 which로 연결한다.

02 (1) 형용사+enough to+동사원형 → so+형용사+that+주어+can+동사원형 (2) too+형용사+to부정사 → so+형용사+that+주어+can't+동사원형 (3) so+형용사+that+주어+cannot+동사원형 → too+형용사+to부정사

03 (1) 주격관계대명사 who가 필요하다. (2) 전치사 다음에는 that을 쓸 수 없다. (3) 사물이 선행사 (a knife)이므로 전치사의 목적어 역할을 하는 목적격 관계대명사 which가 와야 한다. (4) the only가 선행사를 수식하므로 목적격 관계대명사 that이 온다.

시험대비 실력평가 p.75~77

01 ②	02 ①	03 so, can't	
04 (1) which → who(m) [that] (2) that → which			
05 ⑤	06 ④	07 ④	08 so

11

09 ⑤   10 that   11 ①   12 The man gave me all the money that he had.   13 ⑤

14 ④   15 ③   16 too, to carry

17 (1) which → who(m) [that]   (2) were → was

18 ②   19 ③   20 ①   21 ①, ⑤

---

01 선행사가 사람(the gentleman)이고 동사 met의 목적어 역할을 하므로 who(m)나 that이 와야 한다.

02 '상자가 너무 무거워서 나 혼자서 옮길 수 없었다.'고 하는 것이 자연스러우므로 so heavy that I couldn't move ~를 쓰는 것이 적절하다.

03 '걸어가기에 너무 멀다'는 '너무 멀어서 걸어갈 수 없다'는 의미와 같다.

04 (1) 선행사가 사람이므로 knows의 목적어 역할을 하는 who(m) 또는 that을 쓴다. (2) 관계대명사 that은 전치사 뒤에 올 수 없다.

05 '너무 바빠서 그녀를 기다릴 수 없다'는 의미가 자연스러우므로 too busy to wait를 쓴다.

06 ④에서 listen은 자동사이므로 목적어를 취할 때는 전치사 to가 필요하다. (which → to which)

07 ④ '아주 힘이 세서 상자들을 옮길 수 있었다'는 의미이므로 too 대신 so를 써야 한다.

08 so ~ that ... 구문은 '너무 ~해서 …할 수 없다'의 의미를 나타낸다.

09 목적격 관계대명사는 생략할 수 있다. that은 사물과 사람에 모두 쓸 수 있다.

10 선행사가 사람일 때와 사물일 때 모두 쓸 수 있는 관계대명사는 that이다.

11 so that ~ can: ~하기 위해서 / so ~ that ... can't: 너무 ~해서 …할 수 없다

12 선행사 all the money를 목적격 관계대명사 that이 이끄는 절이 수식한다.

13 '너무 ~해서 …할 수 없다'는 so ~ that ... can't로 나타낸다. 또한 too ~ to부정사로 나타낼 수도 있다. ②는 eat의 목적어가 되는 it이 필요하다.

14 ④ 전치사 다음에는 that을 쓸 수 없다.

15 'too+형용사+to부정사'는 'so+형용사+that+주어 +couldn't+동사원형'으로 바꿔 쓸 수 있다.

16 '너무 무거워 내가 옮길 수 없다'는 '내가 옮기기에는 너무 무겁다'로 바꿔 쓸 수 있다.

17 (1) 선행사가 사람이므로 목적격 관계대명사 who(m)이나 that이 와야 한다. (2) 문장의 주어(The knife)는 단수 명사이므로 be동사는 was가 되어야 한다.

18 목적격 관계대명사는 생략할 수 있다. ②의 who는 앞에 나온 The boy를 수식하는 주격 관계대명사이므로 생략할 수 없다.

19 ⓑ enough old → old enough ⓒ solve → solve it

20 ①의 that은 명사절을 이끄는 접속사로 쓰였고, 나머지는 관계대명사로 쓰였다.

21 시제는 과거이고, '너무 ~해서 …하지 못했다'는 「so ~ that+주어+couldn't ~」 또는 too ~ to부정사 구문을 이용하여 나타낸다.

서술형 시험대비

01 (1) I know the man who(m)[that] you are looking for.
　(2) This is the bag which[that] I got from Nancy.
　(3) He is the boy who(m)[that] I meet at the bus stop every morning.

02 (1) so   (2) enough   (3) too   (4) that   03 that

04 (1) too → so   (2) carry it → carry
　(3) enough warm → warm enough   (4) what → that

05 so, that

06 (1) I bought my sister a blouse (which[that] was) made in France.
　(2) Do you know the boy whom I met on the street yesterday?
　(3) This is the city that is famous for its beautiful buildings.

07 (1) so, that, can't   (2) lucky enough to

08 (1) The question is so easy that everyone knows the answer.
　(2) I am so tired that I can't do it right now.

09 (1) to / so, that, can't   (2) enough / so, could blow
　(3) so, couldn't / too, to

10 (1) The girl saw a man and his dog that looked very tired.
　(2) John with whom I played tennis yesterday is the best player in this town.
　(3) This bike which[that] my father bought (for) me last year is my treasure.
　(4) My sister ate the only ice cream that my mother bought for me.
　(5) The house in which we lived two years ago was in Incheon.

11 (1) who[m]   (2) which[that]

---

01 목적격 관계대명사는 접속사와 대명사의 역할을 하며, 선행사가 사람일 경우 who(m)나 that, 사물일 경우 which나 that을 쓴다.

02 (1), (4) so ~ that ... 구문이다. (2) enough to부정사 구문이다. (3) too ~ to부정사 구문이다.

03 선행사가 사람일 때와 사물일 때 모두 쓸 수 있는 관계대명사는 that이다.

04 (1) that절이 있으므로 too 대신 so를 써야 한다. (2) 주어

12 정답 및 해설

The bag이 carry의 목적어이므로 it은 필요 없다. (3) 부사
enough는 형용사 뒤에 위치한다. (4) so ~ that 구문이다.

05 so+형용사+that+주어+동사: 너무 ~해서 …하다

06 (1) 선행사 a blouse가 사물이므로 관계대명사는 which나 that
이 되어야 한다. 과거분사 앞에 있는 <주격 관계대명사+be 동사>
는 생략할 수 있다. (2) whom은 생략할 수 있다. (3) that이 이끄
는 절의 선행사가 단수명사이므로 동사는 is가 되어야 한다.

07 (1) so ~ that ... can't: 너무 ~해서 ...할 수 없다 (2) 형용
사 + enough to + 동사원형: ~할 만큼 충분히 ...한

08 (1) so ~ that ...구문: 너무 ~해서 …하다 (2) so ~ that ...
can't 구문: 너무 ~해서 …할 수 없다

09 (1), (3) 'too+형용사/부사+to부정사'는 'so+형용사/부사
+that+주어+cannot+동사원형'의 형태로 바꿔 쓸 수 있다.
(2) '형용사/부사+enough to+동사원형'은 'so+형용사/부사
+that+ 주어+can+동사원형'의 형태로 바꿔 쓸 수 있다.

10 (1) 선행사가 사람과 동물(a man and his dog)이므로 관계대
명사 that을 쓴다. (4) the only가 선행사를 수식할 때는 보통
관계대명사 that을 쓴다. (5) 선행사가 사물(the house)이므
로, 전치사 in의 목적어 역할을 하는 목적격 관계대명사 which
를 쓴다.

11 (1) 선행사가 사람이고 목적격이므로 관계대명사는 who,
whom 또는 that을 쓸 수 있다. (2) 선행사가 사물이고 목적격
이므로 관계대명사는 which나 that을 쓸 수 있다.

[교과서] Reading

확인문제 p.80

1 F 2 T 3 T 4 F 5 T

확인문제 p.81

1 T 2 F 3 F 4 T 5 F

교과서 확인학습 A p.82~83

01 up, family   02 Since, been
03 friend, driver, cook
04 taught, lessons   05 who, most
06 When, went, got   07 disease
08 Everyone, shock
09 became, over 10 off, that, all
11 got, saw   12 moment, himself, don't, heels

13 that, do   14 create, then, signal
15 tried, materials, socks   16 like, safety
17 After, succeeded
18 worked, that, joy
19 believe, actually   20 For, inventor
21 friend

교과서 확인학습 B p.84~85

1 Kenneth Shinozuka grew up in a big happy family
of three generations.

2 Since he was little, he has always been very close
to his grandfather.

3 He was Kenneth's first friend, his trusty driver, and
his cook.

4 He also taught him many life lessons.

5 He was the person who Kenneth respected the
most in the world.

6 When Kenneth was four, his grandfather went out
for a walk one day and got lost.

7 He had Alzheimer's disease.

8 Everyone in Kenneth's family was in shock.

9 His condition became worse over the next 10
years.

10 He wandered off at night so often that someone
had to keep an eye on him all night long.

11 One night, Kenneth's grandfather got out of bed,
and Kenneth saw it.

12 At that moment, he said to himself, "Why don't I
put pressure sensors on the heels of his socks?"

13 There were many things that Kenneth had to do.

14 He first had to create a pressure sensor and then
find a way to send a signal to his smart phone.

15 Kenneth also tried many different materials to make
comfortable socks for his elderly grandfather.

16 When he felt like giving up, he thought about his
grandfather's safety.

17 After much trial and error, he finally succeeded in
making his device.

18 When it first worked, he was so happy that he
jumped for joy.

19 He could not believe that his invention actually
worked.

20 For his grandfather, Kenneth is the best inventor
in the world.

21 For Kenneth, his grandfather is still his best friend.

01 ④	02 ③	03 driver	04 ①, ②, ⑤
05 ③	06 ⑤	07 lost	08 ②
09 Kenneth의 할아버지가 침대에서 나오는 것			10 ④
11 ⑤	12 ③	13 comfortable	14 ③
15 ①	16 trial	17 ④	18 할아버지

18 ...의 안전에 대해 생각했기 때문이다.   19 ②   20 been

21 그는 또한 그에게 많은 인생 교훈을 가르쳐 주었다.

22 ①, ②	23 ①	24 ③	25 disease

26 ①   27 어느 날 밤 Kenneth의 할아버지가 침대에서 나왔는데, Kenneth가 그것을 보았다.   28 him → himself   29 ②   30 ⑤   31 ②, ④

32 ⑤

01 주어진 문장은 할아버지가 추가적으로 해준 일을 나타내므로 할아버지가 Kenneth의 친구이자 운전기사이자 요리사였다는 문장 다음에 와야 한다.

02 since는 현재완료에서 '~한 이래로'의 뜻으로 쓰인다.

03 drive: 운전하다 / driver: 운전기사

04 선행사가 사람이고 목적격이므로 who, whom, that을 쓸 수 있다.

05 ③ Kenneth의 할아버지가 운전을 잘하는지는 알 수 없다.

06 ①, ②, ③, ④는 Kenneth의 할아버지를 가리키고, ⑤는 Kenneth를 가리킨다.

07 get lost: 길을 잃다

08 so ~ that ... 구문이다.

09 it은 인칭대명사로 앞 문장의 내용을 받는다.

10 ④ 할아버지를 지켜본 것은 Kenneth였다.

11 선행사가 사물이고 목적격이므로 that이나 which를 쓸 수 있다.

12 ⓑ, ③ 형용사적 용법 ①, ④ 명사적 용법 ②, ⑤ 부사적 용법

13 comfort: 편안함 / comfortable: 편안한

14 그의 장비가 처음 작동되었을 때 아주 기뻤다는 문장 다음에 와야 한다.

15 give up: 포기하다

16 try: 시도하다 / trial: 시도, 실험, 시험

17 for[with] joy: 기뻐서

19 grow up: 자라다, 성장하다

20 현재완료이므로 과거분사로 고쳐야 한다.

21 lesson은 여기서 '수업, 과'의 뜻이 아니라 '교훈'의 뜻으로 쓰였다.

22 선행사가 사람이고 목적격이므로 who, whom, that을 쓸 수 있다.

23 '~이었을 때'의 뜻으로 때를 나타내는 접속사가 와야 한다.

24 get lost: 길을 잃다

25 예를 들어 박테리아나 감염에 의해 생기는 것으로 사람, 동물, 식물에 걸리는 병: disease(병)

26 '~에'의 뜻으로 night이나 noon 앞에는 전치사 at이 붙는다.

27 get out of: ~에서 나오다

28 전치사 to의 목적어가 주어 자신이므로 재귀대명사를 써야 한다.

29 Why don't I ~?: ~하는 게 어떨까?

30 to → for

31 선행사가 사물이므로 that이나 which가 알맞다.

32 ⓑ, ⑤ 부사적 용법 ①, ③, ④ 명사적 용법 ② 형용사적 용법

01 giving	02 safety	03 in
04 because[as]		05 inventor
06 Because his device worked.		07 so
08 happiness	09 ① 지역 아이들을 가르친다. ② 지역 아이들을 위한 학교를 세운다.	10 on
11 so	12 which	13 for

14 김도하는 개들을 산보 시키거나 목욕을 시킬 수 있다. 또 그는 개들과 놀 수 있다.

15 up	16 is → has	17 ① 차에 태우고 여기저기를 다녔다. ② 음식을 요리해 주었다
18 to		

19 He respected his grandfather the most in the world.

01 feel like+-ing(동명사): ~하고 싶은 생각이 들다

02 해로움이나 위험으로부터 안전한 상태: safety(안전)

03 succeed in -ing: ~하는 데 성공하다

04 so ~ that ... 구문은 because, as, since와 같은 이유를 나타내는 접속사를 써서 바꿔 쓸 수 있다.

05 invent: 발명하다 / inventor: 발명가

06 그가 만든 장비가 재대로 작동했기 때문이다.

07 so ~ that ... 구문이다.

08 happy: 행복한 / happiness: 행복

10 on TV: 텔레비전에서

11 so ~ that ... 구문은 결과를 나타내는 접속사 so를 써서 바꿔 쓸 수 있다.

12 선행사가 사물인 관계대명사의 목적격 that은 which로 바꿔 쓸 수 있다.

13 look for: ~을 찾다

15 grow up: 자라다, 성장하다

16 현재완료 구문이므로 has+과거분사형이 되어야 한다.

18 teach는 간접목적어가 직접목적어 뒤로 갈 때 전치사 to를 붙인다.

01 ④	02 ③	03 heavy	04 ②
05 ⑤	06 up	07 trial, error	08 ⑤
09 ④	10 ①	11 ⑤	12 to → for
13 ⑤	14 ③	15 ④	

16 ②	17 whom	18 ⑤	19 ④
20 ③	21 ④	22 ③	23 ③
24 ④	25 were → was		26 ②
27 ①	28 ⑤	29 ⑤	30 ④
31 ③	32 나이 드신 분들께 팥빙수를 만들어 드리고 함께 먹는 것이다.		33 ③
34 volunteer	35 so	36 ①, ④	37 ②

01 ④는 명사에 -ly가 붙어 형용사가 된 것이고, 나머지는 형용사에 -ly가 붙어 부사가 된 것이다.

02 • 비가 어느 때보다 더 심하게 내리고 있다. • 그들은 우리를 맞이하기 위해 문에 나와 있었다. • 나는 그가 무슨 말을 하는 건지 모르겠다. • 현지 시각은 오전 10시 50분입니다.

03 반의어 관계이다. 따뜻한 : 시원한 = 가벼운 : 무거운

04 keep an eye on: ~을 계속 지켜보다

05 어떤 사람과 의견이 일치하고 아마도 그들이 성공하기를 바라기 때문에 그들을 돕다: support(지지하다)

06 grow up: 자라다, 성장하다 / come up with: ~을 생각해 내다

07 trial and error: 시행착오

08 A는 상대방에게 도움을 요청하고 있다. 그러므로 상대방의 부탁에 대한 승낙이나 거절의 표현이 들어가야 한다.

09 주어진 문장은 그녀를 격려하고 싶다고 말하는 문장이므로 그녀가 다리가 부러졌다는 문장 다음에 와야 한다.

10 do me a favor: 나의 부탁을 들어주다

11 문맥상 '10월까지는 아니다'라는 뜻이 되어야 한다.

12 get은 직접목적어를 간접목적어 뒤로 보낼 때 전치사 for를 붙인다.

13 ⑤ Kate가 왜 다리가 부러졌는지는 알 수 없다.

14 No problem.은 '천만에요.'의 뜻으로 감사 표현에 답하는 말이다.

15 선행사 the ring이 사물이고 목적격이므로 관계대명사 which[that]가 들어가야 알맞다.

16 so ~ that ... 구문은 '너무 ~해서 …하다'의 의미를 나타낸다.

17 선행사가 사람(friend)이고 앞에 전치사 to가 있으므로 목적격 관계대명사 whom을 쓴다. look to: ~에게 기대하다[기대다]

18 '형용사+enough to+동사원형'은 'so+형용사+that+주어+can'으로 바꿔 쓸 수 있다.

19 ④ 동사 work는 자동사이므로 목적격 whom을 취하기 위해서는 '~와 함께'라는 의미의 전치사 with가 필요하다.

20 ③ enough fast → fast enough

21 <보기>와 나머지는 목적격 관계대명사로 쓰였고, ④는 명사절을 이끄는 접속사로 쓰였다.

22 '너무 ~해서 …할 수 없다'는 「so+형용사/부사+that ~ can't」 또는 「too+형용사/부사+to부정사」로 쓸 수 있다.

23 ③ 관계대명사 that은 전치사(in)의 목적어가 될 수 없다. (that → which)

24 go out for a walk: 산책하러 나가다

25 everyone은 단수동사로 받는다.

26 keep an eye on: ~을 계속 지켜보다

27 Why don't I ~?: 내가 ~하는 게 어떨까?

28 ⑤ Kenneth가 할아버지 양말 뒤꿈치에 압력 센서를 부착했다는 말은 언급되지 않았다.

29 선행사가 사물이고 목적격이므로 that이나 which를 쓸 수 있다.

30 come up with: ~을 제안하다, ~을 생각해 내다

31 make A for B: B에게 A를 만들어 주다

33 개를 위해 할 수 있는 일을 나타내는 문장 앞에 와야 한다.

34 일을 하기를 원해서 보수를 받지 않고 일하는 사람: volunteer(자원봉사자)

35 so: 그래서

36 선행사가 사람인 관계대명사 목적격은 who, whom, that을 쓸 수 있다.

37 ② 김도하의 취미가 무엇인지는 본문에서 언급되지 않았다.

단원별 예상문제
p.98~101

01 ④	02 ②	03 ③	04 queen
05 worse	06 ④	07 ②	08 ④
09 favor	10 weekend	11 ③	12 ⑤
13 ③	14 know them → know		15 too → so
16 This is the book which I borrowed from Paul.		17 ③	18 so, that	19 ⑤
20 ①	21 ③	22 helping	23 지역 아이들을 가르치고 그들을 위한 학교를 세우는 것이다.
24 There were many things that[which] Kenneth had to do.		25 ④	26 ③	27 여러 가지 재료를 써서 양말을 만들어 보았다.	28 like
29 ①	30 ⑤	31 Because his device worked.	

01 ④는 유의어 관계이고 나머지는 반의어 관계이다.

02 look for: ~을 찾다 / be thankful for: ~에 대해 감사히 여기다

03 ③은 support(지지하다)의 영영풀이이다.

04 남성명사 : 여성명사의 관계이다.

05 worse: 더 나쁜, 더 심한

06 Thank you for ~.는 감사를 나타내는 표현이다.

07 책을 대신 반납해 줄 수 있냐고 도움을 요청하는 말에 승낙이나 거절로 답한다.

08 ④ Thank you for ~.는 감사를 나타내는 표현이다.

09 do me a favor: 나의 부탁을 들어주다

10 토요일과 일요일· weekend(주말)

11 take care of=look after: ~을 돌보다

12 앞 문장에는 the doll을 선행사로 하는 목적격 관계대명사 which나 that이 들어가고, 뒤 문장에는 the man을 선행사로

하는 목적격 관계대명사 who(m)이나 that이 들어간다.

13 「so + 형용사/부사 + that ...」구문으로 '너무 ~해서 …하다'의 의미를 나타낸다. 빈칸에 알맞은 말은 so와 that이다.

14 know의 목적어 them은 관계대명사로 바뀌고, 목적격 관계대명사이기 때문에 생략된 형태이다.

15 「so+형용사/부사+that ~」구문으로, so 대신 too를 사용할 수 없다. that절이 있으므로 too를 so로 바꿔야 한다.

16 주절에서 무엇이 선행사인지 찾은 다음, 선행사를 꾸며주는 관계사절을 관계대명사로 연결한다.

17 ③ 선행사가 사람이고 목적격으로 쓰였으므로 관계대명사 who(m) 또는 that이 알맞다.

18 '너무 ~해서 …하다'는 so ~ that 구문을 이용하여 나타낸다.

19 관계대명사 목적격은 생략할 수 있다. ⑤의 who는 주격 관계대명사이므로 생략할 수 없다.

20 아이들을 돕기를 원한다면 Child Care Project에 가입하라는 흐름이 자연스럽다.

21 at first: 처음에는

22 전치사 뒤에는 동명사가 와야 한다.

24 목적격 관계대명사 that이나 which가 생략된 문장이다.

25 a way를 수식하는 형용사적 용법의 to부정사가 와야 한다.

26 make A for B: B에게 A를 만들어 주다

28 feel like -ing: ~하고 싶은 생각이 들다

29 trial and error: 시행착오

30 ⓒ, ⑤ 작동되다, 효과가 있다 ① 일하다 ② 공부하다 ③ 작동시키다 ④ 근무하다

서술형 실전문제 p.102~103

01 do   02 heavy   03 helping
04 (C) - (B) - (D) - (A)
05 (1) whom everyone in my class
   (2) which I want to watch
06 (1) The food was so spicy that Chris couldn't eat it much.
   (2) It was too cold for us to go on a picnic.
   (3) He is rich enough to buy that car.
07 what → which[that]   08 길을 잃었다
09 worse   10 that   11 himself
12 Because Kenneth's grandfather had Alzheimer's disease.
13 which   14 (c)reate   15 to make
16 압력 감지기를 만들어 그의 스마트폰으로 신호를 보낼 방법을 찾으려고 노력했다. 그는 또한 할아버지에게 편안한 양말을 만들어 주기 위해 많은 다양한 재료들을 가지고 만들어 보았다.

01 do me a favor: 나의 부탁을 들어주다

02 무게가 많이 나가는: heavy(무거운)

03 전치사 다음에는 동명사형이 온다.

04 Mark, 부탁 하나 들어줄래? - 물론이지. 부탁할게 무엇이지? - 우리 가족은 일주일 동안 휴가를 갈 거야. 우리 집에 와서 식물들에게 물을 줄 수 있니? - 응, 할 수 있어.

05 (1) 목적격 관계대명사 whom이 이끄는 절이 선행사 a teacher를 수식한다. (2) 목적격 관계대명사 which가 이끄는 절이 선행사 The movie를 수식한다.

06 (1) so ~ that ... 구문을 쓴다. (2) too ~ to ... 구문을 쓴다. (3) enough to ~ 구문을 쓴다.

07 a pen이 선행사이므로 관계대명사는 which나 that을 쓴다.

08 get lost: 길을 잃다

09 bad의 비교급이 와야 한다.

10 so ~ that ... 구문이다.

11 전치사 to의 목적어가 주어 자신이므로 재귀대명사가 와야 한다.

12 할아버지가 알츠하이머병에 걸렸기 때문에 가족 모두가 충격에 빠졌다고 언급되었다.

13 선행사가 사물이므로 that이나 which를 쓸 수 있다.

14 어떤 것이 일어나거나 존재하게 하다: create(창조하다, 만들어 내다)

15 목적을 나타내는 to부정사의 부사적 용법이다.

창의사고력 서술형 문제 p.104

|모범답안|

01 (1) A waiter is someone who serves food in a restaurant.
   (2) A zookeeper is someone who looks after animals in the zoo.
   (3) Dessert is sweet food which is served after a meal.
   (4) The sport (which[that]) Ann plays best is table tennis.
   (5) Show me the camera (that[which]) you got last week.
   (6) Do you remember the woman (whom, who, that) I was talking about?

02 (1) Last year, my sister was too young to go to school, but now she is old enough to go to school.
   (2) Yesterday, my dad was too busy to play with me, but today he is not so busy that he can play with me.
   (3) Last month, my puppy was so light that I could pick it up, but now it is too heavy to pick up.

01 ③	02 ①	03 ①	04 lucky
05 up	06 ⑤	07 ②	08 ④
09 ③	10 for	11 아, 네 여동생에게 생일 선물을 사 줄 거니?	
		12 ②	13 ②
14 ③	15 ②	16 ③	17 ③, ④
18 ④, ⑤	19 too, to	20 ④	21 ③
22 ①	23 ②	24 I like dogs, and there are many things that[which] I can do for them.	
25 ①, ④	26 ⑤	27 ④	28 ②, ③
29 ③	30 actually		

01 at first: 처음에

02 예를 들어 박테리아나 감염에 의해 생기는 것으로 사람, 동물, 식물에게 걸리는 병: disease(병)

03 do A a favor: A의 부탁을 들어주다 / fix: 고치다, 수리하다

04 '명사 : 형용사'의 관계이다. 비 : 비오는 / 운 : 운이 좋은

05 grow up: 자라다, 성장하다 / give up: 포기하다

06 Eric, 이번 주말에 뭐 할 거니? - 특별한 건 없어. 그냥 집에 있으면서 TV를 볼 거야. - 좋아! 이번 주말에 생일 파티를 할거야. 올 수 있니? - 물론이지. 초대해 줘서 고마워.

07 ② 커피 한 잔을 달라는 요청에 '천만에요.'라고 응답하는 것은 어울리지 않는다.

08 Can you do me a favor?는 상대방에게 도움을 요청할 때 사용하는 표현이다.

09 주어진 문장은 그것은 누구에게 줄 것이냐고 묻는 문장이므로 내 여동생에게 줄 것이라는 문장 앞에 와야 한다.

10 for: ~을 (얻기) 위해, ~을 사러

11 현재진행형의 의문문으로 이때의 현재진행형은 가까운 미래의 일을 나타내고 있다.

12 get+직접목적어+for+간접목적어의 어순을 취한다.

13 ② Jaden은 모자를 유리가 아니라 여동생에게 사 주려고 한다.

14 앞 문장은 선행사가 사물이고 주격이므로 which나 that이 알맞고, 뒤 문장은 선행사가 사람이고 목적격이므로 who(m)나 that이 알맞다.

15 so ~ that+S+can't ... 구문은 '너무 ~해서 …할 수 없다'의 의미로 too ~ to부정사 구문으로 바꿔 쓸 수 있다.

16 ③은 주격 관계대명사로 쓰인 that이고, 나머지는 모두 목적격 관계대명사로 쓰였다.

17 ③ enough kind → kind enough ④ solve → solve it

18 선행사가 the writings로 사물이므로 목적격 관계대명사 that 또는 which가 알맞다.

19 '너무 ~해서 …할 수 없다'는 so ~ that ... can't 구문을 이용하여 나타낸다.

20 ④ 관계대명사 목적격은 생략할 수 있다.

21 문맥상 '프로젝트에 합류하다'가 알맞다.

22 on TV: 텔레비전으로

23 ⓒ, ② so ~ that ...과 such ~ that ...은 '아주 ~해서 … 하다'의 뜻을 나타낸다. ① 명사절을 이끄는 접속사 ③, ⑤ 관계대명사 ④ It ... that 강조구문

24 선행사가 사물이고 목적격이므로 which나 that을 보충할 수 있다.

25 선행사가 사람이고 목적격이므로 who, whom, that을 쓸 수 있다.

26 ⑤ 김도하는 자신이 자원봉사 프로젝트에 적합하다고 생각한다.

27 글의 흐름상 Kenneth에게는 그의 할아버지가 여전히 가장 좋은 친구라는 문장 앞에 와야 한다.

28 '~할 때'의 뜻으로 때를 나타내는 접속사가 와야 한다.

29 ⓑ에는 so ~ that ... 구문의 that이, ⓒ에는 명사절을 이끄는 that이 와야 한다

30 actual의 부사형이 와야 한다.

Lesson 5

Bravo! Brava!

01 brave   02 ①   03 ④   04 ⑤

05 ②   06 ⑤   07 (r)iddles

08 beautiful   09 (1) be late for   (2) take, off

01 둘은 반의어 관계이다. 알려지지 않은 : 유명한 = 겁 많은 : 용감한

02 새벽이다. 해가 떠오르고 있어.

03 배경 지식은 당신이 뮤지컬을 감상하는 데 도움이 될 것이다.

04 한 사람에 의해 불러지는 오페라의 음악

05 슬픔이나 공감의 강한 감정을 불러일으키는

06 nothing more than은 '~에 지나지 않은'의 뜻이다.

07 puzzle = riddle: 수수께끼

08 'of+추상명사'는 형용사와 뜻이 같다.

09 (1) be late for: ~에 늦다 (2) take off: (일을) 쉬다

서술형 시험대비   p.113

01 (1) right after   (2) correctly, agree to   (3) marry, riddles   02 (1) appreciate   (2) storyline

03 take   04 (1) most famous   (2) Like

(3) celebrated   (4) performance

05 (1) discount   (2) nothing more than   (3) fails

(4) until[till]

01 (1) right는 부사로 '바로'의 뜻이다. (2) correctly는 부사로 '맞게, 올바르게'의 뜻이고, '~에 동의하다'는 'agree to+동사원형'을 사용한다. (3) '~와 결혼하다'는 marry가 적절하다. 수수께끼는 three가 있으므로 복수형이 적절하다.

02 (1) 어떤 것이나 어떤 사람이 얼마나 좋은지 이해하다 (2) 책, 영화, 희곡 등에서 일어나는 일련의 사건

03 take off: 일을 쉬다, take+교통수단: ~을 타다

04 (1) of the whole opera(전체 오페라 중에서)와 호응이 되려면 'the+최상급' 형태가 적절하다. (2) like는 전치사로 '~와 같이'의 의미로 사용이 되었다. (3) celebrate: (특별한 날·경사 등을) 축하하다, 기념하다 / '그녀는 작년에 내 생일을 축하해 줬다.'는 의미로 과거시제가 적절하다. (4) 소유격 our 뒤에 명사형이 적절하므로 동사 perform의 명사형인 performance가 맞다.

05 (1) discount: 할인 (2) nothing more than: ~에 지나지 않은 (3) fail: 실패하다 (4) until[till]: ~할 때까지

Conversation

1 ③   2 ②   3 ③, ⑤

4 (W)hat about

교과서 대화문 익히기

Check(√) True or False   p.116

1 F   2 T   3 T   4 T

교과서 확인학습   p.118~119

Listen & Speak 1-A

1 hurry up, already / be late for / Why don't we take / faster than

2 wrong / sure, well, Why don't we, celebrate / for / Of course

Listen & Speak 1-B

shall we / Why don't we / good idea

Listen & Speak 2-A

1 let's, parts, play / What time shall we meet / How about, right / Sounds

2 Where shall we / about, near / at

Listen & Speak 2-B

Let's / shall / How about / Let's meet

Communicate A

guess / Why not / anniversary / together / take, off / Why don't we, get, discount if / let's / shall we / How about / best

Communicate B

What shall we / Why don't we / time shall we / How / Let's

Progress Check

1 Why don't we take, faster, at this time of day

2 Let's go swimming / Where / How about

시험대비 기본평가   p.120

01 ④   02 ③   03 ①

04 (C) → (B) → (D) → (A)

01 B의 대답이 '지하철역에서 만나는 게 어때?'라고 했으므로 G는 어디서 만날지 묻는 말이 적절하다.

02 A의 답으로 보아 B는 몇 시에 만날지 묻고 있다는 것을 알 수 있다.

03 비교급 구문으로 faster than이 적절하다.

04 (C) '배드민턴 하지 않을래?'라는 제안 → (B) 승낙의 표현과 어디서 할 것인지 묻고 → (D) 장소 제안 → (A) 동의

시험대비 실력평가 p.121~122

01 ④   02 ②   03 ①
04 ①, ④, ⑤   05 ⑤   06 ④   07 station
08 ①   09 ③   10 anniversary
11 I guess I can take the afternoon off.   12 ②
13 (A) wrong   (B) celebrate

01 B가 '원더 우먼을 보러 가는 게 어때?'라고 답하는 걸로 보아 A는 오후에 무엇을 할 것인지 묻는 것을 알 수 있다.

02 B의 대답으로 보아 시간 약속을 정하는 표현이 적절하다.

03 '~이 어때?'라는 의미로 How about ~?을 사용한다.

04 '~하는 게 어때?', '~하자'는 표현으로 Let's+동사원형 ~, Shall we+동사원형 ~?, Why don't we+동사원형 ~?, What about+동사원형+-ing? 등을 사용할 수 있다.

05 ⑤ 'A: 서둘러. 벌써 10시야.' 'B: 먼저 무엇을 시도해 볼까?'라는 대답은 자연스럽지 못하다.

06 ⓐ '~하자'는 의미로 Let's가 적절하다. ⓑ 만날 장소를 묻는 말이 적절하다.

07 사람들이 타거나 내리기 위해 버스나 기차가 멈추는 건물이나 주변 지역

08 B의 물음은 어디서 배드민턴을 할지 장소를 묻고 있으므로 빈칸에는 장소를 제안하는 말이 적절하다.

09 아빠의 'What do you want to do?'라는 말 다음에 '뮤지컬을 보러 가는 게 어때요?'라는 말이 적절하다.

10 과거의 그 날에 일어난 일을 기억하거나 축하하는 날

11 '~일 것 같다'는 I guess로 문장을 시작한다. '휴무를 하다'는 표현으로 take the afternoon off를 사용한다.

12 Anna와 그녀의 아빠는 다음 주 수요일에 대한 계획에 대해 말하고 있다.

13 대화의 내용은 아들이 한국사 시험에서 한 문제만 틀려서 축하하기 위해 저녁에 외식을 간다는 내용이다.

서술형 시험대비 p.123

01 are going to take the subway

02 The subway will be faster than the bus at this time of day.

03 (L)et's see a magic show.
   (S)hall we see a magic show?
   (W)hat about seeing a magic show?

04 What time shall we meet

05 (A) take   (B) about

06 have a lunch → have lunch

07 a musical, Dad / next, 12 / Bravo Theater

01 지하철이 버스보다 빠르기 때문에 지하철을 탈 것이다.

02 '~보다 빠르다'는 의미로 비교급 than을 이용한다.

03 '~하는 게 어때?', '~하자'는 표현으로 Let's+동사원형 ~, Shall we+동사원형 ~?, Why don't we+동사원형 ~?, What about+동사원형+-ing ~? 등을 사용할 수 있다.

04 약속을 정하는 표현으로 '몇 시에 만날래?'의 의미다.

05 (A)는 '(일을) 쉬다'는 의미로 take off를 사용한다. (B)는 시간을 정하는 표현으로 How about을 사용하여 '12시 어때?'라는 의미이다.

06 식사 이름 앞에는 부정관사 a를 붙이지 않는다.

07 다음 주 수요일 12시에 Bravo 극장에서 아빠와 뮤지컬을 본다.

교과서 Grammar

핵심 Check p.124~125

1 (1) will go   (2) miss   (3) are
2 (1) will exercise → exercise   (2) 틀린 곳 없음
3 (1) clever   (2) interesting   4 ②

시험대비 기본평가 p.126

01 (1) more expensive → expensive   (2) than → as   (3) will answer → answer   (4) won't → don't
02 ⑤   03 ④   04 ③

01 (1) 'as+원급+as' 구문으로 원급인 expensive를 써야 한다.
   (2) 원급 비교는 'as+원급+as'를 사용하므로 than을 as로 고친다. (3), (4) 조건의 부사절을 이끄는 접속사 if절에는 미래시제 대신 현재시제를 사용해야 한다.

02 asked의 직접목적어 자리에 사용된 명사절 접속사 if와 조건을 나타내는 부사절 접속사 if가 적절하다.

03 두 대상의 정도가 같음을 나타낼 때 'as+원급(형용사/부사)+as'를 사용한다.

04 'as+원급(형용사/부사)+as'를 사용하고, 비교급(harder)은 than과 함께 사용된다. hardly는 부사로 '거의 ~ 않다'는 의미이다.

19

01 ①　　　　02 faster　　　03 ⑤
04 (1) as　(2) tall　(3) yours
05 (1) If you have to use earphones, do not play your
　　music loud.
　　(2) If you miss the subway, you will be late for the
　　meeting.
　　(3) My voice is as loud as yours.
　　(4) Nick can run as fast as Peter.
06 ②　　　　07 ④, ⑤　　08 ④　　　　09 ①
10 (1) than → as　(2) more beautiful → beautiful
　　(3) highly → high　(4) will miss → misses
11 (1) friend → friendly　(2) faster → fast
12 ⑤　　　　13 ④　　　　14 (1) as　(2) well
(3) mine　　　15 She is as light as a feather.
16 A tiger is not so big as an elephant.
17 so　　　　18 ②, ③　　19 ①, ⑤
20 go, will eat / meet, will

01 ① 두 대상을 비교할 때는 비교의 대상이 동일해야 한다. His
riddle과 her riddle을 비교해야 하므로 her를 hers(= her
riddle)로 고쳐야 한다.

02 대화의 흐름상 지하철이 버스보다 더 빠르다(faster)는 의미가
적절하다.

03 '~한다면'의 의미로 조건의 부사절 접속사 if가 적절하고, 조건
의 부사절에는 미래시제 대신 현재시제를 사용해야 한다.

04 (1), (2) 'as+원급(형용사/부사)+as' 형태를 사용한다. (3) 두
대상을 비교할 때는 비교의 대상이 동일해야 한다. my room과
your room을 비교해야 하므로 소유대명사 yours가 적절하다.

05 (1), (2) if가 있는 부사절은 '접속사(If)+주어+동사 ~, 주
어+동사 …'의 어순으로 쓴다. (3), (4) 'as+원급(형용사/부
사)+as' 형태를 사용한다.

06 조건의 부사절에서는 미래시제 대신 현재시제를 사용해야 한다.

07 보기의 if는 조건의 부사절이다. ①, ②, ③은 동사의 목적어 자
리에 사용된 명사절 접속사로 '~인지 아닌지'의 뜻이다.

08 두 대상의 동등함을 나타낼 때 'as+원급(형용사/부사)+as' 형태
를 사용한다. ④번은 '민호는 원어민만큼 영어를 잘한다.'는 의
미로 동사 speaks를 수식하는 부사 well이 적절하다.

09 조건의 부사절에서는 미래시제 대신 현재시제를 사용하지만, 주
절에는 미래의 의미일 때 미래시제 will을 사용해야 한다.

10 (1) 두 대상의 동등함을 나타낼 때 'as+원급(형용사/부사)+as'
형태를 사용해야 한다. (2) 'as+원급(형용사/부사)+as' 형태가
적절하므로 비교급을 원급으로 바꾸어야 한다. (3) 'as+원급(형
용사/부사)+as' 형태로 부사 highly는 '매우, 대단히'의 의미이
므로, '높이, 높게'의 의미를 가진 high로 바꾸어야 한다. (4) 조
건의 부사절에서는 미래시제 대신 현재시제를 사용한다. 주어가
she(3인칭 단수)이므로 misses가 적절하다.

11 (1) 'as+원급(형용사/부사)+as' 형태를 사용해야 하므로, 명사
friend를 형용사 friendly로 바꾸어야 한다. (2) 'as+원급(형
용사/부사)+as' 형태로 비교급 faster를 fast로 바꾼다.

12 ⑤ 조건의 부사절에서는 미래시제 대신 현재시제를 사용하지
만, 주절에는 미래의 의미일 때 미래시제 will을 사용해야 한다.
you see the sunrise는 you will see ~.가 되어야 한다.

13 두 대상 간의 동등함을 나타낼 때 'as+원급(형용사/부사)+as'
형태를 사용한다. book은 셀 수 있는 명사이므로 much가 아니
라 many로 수식한다.

14 (1), (2): 두 대상 간의 동등함을 나타내는 동등비교는 'as+원
급(형용사/부사)+as' 형태를 사용해야 한다. (3) 두 대상을 비
교할 때는 비교하는 대상이 동일해야 한다. Your house와 my
house가 비교되어야 하므로 소유대명사 mine이 적절하다.

15 두 대상 간의 동등함을 나타내는 동등비교는 'as+원급(형용사/
부사)+as' 형태를 사용해야 한다.

16 동등비교는 'as+원급+as' 형태를 취하지만 부정문에서는 'not
so+원급+as'를 사용할 수 있다.

17 동등 비교인 'as+원급(형용사/부사)+as'는 부정문에서는 'not
as[so]+원급+as'로 사용할 수 있다.

18 동등비교는 'as+원급(형용사/부사)+as'형태를 취한다.

19 동등비교인 'as+원급(형용사/부사)+as' 형태를 취하고, 부정문
에서는 'not as[so]+원급+as'를 취한다.

20 조건이나 시간의 부사절에서는 미래시제 대신 현재시제를 사용
하지만, 주절에는 미래의 의미일 때 미래시제 will을 사용해야
한다.

01 isn't as[so] big as
02 (1) I can finish the work if you help me.
　　(2) If school finishes early tomorrow, I will go see a
　　movie.
　　(3) If my mom catches a cold, I will do the dishes
　　for her.
03 (1) run as fast as　(2) as, as
04 (1) me → mine[my car]　(2) more popular →
　　popular　(3) won't → doesn't　(4) won't → don't
05 (1) John is as tall as Susan.
　　(2) This apple is as sweet as that pineapple.
　　(3) My bike is not so[as] old as his[his bike].
　　(4) I watch as many movies as Kate.
06 (1) as heavy as　(2) as old as　(3) as tall as
07 (1) If you eat too much chocolate, your teeth will
　　go bad.
　　(2) If Fred walks to school, it will take 40 minutes.

(3) If you follow the map, you'll get to my grandma's house.

08 than her → as hers / will find → finds

09 (1) as old as (2) not so[as] tall as
   (3) not so[as] fast as

10 (1) Her sister is as playful as a kitten.
   (2) My home is as quiet as a grave.
   (3) I'm not so[as] tall as my brother.

01 Mina가 Jenny보다 몸집이 더 크기 때문에 Jenny는 Mina만큼 크지 않다는 'not as[so]+원급+as'가 적절하다.

02 조건의 부사절에서는 미래시제 대신 현재시제를 사용하지만, 주절에는 미래의 의미일 때 미래시제 will을 사용해야 한다.

03 위의 그림은 두 대상 간의 동등한 성질을 나타내고 있으므로 'as+원급(형용사/부사)+as' 형태를 사용한다.

04 (1) 두 대상을 비교할 때는 비교하는 대상이 동일해야 한다. Your car와 my car가 비교되어야 하므로 소유대명사 mine이나 my car가 적절하다. (2) 'as+원급(형용사/부사)+as'를 사용하므로 원급 popular가 적절하다. (3) 조건 부사절에서는 미래시제 대신 현재시제를 사용하므로 won't를 3인칭 단수형 doesn't로 고친다. (4) 조건 부사절에서는 미래시제 대신 현재시제를 사용하므로 won't를 don't로 고친다.

05 두 대상 간의 동등한 성질을 나타내고 있으므로 'as+원급(형용사/부사)+as' 형태를 사용한다. 그리고 부정문은 'not as[so]+원급+as' 형태를 사용한다.

06 (1) Eric과 Amy가 동일한 것은 몸무게이므로 형용사 heavy를 이용한다. (2) Tom과 Amy가 동일한 것은 나이이므로 형용사 old를 이용한다. (3) Tom과 Eric이 동일한 것은 키이므로 형용사 tall을 이용하여 'as+원급+as' 형태를 사용한다.

07 부사절로 시작하는 문장의 형태는 '접속사(If)+주어+동사 ~, 주어+동사 …'이다. 조건의 부사절에는 미래시제 대신 현재시제를 사용한다.

08 첫 번째 틀린 부분은 as difficult 뒤에는 as가 적절하고, 두 대상을 비교할 때는 비교 대상이 같아야 하므로 his riddle과 her riddle을 비교해야 한다. 그러므로 소유대명사 hers가 적절하다. 두 번째 틀린 부분은 시간을 나타내는 부사절에는 미래시제 대신 현재시제를 사용해야 하므로 will find를 finds로 고친다.

09 (1) 수지와 민지는 나이가 같으므로 'as old as'를 사용한다. (2) 민지가 수지보다 키가 크지 않기 때문에 부정문 'not so[as] tall as'를 사용한다. (3) 수지가 민지보다 빠르지 않기 때문에 'not so[as] fast as'를 사용한다.

10 두 대상 간의 능등한 성질을 나타내고 있으므로 'as+원급(형용사/부사)+as' 형태를 사용한다. 그리고 부정문은 'not as[so]+원급+as' 형태를 사용한다.

교과서 Reading

확인문제   p.132

1 T 2 F 3 T 4 F 5 T 6 F 7 T 8 F

확인문제   p.133

1 F 2 T 3 T 4 F 5 T 6 F

교과서 확인학습 A   p.134~135

01 The Most Dangerous   02 Welcome
03 perform   04 Like, in Italian, in Italy
05 I'd like to tell   06 appreciate, if
07 of great beauty, as cold as ice
08 who, marry her   09 fails
10 has ever been   11 falls in love with
12 the first man   13 However, to marry
14 nothing more than   15 of his own
16 What   17 adds, to die, incorrectly
18 before dawn, as difficult as hers
19 until, finds out   20 the most famous aria
21 means   22 sleeps
23 not even you   24 safe
25 will know   26 At dawn
27 prince's   28 in time
29 Let's watch

교과서 확인학습 B   p.136~137

1 Turandot The Most Dangerous Love in the World
2 Welcome, everyone!
3 Tonight, we are going to perform Giacomo Puccini's opera *Turandot*.
4 Like many other famous operas, *Turandot* is in Italian because opera started in Italy in the 16th century.
5 Before we begin, I'd like to tell you the storyline of the opera *Turandot*.
6 You will appreciate it better if you know the story.
7 Turandot, a Chinese princess, is a woman of great beauty, but she is as cold as ice.
8 Any prince who wants to marry her must answer three riddles.
9 If he fails, he must die.
10 No one has ever been able to answer them.

21

11 One day, a brave prince falls in love with her at first sight.

12 He becomes the first man to answer all three riddles.

13 However, Turandot does not want to marry the prince.

14 He is nothing more than a stranger to her.

15 He then gives her a riddle of his own.

16 He asks her, "What is my name?"

17 He adds, "If you answer correctly, I will agree to die. If you answer incorrectly, you will have to marry me."

18 Turandot must find the answer before dawn, but his riddle is as difficult as hers.

19 She says to everyone, "No one will go to sleep until someone finds out his name."

20 The prince then sings the most famous aria of the whole opera, "Nessun Dorma."

21 It means no one sleeps.

22 No one sleeps.

23 No one sleeps, not even you, Princess.

24 My secret is safe.

25 No one will know my name.

26 At dawn, I will win! I will win!

27 The prince's name is Calaf.

28 Will the princess learn his name in time?

29 Let's watch the opera and find out.

시험대비 실력평가   p.138~141

01 (A) Italian (B) to tell (C) know 02 ④
03 ⑤ 04 ① 05 ② 06 ③
07 ③ 08 ② 09 ④ 10 ③
11 ⑤ 12 no one will know his name
13 learn 14 ④ 15 ② 16 ⑤
17 Turandot, a Chinese princess, is a woman of great beauty, but she is as cold as ice.
18 three riddles 19 ②, ③, ⑤
20 ④ 21 (A) to die (B) hers (C) finds
22 What is my name? 23 ① 24 ③
25 are looking for a good musical movie 26 ①, ③

01 (A) '이탈리아어로'라고 해야 하므로 Italian이 적절하다. in Italy: 이탈리아에서, in Italian: 이탈리아어로, (B) would like 다음에는 동명사가 아니라 to부정사를 써야 하므로 to tell 이 적절하다. (C) 조건 부사절에서는 현재시제가 미래시제를 대용하므로 know가 적절하다.

02 시작하기 전에 '오페라 《투란도트》의 줄거리를 알려 드리려고

한다'고 했으므로, ④번이 적절하다.

03 '줄거리'를 알면 이 오페라를 더 잘 감상하게 될 것이라고 했다.

04 앞에 나오는 내용과 상반되는 내용이 뒤에 이어지므로 However가 가장 적절하다. ② 그러므로, ③ 즉, 다시 말해, ④ 예를 들어, ⑤ 그 결과

05 주어진 문장의 a riddle of his own에 주목한다. ②번 다음 문장의 질문을 가리키므로 ②번이 적절하다.

06 ⓐ, ⓒ: Turandot, ⓑ, ⓓ, ⓔ: the prince

07 Turandot는 얼음처럼 차갑고 세 가지 수수께끼에 답하지 못한 왕자들은 죽어야 한다고 했기 때문에 성격이 '무정하고 비정하다'고 하는 것이 적절하다. heartless: 무정한, 비정한, ① 사려 깊은, ② 마음이 따뜻한, ⑤ 부주의한

08 ⓐ와 ②번: [보통 as ... as ~로 형용사·부사 앞에서] …와 같은 정도로, 마찬가지로 (앞의 as는 지시부사, 뒤의 as는 접속사), ① …한 대로(접속사), ③ [비례] …함에 따라, …할수록(접속사), ④ …이라고, …으로(전치사), ⑤ …이므로, …이기 때문에(접속사)

09 ④ Turandot가 물어보는 세 가지 수수께끼가 무엇인지는 대답할 수 없다. ① She is a Chinese princess. ② She is a woman of great beauty. ③ He must answer three riddles. ⑤ A brave prince who falls in love with her at first sight.

10 ⓐ Turandot는 동이 트기 '전에' 답을 찾아야 한다. ⓒ '동틀 녘에', 내가 이길 것이라고 하는 것이 적절하다.

11 글의 흐름상 현재시제로 써야 하고, no one의 경우 3인칭 단수 취급을 하므로 동사 sleep에 -s를 붙인 형태를 쓰는 것이 적절하다.

12 '누구도 그의 이름을 알지 못할 것이기' 때문이다.

13 공주는 그의 이름을 제때 '알아낼' 수 있을까요? 오페라를 보고 '알아봅시다.'라고 했으므로, learn으로 바꿀 수 있다. find out 알아내다, 발견하다

14 위 글은 '감상문'이다. review (책·연극·영화 등에 대한) 논평 [비평], 감상문, ① 독후감, ② 수필, ③ (신문·잡지의) 글, 기사, ⑤ 전기

15 recommend: 추천[천거]하다, 권고[권장]하다, 민수는 미녀와 야수를 마음이 따뜻해지는 사랑 이야기를 좋아하는 사람들에게 '추천한다.' ① 요구하다, ③ 표현하다, ④ 보고하다, ⑤ 충고하다

16 ⑤ 민수가 누구와 그것을 보았는지는 알 수 없다. ① Beauty and the Beast. ② Last Saturday. ③ It is about a beautiful girl and a beast. ④ He enjoyed it a lot.

17 'of'를 보충하고, Turandot와 a Chinese princess는 동격이 므로 a Chinese princess 앞뒤로 콤마를 찍는 것이 적절하다. of+추상명사 = 형용사

18 '세 가지 수수께끼'를 가리킨다.

19 ⓒ와 ①, ④는 형용사적 용법, ②, ⑤ 부사적 용법, ③ 명사적 용법

20 ④ Turandot는 그 왕자의 이름도 모르기 때문에, 그는 그녀에게 단지 '낯선 사람'일 뿐이라고 하는 것이 적절하다. ① 이웃, ⑤ 동료

21 (A) agree는 to부정사를 목적어로 취하므로 to die가 적절하다. (B) 그의 수수께끼는 '그녀의 것'만큼 어렵다고 해야 하므로 hers가 적절하다. (C) 시간을 나타내는 부사절에서는 현재시제가 미래시제를 대신하므로 finds가 적절하다.

22 왕자가 낸 수수께끼는 "제 이름이 무엇입니까?"이다.

23 Turandot는 동이 트기 전에 답을 찾아야 하지만 그의 수수께끼는 그녀의 것만큼 어렵다고 했기 때문에, Turandot의 심경은 절박하다고 하는 것이 적절하다. desperate: 필사적인, 절박한, ② 만족스러운, ③ 지루한, ④ 부끄러운, ⑤ 흥분한

24 ⓐ와 ③: 감동적인, ① 활기적[생기] 넘치는, ② 발랄한, 쾌활한, ④ 정력[활동]적인, ⑤ 우울하게 만드는, 우울한

25 '좋은 뮤지컬 영화를 찾고 있는 사람들'에게 추천하고 있다.

26 ① not only A but also B: A뿐만 아니라 B도, ② not A but B: A가 아니라 B, ③ both A and B: A와 B 둘 다, ④ either A or B: A와 B 둘 중 하나, ⑤ neither A nor B: A와 B 둘 다 아닌

08 주격 관계대명사 who 또는 that이 적절하다.

09 그 누구도 수수께끼에 답할 수 없었고 어떤 용감한 왕자가 세 수수께끼를 모두 맞힌 첫 번째 사람이 된다고 했기 때문에, 'a few'를 'no'로 고치는 것이 적절하다.

10 (A) Turandot와 a Chinese princess는 동격으로 단수로 취급해야 하므로 is가 적절하다. (B) marry는 타동사이므로 전치사 없이 바로 목적어를 써야 하므로 marry가 적절하다. (C) answer는 타동사이므로 전치사 없이 바로 목적어를 써야 하므로 answer가 적절하다.

11 at first sight: 첫눈에, 언뜻 보기에

12 중국의 공주 Turandot는 자기와 결혼하기를 원하는 어떤 왕자에게도 '세 가지 수수께끼'를 낸다. 만약 그가 그것들에 올바르게 대답하지 못하면, 그는 '죽어야 한다.'

13 그의 수수께끼는 '그녀의 것'만큼 어렵다고 해야 하므로 'hers'가 적절하다.

14 '제때에'는 '동이 트기 전에'를 가리킨다.

15 'will'을 보충하면 된다.

16 'as+원급+as'를 사용하여 '그의 수수께끼가 그녀의 수수께끼만큼 어렵다'라고 하는 것이 적절하다. 부정문에서는 'not so+원급+as'도 가능하다.

서술형 시험대비 p.142~143

01 나는 여러분에게 오페라 〈투란도트〉의 줄거리를 알려 드리려고 합니다. 02 the opera *Turandot*

03 opera started in Italy in the 16th century

04 only

05 incorrectly → correctly, correctly → incorrectly

06 someone finds out his name

07 very beautiful   08 who 또는 that

09 a few → no   10 (A) is (B) marry (C) answer

11 at first sight   12 (A) three riddles (B) must die

13 hers   14 before dawn

15 If you answer correctly, I will agree to die.

16 so → as

01 would like to+동사원형: ~하고 싶다

02 '오페라 《투란도트》'를 가리킨다.

03 《투란도트》가 이탈리아어로 되어 있는 이유는 '오페라가 16세기 이탈리아에서 시작되었기' 때문이다.

04 nothing more than: ~에 지나지 않는, ~에 불과한

05 "당신이 '맞게' 대답한다면 나는 죽는 것에 동의하겠습니다. 만약 답이 '틀리면' 당신은 저와 결혼해야 합니다."라고 고치는 것이 직절하다.

06 '누군가 그의 이름을 알아낼 때까지 그 누구도 잠들 수 없다'는 것은 '누군가 그의 이름을 알아낸' 후에야 사람들이 잠들 수 있다는 뜻이다.

07 of+추상명사 = 형용사, of great beauty = very beautiful

영역별 핵심문제 p.145~149

01 ⑤   02 ①   03 ③   04 ③

05 right   06 (A) Where (B) How[What]

07 ④   08 ③   09 What time shall we meet?   10 (B) → (A) → (C) → (D)

11 (A) off (B) if (C) shall we

12 her school's 75th anniversary

13 If you do something special for the world, the world will change.

14 ③   15 He doesn't watch TV as[so] much as   16 ③   17 ⑤   18 ②

19 ④   20 ②   21 ④

22 (1) as[so] fast as (2) as fast as (3) as cheap as

23 ④   24 (1) as small as (2) run as fast as (3) as tall as   25 won't → doesn't

26 (1) will rain → rains (2) comes → will come

27 ②   28 ④   29 ④   30 ①, ③

31 ④   32 (A) more (B) agree (C) difficult

33 ②, ⑤

01 ① 용감한 - 겁 많은, ② 안전한 - 위험한, ③ 어려운 - 쉬운, ④ 실패하다 - 성공하다 / 모두 반의어 관계이고 ⑤는 두 단어 모두 '감동적인'이라는 뜻의 유의어 관계이다.

02 surprising '놀라운' = amazing

03 ① brave: 용감한 / 어느 날, 어떤 용감한 왕자가 그녀에게 첫눈에 반합니다. ② century: 세기 / 오페라는 16세기에 이탈리아

에서 시작되었다. ③ '지하철을 타는 게 어때?'라는 의미로 동사 take가 자연스럽다. ④ dawn: 새벽 / 그녀는 동이 트기 전에 답을 찾아야 한다. ⑤ mean: 의미하다 / Nessun Dorma는 누구도 잠들지 못한다는 뜻이다.

04 celebrate: 축하하다

05 right는 부사로 '바로'의 의미로 사용된다.

06 (A) G의 말로 보아 B는 배드민턴을 칠 장소를 묻고 있다. (B) 상대방에게 제안할 때 사용하는 표현으로 How[What] about ~?을 사용한다.

07 위 대화는 오후에 친구와 무엇을 할 것인지에 대한 계획을 세우는 내용이다.

08 제안할 때 사용하는 표현으로 Why don't we+동사원형?, Let's+동사원형., Shall we+동사원형?, How[What] about+동사-ing?가 있다.

10 오늘 오후에 무엇을 할 건지 묻는 말에, (B) 미술관에 가는 게 어떠냐고 제안을 한다. (A) '좋아'라는 동의의 말을 하고 만날 시간을 물어본다. (C) 2시가 어떤지 시간을 제안하고 (D) 마지막으로 승낙의 표현과 함께 미술관 앞에서 만나자고 제안한다.

11 (A)는 take와 호응하여 '(일을) 쉬다'는 의미로 off를 사용하고, (B)는 의미상 '~한다면'의 의미를 가지는 조건의 부사절 접속사 if가 적절하다. (C)는 시간을 제안할 때 사용하는 표현으로 What time shall we ~?가 적절하다.

13 조건의 부사절에서는 미래시제 대신 현재시제를 사용하고, 주절에는 미래시제를 그대로 사용한다.

14 '~만큼 …한'의 의미로 'as+원급+as'를 사용한다. 부정문에서는 'not as[so]+원급+as'를 사용하지만, 긍정문에서는 as 대신 so를 사용하지 않는다.

15 TV를 보지 않는다는 일반동사 watch의 부정문을 사용해서 He doesn't watch TV를 쓰고, 그 다음 '~만큼 …하게'의 의미로 'as[so]+원급+as' 구문을 이용한다. 이때 watch를 수식하는 부사 much가 적절하다.

16 (1)은 check의 목적어 자리에 사용되는 접속사 if(~인지 아닌지), (2)는 조건의 부사절 접속사 if(만일 ~라면)가 적절하다.

17 ①~④는 동사의 목적어를 이끄는 명사절 접속사 if로 '~인지 아닌지'의 의미이고, ⑤는 조건의 부사절 접속사 if로 '만일 ~라면'의 의미다.

18 ②는 'as+원급+as' 구문으로 so를 as로 바꾸어야 한다.

19 ④ '~만큼 …하지 않다'는 의미로 'not as[so]+원급+as' 구문이 적절하다. 'so heavy so'를 'so[as] heavy as'로 바꾸어야 한다.

20 The subway is as faster as the train.은 as fast as가 되어야 하고, We will go swimming if the weather will be fine tomorrow.는 조건의 부사절에서 미래시제 대신 현재시제를 사용하므로 will be를 is로 고쳐야 한다.

21 조건의 부사절에서는 미래시제 대신 현재시제를 사용하므로 break가 적절하다. 복수 주어 my friends이므로 breaks는 적절하지 않다.

22 (1)은 지하철이 버스보다 빠르지 않기 때문에 'not as[so]+원급+as' 구문을 이용하고, (2)는 버스가 택시와 속도가 같으므로 'as+원급+as' 구문을 이용한다. (3)은 지하철이 버스와 요금이 같기 때문에 'as cheap as'가 자연스럽다.

23 ④는 '나는 너만큼 어리다.'라는 의미이고, 나머지는 모두 '네가 나보다 나이가 많다.'라는 의미이다.

24 '~만큼 …한[하게]'의 의미는 'as+원급+as' 구문을 이용한다.

25 조건을 나타내는 부사절에서는 미래시제 대신 현재시제를 사용해야 하므로, 미래시제 won't를 3인칭 단수 현재형인 doesn't로 바꾸어야 한다.

26 (1) 조건의 부사절에서는 미래시제 대신 현재시제를 사용하고, (2) be sure의 목적어 자리에 사용된 명사절 접속사 if는 미래시제를 사용할 수 있다.

27 시작하기 전에 오페라를 더 잘 '감상하도록' 《투란도트》의 줄거리를 알려 드리려고 한다고 말했기 때문에, 오페라 《투란도트》를 '공연할' 것이라고 하는 것이 적절하다. perform: 공연하다, ① 연습하다, ③ 잘되어 가다, 작동하다, ④ 이루다, 성취하다, ⑤ 완료하다, 끝마치다

28 ⓑ와 ④번은 '~과 같이'라는 의미의 전치사로 사용되었다. 나머지는 다 '~을 좋아하다'라는 의미의 동사이다.

29 ④번 다음 문장의 He에 주목한다. 주어진 문장의 a brave prince를 받고 있으므로 ④번이 적절하다.

30 ⓐ와 ①, ③번은 경험 용법, ② 결과 용법, ④ 완료 용법, ⑤ 계속 용법

31 ④ 수수께끼에 답하지 못하면 죽어야 하는데, 그 누구도 수수께끼에 답할 수 없었다고 했기 때문에, 지금까지 수수께끼에 도전했던 왕자들은 다 죽었다.

32 (A) 그는 그녀에게 '단지 낯선 사람일 뿐'이라고 해야 하므로 more가 적절하다. nothing more than: ~에 지나지 않는, nothing less than: 다름 아닌 바로, (B) 당신이 맞게 대답한다면 나는 죽는 것에 '동의하겠'고 해야 하므로 agree가 적절하다. refuse: 거절하다, (C) 그의 수수께끼는 그녀의 것만큼 '어렵다'고 해야 하므로 difficult가 적절하다. different: 다른

33 give, send, write는 3형식으로 고칠 때 'to'를 사용한다. ①, ③ buy, make는 for를 사용한다. ④ ask는 of를 사용한다. ⑤ thank-you note: 감사장

단원별 예상문제

p.150~153

01 answer   02 nothing more than

03 (1) beauty, cold   (2) perform   (3) incorrectly, marry
   (4) falls in love, sight

04 ②   05 ⑤

06 (1) Why don't we go on a picnic this weekend?
   (2) What about going on a picnic this weekend?

07 ④   08 ⑤   09 get, discount if

10 What time shall we meet?　　　　11 ③

12 ③　　　13 ④　　　14 ②　　　15 ⑤

16 (1) finish　(2) give　(3) changes　　　17 ②

18 ③　　　19 ⑤　　　20 (1) not as[so] tall as

(2) well　(3) as heavy as　　　21 ③　　　22 ①

23 knowing the story　　　24 as sweet as honey →

as cold as ice　　　25 riddles　　　26 ⑤

01 둘은 유의어 관계이다. 제안 : 대답하다

02 nothing more than ~: ~에 지나지 않는

03 (1) of+추상명사 = 형용사. of beauty = beautiful(아름다운)
(2) perform: 공연하다 (3) incorrectly: 올바르지 않게, 틀리게, marry: 결혼하다 (4) fall in love: 사랑에 빠지다. at first sight: 첫눈에

04 예상된 시간보다 더 이르게

05 ⑤번 뒤의 문장에 나오는 See you there.에서 there가 the subway station을 가리키므로 ⑤가 적절하다.

06 상대에게 제안을 할 때 사용하는 표현으로 Let's+동사원형, Why don't we+동사원형?, What about+동명사/명사? 등이 있다.

07 시간이나 장소를 정할 때 How about이나 What about을 이용한다.

08 흥미롭거나 놀라운 일을 말하기 전에 사용되는 표현

09 get a discount: 할인받다, if: ~한다면

10 제안할 때 사용하는 표현으로 shall we ~를 이용하고 시간을 묻는 표현인 What time으로 문장을 시작한다.

12 '~하자'는 제안이나 권유의 의미로 사용할 수 없는 표현은 ③번이다.

13 대화의 흐름상 한국사 시험에서 한 문제 틀린 것에 대해 오늘 밤 축하하러 나가자는 의미로 celebrate가 적절하다. appreciate는 '감상하다'라는 뜻이다.

14 '만일 ~한다면'의 의미로 조건을 나타내는 접속사 if가 적절하다.

15 ⑤ Jane은 Mike보다 성적이 높기 때문에 Mike isn't as smart as Jane.으로 쓰는 것이 적절하다.

16 조건의 부사절에서는 의미가 미래라 할지라도 현재시제를 사용한다.

17 ② 시간을 나타내는 부사절에서는 미래시제 대신 현재시제를 사용한다. will find를 finds로 고쳐야 한다.

18 ③ as ~ as 사이에는 형용사나 부사의 원급을 사용해야 한다. bigger를 big으로 고쳐야 한다.

19 ⑤번은 tell의 직접목적어 자리에 사용된 명사절 접속사 if다. '~인지 아닌지'로 해석한다.

20 두 대상 간의 동등함을 나타낼 때 'as+원급+as'를 사용한다. 부정문은 '~만큼 …하지 않은'의 의미로 'not as[so]+원급+as'를 사용한다.

21 in Italian: 이탈리아어로, in Italy: 이탈리아에서, in the 16th century: 16세기에

22 ⓓ와 ①번은 감상하다, architecture: 건축학[술], 건축 양식, ②와 ④ 고마워하다, ③과 ⑤ (제대로) 인식하다

23 여러분이 '줄거리를 알면' 이 오페라를 더 잘 감상하게 될 것이다. 전치사 By 다음에 동명사로 쓰는 것이 적절하다.

24 수수께끼에 답하는 데 실패하면 죽어야 한다고 했기 때문에, 그녀는 '얼음처럼 차갑다'고 하는 것이 적절하다.

25 riddle: 수수께끼, 터무니없는 것 같지만 영리하거나 재미있는 대답을 지닌 질문을 하는 수수께끼나 농담

26 ⑤ 절차를 통과하지 못한 왕자들이 몇 명인지는 대답할 수 없다. ① 중국의 공주, ② 굉장히 아름답다. ③ 반드시 세 가지 수수께끼에 답해야 한다. ④ 만약 세 가지 수수께끼에 답하지 못하면 죽어야 한다.

01 (A) What time shall we meet?

　(B) Where shall we meet?

02 Why don't we take the subway

03 (A) What shall we do this afternoon?

　(B) Why don't we go see *Wonder Woman*?

　(C) How about 4 o'clock?

04 (1) as expensive as mine[my ring]

　(2) not so kind as　　　(3) comes, take, to

05 (1) will rain → rains　(2) will need → need

06 (1) as old as, not as[so] old as

　(2) as tall as, Mike[Minho] is not as[so] tall as

　(3) as heavy as, is not as[so] heavy as

07 won't pay → don't pay　　08 as cold as ice

09 (A) Any　(B) ever　(C) sight　　　10 failed

11 He is nothing more than a stranger to her.

12 her riddles　　　13 (A) marry him　(B) to die

01 약속을 정할 때 사용하는 표현으로, (A)는 만날 시간을 (B)는 만날 장소를 물어보는 표현이 적절하다.

02 제안을 할 때 'Why don't we+동사원형?'을 이용한다.

03 (A)에는 무엇을 할 것인지 묻는 말로 대화를 시작하는 것이 적절하다. (B)는 구체적으로 무엇을 할 것인지 제안하는 표현이 적절하다. (C)는 '몇 시에 만날래?'라는 물음에 시간을 정하는 표현이 적절하다.

04 (1) 두 대상 간의 동일한 것을 나타낼 때 'as+원급+as'를 사용하고, 비교하는 대상은 같아야 하므로 her ring과 my ring을 비교해야 한다. (2) '~만큼 …하지 않다'는 의미로 'not so[as]+원급+as' 구문을 사용한다. (3) 조건의 부사절에서는 미래시제 대신 현재시제를 사용한다. take A to B는 A를 B로 데려오다라는 의미다.

05 조건 부사절에서는 미래시제 대신 현재시제를 사용한다.

06 두 대상 간의 동일한 것을 나타낼 때 'as+원급+as'를 사용한다. '~만큼 …하지 않다'는 의미로 'not so[as]+원급+as' 구문을

25

사용한다.

07 조건 부사절에서는 미래시제 대신 현재시제를 사용한다.

08 as cold as ice = very cold

09 (A) 그녀와 결혼길 원하는 왕자는 '누구든지'라고 해야 하므로 Any가 적절하다. 긍정문의 any: '어떤 ~이라도', some+셀 수 있는 명사 복수: '약간의', some+셀 수 있는 명사 단수: '어떤(a certain)', (B) 부정의 의미인 No one이 주어이므로 ever가 적절하다. (C) 그녀에게 '첫눈에' 반한다고 해야 하므로 sight가 적절하다. at first sight: 첫눈에

10 목숨을 걸고 세 가지 수수께끼에 답하려고 시도했던 모든 왕자들이 한 왕자를 제외하고는 다 '실패했다.' at the risk of one's life: 목숨을 걸고, except: ~을 제외하고는

11 nothing more than: ~에 지나지 않는, ~에 불과한

12 '그녀의 수수께끼들'을 가리킨다.

13 만약 Turandot가 왕자의 수수께끼에 틀리게 대답한다면 그녀는 '그와 결혼해야 한다.' 만약 Turandot가 맞게 대답한다면 그는 '죽는 것'에 동의할 것이다.

창의사고력 서술형 문제 p.156

|모범답안|

01 (1) A: What shall we do at the park?
　　 B: Why don't we ride the roller coaster?
　　 A: That's a good idea.
　 (2) A: What shall we do at the park?
　　 B: Why don't we visit the flower garden?
　　 A: That's a good idea.

02 (1) The subway fare is as expensive as the bus fare.
　 (2) The subway is not so[as] fast as the bus.

03 (A) Review　(B) the dreams and love
　 (C) beautiful and moving　(D) story

단원별 모의고사 p.157~160

01 ⑤　　02 (1) take, off　(2) practice, play
(3) don't, celebrate　　03 ③　　04 moving
05 late　　06 ③　　07 ②　　08 ④
09 ④　　10 ③
11 What do you want to do?　　12 ③
13 (1) Anna is as beautiful as Julie.
　 (2) I will let you go out if you do finish your job.
14 ③　　15 (1) as not larger → not as large as
(2) as bigger as → as big as　16 not as[so] tall as
17 ④　　18 ⑤　　19 Italian　20 ③
21 ③　　22 ask → answer　　23 ②
24 ④

---

01 ⑤의 appreciate는 'to understand how good something or someone is' (어떤 것이나 어떤 사람이 얼마나 좋은지 이해하다)라는 설명이 적절하다. to do something enjoyable on a special occasion은 celebrate에 대한 설명이다.

02 (1) take off: (일을) 쉬다 (2) practice: 연습하다, play: 연극 (3) Why don't we ~?: ~하는 게 어때?, celebrate: 축하하다

03 빈칸에는 be동사 뒤에 형용사가 보어로 와야 하므로 ①은 적절하지 못하다. as와 as 사이에는 형용사 원급 형태 good이 적절하다. ⑤의 the best는 셋 이상에서 '가장 ~한'의 의미인 최상급이다.

04 moving: 감동적인

05 '계획되고, 예상되고, 일상적인 또는 필요한 시간 후에 발생하거나 도착하는', 즉 '늦은'의 의미이다.

06 콘서트가 언제 시작되는지는 대화에 언급되어 있지 않다.

07 한국사 시험에서 한 문제만 틀렸다고 했으므로, 시험을 못 본 것이 아니라 잘 봤다는 것을 알 수 있다. poorly를 well로 바꾸어야 한다.

08 ④ 시험을 잘 본 사람은 Joe다.

09 '몇 시에 만날래?'라는 물음에 장소를 말하는 것은 어색하다.

10 다음 주 수요일에 학교를 가지 않는다는 말에 이유를 물어보는 것이 자연스럽다.

11 의문사 what으로 문장을 시작하고, '~하고 싶다'는 'want to+동사원형'을 이용한다.

12 ③ Ann과 아빠는 뮤지컬을 보러 갈 것이다.

13 (1) 'as+원급+as' 구문으로 형용사 beautiful은 as와 as 사이에 넣는다. (2) 접속사 if 뒤에는 '주어+동사'가 나와야 한다.

14 ③ 두 대상인 Her hair와 my hair를 비교하는 문장이므로 I를 mine이나 my hair로 바꾸어야 한다.

15 'as+원급+as' 구문으로, 원급은 형용사와 부사를 사용해야 한다.

16 Ann이 Tom보다 키가 작으므로 'not so[as]+원급+as' 구문을 사용한다.

17 조건의 부사절에서는 미래시제 대신 현재시제를 사용하지만 주절에는 미래시제를 그대로 사용한다.

18 ⑤번은 '테니스는 축구만큼 인기가 없다'는 의미로 is not as[so] popular as가 되어야 한다.

19 'Italy'의 언어를 나타내는 'Italian'을 쓰는 것이 적절하다. in Italian: 이탈리아어로

20 storyline: (소설·연극·영화 등의) 줄거리, ③ plot: (소설, 극, 영화 등의) 구성[플롯/줄거리], ① 주제, 테마, ② 배경, ④ 개념, ⑤ (논의 등의) 주제[대상/화제]

21 ⓐ of+추상명사 = 형용사, of great beauty = very beautiful, ⓒ fall in love with: ~와 사랑에 빠지다

22 그녀와 결혼길 원하는 왕자는 누구든지 반드시 세 가지 수수께끼에 '답해야' 한다고 해야 하므로 ask를 answer로 고치는 것이 적절하다.

23 ⓐ와 ②, ⑤는 명사적 용법, ①, ③은 부사적 용법, ④는 형용사적 용법

24 ④ 만약 Turandot의 답이 틀리면 '그녀는 왕자와 결혼해야 한다.'

교과서 파헤치기

단어 TEST Step 1 p.02

01 완전한	02 놀라운	
03 ～(해)지다, ～이 되다		
04 잡다, 포착하다,담아내다		05 해산물
06 여행; 여행하다	07 간단한, 단순한	08 번지 점프
09 예측, 예보	10 지구, 땅	11 또 다른, 다른
12 유명한	13 초상화	14 마침내
15 식량, 음식	16 졸업하다	17 가능성, 기회
18 섬	19 남다, 남아 있다	20 날씨
21 추측하다, 짐작하다		22 시장
23 외국의	24 수수께끼, 미스터리	
25 꽁꽁 얼게[너무나] 추운		26 실제로, 정말로
27 예상[기대]하다	28 일기	29 무서운, 겁나는
30 실내에, 집안에	31 창조[창작/창출]하다	
32 대학교	33 방학, 휴가	
34 나타나다, 출연하다		35 ～에 도착하다
36 ～으로 가득 차다	37 ～에 들어가다, ～에 타다	
38 지금, 당장	39 많은	40 ～와 같은
41 ～에 발을 들여놓다		42 좀, 약간, 약간의
43 나타나다		

단어 TEST Step 2 p.03

01 touch	02 plate	03 check
04 cloudy	05 pack	06 decide
07 during	08 foreign	09 around
10 drive	11 windy	12 invite
13 huge	14 avatar	15 field trip
16 object	17 college	18 weather
19 moment	20 relax	21 drawing
22 trip	23 turtle	24 market
25 admire	26 diary	27 perfect
28 expect	29 capture	30 graduate
31 freezing	32 scary	33 simple
34 island	35 a few	36 right now
37 get to	38 be full of	39 at last
40 show up	41 set foot at[in]	42 get into
43 such as		

단어 TEST Step 3 p.04

1 food, 식량, 음식 2 chance, 가능성
3 island, 섬 4 market, 시장 5 admire, 존경하다
6 drawing, 그림, 소묘 7 amazing, 놀라운
8 beach, 해변, 바닷가 9 create, 창조[창작/창출]하다
10 invite, 초대하다 11 mystery, 수수께끼, 미스터리
12 strange, 이상한, 낯선 13 travel, 여행하다
14 decide, 결정하다 15 relax, 휴식을 취하다
16 pack, (짐을) 싸다

대화문 TEST Step 1 p.05~06

Listen & Speak 1 A. Listen and Check

1 Have, tried / have, only tried / How it / hot, but
2 have, gone / No, haven't, How about / When, visited, tried once / Wasn't, scary / want to, again

Listen & Speak 2 A. Listen and Answer

1 how's weather, need / cloudy outside, check, forecast / Thank / going to rain / don't need
2 welcome to, sunny outside, expectiong, Don't leave, without, weather forecast, Have

Communicate A~B

A have, been to / have, lived, for / How's, there, going to, on vacation / to visit, autumn / planning to spend, relax / often rains, may, sunny days / take, pack, too / good idea, Have
B Have, been to, places / have, went to, last, with / How, weather / mostly sunny, changed

Progress Check

1 Have, ridden / have, How about / haven't, How / fun, a little, too
2 weather / cloudy outside, check, forecast / going to rain
3 welcome to, raining right now, expecting, leave, without

대화문 TEST Step 2 p.07~08

Listen & Speak 1 A. Listen and Check

1 G: Have you ever tried Indian food?
  B: Yes, I have, but I've only tried Indian curry.
  G: How was it?
  B: It was really hot, but I loved it.
2 G: Bill, have you ever gone bungee jumping?
  B: No, I haven't. How about you, Katie?
  G: When I visited New Zealand, I tried bungee jumping

once.

B: Wasn't it scary?

G: No, I liked it. I want to do it again.

Listen & Speak 1 A. Listen and Answer

1 B: Mom, how's the weather today? Do I need an umbrella?

W: It's quite cloudy outside. I'll check the weather forecast.

B: Thank you, Mom.

W: Well, it's not going to rain today.

B: Good! Then, I don't need an umbrella today.

2 W: Good morning, and welcome to the weather forecast. It's sunny outside, but we're expecting some rain in the afternoon. Don't leave home without your umbrella. That's the weather forecast for today. Have a nice day.

Communicate A~B

A Suho: Anna, have you been to Australia before?

Anna: Yes, I have. Actually, I lived in Sydney for a year.

Suho: Great! How's the weather there in April? I'm going to visit Sydney on vacation next week.

Anna: April is a great time to visit Sydney. In April, it's autumn in Australia.

Suho: Good. I'm planning to spend some time on the beach and relax in the sun.

Anna: Well, it often rains in April, but you may have some sunny days.

Suho: I'll take my hat and pack an umbrella, too

Anna: That's a good idea. Have a great time.

B A: Have you been to any special places in Korea?

B: Yes, I have. I went to Ulleungdo last summer with my family.

A: How was the weather there?

B: It was mostly sunny, but the weather changed often.

Progress Check

1 G: Have you ever ridden a horse?

B: Yes, I have. How about you?

G: No, I haven't. How was it?

B: It was fun, but it was a little scary, too.

2 B: Mom, how's the weather today?

W: It's quite cloudy outside. I'll check the weather forecast.

B: Thanks, Mom.

W: Well, it's going to rain in the afternoon.

3 M: Good evening, and welcome to the weather forecast. It's raining right now, but we're

expecting a sunny day tomorrow. Don't leave home tomorrow without your hat.

01 am, live in
02 Last, on, for
03 During, simple, journal
04 way, capture, special
05 last, set, mysterious
06 After, drive, finally
07 amazing, ring, huge
08 stones, thousands, ago   09 What, for
10 guess, remain, mystery   11 try, perfect
12 few, enough   13 In, around
14 started, so, decided   15 popular, stay
16 like, than   17 invited, for
18 dining, full, and
19 busy, admiring, plates
20 much, anything
21 draw, like, journal   22 Our, stop
23 visited, College
24 become, since, appeared
25 movies, else, dinner
26 also, portraits, graduated
27 outside, walked, touched
28 Because, touched, get
29 said, smile, wait   30 Create, own
31 drawing, much, interesting

01 am, live in   02 Last week, went on, for
03 During, drawings, journal
04 to capture, special moments
05 set foot at, one of, places
06 After, drive from, got to   07 amazing, ring
08 huge stones, thousands, ago   09 What, for
10 guess, remain, for
11 Don't try, perfect   12 A few, enough
13 In, walked around
14 to rain, decided to stay
15 popular, stay in
16 feels, like, than   17 owner, invited
18 dining, was full of
19 busy eating, admiring, plates

20 ate, so, couldn't eat

21 to draw, like, journal　　　　22 last stop

23 first visited

24 has become, famous place, since

25 everyone, eat dinner

26 saw portraits, graduated from

27 When, outside, walked to, touched

28 Because, touched, get into

29 with a smile, can't wait to　　30 Create, avatar

31 drawing journal. much more

보았다.

27 우리가 건물 밖으로 나왔을 때, 나는 유명한 올리브 나무로 걸어가서 그것을 만졌다.

28 "이 나무를 만졌기 때문에, 난 옥스퍼드 대학교에 들어갈 거야!"라고 말했다.

29 그러자 오빠가 웃으면서 "벽에 걸린 네 초상화가 빨리 보고 싶어."라고 말했다.

30 여러분 자신의 아바타를 만드세요.

31 그림일기가 훨씬 더 재미있을 거예요.

1 안녕, 나는 Lucy Hunter이고 런던에 살아요

2 지난주에 우리 가족은 3일 동안 휴가를 갔습니다.

3 여행 중에 나는 일기에 간단한 그림을 그렸어요.

4 그것은 모든 특별한 순간을 포착하는 훌륭한 방법이었어요.

5 마침내, 우리는 지구에서 가장 불가사의한 장소 중 하나인 스톤헨지에 발을 디뎠다.

6 런던에 있는 집에서 차로 두 시간을 달려서 우리는 마침내 스톤헨지에 도착했다.

7 원형으로 둘러서 있는 거대한 돌들을 보는 것은 정말 놀라웠다.

8 어떻게 그 거대한 돌들이 수천 년 전에 그곳에 도착했을까?

9 그것들은 무엇을 위한 것이었을까?

10 완벽한 그림을 그리려고 하지 마세요.

11 몇 가지 색깔이면 충분할 것입니다.

12 스톤헨지는 오랫동안 미스터리로 남을 것 같다.

13 아침에 우리는 코츠월드 언덕을 돌아다녔다.

14 오후에 비가 오기 시작해서, 우리는 B&B의 실내에서 머물기로 결정했다.

15 B&B는 영국에서 체류하는 곳으로 인기가 있다.

16 그것은 호텔이라기보다는 집처럼 느껴진다.

17 주인은 오늘 오후의 다과회에 우리를 초대했다

18 식탁에는 쿠키, 케이크, 빵, 그리고 치즈가 가득했다.

19 내가 먹느라 바쁠 때, 엄마는 아름다운 컵과 접시를 감탄하며 바라보고 계셨다.

20 나는 너무 많이 먹어서 저녁으로 아무것도 먹을 수 없었다.

21 당신의 일기에 컵과 접시 같은 일상적인 물건들을 그려도 괜찮습니다.

22 우리가 마지막으로 머문 곳은 옥스퍼드였다.

23 우리는 먼저 Christ Church College를 방문했다.

24 이곳은 해리포터 영화에 등장한 이후 방문해야 할 세계적으로 유명한 장소가 되었다.

25 영화에서 Harry와 다른 모든 사람들이 Christ Church의 회관에서 저녁을 먹는다.

26 우리는 또한 그 대학을 졸업한 유명한 사람들의 초상화를

1 Hi, I am Lucy Hunter, and I live in London.

2 Last week, my family went on a vacation for three days.

3 During our trip, I made simple drawings in my journal.

4 That was a great way to capture all the special moments.

5 At last, we set foot at Stonehenge, one of the most mysterious places on Earth.

6 After a two-hour drive from our home in London, we finally got to Stonehenge.

7 It was just amazing to see the ring of huge stones.

8 How did those huge stones get there thousands of years ago?

9 What were they for?

10 Don't try to make a perfect drawing.

11 A few colors will be enough.

12 I guess Stonehenge will remain a mystery for a long time.

13 In the morning, we walked around the Cotswolds.

14 It started to rain in the afternoon, so we decided to stay indoors at our B&B.

15 A B&B is a popular place to stay in England.

16 It feels more like a home than a hotel.

17 The owner invited us for afternoon tea today.

18 The dining table was full of cookies, cake, bread, and cheese.

19 While I was busy eating, Mom was admiring the beautiful cups and plates.

20 I ate too much, so I couldn't eat anything for dinner.

21 It is O.K. to draw everyday objects like cups and plates in your journal.

22 Our last stop was Oxford.

23 We first visited Christ Church College.

24 It has become a world famous place to visit

since it appeared in the Harry Potter movies.

25 In the movies, Harry and everyone else eat dinner at the Hall of Christ Church.

26 We also saw portraits of famous people who graduated from the college.

27 When we were outside the building, I walked to the famous olive tree and touched it.

28 "Because I touched this tree," I said, "I will get into Oxford University!"

29 Then, my brother said to me with a smile, "I can't wait to see your portrait on the wall."

30 Create your own avatar.

31 Your drawing journal will become much more interesting.

2. We visited a lot of beautiful temples and went to the night market in Vientiane.

3. Then, we moved to Vang Vieng and went river tubing.

4. We also enjoyed their traditional food.

5. It was a lot of fun to try new things in a foreign country.

6. I hope I will have a chance to visit Laos again.

Culture Project

1. September 15, 1835

2. We finally arrived on this island.

3. There are many animals to study here.

4. Today, I saw some strange turtles.

5. It was amazing to watch them.

구석구석지문 TEST Step 1   p.19

Link - Share

1. went on, last

2. It, amazing, islands

3. also visitied, Village

4. never forget

Write

1. Last winter, went, with

2. lot, temples, market

3. moved to, went

4. enjoyed, traditional

5. lot of, to try, foreign

6. chance to visit

Culture Project

1. September

2. arrived on

3. are, to study

4. asw, strange

5. amazing, watch

구석구석지문 TEST Step 2   p.20

Link - Share

1. We went on a field trip to Namhae last month.

2. It was just amazing to see so many beautiful islands.

3. We also visited Namhae German Village.

4. We'll never forget that trip.

Write

1. Last winter, I went to Laos with my family.

단어 TEST Step 1   p.21

01 발명가, 창안자　　02 압력, 압박　　03 활동
04 지지하다, 지원하다　　　　　　05 목욕, 욕조
06 쇼핑　　07 어린 시절　　08 목적
09 시험, 실험　　10 정말로, 진심으로　　11 운전자, 운전기사
12 충격; 쇼크[충격]를 주다　　　　13 프로젝트, 과제
14 호의, 친절　　15 고정시키다, 수리하다
16 선물, 재능　　17 가까운, 친한　　18 노숙자의
19 발명, 발명품　　20 기쁨, 환희
21 (특정) 지역의, 현지의　　　　22 편한, 편안한
23 완전한, 완벽한　　24 아직(도), 여전히　　25 판자, 널
26 사람, 개인　　27 식물, 초목　　28 성공하다
29 운이 좋은, 행운의　　30 안전, 안전성　　31 항상, 언제나
32 센서, 감지기　　33 상태　　34 이해하다
35 포기하다　　36 성장하다, 자라다
37 ~에 대해 감사히 여기다　　　　38 ~하고 싶다
39 기뻐서　　40 여기저기 쏘다니다
41 (해답 등을) 찾아내다[내놓다]　　　　42 ~에 오다
43 ~을 돌보다, 뒷바라지하다

단어 TEST Step 2   p.22

01 worry　　02 believe　　03 daughter
04 disease　　05 proud　　06 error
07 share　　08 clean　　09 generation
10 happiness　　11 worse　　12 pleasure
13 just　　14 material　　15 heel
16 signal　　17 understand　　18 wander
19 bath　　20 respect　　21 actually
22 heavy　　23 trusty　　24 condition
25 until　　26 volunteer　　27 safety
28 homeless　　29 succeed　　30 support
31 comfortable　　32 pressure　　33 invention
34 joy　　35 take care of　　36 come over to
37 look for　　38 thank A for B　　39 come up with
40 at first　　41 wander off　　42 cheer up
43 keep an eye on

단어 TEST Step 3   p.23

1 heavy, 무거운　　2 always, 항상, 언제나　　3 joy, 기쁨, 환희
4 heel, 발뒤꿈치　　5 create, 창조하다
6 driver, 운전자, 운전기사　　7 perfect, 완벽한, 완전한

8 believe, 믿다　　9 gift, 선물　　10 pressure, 압력, 압박
11 safety, 안전　　12 childhood, 어린 시절
13 inventor, 발명가　　14 comfortable, 편안한
15 support, 지지하다, 후원하다　　16 worry, 걱정하다

대화문 TEST Step 1   p.24~25

Listen & Speak 1 A. Listen and Check

1 do me a favor / What / family, going on vacation, come, water / can

2 can, favor / it / help me with, project / Sorry, can't, have to visit, with

Listen & Speak 2 A. Listen and Check

1 Hi, As you know, birthday, haven't had, to, beging, been, and, for supporting, trying, proud, daughter

2 are, doing, weekend / Nothing special, stay, watch / having, party / for inviting

Listen & Speak 1-B

Can, do, favor / What / move, with, heavy / No problem / Thank, for helping

Communicate A. Listen and Answer

Can, do me a favor / What / go shopping, for / of course, Who, for / for my little sister / getting, a birthday gift / isn't until October / why are, getting, cap / broke, while she was riding, last, just, cheer her up / see, can go / sounds perfect

Progress Check

1 can you do, favor / What, it / going to go, this, weekend, take care of, during / worry, enjoy

2 Hello, haven't, a chance to thank, for being, Every, welcome, always teach, things, lucky to have, proud to be, students

3 any special plans, just going to stay, then, come over, for dinner

대화문 TEST Step 2   p.26~27

Listen & Speak 1 A. Listen and Check

1 G: Mark, can you do me a favor?
  B: Sure. What is it?
  G: My family is going on vacation for a week. Can you come to our house and water the plants?
  B: Yes, I can.

2 G: Kevin, can you do me a favor?
  B: O.K. What is it?
  G: Can you help me with my science project this

31

afternoon?

B: Sorry , but I can't . I have to visit my grandma with my mom.

Listen & Speak 2 A. Listen and Check

1 G: Hi, Mom! Hi, Dad! As you know, today is my 15th birthday. I haven't had a chance to thank you for being my parents. You've truly been my friends and my teachers. Thank you for supporting me and always trying to understand me. I'm really proud to be your daughter.

2 G: What are you doing this weekend, Eric?

B: Nothing special. I'll just stay home and watch TV.

G: Great! I'm having a birthday party this weekend. Can you come?

B: Sure. Thank you for inviting me.

Listen & Speak 1-B

A: Can you do me a favor?

B: Sure. What is it?

A: Can you move this table with me? It's too heavy.

B: Sure. No problem.

A: Thank you for helping me.

Communicate A. Listen and Answer

Jaden: Can you do me a favor, Yuri?

Yuri: Sure. What is it, Jaden?

Jaden: Can we go shopping together for a baseball cap for a girl?

Yuri: Yes, of course. Who is it for?

Jaden: It's for my little sister Kate.

Yuri: Oh, are you getting her a birthday gift?

Jaden: No, her birthday isn't until October.

Yuri: Then, why are you getting a baseball cap for her?

Jaden: She broke her leg while she was riding her bike last week. I just want to cheer her up.

Yuri: Oh, I see. I can go this Friday afternoon.

Jaden: That sounds perfect. Thank you.

Progress Check

1 G: Andrew, can you do me a favor?

B: O.K. What is it?

G: My family is going to go to Jejudo this weekend. Can you take care of my cat during the weekend?

B: Sure. Don't worry about her. And enjoy your trip.

2 G: Hello , Mr. Smith. We haven't had a chance to thank you for being our teacher. Every morning, you welcome us in the classroom. You always

teach us important and interesting things. We're lucky to have you, and we're proud to be your students.

3 G: Do you have any special plans this weekend?

B: No, I'm just going to stay home.

G: Oh, then can you come over to my house for dinner?

01 up, family, generations

02 little, been, close

03 first, trusty, cook

04 taught, lessons

05 person, respected, most   06 went, for, got

07 had, disease   08 Everyone, was, shock

09 became, over 10 wandered off, keep, all

11 One, got, saw 12 moment, himself, don't, heels

13 were, that, do 14 sensor, way, signal

15 tried, materials, comfortable, elderly

16 like, up, safety 17 trial, error, succeeded

18 worked, so, that

19 believe, invention, worked

20 For, inventor, world   21 his, still, best

01 grew up, family, three generations

02 Since, was little, been, close to

03 first friend, trusty driver, cook

04 also taught, life lessons

05 who, respected the most

06 When, went out for a walk, got lost

07 had, disease   08 Everyone, was in shock

09 became worse over

10 wandered off, so, that, keep an eye, all

11 got out of, saw

12 moment, said to himself, don't, heels

13 were, that, had to do

14 had to create, then, a way to send, signal

15 tried, materials, socks

16 felt like giving up, safety

17 After, trial, error, succeeded in making

18 worked, that, jumped for joy

19 could not believe, actually worked

20 For, the best inventor

21 is still, best friend

1 Kenneth Shinozuka는 3대의 행복한 대가족에서 자랐다.

2 그는 어렸을 때부터 항상 할아버지와 매우 친했다.

3 그는 Kenneth의 첫 친구이자, 신뢰할 수 있는 운전기사이자, 요리사였다.

4 그는 또한 그에게 많은 인생 교훈을 가르쳐 주었다.

5 그는 Kenneth가 세상에서 가장 존경하는 사람이었다.

6 Kenneth가 네 살이었을 때, 그의 할아버지는 어느 날 산책을 나갔다가 길을 잃었다.

7 그는 알츠하이머병에 걸렸다.

8 Kenneth의 가족 모두는 충격에 빠졌다.

9 그의 상태는 10년 동안 더 악화되었다.

10 그는 자주 밤에 여기저기 돌아다니기 때문에 누군가가 그를 밤새 감시해야 했다.

11 어느 날 밤, Kenneth의 할아버지가 침대에서 일어났는데, Kenneth가 그것을 보았다.

12 그 순간, 그는 혼잣말을 했다. "내가 할아버지의 양말 뒤꿈치에 압력 감지기를 설치하는 게 어떨까?"

13 Kenneth가 해야 할 많은 일들이 있었다.

14 그는 처음에 압력 감지기를 만들고 나서 그의 스마트폰으로 신호를 보낼 방법을 찾아야 했다.

15 Kenneth는 또한 그의 연로한 할아버지에게 편안한 양말을 만들어 주기 위해 많은 다양한 재료들을 가지고 만들어 보았다.

16 그는 포기하고 싶은 생각이 들 때 할아버지의 안전에 대해 생각했다.

17 많은 시행착오 끝에 그는 마침내 자신의 장치를 만드는 데 성공했다.

18 그것이 처음 작동했을 때, 그는 너무 행복해 기뻐서 펄쩍 뛰었다.

19 그는 자신의 발명품이 실제로 작동했다는 것을 믿을 수 없었다.

20 그의 할아버지에게 Kenneth는 세계 최고의 발명가이다.

21 Kenneth에게 그의 할아버지는 여전히 그의 가장 친한 친구이다.

1 Kenneth Shinozuka grew up in a big happy family of three generations.

2 Since he was little, he has always been very close to his grandfather.

3 He was Kenneth's first friend, his trusty driver, and his cook.

4 He also taught him many life lessons.

5 He was the person who Kenneth respected the most in the world.

6 When Kenneth was four, his grandfather went out for a walk one day and got lost.

7 He had Alzheimer's disease.

8 Everyone in Kenneth's family was in shock.

9 His condition became worse over the next 10 years.

10 He wandered off at night so often that someone had to keep an eye on him all night long.

11 One night, Kenneth's grandfather got out of bed, and Kenneth saw it.

12 At that moment, he said to himself, "Why don't I put pressure sensors on the heels of his socks?"

13 There were many things that Kenneth had to do.

14 He first had to create a pressure sensor and then find a way to send a signal to his smart phone.

15 Kenneth also tried many different materials to make comfortable socks for his elderly grandfather.

16 When he felt like giving up, he thought about his grandfather's safety.

17 After much trial and error, he finally succeeded in making his device.

18 When it first worked, he was so happy that he jumped for joy.

19 He could not believe that his invention actually worked.

20 For his grandfather, Kenneth is the best inventor in the world.

21 For Kenneth, his grandfather is still his best friend.

Link - Share

1. volunteer work, planning, elderly

2. came up with

3. One of, for

Write - Write

1. would like, volunteer

2. One, on

3. so, that, to help

4. there are, that

5. walk, bath, with

6. who, looking for

Culture Project

1. to help

2. John, Oare

3. local

4. build, for

5. so, that, at, happiness, helping

Link - Share

1. I'd like to talk about the volunteer work that we're planning to do for the elderly people in our city.
2. We came up with three activities.
3. One of them is to make patbingsu for them and eat it together.

Write - Write

1. Hello, I am Kim Doha, and I would like to join your volunteer project.
2. One day, I saw some poor dogs on TV.
3. They looked so sad that I wanted to help them.
4. I like dogs, and there are many things that I can do for them.
5. I can walk the dogs, give them a bath , and play with them.
6. I am the person who you are looking for !

Culture Project

1. Do you want to help children?
2. Join our Child Care Project in Laos.
3. You'll teach local children.
4. You'll also build a school for them.
5. The work is so hard that you'll want to go home at first, but you'll find h`appiness in helping these children.

단어 TEST Step 1   p.40

01 연습하다   02 지하철

03 진가를 알아보다, 감상하다, 감사하다   04 용감한

05 세기   06 실은, 사실은, 실제로

07 ~와 결혼하다   08 새벽   09 공연하다, 수행하다

10 실패하다   11 줄거리   12 수수께끼

13 공주   14 기념하다   15 이미, 벌써

16 공연   17 비밀   18 정확하게, 바르게

19 제안   20 유명한   21 추측하다

22 정확하지 않게, 틀리게   23 낯선 사람, 이방인

24 할인   25 어려운   26 의미하다

27 놀라운   28 타조

29 (말을) 덧붙이다, 더하다   30 기념일

31 즉시, 곧바로   32 안전한   33 극장

34 전체, 모든, 전부의 35 서두르다   36 ~에 늦다, 지각하다

37 ~하는 게 어때?   38 ~하고 싶다   39 …만큼 ~한

40 ~와 사랑에 빠지다   41 ~에 지나지 않는

42 제시간에, 늦지 않게   43 알아내다, 발견하다

단어 TEST Step 2   p.41

01 secret   02 guess   03 century

04 incorrectly   05 actually   06 princess

07 brave   08 ostrich   09 discount

10 appreciate   11 stranger   12 correctly

13 agree   14 play   15 storyline

16 already   17 anniversary   18 marry

19 perform   20 fail   21 whole

22 subway   23 add   24 celebrate

25 famous   26 safe   27 performance

28 suggestion   29 practice   30 moving

31 difficult   32 amazing   33 riddle

34 beauty   35 be late for ~   36 in time

37 find out   38 hurry up   39 fall in love with ~

40 take off   41 one day   42 at first sight

43 would like to+동사원형

단어 TEST Step 3   p.42

1 century, 세기   2 already, 이미

3 perform, 수행하다, 공연하다   4 amazing, 놀라운

5 storyline, 줄거리   6 aria, 아리아, 영창   7 brave, 용감한

8 discount, 할인   9 appreciate, 진가를 알아보다

---

10 celebrate, 축하하다, 기념하다   11 moving, 감동적인

12 guess, 추측하다   13 secret, 비밀   14 marry, 결혼하다

15 anniversary, 기념일   16 riddle, 수수께끼

대화문 TEST Step 1   p.43~44

Listen & Speak 1-A

1 hurry up, already / going to be late for / Why don't we take, faster than / good idea

2 got only, wrong / sure, well, Why don't we go out to celebrate / have pizza for / Of course

Listen & Speak 1-B

What shall we do / Why don't we see / a good idea

Listen & Speak 2-A

1 let's practice, parts, school play / What time shall we meet / How about, right after school / Sounds

2 play badminton / Where shall we / How about, near / See you there at

Listen & Speak 2-B

Let's go on a picnic / What time shall we meet / How about, on / Let's meet

Communicate A

guess what, have no school / Why not / anniversary / together / take, off, What, want to / Why don't we go see, near your work, get, discount if, go on a Wednesday / let's just meet / shall we / How about, have lunch / best

Communicate B

What shall we / Why don't we / time shall we meet / How about / Let's meet

Progress Check

1 hurry up, already / be late for / Why don't we take, faster than, at this time of day / good idea

2 hot today, Let's go swimming / Where shall, meet / How about / See, tere

대화문 TEST Step 2   p.45~46

Listen & Speak 1-A

1 M: Liz, hurry up. It's already 6 o'clock.

W: Oh, we're going to be late for the concert.

M: Why don't we take the subway? The subway will be faster than the bus at this time of day.

W: That's a good idea.

2 B: Mom, I got only one question wrong on the Korean history exam!

W: Great! I was sure you would do well. Why don't

we go out to celebrate tonight?

B: Yes! Can we have pizza for dinner?

W: Of course, Joe. I'll call your dad.

A: What shall we do at the park?

B: Why don't we see a magic show?

A: That's a good idea.

1 B: Karen, let's practice our parts for the school play today.

G: O.K. What time shall we meet?

B: How about 4 o'clock, right after school?

G: Sounds good.

2 G: Do you want to play badminton together this afternoon, Mark?

B: Sure. Where shall we play?

G: How about at the park near your place?

B: O.K. See you there at 3 o'clock.

A: Let's go on a picnic this weekend.

B: Good idea. What time shall we meet?

A: How about 10 o'clock on Saturday?

B: O.K. Let's meet at the subway station. See you there.

Anna: Dad, guess what! I have no school next Wednesday.

Dad: Really? Why not?

Anna: It's our school's 75th anniversary.

Dad: Oh, I see.

Anna: Can we do something together that day?

Dad: I guess I can take the afternoon off. What do you want to do?

Anna: Why don't we go see a musical at Bravo Theater near your work? We can get a discount if we go on a Wednesday.

Dad: Good idea, Anna! Then, let's just meet at the theater.

Anna: O.K. What time shall we meet?

Dad: How about 12? Then, we can have lunch together, too.

Anna: You're the best, Dad!

A: What shall we do this afternoon?

B: Why don't we go see *Wonder Woman*?

A: Good idea! What time shall we meet?

B: How about 4 o'clock?

A: O.K. Let's meet at Moon Theater.

1 G: Jim, hurry up. It's already 10 o'clock.

B: Oh, we're going to be late for the movie.

G: Why don't we take the bus? The bus will be faster than the subway at this time of day.

B: That's a good idea.

2 B: It's very hot today. Let's go swimming, Julie.

G: Good idea! Where shall we meet?

B: How about at the subway station near my place?

G: O.K. See you there at 11 o'clock.

01 Most Dangerous, World

02 Welcome, everyone

03 going, perform, opera

04 Like, other, Italian because

05 Before, like, storyline

06 appreciate, better if

07 of, beauty, cold as

08 who, marry, must

09 fails, die   10 has, been able

11 One, falls, at, sight

12 becomes, answer, riddles

13 However, marry, prince

14 nothing more than   15 then, of, own

16 asks, What

17 adds, correctly, die, incorrectly

18 before dawn, as, hers

19 to, until, finds out

20 most famous aria, whole   21 means, sleeps

22 No, sleeps   23 one, not even   24 secret, safe

25 No, will know   26 At dawn, will   27 prince's, is

28 learn, in time   29 watch, find out

01 The Most Dangerous, World

02 Welcome, everyone

03 are going to, perform

04 Like, other famous operas, in Italian because, in Italy, 16th century

05 I'd like to tell, storyline of the opera

06 appreciate, better if

07 of great beauty, as cold as ice

08 who, marry her, three riddles

09 fails, must die 10 has ever been able to

11 falls in love with, at first sight

12 the first man to answer

13 However, to marry

14 nothing more than

15 her a riddle of his own

16 asks her, What

17 adds, correctly, agree to die, incorrectly, have to marry

18 before dawn, as difficult as hers

19 go to sleep until, finds out

20 the most famous aria, whole opera

21 means, sleeps

22 No, sleeps   23 not even you

24 My secret, safe

25 No one will know

26 At dawn, will win   27 prince's name

28 Will, learn, in time

29 Let's watch, find out

---

1 투란도트, 세상에서 가장 위험한 사랑

2 여러분, 환영합니다!

3 오늘 밤, 우리는 지아코모 푸치니의 오페라 《투란도트》를 공연할 것입니다.

4 다른 많은 유명한 오페라들처럼 《투란도트》는 이탈리아어로 되어 있는데, 오페라가 16세기 이탈리아에서 시작되었기 때문입니다.

5 시작하기 전에 오페라 《투란도트》의 줄거리를 알려 드리려고 합니다.

6 여러분이 줄거리를 알면 이 오페라를 더 잘 감상하게 될 것입니다.

7 중국의 공주 Turandot는 굉장히 아름다운 여인이지만, 그녀는 얼음처럼 차갑습니다.

8 그녀와 결혼하길 원하는 왕자는 누구든지 반드시 세 가지 수수께끼에 답해야 합니다.

9 만약 실패하면 그는 죽어야 합니다.

10 그 누구도 수수께끼에 답할 수 없었습니다.

11 어느 날, 어떤 용감한 왕자가 그녀에게 첫눈에 반합니다.

12 그는 세 수수께끼를 모두 맞힌 첫 번째 사람이 됩니다.

13 그러나 Turandot는 그 왕자와 결혼하길 원하지 않습니다.

14 그는 그녀에게 단지 낯선 사람일 뿐입니다.

15 그러자 그는 그녀에게 자신의 수수께끼를 냅니다.

16 그는 그녀에게 "제 이름이 무엇입니까?"라고 묻습니다.

17 그는 "당신이 맞게 대답한다면 나는 죽는 것에 동의하겠습니다. 만약 답이 틀리면 당신은 저와 결혼해야 할 것입니다."라고 덧붙입니다.

---

18 Turandot는 동이 트기 전에 답을 찾아야 하지만 그의 수수께끼는 그녀의 것만큼 어렵습니다.

19 그녀는 모두에게 "누군가 그의 이름을 알아낼 때까지 그 누구도 잠들 수 없다."라고 말합니다.

20 그리고 왕자는 이 오페라 전체에서 가장 유명한 아리아, Nessun Dorma를 부릅니다.

21 그것은 누구도 잠들지 못한다는 뜻입니다.

22 누구도 잠들지 못하네.

23 누구도 잠들지 못하네, 당신조차도, 공주여.

24 나의 비밀은 안전하다네.

25 누구도 나의 이름을 알지 못할 것이네.

26 동틀 녘에, 내가 이길 것이라네! 내가 승리할 것이라네!

27 왕자의 이름은 Calaf입니다.

28 공주는 그의 이름을 제때 알아낼 수 있을까요?

29 오페라를 보고 알아봅시다.

---

1 Turandot The Most Dangerous Love in the World

2 Welcome, everyone!

3 Tonight, we are going to perform Giacomo Puccini's opera Turandot.

4 Like many other famous operas, Turandot is in Italian because opera started in Italy in the 16th century.

5 Before we begin, I'd like to tell you the storyline of the opera Turandot.

6 You will appreciate it better if you know the story.

7 Turandot, a Chinese princess, is a woman of great beauty, but she is as cold as ice.

8 Any prince who wants to marry her must answer three riddles.

9 If he fails, he must die.

10 No one has ever been able to answer them.

11 One day, a brave prince falls in love with her at first sight.

12 He becomes the first man to answer all three riddles.

13 However, Turandot does not want to marry the prince.

14 He is nothing more than a stranger to her.

15 He then gives her a riddle of his own.

16 He asks her, "What is my name?"

17 He adds, "If you answer correctly, I will agree to die. If you answer incorrectly, you will have to marry me."

18 Turandot must find the answer before dawn, but his riddle is as difficult as hers.

19 She says to everyone, "No one will go to sleep until someone finds out his name."

20 The prince then sings the most famous aria of the whole opera, "Nessun Dorma."

21 It means no one sleeps.

22 No one sleeps.

23 No one sleeps, not even you, Princess.

24 My secret is safe.

25 No one will know my name.

26 At dawn, I will win! I will win!

27 The prince's name is Calaf.

28 Will the princess learn his name in time?

29 Let's watch the opera and find out.

구석구석지문 TEST Step 1   p.57

Link
1. How, our performance
2. amazing, seen, as great as, musical's

Write
1. Review of
2. saw, last Friday
3. is about, dreams, love
4. its beautiful, moving songs
5. was also as good as
6. are looking for, should see
7. by, on

Write
1. Review of
2. saw, last Saturday
3. beautiful girl, beast
4. it a lot
5. as beautiful as a gem
6. like heart-warming stories, will like, too
7. by, on Aug

구석구석지문 TEST Step 2   p.58

Link
1. A: How was our performance?
2. B: It was amazing ! Actually, I've seen the musical *Cats* before, and your song was as great as the musical's.

Write
1. Review of *La La Land*
2. I saw *La La Land* last Friday.
3. It is about the dreams and love of Mia and Sebastian.

---

4. I enjoyed its beautiful and moving songs.
5. The story was also as good as the songs.
6. If you are looking for a good musical movie, you should see this movie.
7. by Kim Jisu on Aug. 11

Write
1. Review of *Beauty and the Beast*
2. I saw *Beauty and the Beast* last Saturday.
3. It is about a beautiful girl and a beast.
4. I enjoyed it a lot.
5. The songs were great, and the love story was as beautiful as a gem.
6. If you like heart-warming stories about love, you will like it, too.
7. by Lee Minsu on Aug. 12

적중100
영어 기출 문제집

정답 및 해설

미래 │ 최연희